DIVE!

Also by Mike Carlton

Cruiser: The Life and Loss of HMAS Perth *and Her Crew*

First Victory 1914: HMAS Sydney's Hunt for the German Raider Emden

Flagship: The Cruiser HMAS Australia II *and the Pacific War on Japan*

On Air

The Scrap Iron Flotilla

MIKE CARLTON
DIVE!

AUSTRALIAN SUBMARINERS
AT WAR

Foreword by the Chief of Navy,
Vice Admiral Mark Hammond, AO, RAN

PENGUIN BOOKS

UK | USA | Canada | Ireland | Australia
India | New Zealand | South Africa | China

Penguin Books is part of the Penguin Random House group of companies whose addresses can be found at global.penguinrandomhouse.com

First published by Penguin Books in 2024

Copyright © Mike Carlton, 2024

The moral right of the author has been asserted.

All rights reserved. No part of this publication may be reproduced, published, performed in public or communicated to the public in any form or by any means without prior written permission from Penguin Random House Australia Pty Ltd or its authorised licensees.

Cover photography: HMS *AE1* with crew on deck, Royal Navy, courtesy of the Imperial War Museum
Cover design by Luke Causby © Penguin Random House Australia Pty Ltd
Author photograph © Carol Gibbons
Maps and diagrams by James Carlton
Internal design by Midland Typesetters, Australia
Typeset in 11.5/15 pt Janson Text LT Std by Midland Typesetters

Printed and bound in Australia by Griffin Press, an accredited ISO AS/NZS 14001 Environmental Management Systems printer

 A catalogue record for this book is available from the National Library of Australia

ISBN 978 1 76134 288 2

penguin.com.au

We at Penguin Random House Australia acknowledge that Aboriginal and Torres Strait Islander peoples are the Traditional Custodians and the first storytellers of the lands on which we live and work. We honour Aboriginal and Torres Strait Islander peoples' continuous connection to Country, waters, skies and communities. We celebrate Aboriginal and Torres Strait Islander stories, traditions and living cultures; and we pay our respects to Elders past and present.

CONTENTS

Foreword by Vice Admiral Mark Hammond — ix
Author's Note — xiii
Submarines — xvii
Maps — xx

1. Damned Un-English — 1
2. Straws in the Wind — 21
3. Australia Welcomes Her Defenders — 40
4. The Unthinkable — 59
5. Goodbye to *AE1* — 79
6. Generally Run Amuck — 100
7. Abandon Ship! — 120
8. Arrival at Prisoner Avenue — 140
9. Entrances and Exits — 161
10. First to the Perisher — 177
11. Lifeboat Number Seven — 195
12. Special and Hazardous Service — 215
13. Attack the *Tirpitz*! — 234
14. More Frightened Than I Have Ever Been . . . — 255
15. Operation Postage Able — 275
16. 'Okay. We'll go.' — 295

17.	Operation Sabre	315
18.	To the Saigon River	332
19.	Enter the Oberons	352
20.	The Cold War	378
21.	In Memoriam	399

Acknowledgements	421
Bibliography	424
Endnotes	429
Index	443

This book is dedicated to my good friend the late
Rear Admiral James Goldrick AO, CSC, RAN, who died
of leukaemia – far too young – in March 2023.

James was a unique combination of sailor and scholar, a man of action and a man of intellect. In his naval career he held important commands at sea and ashore. His work as a writer, historian and strategist rightly won him global renown.

It was he who got me into the naval history business with sound advice and warm encouragement, beginning with *Cruiser*, my first book in 2008. I owe him a great debt.

James, may you have fair seas and following winds.

FOREWORD

'The fair breeze blew, the white foam flew,
The furrow followed free;
We were the first that ever burst
Into that silent sea.'
    Samuel Taylor Coleridge, *The Rime of the Ancient Mariner*, 1798

Four hundred years have passed since the world's first submarine prototype dived silently beneath the murky surface of the River Thames. We have come a long way since Cornelis Drebbel's greased leather submersible rowboat, but the fascination with submarines has only gathered strength over time. We live in a world where the land has been explored and mapped in great detail. Submarines are the vehicles that enable us to visit the depths of the oceans, Earth's last frontier, hiding vast ecosystems and geographic mysteries. It is no surprise then that submarines continue to be an attractive option, providing strategic deterrence for coastal states and uncertainty for their adversaries.

As interest in submarines has increased, so has the number of publications about them. From books on the first offensive use of a submarine during the American Revolution, to their proliferation since World War I, to the development of propulsion, weapons, communications and quieting technologies, and their role in deterrence in the competition of our era, to the submarines of any particular nation, the silent service has peeked out of the shadows. Apart, that is, from in Australia, where it has remained the silent service indeed. The number of commercial books on our submarine service and history can be counted on one hand.

Perhaps one of the reasons why is part of a broader trend: that our three-ocean, island-trading nation forgets it is a maritime one. As incongruous as that sounds, Australia inherited a continental identity. A 2004 Parliamentary Library research brief on Australian maritime strategy observed that:

> If our nature is characterised by our myths and legends, then Australia is not a maritime nation. As a people, we are happy to lie at the beach and toss pebbles at the waves, or turn our back upon it and fix our gaze on the dusty enormity of our island continent.

Sadly, the service and sacrifice of Australian submariners have not captured the public memory. The call to the profession of arms in Australia has traditionally been seen through a land warfare lens. This is partly due to the role the Gallipoli landings played in forming the national identity of a young Australia. However, part of it also boils down to pure numbers. In World War I, the greatest concentration of Australian service personnel fought on land. The Australian Imperial Force had 412,953 Australians, compared to the 5275 in the Royal Australian Navy, with a number of sailors also contributing to the 3651 personnel in the Australian Naval and Military Expeditionary Force.

Despite numerous examples of gallantry at sea, Australia lacks an abiding Jutland, Midway or Trafalgar narrative that psychologically binds the national identity to the sea. Perhaps if Peter Weir's 1981 film *Gallipoli* had commenced with scenes of HMAS *AE2* quietly slipping into the heavily mined and fortified Dardanelles prior to the Anzac beach landings, Australians would have a greater understanding of our maritime identity. The *AE2*'s Commanding Officer, Lieutenant Commander Henry Stoker, was tasked to make the hazardous transit through the Dardanelles in order to prevent enemy shipping from resupplying Turkish troops on the Gallipoli Peninsula. He successfully completed the treacherous journey amid constant danger and under heavy enemy fire, the first submarine to do so. It is pleasing to see the story of Stoker and the *AE2* detailed in this book. The story is one of many examples that highlight the unique challenges and dangers associated with naval service. As United States Marine Corps private and World War II veteran Clifford C. Spencer eloquently described:

> Imagine your living room is made of steel, the windows are your lookout posts and you have been there for two weeks. With very little rest and less sleep, you stare out day and night for an attack from the air, from across the street, or up from your basement, that you know will destroy your home and probably take you or your family's life. This might give you a small idea of what the mental and physical conditions are like in sea warfare.

Mike Carlton is already an accomplished author of the Royal Australian Navy's history. His previous works have done more than most to tell the story of the RAN's service to the nation and the gallantry of sailors who brought Australian warships to life. In this latest book, he places the tenacity of Australian submariners in pride of place, for all to see. *Dive!* is a comprehensive treatise on Australian submarines, from their initial development and Australia's first submarine capability to the present day Collins-class boats.

Dive! has come at an opportune time as it reminds us that we are, and will always be, a maritime nation. As a three-ocean, island-trading nation, the majority of Australian commodities are imported or exported by sea. The energy that powers our homes, cars and phones comes from or over the sea. The crucial medical equipment, machinery and vehicles that sustain prosperous, healthy and fulfilling lives for Australians come by the sea. The internet connection that secures our access to global financial markets is carried by cables under the sea. Australia derives its economic wellbeing and, accordingly, its national security from the sea.

The rules-based order that has enabled good order at sea and underpinned Australian and global prosperity since the end of World War II is now challenged. In our times, free and open access to the sea can no longer be assumed, so it must be assured. This is why the RAN will continue to cultivate and progress our world-renowned submarine capability, through the character and competence of our people. Our navy is charged with safeguarding our national prosperity; it is not a responsibility taken lightly. It is also something that requires constant investment and time, and cannot be surged at the final hour. Pericles' address to the Athenians in the Peloponnesian War echoes to us today:

> As for naval skills, they [the Spartans] will not find them easy to acquire ... Seamanship is an art like any other; it is not something which can be picked up in one's spare time, indeed, it leaves no leisure for anything else.

It is my hope that this book inspires young and old minds alike to understand Australia's maritime identity, and to know more of the Australian submariners who have and continue to serve our nation with courage, competence and character. *Dive!*

Vice Admiral Mark Hammond, Chief of Navy
Canberra, 2024

(The views expressed in this foreword are personal views only and do not represent the official position of the Commonwealth of Australia.)

AUTHOR'S NOTE

After four books of naval history I felt I had surface warships pretty much worked out. Submarines were a new learning curve, and a steep one. I thought a few simple notes might help the reader.

First, submarines are boats, not ships. That's because the earliest, primitive underwater craft were modified small boats and the name stuck. Today's giant American, British, Russian or Chinese nuclear submarines are still boats.

All the submarines in this book are diesel electric, meaning they have two sources of power. On the surface, noisy diesel generators produce electricity to drive their motors, pushing them along. But the diesels cannot be used submerged because there is no way for fresh air to be drawn in to run them, or for the toxic exhaust gases to escape. Instead, big banks of batteries provide electric power, which is both cleaner and, happily, very much quieter.

The batteries have to be recharged every so often. In the early days a boat would need to fully surface, usually at night, to suck in air and run the diesels to top up the batteries. In World War II the Germans fitted the *Schnorchel* – or snorkel – to their U-boats, an invention they stole from the Dutch when they invaded Holland. This was a long tube which could be raised in the air above the waves. The U-boat would remain concealed at periscope depth, using its diesels to recharge, with the snorkel sucking in air and expelling the exhaust fumes. Everyone adopted the idea and it still exists, using more advanced technology. The English language navies call it 'snorting'.

Like any vessel, a submarine will float on the surface if it weighs *less* than the weight of the water it displaces. To dive it has to become heavier. This is done by allowing sea water into tanks – called ballast tanks – mounted on its hull. As the water enters, down she goes.

To help her submerge there are hydroplanes – generally just called planes – mounted outside the hull. One man – usually an experienced petty officer – controls them like horizontal rudders or the flaps on an aircraft wing, angling the bow down. With the diesels stopped, electric power drives her forward.

The order from the captain might be 'Ten down, keep 200 feet.' The boat will move ahead and downwards at an angle of 10 degrees below the horizontal until it reaches a depth of 200 feet. This is both science and art. In the control room there is a gauge, known as a clinometer, which has a bubble of air floating in a fluid. It works exactly the same way as a carpenter's spirit level: when the submarine reaches the required depth, the bubble has to be brought to dead centre. 'Zero bubble', they call it. The boat's 'trim' must be adjusted by taking on or pumping out water until it has become exactly the same weight as the water she has displaced. The fore and aft balance is adjusted by pumping water between trim tanks in the bow and stern until the boat is hovering horizontally on an even keel, neither sinking nor rising. This is called 'a stopped trim'.

Making it harder is the fact that the submarine is squashed by the water pressure as it goes deeper, so it displaces less. The opposite happens when it rises. Speed also has an impact. As the submarine goes faster it generates lift from its hull shape, requiring added water to compensate.

And not all water is equal. It is changed by depth, temperature and salinity, all of which can affect a boat's trim. As any swimmer knows, salt water is more supportive than fresh water. A boat running from sea water into a harbour and suddenly encountering fresh water flowing from a river could abruptly plunge to the bottom. Managing that takes fine judgement.

Ocean currents can also be a problem. It is quite common for warmer surface water to be moving in one direction, with deeper, colder water going in another. This also has to be taken into account.

Surfacing is another art. Submarines carry supplies of high pressure compressed air, which is blown into the ballast tanks. That expels the sea water. The boat becomes lighter, the planes angle the bow upwards and she heads for the surface. This again takes care. Too fast or at too sharp an angle and the submarine will leap out of the water like a playful porpoise, then crash back down.

For this book, old measures have been mostly converted to metric. Nautical miles have become kilometres, for example. One nautical mile is 1.85 kilometres. A knot is a measure of speed at sea, one nautical mile per hour. A submarine moving at 10 knots is doing 10 nautical miles per hour or 18.5 kilometres per hour.

Some things do not change. Port is the left-hand side of the boat as you look forward, starboard is the right-hand side. If you turn to face the other way, port and starboard stay the same.

The first time I went down in a submarine I knew what to expect. I had seen all the movies. There would be klaxons blaring, lots of shouting, people tumbling down ladders and running this way and that, a great whoosh of water into the control room before the hatch was closed. One young sailor would lose his nerve and scream to be allowed out.

There was nothing of the sort. With just a few quiet orders the boat angled gently downwards, almost imperceptibly at first. The control room was as calm as a cathedral. It was no more exciting than riding the escalator at your local shopping mall.

Greatly disappointed, I asked the captain if they ever had to do an emergency crash dive with all the Hollywood drama.

'If it gets that bad,' he said, 'we're already dead.'

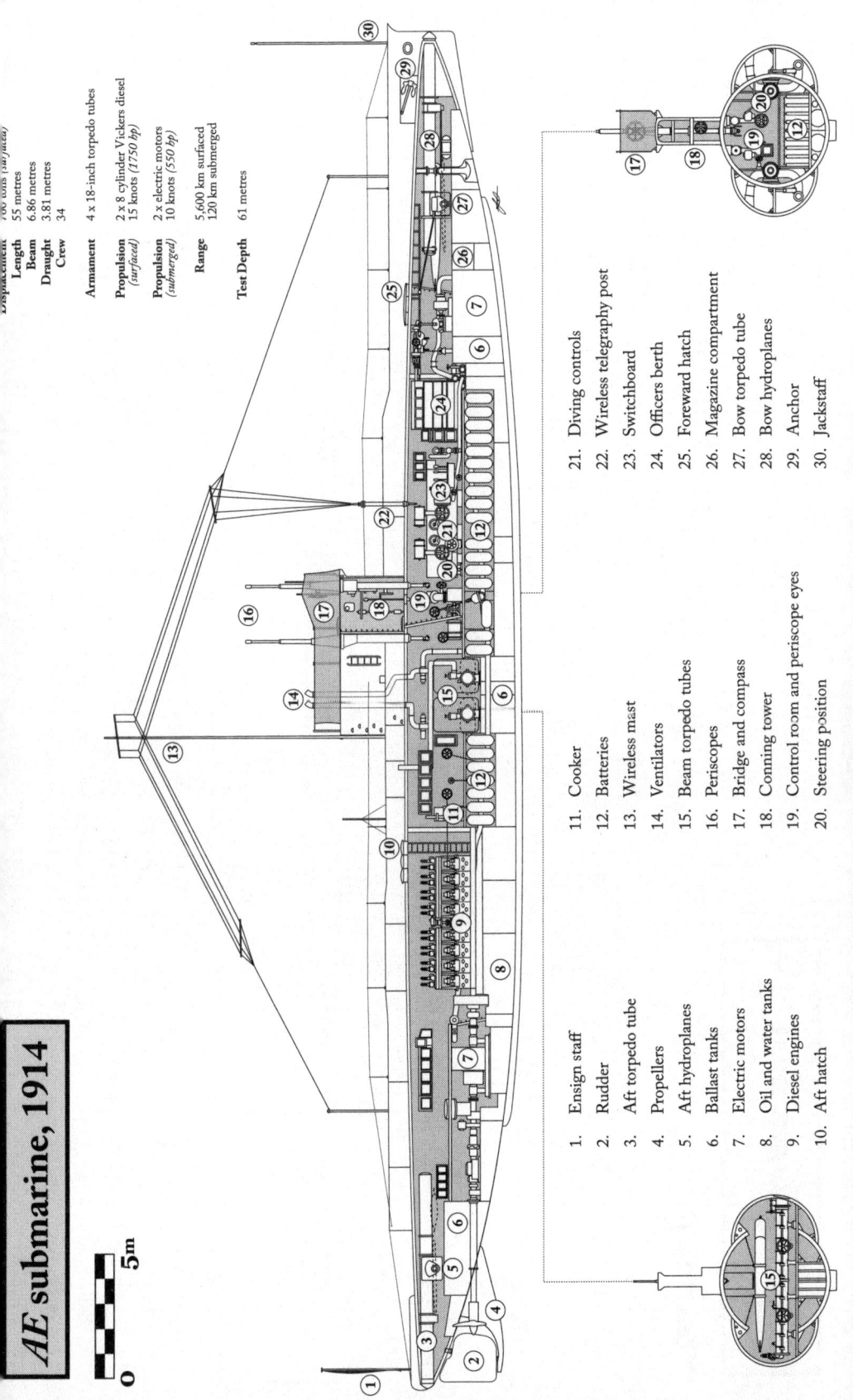

X-class submarine, 1943
(X5 - X10 shown)

Displacement	27 tons *(30 tons submerged)*
Length	15.62 metres
Beam	1.75 metres
Draught	1.60 metres
Crew	4
Armament	2 x 2000 kg detachable amatol charges
Propulsion *(surfaced)*	1 x Gardner 4LK Diesel engine 42 hp at 1,800 rpm 6.5 knots
Propulsion *(submerged)*	1 x Keith Blackman electric motor 30 hp at 1,650 rpm 5.5 knots
Range	926 km surfaced 152 km submerged
Test Depth	91.5 metres

1. Rudder
2. Propeller
3. Hydroplanes
4. Exhaust muffler
5. Electric motor and air compressor
6. Ballast tanks
7. Fuel tanks
8. Diesel engine
9. Impeller log
10. Magnetic compass
11. Dive/engine controls *(first lieutenant)*
12. Aft hatch
13. Compensating tank
14. Compressed air cylinders
15. Side cargo release wheel
16. Day periscope *(commanding officer)*
17. Night periscope
18. Steering controls *(helmsman/engineer)*
19. Induction trunk and aerial
20. Wet and dry hatch
21. Batteries
22. Sleeping position *(diver)*
23. Tow hooks
24. Amatol charges

Oberon-class submarine, 1987
(HMAS Ovens shown)

Displacement	2186 tons *(surfaced)*
Length	89.91 metres
Beam	8.07 metres
Draught	5.48 metres
Crew	8 officers, 60 sailors
Armament	6 x 21-inch torpedo tubes firing MK-48 Mod 4 torpedoes or UGM-84 harpoon missiles
Sensors	Kelvin Hughes Type 1006 surface radar; Atlas Elektronik CSU3-41 bow attack sonar; Sperry AN/BQG-4 rangefinding sonar; BAC Type 2007 long range passive sonar
Propulsion *(surfaced)*	2 x 1,840 hp Admiralty Standard Range V16 diesels; 12 knots
Propulsion *(submerged)*	2 x 3000 hp English Electric motors; 17 knots
Range	19,170 km at surface cruising speed
Test Depth	200 metres

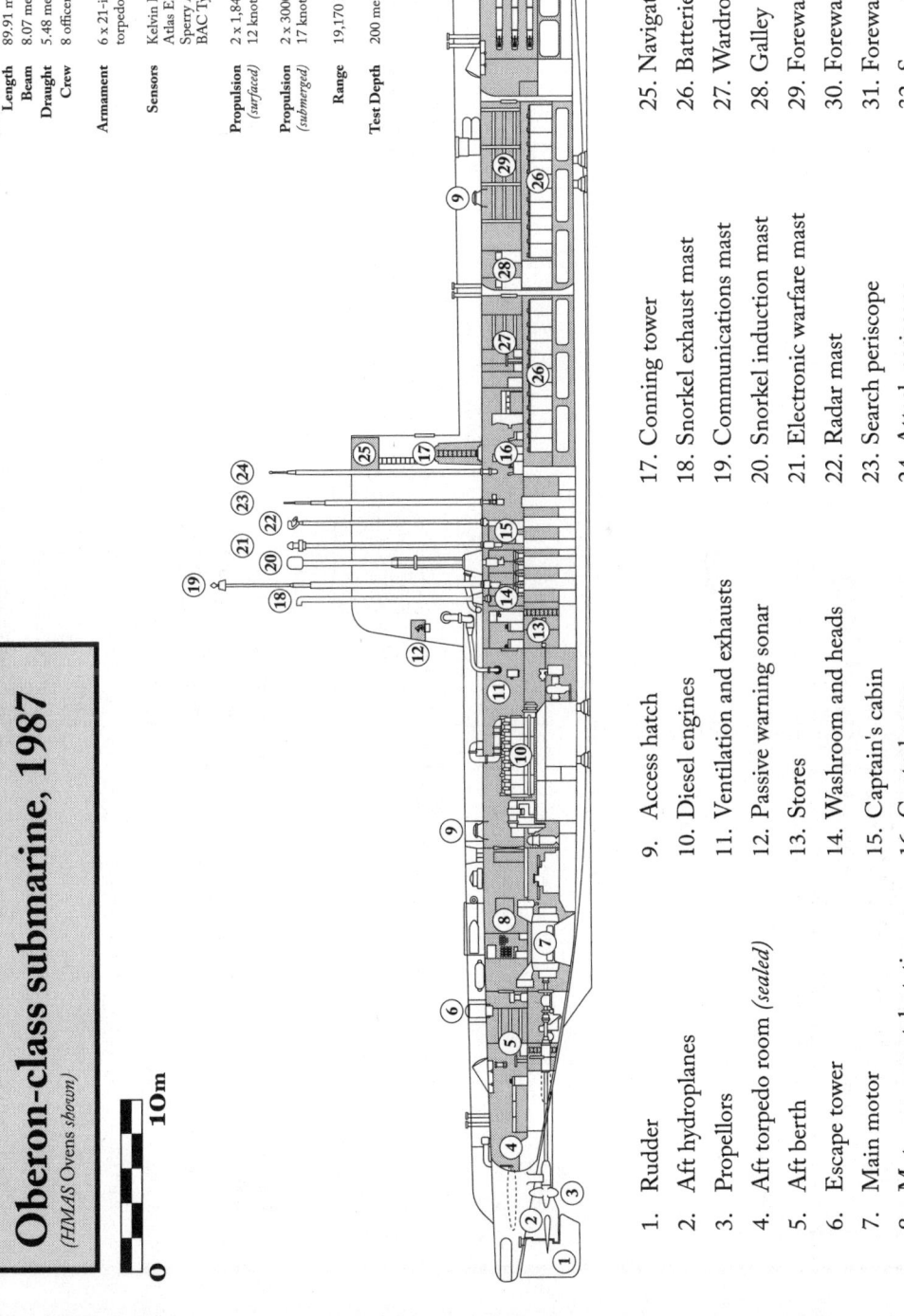

1. Rudder
2. Aft hydroplanes
3. Propellors
4. Aft torpedo room *(sealed)*
5. Aft berth
6. Escape tower
7. Main motor
8. Motor room watch station
9. Access hatch
10. Diesel engines
11. Ventilation and exhausts
12. Passive warning sonar
13. Stores
14. Washroom and heads
15. Captain's cabin
16. Control room
17. Conning tower
18. Snorkel exhaust mast
19. Communications mast
20. Snorkel induction mast
21. Electronic warfare mast
22. Radar mast
23. Search periscope
24. Attack periscope
25. Navigation position
26. Batteries
27. Wardroom
28. Galley
29. Foreward berths
30. Foreward torpedo room
31. Foreward hydroplanes *(stowed)*
32. Sonar chamber

German New Guinea, 1914

BISMARCK SEA

NEW IRELAND

AE1 last seen by HMAS Parramatta 1520, 14 September

AE1 approximate wreck location

DUKE OF YORK IS.

Most probable return track

CREDNER IS.

BLANCHE BAY

CAPE GAZELLE

RALUANA POINT

Rabaul

NEW BRITAIN

0 — 10 km

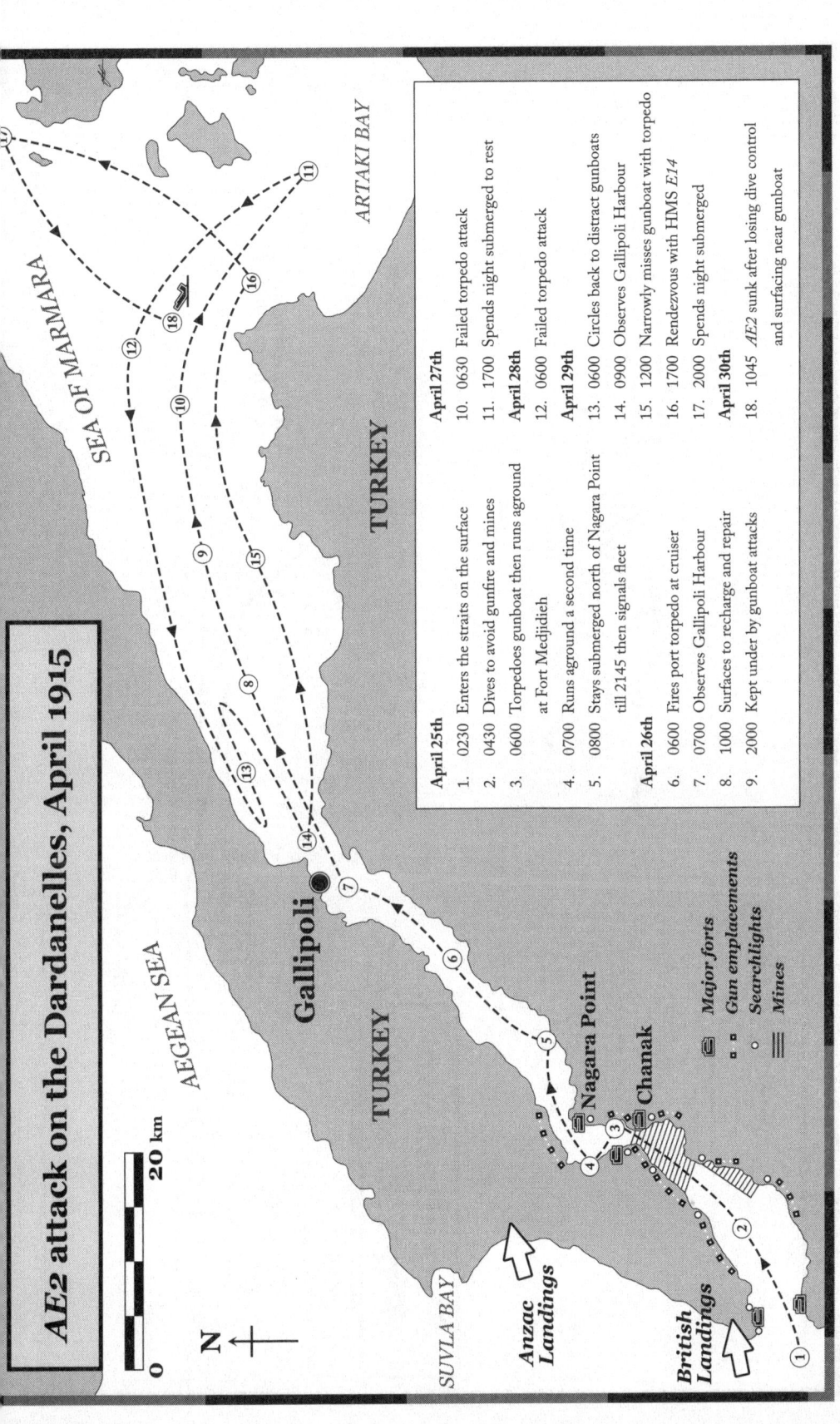

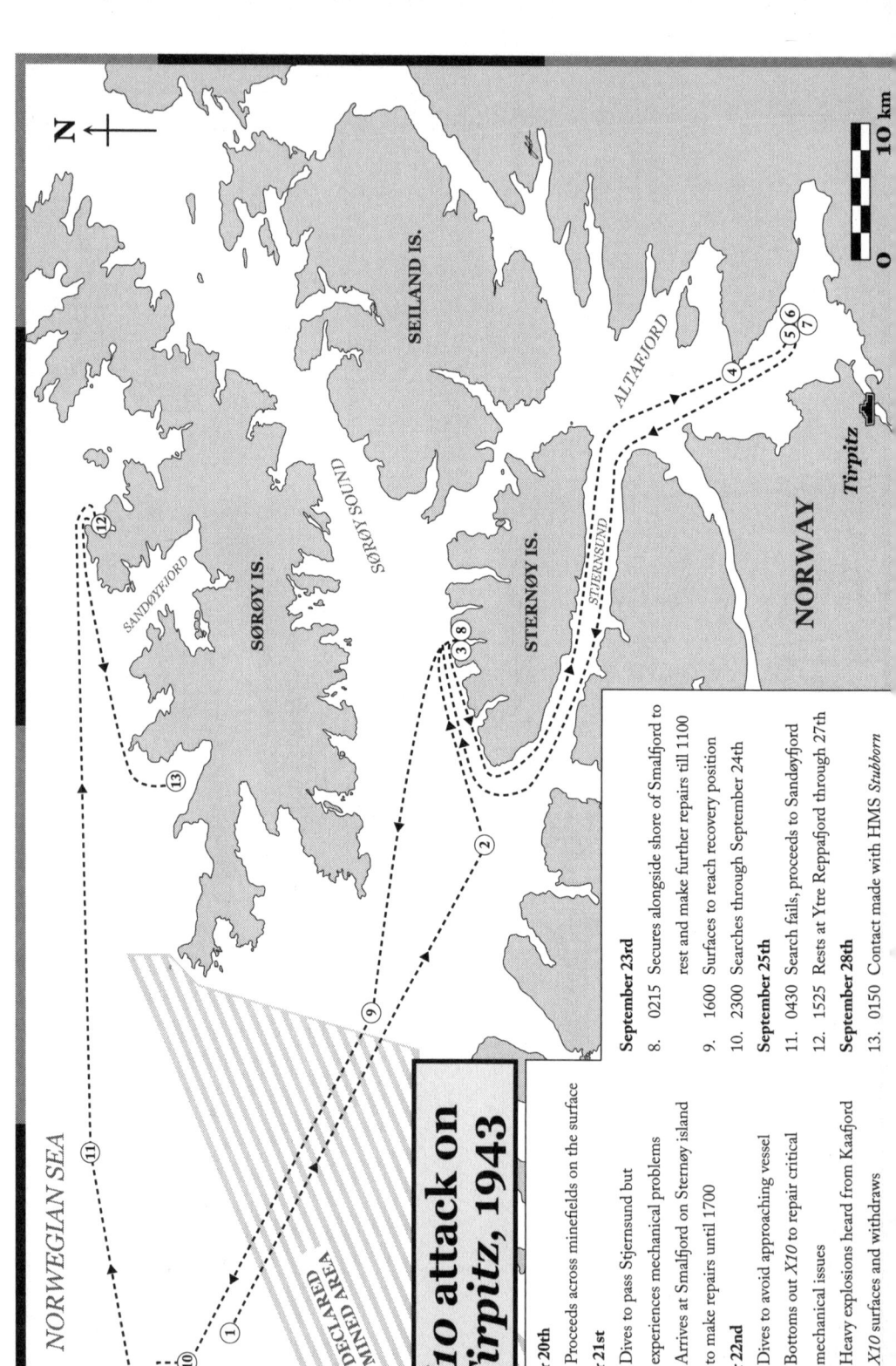

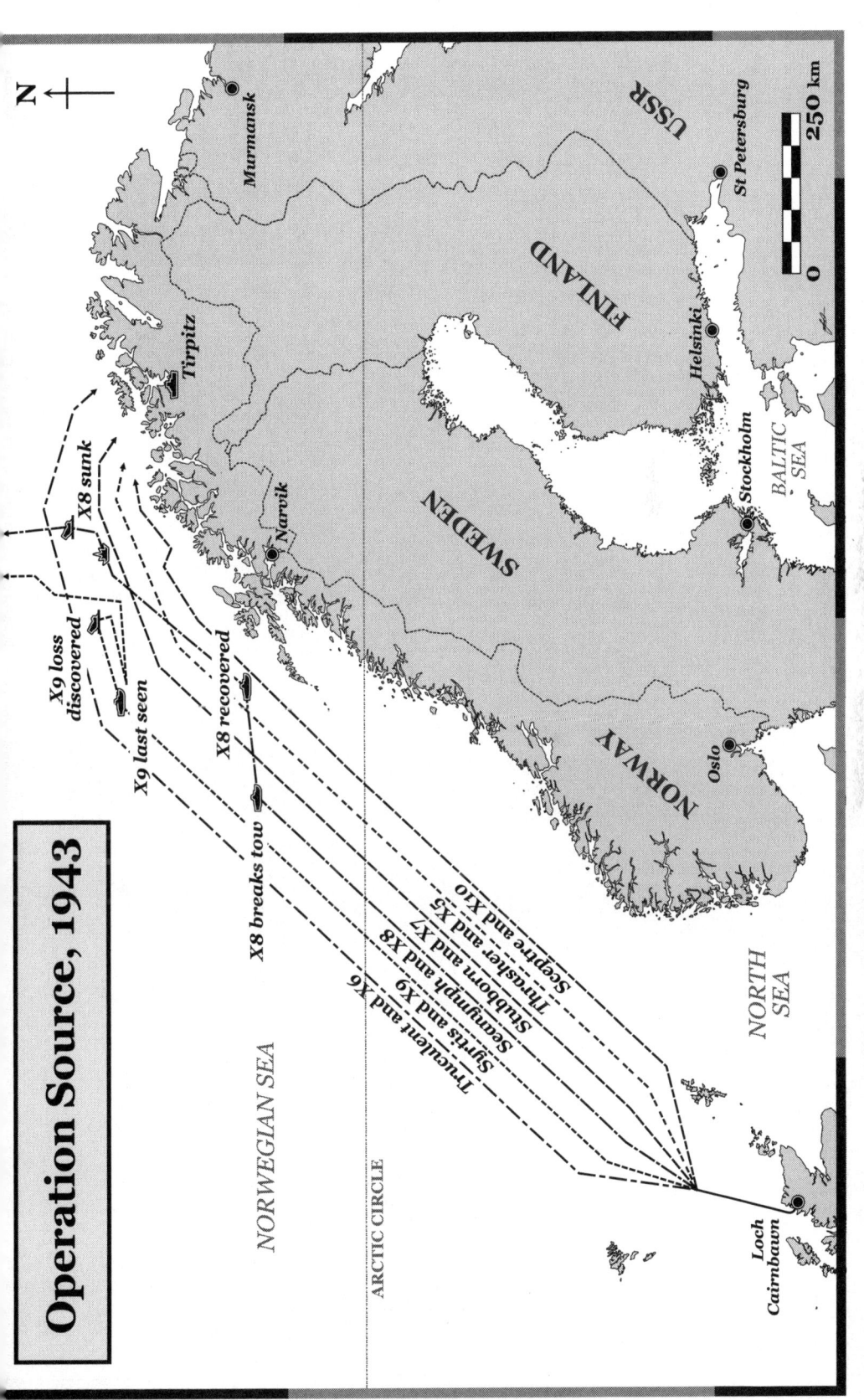

1

DAMNED UN-ENGLISH

[P]erhaps it will not be impertinent if I acquaint your Lordship with a Conceit of that deservedly Famous Mechanician and Chymist, Cornelis Drebel, who among other strange things that he performed, is affirmed (by more than a few credible Persons) to have contrived for the late learned King James, a vessel to go under Water; of which tryal was made in the Thames with admirable success, the vessel carrying twelve Rowers besides Passengers; one of which is yet alive . . .[1]

It was the first submarine. The year was 1624, and the famous Mijnheer Drebbel – he was a Dutchman – apparently persuaded James I to go for a ride in it. A contemporary painting depicts a boat like a fat wooden porpoise with six oars on each side. There are other written accounts of this exploit, one reporting that it travelled 'under water from Westminster to Greenwich, the distance of two Dutch miles; even five or six miles, or as far as one pleased. In this boat a person could see under the surface of the water and without candle-light, as much as he needed to read in the Bible or any other book.'[2]

We do not know how this craft dived or surfaced, and how the crew breathed is also a mystery, for Drebbel would offer only that he had discovered a 'Chymicall liquor' that somehow cleaned the air. Another Dutch writer, though, saw the future:

[I]t is not hard to imagine what would be the usefulness of this bold invention in time of war, if in this manner (a thing which

> I have repeatedly heard Drebbel assert) enemy ships lying safely at anchor could be secretly attacked and sunk unexpectedly utilizing a battering ram – an instrument of which hideous use is made nowadays in the capturing of the gates and bridges of towns.[3]

But there the matter rested. England's admirals, less perceptive, stuffily declined to take up Drebbel's invention.

Down the centuries, other dreamers – French, Russian, German, Italian – had a shot at producing a working submarine, with varying success. In 1775 an American inventor, David Bushnell, designed and built the *Turtle*, which he offered to George Washington for the revolutionary war against the British. Shaped like an egg, not quite two metres tall and built of oak planks covered with tar, it was driven by one man pedalling a screw propeller.

The next year, at 11 p.m. on 6 September 1776, Sergeant Ezra Lee of Washington's army conned *Turtle*, this 'infernal machine', beneath New York Harbor, intending to screw a charge of gunpowder into the wooden hull of the British flagship, HMS *Eagle*. The attack failed because Lee could not get the screw to penetrate the ship's timbers, but it was, nonetheless, a leap forward: the first time a submersible craft had been used in war.

Other Americans took longer leaps. In 1800 Robert Fulton of Pennsylvania demonstrated his *Nautilus* submarine to the French in the River Seine and again at Le Havre. Built of copper sheets over a cylinder of iron ribs, driven underwater by a hand-cranked propeller, it submerged with a crew of three to the amazing depth of 7.5 metres and stayed there for an hour. Again the idea was to sink British warships with explosives, but Napoleon Bonaparte, who knew nothing of the sea, was unimpressed, informing the *Académie des sciences*:

> There are in all the capitals of Europe, a crowd of adventurers and men with plans who roam the world, offering to every sovereign their so-called discoveries which only exist in their imaginations. They're no more than charlatans or imposters, who have no other goal except to grab money. This American is one of that number. Do not speak of him to me any more.[4]

Like any arms dealer before or since, Fulton deftly switched sides and in 1805 took himself off to London, where he explained his underwater bombs to the prime minister, William Pitt the Younger. Torpedoes, he called them. Pitt was interested but, again, the admirals were not. The gouty and irascible Earl of St Vincent, the recently retired First Lord of the Admiralty, grumbled: 'Pitt was the greatest fool that ever existed, to encourage a mode of war which they who commanded the seas did not want, and which, if successful, would deprive them of it.'[5]

And that was that. Failing to get the handsome fee the British had promised him, Fulton returned to America to a successful career building the first steamboats to ply the Mississippi River.

But from the middle of the nineteenth century the drive to build a better underwater boat accelerated. The French navy launched *Plongeur* in 1863, the first submarine to be propelled not by human muscle pedalling or cranking but an engine powered by compressed air. Looking rather like a swordfish, it had a long ram to penetrate an enemy hull but also an annoying tendency to nosedive straight to the bottom, and it was eventually abandoned. The writer Jules Verne saw a model of it, though, at the Paris Exposition of 1867, and took it as the inspiration for his bestselling science-fiction novel *Twenty Thousand Leagues Under the Sea*, with its stirring tales of a battle with giant squids and the lost city of Atlantis.

Across the Atlantic, Americans were still striving for a successful undersea weapon. During the Civil War, the Confederate government offered a bounty of US$50,000 to anyone who could sink a Union ship. Horace Lawson Hunley, a marine engineer from Tennessee, produced a cylindrical vessel worked by eight men straining and sweating to turn a hand-cranked propeller.

Named for its creator, *H.L. Hunley* wielded a spar torpedo – an explosive charge at the end of a long wooden pole – but it was a mixed success. On its first test run, in 1863, five of the crew were drowned when the boat went down with a hatch left open. At the second run a few months later, all eight crewmen were killed, including Hunley himself. Undeterred, a fresh crew tried for a third time and managed to sink a steam-powered sloop, USS *Housatonic*, off Charleston, North Carolina. But again disaster struck: the pressure wave from the explosion ruptured their boat and killed all of them as well. More work needed. But it was the first time a warship had been sunk by a submarine.[6]

As the last quarter of the century rolled along, the technology evolved at dizzying speed. A Polish engineer developed an electric battery for submerged power and coal-fired steam engines arrived for travel on the surface. A British engineer, Robert Whitehead, came up with the first workable self-propelled torpedo to carry a warhead. Driven by compressed air, it bubbled along at a spanking seven knots and could hit a target 600 metres away. In 1885 a Swedish industrialist living in London, Thorsten Nordenfelt, financed the building of four submarines in Britain, each more advanced than its predecessor. One of them, steam-powered and commissioned into the Ottoman navy as *Abdül Hamid*, became the first submerged submarine to sink a target ship with a Whitehead torpedo.

Remarkably, it was an Irishman who emerged to establish the dominant template that would carry submarine design forward into the twentieth century. He was a wildly unlikely candidate for the role. Growing up in County Limerick and speaking only Gaelic in his early childhood, John Philip Holland left school to spend fifteen years wearing the habit of the Christian Brothers as a teacher of singing, mathematics and drawing. He had a fascination with 'mechanical contrivances' and, tiring of the religious life, he emigrated to Boston, Massachusetts, where, still teaching by day, he spent his leisure hours designing and eventually building the submarines that would take and make his name.

He struck setbacks and rejection. For a while he was subsidised by the Fenian Brotherhood, Irish republican revolutionaries in the United States, who wanted his submarines to confront the Royal Navy. After falling out with them, Holland linked up with two men who saw the potential in his creations, one a financier, the other a lawyer, and the Electric Boat Company was born. He kept dreaming, drawing, building. In 1897 his latest design, *Holland VI*, was launched in a New Jersey shipyard and, after more rigorous tests and negotiation, more hope and disappointment, it was bought by the United States Navy for US$150,000. On 12 October 1900, *Holland VI* was commissioned as USS *Holland* and another seven boats were ordered.

For most of the nineteenth century Britannia had watched and waited. Ruler of the waves, master of the most mighty fleet the world had known, the Admiralty in London flip-flopped between embracing the submarine revolution and hoping it would quietly go away. The ethos of Queen Victoria's navy was ostentatious display, swank and pomp, an endless pageant of coloured flags, scrubbed white decks, gleaming brass and long lines of majestic battleships wheeling in perfect order. For some it was preposterous, outrageous, that a tiny underwater craft might attack and sink these Hearts of Oak. Submarines were 'revolting to every noble principle', fumed an anonymous writer in the *Naval Chronicle*:

> Guy Fawkes is got afloat, battles in future may be fought under water; our invincible ships of the line may give place to horrible and unknown structures, our projects to catamarans, our pilots to divers, our hardy, dauntless tars to submarine assassins; coffers, rockets, catamarans, infernals, water-worms, and fire-devils! How honourable! How fascinating is such an enumeration! How glorious, how fortunate for Britain are discoveries like these! How worthy of being adopted by a people made wanton by naval victories, by a nation whose empire are the seas![7]

Pragmatism won the day. The British naval attaché at the embassy in Washington DC had been sending glowing reports of the American innovation. In Europe, Britain's ancient rivals at sea, the French and Spanish, were building their own submarines, and perhaps the Germans were too. Yet Britain did not have even a design. Never in 300 years had the Royal Navy bought a ship from a foreign builder, but there was nothing else for it. In 1900 the Admiralty took a collective deep breath, swallowed its pride, and quietly placed an order with the Electric Boat Company for five Holland submarines, to be built by the Vickers shipyard at Barrow-in-Furness, in England's northwest. They would each cost £35,000. Secrecy was paramount.

A year later, Rear Admiral Arthur Wilson, the Third Naval Lord and Controller of the Navy, wrote to an enquiring member of parliament:

> They call them underwater weapons. I call them underhand, unfair and damned un-English. They will never be of any use in war, and I'll tell you why. I am going to get the First Sea Lord to announce that we intend to treat all submarines as pirate vessels in wartime, and that we will hang all the crews.[8]

Wilson was famously abrasive and choleric, and that broadside has echoed in history as evidence of blockheaded stupidity in the highest naval ranks, but he would have known that the Holland boats were already being built, and it is likely he was merely trying to keep the secret from possible foes and competitors. HMS *Holland 1* was launched at Barrow on 2 October 1901.

Shaped like a cigar, not quite twenty metres long and displacing 107 tonnes submerged, she could dive to a designed depth of thirty metres. She carried a crew of eight, was armed with one eighteen-inch torpedo tube, and had a 160-horsepower petrol engine for eight knots on the surface and a seventy-horsepower battery electric motor that, in theory, would drive her at seven knots underwater. A new feature was a small 'conning tower' with windows; it was more of a blister or a bubble on the top of the boat, but this improvement allowed you, remarkably, to see where you were going. The first test dive and run was in Morecambe Bay, not far from Barrow, with an American crew sent over to help out. *Holland 1*'s British captain, Lieutenant Forster Delafield Arnold-Forster, recorded the experience:

> After the boat was carefully trimmed down everyone except the American working the diving rudder wheel, the 'boss diver' as he called himself, was seated about the boat on canvas stools opposite their work and warned that if they moved they might upset the balance and perhaps cause a nose-dive into the mud.
>
> Then the motor went ahead, the diving rudder was put down and green water was seen through the conning tower windows. Gradually the depth gauge showed we were running under water for the first time and those who could see watched it anxiously

whilst listening to the hum of the motor and the queer sounding American orders given by our temporary captain.

The boat ran, as these boats always did, with her nose well down and to those who could not see the depth gauge it seemed as though we were bound for the bottom and when a bucket got loose and clattered down the engine room floor plates it sent their hearts into their mouths.

After a little practice the boat was found to be very handy under water but on the surface she was a brute. Being short and stumpy she was awkward to steer on the surface and one day she alarmed the inmates of the sick-bay in her parent ship by poking her big nose right through the ship's side into the berths.

When it was at all rough the boat was all awash and nothing could be seen from the little conning tower. Everything had to be battened down. Those below had to stop there and those on deck, the captain and the coxswain, had their work cut out to hang on by the wheel and ventilators when their feet were washed from under them by the seas.[9]

It was the future and it worked. The question now was what to do with *Holland* and her sisters: how and where and when to deploy them in wartime, which strategies and tactics might be devised and used.

Submarines were too slow and had too little range to keep up with the main fleet or a squadron of battleships. They were not ocean-going vessels; the prevailing view was that they might be useful along a coastline for attacking an enemy harbour or defending your own. There was also the problem of hunting for an enemy boat; there was no known way of finding a submarine below the surface, let alone destroying it there. The writer H.G. Wells, admired at the time as a great thinker and visionary, was scathingly dismissive in 1902:

> I must confess that my imagination, in spite even of spurring, refuses to see any sort of submarine doing anything but suffocate its crew and founder at sea. It must involve physical inconvenience of the most demoralizing sort simply to be in one for any length of time . . .

> You may, of course, throw out a torpedo or so, with as much chance of hitting vitally as you would have if you were blindfolded, turned round three times, and told to fire revolver-shots at a charging elephant . . .
>
> In no way can a submarine be more than purblind, it will be, in fact, practically blind. Given a derelict ironclad on a still night within sight of land, a carefully handled submarine might succeed in groping its way to it and destroying it; but then it would be much better to attack such a vessel and capture it boldly with a few desperate men on a tug. At the utmost the submarine will be used in narrow waters, in rivers, or to fluster or destroy ships in harbour . . .[10]

Wells would live until 1946, more than long enough to see himself proved spectacularly wrong.

Other, more qualified minds had different ideas. The *Holland* boats were demonstrably a success, and from its cautious, hesitant start – typically English – the Admiralty now hurled itself into submarine development with gusto. Much of the impetus for progress came from Admiral Sir John Arbuthnot Fisher, known to one and all as Jacky, a turbulent, impulsive firecracker of a man, perhaps a genius, who at the turn of the century held the navy's most prestigious post at sea as Commander-in-Chief of the Mediterranean Fleet.

Jacky Fisher had entered the navy in 1854 at the age of thirteen by passing an examination which required him to write out the Lord's Prayer and, reputedly, to jump naked over a chair. It was an unconventional start to an unconventional career, in which Fisher's drive for radical improvement and efficiency and his sometimes brutal, suffer-no-fools manner would win him ardent admirers and mortal foes in large and equal measure.

From his flagship in the Mediterranean, HMS *Renown*, he bombarded his juniors, equals and superiors, including influential politicians, with passionate suggestions, schemes and demands for reform, urging upon them his conviction that the submarine and the torpedo were the weapons of the future. Instinct and reason told him that they would entirely change the rules of the game at sea. In a second string to his bow, he quietly (and unusually, for a senior naval officer) kept up a prolific backdoor correspondence with influential Fleet Street journalists, who would push his ideas in the newspapers.[11]

In this he was assisted by a new man in a new job. In 1901 Captain Reginald Bacon was appointed the Inspecting-Captain of Submarine Boats, which put him in charge of the growing underwater fleet. Fisher described him as 'the cleverest officer in the navy'.[12]

Bacon saw a stream of new submarine designs and classes glide down the dockyard slipways, each one a quantum improvement, bigger and better than the last. In almost bewildering succession, in the space of just ten years came the A-class, the B-class, the C-class and the D-class, most of them built at Barrow, where the *Holland* boats had started life.

Much was trial and error, and not without setbacks, accidents and disasters. A build-up of poisonous gases was always a risk, and explosions of one sort or another were not uncommon. For a while white mice were carried in cages to warn if the air was turning foul. In 1904, HMS *A1* was rammed and sunk by a passenger liner off Spithead, with the loss of eleven men. In 1905, five men died when a spark ignited petrol fumes in *A5*, and an accident sank *A8* at Plymouth, with fifteen dead. *A8*, *B2*, *C11* and *C14* were all lost in collisions with surface vessels over the ten years before 1913. The hazards were plenty.

Yet lessons learned brought innovation, and swiftly. The sinking of *A1* saw watertight hatches installed at the bottom of the conning towers, and this saved *A9* when she too was rammed by a steamer at Plymouth two years later. An instrument designer from Dublin, Sir Howard Grubb, produced the first workable periscope, which was gradually improved. Two were fitted in each of the C-class boats, raised and lowered by hand crank at first and later by electric power. The D-class boats were the first to have the new Marconi wireless transmitters and twin propellers. Notoriously unreliable magnetic compasses were replaced by a much more accurate American invention, the Sperry gyrocompass, which used the Earth's rotation to find direction.

In 1904 Jacky Fisher rose yet again to become First Sea Lord, the professional head of the Royal Navy. To the fury of his enemies and the elation of his disciples, he arrived at the Admiralty like a tornado, alternately radiating charm and spitting venom, slashing waste and deadwood in ships, dockyards and officers. 'If any subordinate opposes me, I will make his wife a widow, his children fatherless and his home a dunghill,' he famously snarled.[13] Convinced that war with Germany was inevitable – even perhaps necessary[14] – he set to preparing for it, scrapping no fewer than 160 ships 'that could neither fight nor run away', and embarking on a massive new construction program.[15]

The *Dreadnought* battleship was his baby. Built in just over a year, a stunning achievement, and commissioned in 1906, she was a leviathan whose main armament of ten twelve-inch guns and new steam turbine engines rendered all else obsolete and went a long way towards igniting the naval arms race with Germany. Another new class of ship, the battlecruiser, was his as well. Boasting a battleship's big guns, but less heavily armoured and therefore much faster, it was designed to strike, hit hard and run.

Yet submarines and the men who served in them were an overarching passion for Fisher, displayed in a typically exuberant diary note he made after an inspection tour in 1904:

> Just back from the English Channel with the Submarines and am very enthusiastic! . . .
>
> Yesterday all the mice died in their cages and two of the crew fainted, but the young Lieutenant of the Submarine didn't seem to care a damn whether they all died so long as he bagged the Battleship he was after, and he practically got her and then he came up in his Submarine to breathe!
>
> Depend on it we shall have more 'Niles' and 'Trafalgars' so long as we continue to propagate such 'young bloods' as this! . . .
>
> Another submarine had an explosion which made the interior 'Hell' for some seconds (as the Submarine was bottled up and diving to evade a Destroyer who had caught her with a hook), but

the Submarine Lieutenant saw them all damned first before he would rise up and be caught. Another young fire-eater had his periscope smashed but bagged a battleship nevertheless by coming up stealthily to blow just like a beaver, and look round.

It really is all lovely![16]

Jacky Fisher reluctantly retired from the Admiralty on his sixty-ninth birthday, 25 January 1910, a fully fledged Admiral of the Fleet, a peer of the realm, laden with ribbons and honours, and certain that he had done all he could to ready the Royal Navy for war.

As he left the stage, the arms race was at full pace, the shipyards of Kiel, Hamburg and Bremerhaven, and at Chatham, the Tyne and the Clyde straining to produce battleships, battlecruisers, cruisers, destroyers, submarines. The German kaiser, the strutting and erratic Wilhelm II, a grandson of Queen Victoria and nephew of King Edward VII, displaying an almost pathological envy of all things English, had determined to have a grand navy of his own, to secure Germany's 'place in the sun', as he saw it. In this he was egged on by his navy minister, the talented and scheming Großadmiral Alfred von Tirpitz, who threw his considerable energies into creating a modern and powerful *Hochseeflotte*, or 'High Seas Fleet'.

It had long been a cardinal rule of British imperial policy that the Royal Navy should be large enough and strong enough to match and meet the navies of any two possible enemies, which, in unspoken practice, meant Germany and France. Tirpitz in turn constructed his own 'risk theory', which argued that while Germany could not expect to defeat the Royal Navy, the High Seas Fleet could choose a battle that would inflict enough damage on the British to allow Germany to pursue her imperial ambitions at sea unhindered. The two nations were on a collision course.

Like Fisher, Tirpitz was an enthusiast for underwater warfare. The next generation of British submarines and German U-boats was on the drawing boards.

Britain's first E-class boat in the water should have been *E1*, being built at the Chatham dockyard in Kent, but *E4*, built by Vickers at Barrow, was completed first and commissioned on 28 January 1913. The evolution from those first stumpy little *Hollands* in so few years was nothing less than spectacular: the E-class boats were at the cutting edge of naval science, engineering and art, and crammed with new ideas and new technology.

They were also marvellous to look at, even at rest, tied up to a dock. Long and low and lean, the E-class hull was surmounted by a bold new conning tower, topped by a bridge with more than enough space for the captain to con the boat on the surface with the coxswain at the wheel and a bridge crew of lookouts and a signalman. To landsmen and seamen alike, the boats radiated a powerful aura of menace.

The E-boats were bigger than anything that had come before, displacing 808 tonnes when submerged. The old petrol engines, always at risk of explosion and fire, had been supplanted by two much less volatile British-built Vickers-Admiralty diesels, each of eight cylinders, delivering a total of 1600 horsepower to drive twin-screw propellers. The diesels themselves were a giant stride into the future: the German engineer Rudolf Diesel had devised, tested and run his first successful engine, the Motor 250/400, only in 1897, less than twenty years before. Their best speed was a more-than-respectable fifteen knots on the surface and ten knots below, with a rated safe depth of 100 feet or thirty-three metres. With a range of 3000 nautical miles (5600 kilometres) at ten knots on the surface, they were in theory no longer a mere coastal vessel but ocean-going, although this had yet to be proven. There were two periscopes and, for the first time in a submarine, internal watertight bulkheads that strengthened the hull against the pressure of water.

Most striking – and this again was new – there were four torpedo tubes, one fore and one aft, and another two laid transversely, or across the beam amidships, enabling the eighteen-inch Whitehead torpedoes to be fired on the broadside as well, one to port and one to starboard. Each boat carried eight torpedoes. Curiously, though, the early models did not have a deck gun, an omission that would prove costly.

The Admiralty's first order was for ten boats. Eventually, fifty-six would be built between 1911 and 1917, with each new batch incorporating improvements upon its predecessors.

In Australia, debate about the defence of the nation at sea, its trade and communications and harbours, waxed and waned and waxed again. Since the first settlement in 1788, the colonies had grown and flourished under the protection of ships of the Royal Navy – at first a mere handful of them, but in time a squadron based at what became known as the Australian Station, commanded by a British admiral in Sydney.

From around the middle of the nineteenth century, all the colonies except Western Australia began to set up their own naval forces, a motley collection of vessels that ranged from the small and largely impotent to the aged and infirm and the absurdly comical. The centrepiece of Her Majesty's Victorian Navy was the monitor *Cerberus*, an ugly beast of a thing with ancient muzzle-loading guns. She sat so low in the water that after she lurched into Port Phillip Bay in 1871, no one ever dared take her to sea again.[17]

With Federation, the states handed their vessels over to the new national government to form the Commonwealth Naval Forces. In salty circles there was wild talk that perhaps, at some time in the future, there might be an Australian naval squadron, even an Australian navy. For most, though, that was a pipe dream. The first prime minister, Edmund Barton, was a Sydney lawyer little interested in defence and knowing less; he was content to keep paying a subsidy of £200,000 a year to help maintain the Royal Navy in Australian waters.

The second prime minister changed everything. Alfred 'Affable Alfie' Deakin, a gifted Melbourne barrister, journalist and former Victorian cabinet minister, took office in 1903. As he turned his agile mind to the question of defence, he gradually became convinced that an Australian navy would be a very good idea. He set about to make it happen. What he needed was sound professional advice. He did not have to look far.

William Rooke Creswell, born on the Mediterranean island of Gibraltar in 1852, had entered the Royal Navy as a cadet at the customary age of thirteen. Bold and dashing, as a young lieutenant he had skirmished with Malay pirates, who shot him in the hip, and he battled the slave trade off Zanzibar. A fever cut short his career and in 1878 he left the navy – he 'swallowed the anchor', as the old saying had it – emigrated to Australia and went bush, joining his brother droving cattle and exploring in Queensland and the Northern Territory. The sea, though, kept calling him. When the South Australians asked him to return to uniform in their flagship, the little gunboat HMCS *Protector*, he jumped at the offer.[18] As her captain, he took her in 1900 to serve in the Boxer Rebellion in the waters off Shanghai, flying the Royal Navy's White Ensign.

He was just the man Deakin wanted. In 1904 Captain Creswell was appointed to the newly created job of Naval Officer Commanding the Commonwealth Naval Forces. An articulate speaker with a flowing pen, a forceful presence and the courage of his convictions, with the prime minister's support he began to mount a skilful public and private campaign for Australia to have a navy of its own.

Not everyone approved. In distant Whitehall and Westminster, it was commonly held that the descendants of convicts, while they might be trained as useful seamen, could hardly understand high policy and naval doctrine, that knowledge of the command of the seas and oceans acquired over centuries. At the Admiralty, they viewed Creswell as a colonial upstart on the make for publicity and promotion.

As always, the devil was in the detail. How many ships would be needed, and of what type? How would officers and men be recruited and trained, and where? Who would pay for it all? The decisions were not made any easier by a revolving door of defence ministers in Australia – there were no fewer than eleven of them in the ten years following Federation. Gradually, though, British intransigence began to soften. In 1907 Deakin travelled to the Colonial Conference of Prime Ministers and Premiers in London to hear the news that 'His Majesty's government recognise the natural desire of the self-governing colonies to have a more particular share in providing the Naval defence of the Empire'.[19] On a visit to Portsmouth, Deakin was shown the Royal Navy's latest submarines, the C-class, and went home mightily impressed.

William Creswell, however, had no faith in these newfangled boats. Essentially, he saw a squadron of surface vessels, of three small cruisers, sixteen destroyers and thirteen torpedo boats. In a closely reasoned report to the defence minister in September 1907, Creswell argued that he was 'against the adoption of the submersibles' on the grounds that they were experimental, unstable, of limited range, unsuitable for use in the big seas off the Australian coast, and largely useless at night.[20]

In December, *The Age* in Melbourne published a significant scoop, quite clearly having enjoyed a tip-off from the prime minister's office. Deakin was planning a major speech to parliament that would be 'the first complete pronouncement on defence policy made since Federation was consummated'.[21] He would announce 'the acquisition of an Australian coastal navy', said the paper, and it was expected that he would 'be able to state that the fleet will embrace the very latest in submersibles or submarines, as well as torpedo boats and coastal destroyers'.

Creswell, caught unawares, read this with rising dismay, and the next day fired off a starchy letter to the defence minister:

> My reasons for using every endeavour to dissuade the Government from including submarines in any of their proposals are:
> 1) That submarines will be useless for Australia under present conditions or against any attacks possible to occur.
> 2) They will be unsuitable under weather and sea conditions of common occurrence with us; and
> 3) They will in no way contribute to that Naval development (so vital to the future of Australia) and valuable by-product of the Naval Defence Scheme already submitted to the government by myself and a Committee of Naval Officers.

To add insult to injury, *The Age*'s report revealed that Deakin had gone over Creswell's head to ignore his professional advice – there could be no doubt about it:

> I understand from the public press that the decision of the Government to acquire submarines for Australia has been arrived at after long and frequent communication with the Admiralty. I can only express my regret that I have not been privileged to see the views on which the Prime Minister has based his reasons for a change so radical in the Australian Naval Defence proposals before the government.

It was to no avail. That same evening, Deakin made his speech to the House of Representatives exactly as *The Age* had foreshadowed. It was stirring stuff. There would be an Australian naval squadron, manned by Australians and including destroyers, torpedo boats and the submarines he had seen in Britain. No fewer than nine of the C-class submarines would be built, three a year for three years, at a cost of £55,600 each.[22]

The prime minister's speech was enthusiastically endorsed by the Labor opposition and its leader, Andrew Fisher, but as in every defence debate then and ever since, ignorance reared its foolish head. The Sydney *Evening News* dismissed the speech as 'high falutin bunkum' and snapped: 'It is more than doubtful whether the Admiralty wishes to be bothered with the thankless task of breaking in raw Australians to become men o'-warsmen.'[23]

The inevitable armchair experts harrumphed in letters to editors that an Australian navy would be a scandalous waste of money and a disloyal insult to King and Empire, while a peppery military faction – khaki, polished brown leather and fierce moustaches – maintained that any invader could be sent packing by artillery batteries mounted on cliffs and harbour headlands.

To move public opinion his way, Deakin came up with a masterstroke. The President of the United States, Theodore Roosevelt, had despatched his 'Great White Fleet' of battleships on a world cruise to demonstrate that America was a naval power to be reckoned with. Deakin asked Roosevelt to send the fleet to Australia, which he readily did. News of the visit put noses severely out of joint in Britain, but when sixteen warships of the US Navy steamed through the Heads of Sydney Harbour in August 1908, their white hulls and buff-painted upperworks splendid in the winter sunshine, a forest of flags flying beneath sulphurous clouds of coal smoke, they met a rapturous welcome. The city streets were decked with flowers, flags and festive arches, there were parades and parties, dinners and picnics, church services and receptions, and windy speeches about brotherhood in the Pacific, the eternal kinship of eagle and kangaroo. It was, as Sydney's *Lone Hand* magazine stoutly proclaimed, 'an armed assertion that the white race will not surrender its supremacy on any of the world's seas'.[24] The reception in Melbourne a week later was equally fervent, and again at Albany in Western Australia.

Public sentiment swung exactly as Deakin had hoped: if the American cousins could maintain their own fleet, surely Australians could too. Eloquent as ever, he rammed home the point:

> But for the British Navy there would be no Australia. That does not mean that Australia should sit still under the shelter of the British Navy – those who say we should sit still are not worthy of the name of Briton. We can add to the squadron in these seas from our own blood and intelligence something that will launch us on the beginning of a naval career, and may in time create a force which shall rank among the defences of the Empire . . .[25]

The defence of the British Empire took on added urgency after what became known as the Naval Scare of 1909, when the First Lord of the Admiralty, Sir Reginald McKenna, rose in the House of Commons with a dire warning of Germany's accelerating drive to build battleships that could only be intended to challenge the British fleet. Britain must increase her construction or the Royal Navy would lose its supremacy at sea by 1912.

The speech caused a sensation, arousing alarm throughout the empire, including in Australia. For all their pride in their newfound nationhood, Australians still saw themselves as Britons, loyal members of 'the British race', with unbreakable bonds to what many still called 'the Mother Country' or even 'Home'. Even at this other end of the Earth, the spectre of a belligerent Germany was too close for comfort, and bound to raise hackles. Australia was well aware of the Pacific outposts of the Kaiser's empire to the near north, in German New Guinea, Nauru and the

North Solomon Islands and more, patrolled by modern cruisers of the East German Asia Squadron, based in Tsingtao, China.

In Melbourne – Australia's temporary national capital at this time – the Town Hall was packed one Friday evening by what *The Argus* approvingly called 'a monster meeting ... of the hard-working part of the population', attended by the premier, the state treasurer and the lord mayor, to pledge donations from the Victorian people to buy Britain a battleship.

> When the organist broke into 'Rule Britannia' the great audience, moved as if by one impulse, rose and cheered and cheered again, waving hats and handkerchiefs. On the chorus being repeated the audience stopped from cheering to sing the words, the concluding line 'Britons, never, never, never shall be slaves' coming with a great roll of sound.[26]

Nothing came of the meeting, but the British patriotism was real enough. Jacky Fisher was invited to visit Australia to make yet another assessment of naval defence, but he declined and instead the recently retired admiral Sir Reginald Henderson was sent out in 1910 to provide advice. A dockyard expert who had never actually commanded a fleet, he came up with a vision for a naval force and bases so vast and expensive that the Commonwealth could never have afforded it, nor found the sailors to man it.

Fisher did offer his thoughts from a distance, proposing that Australia should have one of his brand-new battlecruisers, three supporting light cruisers, a flotilla of six destroyers and three submarines. 'We manage the job in Europe,' he wrote to a friend. 'They'll manage it against the Yankees, Japs and Chinese as occasion requires out there.'[27]

A long and meandering course through stormy political and naval professional waters was nearing its end. After no little prodding, the Admiralty agreed to do all in its power to assist the young Commonwealth to lay the foundations for its own navy, and the Deakin government ordered the building of what was called a fleet unit – one of Fisher's new battlecruisers, two light cruisers and three destroyers. On 10 July 1911, King George V was 'graciously pleased' to grant the Commonwealth Naval Forces the title of Royal Australian Navy (RAN).

A torrent of official paperwork rained down from on high to make this happen, orders great and small, including such vital gems as: 'Officers of the Royal Australian Navy shall wear the same uniform as prescribed for Officers of the Royal Navy except that the buttons worn by the former shall be of a special design (information as to which will be communicated later).'[28]

Creswell, by now a rear admiral, was the government's professional naval adviser as First Naval Member of the Australian Commonwealth Naval Board. In March 1913 the inaugural class of twenty-eight officer cadet midshipmen, thirteen-year-old boys, arrived at the Royal Australian Naval College at its temporary home in Geelong, and that same year this new RAN took tangible, living form in grey steel.

On Saturday, 4 October there began another ecstatic week of welcome in Sydney as the fleet unit made its first grand entrance. In brilliant spring sunshine, HMAS *Australia*, the battlecruiser and flagship, the cruisers HMAS *Sydney* and *Melbourne*, and the destroyers HMAS *Warrego*, *Parramatta* and *Yarra* steamed up the harbour, at first to an awed silence and then to rousing, rolling cheers from the crowds thronging every vantage point on the foreshores. The great guns thundered in salute.

The defence minister, Senator Edward Millen – another former journalist – proclaimed that:

> The Australian fleet is not merely the embodiment of force. It is the expression of Australia's resolve to pursue, in freedom, its national ideals, and to hand down unimpaired and unsullied the heritage it has received, and which it holds and cherishes as an inviolable trust. It is in this spirit that Australia welcomes its fleet not as an instrument of war but as the harbinger of peace.[29]

Some unfinished business remained. Deakin had got his way with the submarines, too, but technology had moved on from the C-class, and with the rising costs of the new designs the original idea of nine boats was now beyond reach. The government ordered two of the new E-class boats, then still on the drawing board, to be built by Vickers at Barrow. The original price quoted was £115,000 per boat but after some negotiation that was wound back to £105,415. The first was to be delivered in December 1912, and the second a month later. They would be named HMAS *AE1* and HMAS *AE2*, with the A signifying 'Australia'.

At home, Australian sailors were asked to volunteer to man them. They would become the nation's first submariners.

2
STRAWS IN THE WIND

Harry Kinder had already been posted in Britain when the word went out that they were looking for men to serve in the new Australian submarines; his name was on the books of HMS *Victory*, Nelson's old flagship at the great Portsmouth Naval Base in Hampshire. A notice calling for volunteers appeared in the Portsmouth Barracks and caught his eye. It was the autumn of 1912. At the age of twenty-one, Harry was a leading stoker, fit and healthy, which was what they said they wanted. And so, out of curiosity more than anything else, he put his hand up.

He did a medical examination so stringent that of the twenty-eight sailors lined up before the doctors, only he and one other man passed it. He was in. The next day he was told to pack his kit and get across the harbour to Fort Blockhouse, the home of the Royal Navy's submarine fleet, where, with some other successful volunteers, he was issued with extra submarine clothing: a thick white woollen jumper with a rollneck, and warm woollen underwear. Submarines could get cold, they said. There was a heavy pair of leather seaboots as well, two sizes too big so that if you fell overboard you could kick them off easily – a cheerful thought.

Harry – full name Henry James Elly Kinder – was born on 17 January 1891, the third of four children. Their father, George, an immigrant from Lancashire, was a stonemason, and the family lived in Railway Parade at Kogarah, not far from the western shore of Botany Bay, where you could picnic, swim and go fishing. When Harry left school, he worked for a while as a fireman, but a life at sea caught his imagination and at the age of eighteen he signed on as a stoker second class in the Commonwealth Naval Force. Stokers were pretty much the lowest form of naval life, employed to shovel or 'stoke' coal into the furnaces that fired a ship's boilers, backbreaking work deep below the waterline. His first ship was HMS *Challenger*, a three-funnelled cruiser based at the Australian Station, where the temperature in the stokehold at the height of summer might reach fifty degrees or more. Submarines must have seemed appealing after that.

Stokers were usually chosen for brawn, not brain, but Harry had both. His memoir is a vivid, observant picture of life underwater. The Royal Navy's Portsmouth submarine school – officially the shore establishment HMS *Dolphin*, but invariably known to its inmates and graduates as just plain Blockhouse – had its beginnings as a fort against the French back in the sixteenth century under the Tudor monarchs, with its bastions and parapets and batteries fortified again during the Napoleonic Wars of the nineteenth century. The navy took it over in 1907 to teach generations of submariners the basics before they went to sea. After his first stretch of training, Harry was assigned to the crew of a D-class boat, *D2*. '[M]y first impressions,' he wrote, 'were of a jumble of wheels, pipes and electrical gear.'

> There was hardly room to move about and it would take me more than a few months to sort it out and digest its workings. At first one wonders what so many wheels and electric switches jammed in every hole and corner could be used for but one soon gets used to their different workings.
>
> I am not likely to forget my first dive in a submarine off the Isle of Wight. When submerging, the boat seemed to go down at angles and the crew looked a bit anxious. My hair seemed to be standing on end. I wasn't sure when we reached the surface and returned to harbour again and I could feel solid ground under my feet once more. A lot of men's enthusiasm for submarines evaporated on that trip and I would have willingly returned to general service again, as the sensation of diving for the first time especially when the boat is not under proper control is not a pleasant one.

I was not altogether pleased to have volunteered. All crews of submarines are drawn from the ships in the fleet by calling for volunteers. They draw an extra allowance as danger money, or as it is commonly called in submarines, Blood Money.[1]

There was nothing to do but stick at it, picking up knowledge as you went. Harry would learn that even on a training exercise there was danger for the unwary, when *D2* came within a hair's breadth of a collision at sea, with – of all things – the battlecruiser HMAS *Australia*. The boat was shallow, at a depth of only twenty-two feet, with the captain away from the control room to check something up for'ard:

> *D2* had been submerged for about half an hour when one of the men, out of curiosity, looked through the periscope and saw a man o'war bearing down on us. It proved to be HMAS Australia doing her steering trials.
>
> *D2*'s captain happened to be coming aft at the time so orders were soon flying around, the tanks put hard to blow and the helm to port. *D2* rose to the surface practically under the bows of the Australia but luckily officers on the Australia's bridge saw *D2*'s periscope rising and evidently gave the order to swing to starboard.
>
> As the Australia swung off, just missing ramming *D2*, we could hear her huge propellers churning the water as she raced by. It seemed as though they would crash through the thin shell of the *D2* at any moment and we gave a sigh of relief when the churning propellers sounded further away.
>
> It is not pleasant having a boat of 20,000 tons racing toward you and it seemed strange that it was to be our future flagship. We were not sorry when orders were given to return to harbour, as a shock like that is enough for one day.

In truth, for all the advances in technology and all the hard-won experience accumulated by officers and men in these early years, it was an unavoidable fact of submarine life that accident and hazard hovered not far from their shoulders. Harry had transferred to the newly commissioned *E4* and was in his final months of training at Blockhouse when they learned in June 1913 that *E5*, still on her trials in the Bristol Channel, had suffered a catastrophic explosion in her engine room, with one man killed instantly and two more who died later from their injuries. It cast a dark cloud, especially over the Royal Navy (RN) sailors. The victims were people like themselves, young men doing the same job, some of them former shipmates or names they knew.

'Every conceivable measure to prevent accidents is taken by the officers and men on board these vessels,' the First Lord of the Admiralty, Winston Churchill, told the House of Commons after the accident. 'They know that their lives depend upon the care with which dangerous instruments are handled . . .'[2]

This was not necessarily all that reassuring. There but for the grace of God . . .

Four months later, in October 1913, and having been promoted to stoker petty officer, Harry took a train north to Barrow-in-Furness to join the commissioning crew of *AE2*. By this time, both boats had been launched, *AE1* in May that year and *AE2* in June. They were in the water, but still with a daunting amount of work to be done both above and below decks. Bit by bit, the crews were coming together, to 'stand by the build', as the navy called it: thirty men for each boat, including two officers. With not enough RAN sailors able or available to fill all the jobs, there was a draft of mostly well-experienced RN sailors, all volunteers, who were 'lent to the Royal Australian Navy for three years'.

Typical of the Brits was Chief Petty Officer Charlie Vaughan, a veteran of twenty-three years in 'the Andrew', an old slang term for the RN.[3] After joining as a Boy 2nd Class in 1890, he had served on battleships, cruisers and torpedo boats and begun his submarine training in 1907. He was a qualified torpedoman, forty years old, still speaking with an engaging West Country burr from his birthplace in Somerset. Charlie would be *AE2*'s coxswain, the senior sailor in the boat, known to one and all as 'Swain, the sort of man who is the heart and soul of a well-run ship.

The Australians were generally younger and newer. Jack Bray, a stoker first class, was twenty-two when he arrived in Barrow to join *AE1*. He was from Eaglehawk, north of Bendigo, in country Victoria, and a blacksmith before he signed up for the RAN.

His service record noted that he was five feet five inches tall, with brown hair, blue eyes and a fresh complexion. In submarines, it helped to be a bit on the shorter side.

Many of them were boys from the bush. Able Seaman Jack Jarman, a fair-haired, good-looking officers' steward, had grown up at Dookie, east of Shepparton, Victoria, and had enlisted in 1911. The RAN carefully noted his tattoos on his service record, a splendid display: 'Nellie over clasped hands, 3 horseshoes, heart and cross, ship in wreath on left arm, full rigged ship, shield and heart, floral design on left hand.' This might have been useful to identify him, for he deserted from *Parramatta* very early in the piece and was on the run for almost a year until October 1912, apparently to care for an invalid mother and his baby sister. When the navy got him back – and curiously there's no record of any punishment – they sent him off for *AE1*. He was just twenty years old.

The officers were all RN. No RAN officer had yet qualified for submarines, let alone at a level to command one, and there was no time for learning on the job. *AE1*'s captain would be Thomas Besant, born in Liverpool into a well-known middle-class family and thirty years old when he was promoted to lieutenant commander in December 1913. One of his uncles, Sir Walter Besant, was a novelist and historian, forgotten now but in his day a celebrated figure knighted by Queen Victoria. An aunt, Annie Besant, an outspoken socialist and feminist, had scandalised polite society by walking out on her husband, a respectable country vicar, leaving their two children for him to bring up while she travelled the world to campaign noisily for women's rights and birth control. A stirring orator, she preached the shining virtues of 'theosophy', a crank quasi-religious cult fashionable at the turn of the century. Annie, whipping up still more scandal, eventually took herself off to India, where she became a friend of Mahatma Gandhi and agitated for Indian independence from the British Raj. She also toured Australia twice, drawing big audiences.

Tom Besant's upbringing was rather more conventional. His father, Edgar, is usually referred to as a naval storekeeper, suggesting a humble occupation, but in fact he was a civilian administrator in Royal Navy dockyards who served as far afield as Portsmouth, Malta, Hong Kong and Chatham, rising in seniority and authority until he retired at Devonport in 1900, after which he moved first to Switzerland and then into a handsome villa in Ladbroke Grove, London.

Oddly, the youngster's family called him by his middle name, Fleming, but he was Tom to everyone else.[4] Living in or near the bustling dockyards, he grew up familiar with foreign ports and sailors, ships and the sea, and his father would certainly have known the right people, admirals and captains with the influence needed to win his son a position as a naval cadet. Tom duly entered the RN training ship *Britannia* in 1898.

His career was moving steadily upwards, nothing less but nothing more either. He finished his exams for sub-lieutenant in 1904 with first-class passes for seamanship and torpedo but only a third for navigation and gunnery. He did submarine training in 1905 and gained his first command, on *C12*, as a lieutenant in 1907. Then, after a spell on the surface in a battleship, he was given *C30*, one of the last of the boats with those frighteningly volatile petrol engines.

He must have done it well enough, for one of his superiors in a performance report marked him as an excellent submarine commander and very good divisional leader, strongly recommended. Another remarked that he was 'zealous and very able, slow but sure'.[5] His colleague and friend Harry Stoker, captain of *AE2*, described him as 'skillful, cautious and experienced'.[6] He added the half-stripe of a lieutenant commander to his uniform in December 1913.

Tom Besant was unmarried, and if he kept a diary it is lost, but we get a glimpse of the man from his personal possessions. In those early days, submarines had a depot ship or tender, a floating base which carried supplies and engine stores and the like, and also the crews' kit that was too bulky to take with them to sea. Lieutenant Commander Besant's belongings included Shakespeare's plays and the works of Rabelais and Voltaire in French; books on chess, engines and public speaking; a camera; tennis racquets, riding jodhpurs and a fishing net; a chess set;

a typewriter and Masonic regalia; and a small collection of silver in cigarette cases, boxes and a watch and chain. It is the picture of a self-contained and bookish yet vigorous young officer and gentleman.

Harry Stoker stands out more brightly, for he wrote a delightfully entertaining memoir, *Straws in the Wind*. His foreword begins:

> This is the attitude towards life that attracts me. With indulgent smile and jest on lip, I like to wave an airy hand and murmur: Look at it all, what funny little folk we are – how seriously we take ourselves! We live, we laugh, we love, we weep, we war, we waste away – oh! so seriously! As if the world hinged on our petty doings! We strut with such an air of importance round our tiny spinning ball – a speck in the inscrutable, unfathomable depths of the universe.[7]

Dublin was his home, for he was an Irishman, born Henry Hugh Gordon Stoker in 1885, the son of a prominent physician.[8] Like Tom Besant, he had a literary connection: a cousin, Bram Stoker, was the author of the hugely popular novel *Dracula*, a Gothic horror story of a Transylvanian vampire published in 1897. Inspired by a relative who had tried but failed to join the navy, young Harry entered the service in 1900 as a cadet of fifteen after a spell at a college in England. He was mocked there for his Irish accent and quaintly odd clothing but the training got him through his entrance exam with flying colours. As he described it:

> 'Twas a good life on board the old *Britannia*, the training ship. Moored in the river at Dartmouth, midst beautiful Devon scenery, about 250 cadets lived aboard, and messed, and drilled, and worked at the intricacies of navigation and seamanship, landing only for games, and ending the day in happy weariness by climbing into one of the closely hung hammocks. A strange life, too, with its uniforms, its minutely graded officers, its strict discipline; but even to an Irish boy the discipline seemed a fair and good thing and inspired no rebellious spirit. Thus young does the Navy breed a pride in the Service in its sons.[9]

As a cadet, Stoker attended that tremendous climax of Victoriana, the pomp and circumstance funeral of the great Queen – 'such a lump came to my throat'[10] – and as a teenage midshipman in a battleship of the Channel Fleet, HMS *Jupiter*, he was regularly beaten by the two sub-lieutenants in charge of the gunroom, who, for sins real or imagined, would stretch him out over a table and whack him with a cane or a sword scabbard.[11] It was normal, expected, the custom, did you a lot of good. 'The victim was generally a mild hero to his fellows who would, with critical interest, inspect the striped and bruised portion at the first opportunity in the midshipmen's bathroom,' Stoker reported.[12]

Next came a spell in the Mediterranean Fleet aboard the brand-new battleship *Implacable*, with no less than His Serene Highness Prince Louis of Battenberg as captain. Of this time, Stoker recalled:

> We roamed the Mediterranean, visited a hundred foreign ports, played our cricket and football and hockey and rackets and tennis; we rode and we danced, and we lost our youthful hearts with ease and regularity, retrieving them only for the purpose of losing them again.
>
> A midshipman's love affair is a very delightful business. The ship enters a harbour and he lands and immediately gives his heart to the most presentable of the local ladies. For a couple of days he adores her and then the ship sails away. He is beautifully miserable, and writes her a long, long letter telling her how wonderful she is and how he will never be able to forget her. But the ship must reach a new port before the letter can be posted. And in the new port there is a new lady . . .[13]

By now the young man was slender, fit and darkly handsome, with a winning smile and lashings of Irish charm. A philanderer, he liked to call himself. He complained that the Commander-in-Chief, Jacky Fisher, kept cutting in on his dancing partners – although not to the man himself.[14]

Promotion followed in the normal course of events: sub-lieutenant in 1904, and lieutenant in 1906. Also in that year he went into submarines. He got his first command as a 23-year-old lieutenant in *A10*, which he proceeded to ram full tilt into the dockyard wall at Devonport. Evidently he was forgiven.

In 1908 he married Olive Leacock, the daughter of an Indian Army officer. She was a divorcee, which caused some thin lips. They settled in Portsmouth and had three daughters, Hope, Joan and Iris, but it was not a happy marriage – it seems his philandering went on untroubled – and Stoker never mentions his family in his memoirs. He took his second command, *B8*, to Gibraltar in 1911, to revel, yet again, in the glittering pleasures of the naval life abroad:

> I well remember an evening on the north front racecourse when a Navy and Army cricket match was in progress. I had collected some runs and was having a late tea, at peace with the world. A band was playing, the Governor and the beauteous ladies of the garrison were making a social function of the occasion; the sun was sinking in the west, but a nearly full moon had already risen in the east; a football match was being played upon an adjacent ground; some polo ponies were exercising and a couple of racehorses doing gallops around the track; I noted it all; and, as a last touch, hounds came into sight returning to kennels from exercise. Sun and moon, cricket and football, horses and hounds, bands and beauteous ladies – all at the same moment. What more can anyone ask?[15]

The polo playing attracted him but there was no way he could afford the eyewatering expense of keeping the ponies. His career moved onwards and upwards. In 1913 a note on his service record commended him as 'a very clever, brilliant submarine officer, good judgement, excellent nerve', although there was a little sting in the tail: 'His complete success as a submarine officer is rather marred by the neglect of small though important details of preparation.'[16]

One day he heard on the grapevine that there was a wealthy man in Australia who would meet all the bills if you would play for his team. It was another of those straws in the wind. By happy coincidence, the RN was advertising for qualified officers to take command of two new Australian submarines. For all his headlong enjoyment of wine, women and sport, Stoker was an able and well-regarded officer who took his profession seriously. He applied and was accepted. And so, in October 1913, he too was in Barrow to stand by *AE2*.

With the dark northern winter coming on, it must have seemed a long way from the sunny pleasures of Gibraltar and Malta. Barrow had been a quiet rural village on the coast of Lancashire until the mid-nineteenth century, when iron ore was discovered nearby. Local magnates threw their money in and built railways and factories and workshops, and towards the end of the century the town could boast a giant blast furnace in the largest steelworks in the world. The Vickers shipyard began operating at around the same time. As the curtain rose on the twentieth century, Barrow was a clanging, roaring, thundering, grimy, soot-stained industrial titan almost perpetually shrouded in coal smoke from its towering chimneys. Ships large and small rolled down its slipways.

For the young Australians there, it was purgatory. There were no dark satanic mills like this in the sunlit country they had come from. In truth, though, there were some compensations to make life a little easier. Naval barracks had not been built so they were billeted out with private families, which meant – if your landlady was up to it – that you got a decent bit of home cooking. Lancashire hotpot was good tucker, lamb and potatoes. And there was always a pub or one of those workingman's clubs typical of the north of England around the corner. After a while you got accustomed to the flat, dark brown brew the English called beer. And if you had a mind for it and could snatch the time, you could escape the grime and go further afield into the lovely countryside of the Lakes District around Coniston Water and Windermere.

There was one night in January 1914 that thrilled them all. The world famous American escape artist Harry Houdini came to town. Barrow was his first stop in a tour of Britain, playing five nights at the Tivoli Theatre, just a few blocks from the docks.

The town woke one morning to find the streets plastered with placards headlined:

CHALLENGE
from the
PETTY OFFICERS AND MEN
of the
AUSTRALIAN SUBMARINES.

We, the undersigned Petty Officers and Men of the Australian Submarines now building in Barrow, happening to have in our possession an old straightjacket which used to be used for the criminally insane, challenge Houdini to escape from the same. The only conditions we wish to enforce are that we should personally strap Houdini in the jacket and that he should remain on stage in full view of the audience during the whole time he is endeavouring to escape.

It was a put-up job, a publicity stunt, and everyone knew it, but the excitement mounted the next day when more placards appeared, in which Houdini accepted the challenge and promised to pay the men £250 if he failed to free himself. On a Friday night – it was 16 January – the crews duly filed into the reserved front rows of the Tivoli, many of them fortified with a few beers to combat stage fright. Houdini invited them up, introduced them by name and commanded them to strap him in.

An amused Harry Stoker was there for the show:

> The great attempt started. Houdini writhed and twisted, and tugged and strained. After about half an hour, when he had apparently made little progress and was lying on the floor with hands and legs still bound, one of the sailors produced a suspiciously clean-looking handkerchief and, walking over, wiped the worker's heated brow. This, of course, produced absolute hurricanes of applause from the audience in appreciation of the gallant tar's kindly act.[17]

In another half-hour the great man had struggled free and his money was safe. It was back to work for the crews the next day, for delivery of the boats was well behind schedule and the rush was on to keep things moving. *AE1* was due to leave Barrow for Portsmouth in a few days, and *AE2* just a couple of weeks later, early in February.

The RAN had sent two engineer officers, Lieutenants Halliday Paterson and Douglass Herbert, to supervise the more technical aspects of the construction, and that took a lot of the weight, but each captain still had to learn every nut and bolt in his boat. He had to get his crew into shape and begin thinking hard about the long voyage to Australia, where no submarine had been before. The testing had all been done, as much as possible in the time available: engines running, diesels and batteries, electricals, periscopes. Trim and inclining tests, and diving tests in Morecambe Bay. Everything seemed to be working, as far as you could tell. It was hardly rigorous, but the most that time would allow.

There were two more officers to help shoulder the burden. Each captain had been allowed to choose his own man. In *AE1*, Besant's first lieutenant was another Irishman, 25-year-old Lieutenant Charles Moore. Stoker had picked Lieutenant Geoffrey Haggard, also twenty-five, for his 'number one', as the captains informally called their executive officers. Tall and athletic, he too had a literary link: an uncle was H. Rider Haggard, author of *King Solomon's Mines*, a novel of exploration in darkest Africa advertised by its publishers in 1887 as 'the most amazing book ever written' and duly devoured by readers around the world.

Both these young officers had trained for submarines, but they would be at full stretch. Hallowed naval routine and practice was for a ship's company to work in watches of four hours on and four hours off, save for what were known as the 'dog watches', which were two hours: the first beginning at 4 p.m., followed by the second at 6 p.m. In a large surface vessel, a battleship or a cruiser, the captain did not stand a regular watch and would normally leave conning the ship to his watchkeeping officers: at least half a dozen of them would take turns. In submarines there simply weren't the numbers. At sea it would be watch on and watch off for each officer, turn and turn about, with never more than four hours' sleep. It was an arduous, draining regime.

Every sailor had to know his boat, too, from the most junior hand upwards. Safety was paramount, teamwork was vital, and with experience each man would learn and understand what his shipmates' jobs involved. There was a lot to take in.

AE1 and *AE2* were identical twins, each 55.17 metres long from stem to stern and 6.8 metres in the beam. On the outer hull there were four bulbous tanks on each side, port and starboard, known as saddle tanks, which could be filled, individually, with up to 100 tonnes of sea water to dive the boat. To surface again, the water would be pumped out with compressed air.

You could enter the boat through the conning tower, but would more likely use the main hatch on the casing aft. Down the ladder and your feet landed on a deck covered in canvas to help keep your foothold, and also to waterproof the great bank of batteries that lay beneath. Saltwater and batteries could be a deadly combination, producing poisonous chloride gas that could choke and kill a crew with frightening speed. There were 224 separate battery cells, weighing in total around ninety tonnes and pumping out 300 volts at maximum charge to power the engines beneath the surface and provide light. Beneath the batteries there were still more tanks for engine fuel and fresh water.

Harry Kinder, ever the discerning observer, described *AE2* in his diary, what she looked like and how she worked. It is an account so vivid that it can't be bettered and deserves reading in full:

> The boat is divided vertically into three sections by two bulkheads fitted with watertight doors. The front section contains a bow torpedo tube for firing straight ahead, a reciprocating pump for emptying out the ballast tanks and the motors for hauling up the anchors. One anchor could be let go while the submarine was on the bottom to prevent her from drifting.
>
> Around the torpedo tubes were stored the engine room stores and spare gear for the engines. When anything was wanted it was a Chinese puzzle to get it out as everything was bolted onto plates to prevent it moving in rough weather.
>
> On going through the watertight doors you come to the officers' quarters. They have three bunks in the form of a big set

of drawers, but otherwise they have very little more comfort than that provided for the remainder of the crew.

The wireless cabin was jammed up against the wardroom. It took up a lot of room as it had to be made soundproof. By the time the operator wedged himself in there wasn't much room. Our wireless never seemed to be much good but probably it was owing to so much electrical gear around it on both sides.

As you went aft, you came to the main motor switches for controlling the motors and lights throughout the boat. Opposite are the two big hydroplane motors and the big brass wheel to operate the hydroplanes by hand. These planes are fitted on the outside of the boat, two in the bow and two in the stern, and are used to dive the boat. They look like big fins sticking out.

Over the hydroplane wheels are two big depth gauges which indicate the depth of the boat. They register up to 120 ft [36.5 metres] and after that depth air pressure indicates the depth. Inside these gauges are curved spirit levels to tell when the boat is level.

When the boat submerges, the bow hydroplanes force her under to the required depth and the stern hydroplanes keep the boat level. A fair amount of practice is required, chasing the spirit bubble, to keep the boat level, and generally the two coxswains are stationed on the hydroplanes.

In the middle of the boat and under the conning tower are the two periscopes, the eyes of the submarine and the only means of seeing the outer world when the conning tower doors are shut down. They are only of use while the submarine is submerged above 22 ft [6.71 metres]. Any depth greater than that, and the boat can only be steered by compass and judgement. When the submarine is submerged the periscopes can be lowered down into the boat either by electric motor or by hand to prevent them catching in any wreckage or wires and getting broken.

On either side of the conning tower are the two big rotary pumps for emptying the 105 tons of water in the ballast tanks in just three minutes.

Just aft of the periscopes are the beam torpedo tubes, one firing each side. The piping around these tubes is very complicated as a lot of valves are attached to them.

Going aft again, you come to the Chiefs' and 1st class Petty Officers' messes, with their two little tables and also the electric oven. Very handy for cooking but I never knew our cook to distinguish himself on it. He might have been a good signalman but in the culinary arts he was a hopeless failure.

No cooking is allowed when a submarine is submerged on account of the smell and the air. The most objectionable thing to cook is cabbage. The smell will make you feel sick, even in harbour.

Passing through the second bulkhead door, you are in the engine room and facing you are the two big eight cylinder diesel engines. The engines are only used when the submarine is running on the surface. The two main motors are used when submerged or going astern.

The flywheels on the engines weigh two tons each. Between the engines and main motors, which are both on the one shaft, is a clutch. This clutch allows the main shaft to be broken and allows the motors to work the propeller independent of the engine. Aft of the motors is an air compressor for filling up the air bottles, then another clutch.

With these two clutches on the shaft, the engine can drive the motor and charge up the batteries without turning the propeller, or the motor to drive the compressors without engine or propeller.

Over the main motors is a platform where the remainder of the crew mess in a very cramped condition. They also have an electric stove to cook with. Last comes the aft torpedo tube. In every spare nook and corner lockers were fitted spare gear and spanner racks and the 48 air bottles, which are kept pumped up to 3,300 pounds pressure.

The air is used to blow the water out of the tanks when bringing the boats to the surface as the pumps cannot be used until the conning tower door or air vents are opened. Otherwise, the pumps would suck all the air out of the boat and leave the crew without any to breathe. The torpedoes, which are also driven by air are also filled from these bottles to 3,000 lbs pressure.

Overhead there is a network of pipes and electric wires. You wonder what they could all be used for. The sleeping accommodation for the crew is just where you can get your head down.

When the engines are running the noise is deafening, and it is impossible to hear anyone shouting in the engine room. Signs have to be used if you want anything. A man can sing at the top of his voice without waking anyone up, so it has its advantages.

At each end of the boat were tanks, kept about half full, and connected by a pipe so that if the boat was down by bow or stern, the water could be blown from one tank to the other until the boat was on an even keel. The same process was used if the boat had a list to port or starboard. Levels were fitted for this purpose as it was essential that the boat be level when diving.

To get a submarine into trim for diving all stores, oil and spare gear are stowed in board and the eight main ballast tanks filled with 105 tons of water. Then the compensating tanks are filled slowly, keeping the boat level, until the boat is just buoyant enough to float. Then the compensating tanks are closed.

By going ahead on main motors and turning the for'ard hydroplanes down to catch the resistance of the water, it gradually forces the bow of the boat down. The after hydroplanes are turned up to lift the stern up and when the required depth is reached the resistance is gradually taken off the planes, just sufficient being kept on to stop the boat from rising.

When coming to the surface the planes are reversed and the main ballast tanks blown, but the compensating tanks are not touched, as a boat only requires trimming once a month, according to the amount of engine oil used. A corresponding amount of water is taken into the compensating tanks and so keeps the boat trimmed.

One always has his food flavoured with engine oil, so perhaps a good cook would only be wasting his time.[18]

AE1 kept to her timetable. On the afternoon of Tuesday, 20 January 1914, four days after the Houdini escape, a little after 4 p.m., Tom Besant eased her away from Barrow's Devonshire Dock, past the great crane that had towered above her for so many months, and out into the Irish Sea on her first voyage, destination Portsmouth.

It was the first leg of the long journey to Australia. There were rousing cheers from the dock workers who had built her and from the *AE2* men, who would soon be leaving themselves.

The trip would be all on the surface, about 800 kilometres, accompanied for safety's sake by the brand-new submarine tender HMS *Adamant*. They were taking every precaution: everyone was aware that it was on this same journey that E_5 had suffered her fatal engine room explosion. But it went without incident in fine, clear weather and they arrived in Portsmouth two days later. Remarkably, this was the longest journey yet taken by an E-class submarine without mishap, a new record, something to celebrate.

AE2 was not so lucky. She farewelled Barrow at 10 p.m. on the night of Tuesday, 10 February, also in company with *Adamant*, heading south-west in foul weather that grew worse as the night wore on, both vessels pitching and tossing in a big swell. On the bridge, in heavy oilskins, Harry Stoker strained to keep station astern of *Adamant*, his coxswain, Charlie Vaughan, wrestling with the wheel, the lookouts peering through the mist and scudding drifts of rain. Below, the crew struggled to keep their feet or snatch what sleep they could. Some were sick, the smell of vomit pervading their quarters.

By morning it was too much. The first feeble light of dawn showed a tumbled, tossing seascape, grey and forbidding. There was no point in going on like this, not with boat and crew so new and raw, and at 5 a.m., an hour into the morning watch, reluctantly they put into the little Welsh harbour of Holyhead to find some respite. They stayed overnight there and made another attempt to get going the next morning at 5 a.m.

Again the weather turned treacherous, and they ploughed on for as long as they could until they had to seek shelter once more, this time at Fishguard. There they remained for four nights, resting and regrouping, waiting for the weather to ease, which it eventually did. Weary and worn, *AE2* reached Portsmouth on Tuesday, 17 February.

There was no rest for the wicked. The very next night the officers were expected, in best uniforms, at a formal mess dinner, where the senior guest was no less than the Royal Navy's Commodore

Submarines, Roger Keyes. A tall, assertive figure, ever thirsting for action, Keyes had celebrity status in the RN for his dashing deeds during the Boxer Rebellion, when, as a destroyer captain, he was the first British officer into Peking, coming to the rescue of Western diplomats besieged in their legations. Some of the submariners at dinner that evening would encounter the commodore again a year later, in the waters off Gallipoli.

The next fortnight passed in a whirl of preparation for their voyage, the details big and small of making ready for sea. They would be accompanied by the light cruiser HMS *Eclipse*, whose captain, Frank Brandt, had commanded submarines himself. Famous in the navy for his salty vocabulary and with a voice like a bull's roar, he knew the ropes. Brandt and *Eclipse* would be with *AE1* and *AE2* all the way south through the Suez Canal and into the Indian Ocean, carrying supplies and personal belongings and relief crewmen, and taking turns to tow each submarine to ease the load on their engines.

Their sailing orders had already arrived:

> You are hereby directed to use every effort to complete H.M.A. Submarines under your command with all stores as necessary, so as to be ready in all respects to leave Portsmouth on the 28th February or as soon after that date as is practicable . . .
>
> [U]nless unforeseen circumstances arrive, the voyage to Gibraltar should be made by H.M.A. Submarines under their own motive power, and, subject to the weather conditions and the directions of the commanding officer of HMS Eclipse, it is considered a speed of 11 to 12 knots should be maintained . . .[19]

Both boats had a Sperry gyrocompass and a wireless installed. At a cost of £75 each, a bulky one-kilowatt Marconi Type 10 Morse spark transceiver, with its impressive array of valves, dials and knobs, and a cabinet was squeezed into a space next to the already cramped wardroom. Room also had to be found for the large and cumbersome wireless mast and aerials that would be erected when the boats were surfaced.

On 28 February, in a low key ceremony, *AE1* and *AE2* were formally commissioned into the Royal Australian Navy, the White

Ensign broken out on the small staff astern. The next day, Stoker took *AE2* to sea for a quick engine trial and found that the port thrust block (a support for the shaft that turned the propeller) was overheating. That had to be hurriedly worked on. It seemed they were never going to be free of civilian dockyard workers.

The sailing date was now set for Monday, 2 March. If all went as planned – and that was a big if – they should arrive in Sydney Harbour in the second week of May, after a journey of 21,000 kilometres, an odyssey never before undertaken by a submarine. There would be stops at Gibraltar and Malta in the Mediterranean; at Port Said, at the head of the Suez Canal; at Aden, at the mouth of the Red Sea; at Colombo, in Ceylon; at Singapore; and at Batavia, the capital of the Dutch East Indies. The first Australian landfall would be Port Darwin, then it was on to Cairns and finally Sydney.

Each man was keenly conscious that he was taking part in a historic undertaking. The excitement was real, almost tangible. The Australians would be going home, at last. The British submariners, officers and men, would be off to a new and faraway world, a country and a future they could only imagine.

3
AUSTRALIA WELCOMES HER DEFENDERS

They breakfasted before dawn on a cold, grey Monday morning with a fresh wind blowing, the waters of Portsmouth harbour ruffled and choppy. Then began the familiar ritual of readying the submarines for sea. Both boats were alongside at Blockhouse. The first lieutenants, Charlie Moore and Geoff Haggard, ran down the list of orders for harbour stations and received the checks and reports from the coxswain, the chief engine room artificer, the leading torpedoman, the signalman and more:

> Fresh water tanks full, 14 days provisions on board, sir . . . Oil fuel tanks full, lubricating oil tanks full, No: 1 tank online, both main engines available, clutches open . . . Both batteries at 85%, periscopes correct and cleaned, hydroplanes and steering gear correct, navigation and flashing lights tested and correct, gyrocompass started, spare lamps and fuses stowed, sir . . .

The traditional acknowledgement was 'Very good'. It went smoothly, no hitches. The boats soon rumbled to the deep throb of the diesel engines warming up. That in itself was a minor blessing. There were no long hours of shovelling coal, of firing boilers and bringing them online, of raising steam, as there were in a surface vessel.

More reports: 'Towing slips and pendants correct, bridge rigged for sea, sir, upper deck gear correct . . . Signal gear on the bridge, Captain's glasses cleaned and on the bridge, challenge and reply correct . . .'

In *AE2*, Haggard reported to his captain that the boat was ready to proceed. The nine 'special sea duty' men were closed up and waiting on the casing fore and aft under the direction of the second coxswain, Chief Petty Officer Harry 'Scratcher' Abbott. Their job was to cast off the lines that held the boat to dry land. The submarine would begin to move first on the battery motors, and then switch to the diesels.

Stoker now took charge: 'Let go aft, let go back spring . . .'

The lines snaked through the air to the dock. Next the helm and engine orders. 'Starboard thirty, slow ahead port.'

With the bow lines still in place, that moved the stern gently out so she could back away from the berth.

'Stop port, let go for'ard, let go the head spring. Midships. Slow astern starboard.'

AE2 was now free, her wake lightly churning and bubbling. Clear of the berth, Stoker gave the order to engage the diesels, then 'Slow ahead both', and the submarine nosed her way out past Spithead towards the open sea, where she would take station astern of *AE1* and their chaperone, *Eclipse*. It was from this same harbour, these same waters, in 1787, that Captain Arthur Phillip's First Fleet of eleven ships had begun its journey to Botany Bay. Horatio Nelson, too, had sailed from here in 1805, for his victorious but fatal encounter with the French at Trafalgar. The tall, bare masts of his flagship, HMS *Victory*, still at anchor in Portsmouth, though sadly neglected, faded into the haze.

Sou'west they went at around eleven knots, the wind picking up in the afternoon, with a rising swell coming at them two points before the beam. 'A most uncomfortable motion was set up, combined pitch and roll and very jerky,' Lieutenant Commander Besant noted in his diary.[1] Both submarines were having intermittent, tiresome trouble with engine valve springs breaking. It was annoying work for the engine room artificers, but by stopping the offending engine and going up to full speed on the other, they could get the repair done in a few minutes without losing speed.

Real trouble struck on the second day out, in the Bay of Biscay. On 4 March, at 4 p.m., the start of the first dog watch, *AE2* was gripped by a sudden and violent convulsion. She throbbed and quivered, vibrating alarmingly. Harry Kinder, who was on watch at the time, 'thought the boat would shake to pieces with the vibrations until the engine was stopped'.² It was the port propeller. A blade must have fallen off, or something like it, but at sea there was no way of telling for sure. *Eclipse* took them in tow and they limped into Gibraltar two days later, where a diver went down and confirmed that, yes, a blade had gone. They would have to go into dry dock to replace it. Fortunately, *Eclipse* was carrying a couple of spare propellers for just this possibility. *AE1* was still having problems with valve springs and her Sperry compass seemed to be a bit out of whack, but her crew were coping.

'With the exception of the Leading Signalman who is afflicted with a stricture and one AB [able seaman] who has developed gonorrhoea the crews are very healthy,' Besant noted in his diary. 'The two ratings mentioned have been relieved by spare crew.'³

Most of the men got shore leave, a chance to stretch their legs and get a meal and a drink, but *AE2*'s engine room staff had no such luck. The boat went into dry dock at 10 a.m. on 7 March but it took hours for the water to be pumped out and the boat to be settled on wooden blocks, so work on the propeller couldn't start until 2 p.m. Stoker was angered to find that, for some reason, there were no local dock workers who could pitch in; his men would have to do the job themselves. The 'exigencies of the Service' was the usual phrase – the stuff that kept cropping up just when you least expected it and had to be dealt with, for better or worse. This job asked a lot of men, but there was nothing for it. Mustn't grumble.

The chief engine room 'tiffy', or artificer – the senior engineer in the boat – Harry Broomhead, a stalwart Yorkshireman, set his men to the task, to their captain's gratitude:

> This work should have been performed by dockyard labour, as it was not right that ERAs [engine room artificers] etc should be working all day in the bottom of a hot dock and then proceed to sea straight and have to keep their watches.
>
> By working straight on with no Stand Easy, work was completed by 8pm. Flooded dock immediately. Undocked at 10pm and sailed for Malta at 11pm.⁴

The course was eastwards now, heading into the sunrise, with *AE2* striking no further difficulties but *AE1* having more engine problems and requiring a tow. The sea got up again as they neared Malta, all three vessels butting into a strong easterly wind, but by 10 p.m. on 13 March they were gliding in between the massive stone forts guarding the entrance to Grand Harbour, with the lights of Valletta and the 'Three Cities' – Vittoriosa, Senglea and Cospicua – twinkling in welcome.

Lieutenant Stoker was in his element, back to his old stamping ground, looking up old friends. For everyone there was the luxury of hot baths and hot meals at the Submarine Depot, cabins ashore with bunks for the officers to sleep in and comfortable quarters for the men, too. Malta had been a British colony for a century, since the first Treaty of Paris brought a temporary halt to the Napoleonic Wars in 1814. It was home to the Royal Navy's Mediterranean Fleet. The younger men found their way to Strait Street, known to every sailor as 'The Gut', a narrow, cobbled lane of cafés, bars and brothels where, from long experience, the Maltese understood very well what the navy wanted on a run ashore and happily provided it. For a price.

Other sailors, often the married men, were more eager to see the sights. John Marsland, a 34-year-old Yorkshireman from Leeds and an engine room artificer in *AE2*, had volunteered for service with the RAN to see the world, farewelling his wife, Nellie, from their home in Southampton. He too kept a diary and later wrote an account of his travels to Australia for Sydney's *Sunday Times*. In Malta he and some mates took a train inland to the ancient walled city of Città Vecchia, where they took hotel rooms and hired a guide to show them around.

> The first place he called our attention to was a large convent, saying that if you once enter you never come out again, so we went past there. The next place was St John's church, where I must say I saw the finest paintings, mosaic and marble work in my life.
>
> While we were in there the afternoon service commenced and there were at least 30 bishops, priests and other grades of clergy, all dressed in beautiful robes, with facings of the finest Maltese lace,

and then the Dean and a very old, white-haired gentleman arrived and prayers commenced. The singing was very nice indeed.[5]

After three relaxing days and nights, they were away again, heading east-south-east across the Mediterranean towards Port Said and the Suez Canal, the weather growing hotter with each new dawn. *Eclipse* towed her charges turn and turn about, mostly without incident, although occasionally a tow line might chafe or break and have to be replaced. There was a nasty scare when *AE1*'s steering gear suddenly jammed hard a'starboard and she nearly rammed her sister boat. They missed each other by a whisker.

On 20 March they were at dreary Port Said – 'hard to praise', thought Stoker wryly[6] – and then into the canal proper. The heat by now was intense, blasting, searing. It was blinding hot on deck and on the bridge, where *AE2* spread a makeshift canvas awning to get some shade, and it was worse below as they headed down the canal towards Aden, at the mouth of the Red Sea. The mood was lightened a little when Petty Officer Harry Hodge, the second coxswain and a veteran three badge man who should have known better, somehow managed to lose his footing on *AE1* and fell overboard into the canal; he was fished out by a French steamer following behind them.[7]

The mercury continued to soar. On 27 March, *AE2* recorded temperatures of 120 degrees Fahrenheit (48.9 degrees Celsius) in the engine room, 104 degrees Fahrenheit (40 degrees Celsius) at the switchboard and 92 degrees Fahrenheit (33 degrees Celsius) in the wardroom.

And then it happened again. When they were almost at Aden, *AE2* was shaken by those juddering vibrations which almost certainly meant another propeller blade gone, this time on the starboard side. She trudged into harbour on her port engine, arriving in the afternoon of 29 March. A diver went down and confirmed their fears.

Stoker was downcast. 'Consider it hard lines that after steaming [*sic*] nearly 3,000 miles without internal hitch the propeller should give in,' he lamented. 'No dock at Aden capable of taking boat.'[8]

No dock meant they would have to work out some way of replacing the propeller while the boat was still afloat. Stoker conferred with Tom Besant and Captain Brandt of *Eclipse*, and they came up with a masterly solution. If they could somehow weigh *AE2* down by the bow, it might be enough to bring her propellers at least partly out of the water, where the faulty one could be removed and replaced by another spare from the cruiser.

They got down to it. First the submarine's for'ard ballast tanks were pumped full, which brought her stern up a little, although not enough. So to add more weight they draped the bower and sheet anchors from *Eclipse* over the bow, with lengths of heavy cable as well, and that did the trick. The tips of the propeller blades were awash and reachable. It was a superb piece of seamanship. The divers got to work.

The task was daunting. The propeller, cast in bronze, weighed almost 400 kilograms. In the steamy heat, divers and other men in ship's boats from *Eclipse* struggled to draw it off the shaft for most of 30 March, quitting in defeat at 8 p.m. but intent on having another go the next day. They started again at 6 a.m., hitting and hammering and levering until finally, at noon, they got it off and the shaft was bare.

Then came their next shock. The replacement propeller was also flawed. When it was taken from its protective covering, they discovered a crack in it, twelve centimetres long. They could hardly believe it. Faulty workmanship could be the only explanation – a bad job at Vickers back in Barrow. But it was the only one they had, and they would have to live with it, fingers crossed.

It took another day and a half of sweating and swearing to get the new propeller onto the shaft and secured. On the evening of 1 April, they sailed out into the Indian Ocean for the crossing to Colombo, *AE2*'s hull oddly painted a shabby white in the hope of reflecting the heat better than her regulation dark grey.

Luck now looked their way. The weather and sea were kind, gentle, to the relief of all, including Harry Stoker:

> So calm was it that almost nightly I had my bed brought up and placed on the small strip of 'upper deck'; as this was only three to

four feet above the water's level it can be imagined how quiet the ocean must have been. The only exciting incident occurred when a flying fish flew into my bed. A fish in its proper place, at the end of your line or on a breakfast plate, is a most estimable animal; as a companion of your bed it is a failure.[9]

Five days in Colombo provided more balm for body and soul, the rich tropical greenery a delightful change from the barren rocks of Aden. Drinks on the terrace of the renowned Galle Face Hotel, overlooking the seafront, were a treat for the officers. At Colombo they farewelled the faithful *Eclipse*, who had done her job and was returning to the UK. Another ship, the four-funnelled cruiser HMS *Yarmouth*, from the Royal Navy's China Station, would escort them to Singapore.

The next leg was another pleasure cruise, happily lodged in Stoker's memory:

> [T]he beautifully calm weather still holding. The nights, with their starlit sky, dead smooth sea, and phosphorescent water swishing musically by, used greatly to affect our red-haired but sentimental sub-lieutenant;[10] every evening, on coming on deck to smoke an after-dinner pipe, he would lean on the rails, look around and deliver himself of the same remark: 'This is a night on which every woman wishes to be loved . . .'
>
> Such great thoughts lose their value when in a submarine one thousand miles from the nearest point of land . . .[11]

Not everyone was so enraptured. By now boredom was hanging heavily, for in truth there was very little to do for most of the men but eat and sleep. The engineers tended to their charges but for the rest there was no navigation to be done, no real maintenance between ports, none of the normal drills or routines of a submarine on patrol at sea. They could not have dived their boats even had they wanted to, because the hydroplanes, which directed the vertical motion, had been unshipped before they left Portsmouth to provide greater stability for surface travel.

Monotony gripped the men: the sameness of the meals, tasting always of engine oil; the sameness of watch on and watch off; the sameness of the distant circle of the horizon; the sameness of the faces; the sameness of having nothing new to chat about. Living cheek by jowl, if you were not carefully tolerant, some minor irritant could easily and quickly blow up into a major personal confrontation. It did not often happen, but when it did it could be ugly.

As they were passing the Nicobar Islands, heading for the Straits of Malacca, Harry Stoker asked the coxswain if he could arrange a concert. John Marsland took a leading role, as he later detailed:

> The program was put up on the notice board, and after supper a platform and mess stools were got in order, and we started off with a banjo, violin and mandolin march, but something went wrong with it, anyhow I put it down to that and the excuse was accepted.
>
> The next item was a Comic Song by myself entitled Ding Dong, with banjo accompaniment, and then we had The Flight of Ages and Star of My Soul, after that a gramophone selection, then the Captain sang a song and played the banjo, which went down very well.
>
> We had an interval during which the gramophone played a prominent part, and we adjourned to our Mess for a glass of water, there being no refreshment bar in submarines...[12]

The highlight of the night was an old sailors' song called 'Captain Nipper':

> 'Twas the fifteenth of September,
> How well I do remember,
> It nearly broke my poor old mother's heart,
> For I shipped with Captain Nipper
> In a big four-masted clipper
> Bound away down south for foreign parts...

Yarmouth left them at Singapore. Their companion for the rest of the journey to Australia would be one of the RAN's two new and modern cruisers, HMAS *Sydney*, specially despatched to meet them. Stoker was hoping to get hold of a new propeller being shipped out to him from the UK but discovered that it would take another fortnight to arrive. *AE2* would have to make do with the one she had.

They found Singapore unpleasantly hot and foul-smelling, and after four days it was a relief to get to sea again, heading for Batavia. *Sydney*, though, had taken on poor quality coal and the submarine taking its turn to be towed was smothered in clouds of stinking black smoke from her funnels, the helmsman and officer of the watch coughing and spluttering and forced to wear goggles.

The Dutch welcomed them warmly. The men took steam trams from the port of Tanjung Priok to the city of Batavia itself, where they goggled at the Javanese women, young and old, bathing naked in the canals. The local Dutch admiral, portly and affable, laid on an enormous *rijstaffel* banquet for an officers' luncheon at another of those luxurious colonial palaces, the Hotel des Indes, sixteen spicy courses in all. They would very happily have stayed another week, but the pressure was on now for them to arrive in Sydney before Empire Day, in late May.

They sailed the next day, east across the Java Sea and then south into the narrow, turbulent strait between Bali and the neighbouring island of Lombok. It was a prelude to disaster, a frightening coincidence of mishaps and bad luck that came close to claiming them all.

The Lombok Strait is the artery for what mariners know as the Indonesian Through Flow, which drives water down from the Pacific Ocean towards the Indian Ocean in a fierce, southerly current, often with strong northerly countercurrents to make life even more difficult. It was 1.30 a.m. on 1 May, a pitch-black, moonless night, in the narrowest part of the strait. *AE1* was being towed by *Sydney*, with *AE2* following them astern and a little out to port, the helmsmen in each boat struggling to keep a course in the swirls and eddies.

Without warning, *AE1* lunged to port so sharply that the tow rope parted, sending her drifting out of control right across the bow of *AE2*. Lieutenant Stoker ordered his helm hard a'starboard but nothing happened:

Being caught by the eddy, the boat did not diverge one iota from her course and held straight on for the centre of the other submarine. It looked as if a collision was absolutely inevitable, as there could be no hope of the engines answering to the order 'Full Speed Astern' before the boats struck. As a last resort we in AE2 put the helm hard over the other way; a lucky swirl caught the boat's nose at the same moment, helping to swing her off to starboard – and we whizzed past AE1's stern at a distance of some three feet.[13]

But it was not over yet. Stoker now found that his helm had jammed and that he was drifting out of control, helpless, the current taking him towards the rocky Lombok shore. *Sydney* was too far away to help, while *AE1*, out in the blackness, was having her own steering troubles. The only hope was to use the engines: now ahead, now astern, now port, now starboard, Stoker barking the orders down the voicepipe to the engine room. It worked, and gained them just enough time to get the steering up again – a blown fuse was the culprit – and the boat back under control. *AE1* sorted herself out as well, and both submarines carried on down the strait to pass *Sydney*, who was hauling in the tow line.

Trouble, though, comes in threes. Picking up speed, *Sydney* was now shaping to move ahead of her two charges. Thinking the drama was over, *Sydney*'s captain, John Glossop, made to leave the bridge for some sleep. Suddenly, without warning, the cruiser swung sharply to starboard. The tow line had fouled her rudder and she was heading straight for *AE2*, all 6100 tonnes of her, that towering bow threatening to cut the little boat in half like a knife through a banana.

It must have been a heart-stopping moment. If Glossop thought as much, he never said it, but whatever the reason, whatever the fault, to ram and sink one of these precious submarines, with certain loss of life, would have been an Australian and British national tragedy and, for him, professional ruin, to be neither forgiven nor forgotten. With the officer of the watch and the bridge crew looking on in frozen horror, the captain ordered 'full astern all'. *Sydney* had four propellers. There was a chance, a slender chance, that it might take enough weight off the ship at least to lessen the impact. Then came a pipe for 'collision stations', to get the sleeping men out of the messdecks in the fo'c'sle, where they might be killed or injured.

On *AE2*'s bridge, Stoker could see both of *Sydney*'s navigation lights, red and green, port and starboard, an alarming sign that she was coming straight at him. He reacted too. Hanging on for dear life, he ordered full speed ahead on both engines. The stern dug deep and she surged forward.

It was enough – just. Both captains had made the right call. *Sydney* passed astern of *AE2*, her menacing grey bulk receding in the dark.

That was enough excitement for one night. It had been a near-run thing, all of it. In the morning Glossop sent down divers, who cleared *Sydney*'s rudder. That took a few hours, but in the afternoon they resumed their journey east into the Timor Sea, with the keen anticipation of their first Australian landfall, Port Darwin. It would be the morning of Tuesday, 5 May. None of them had been there before, and they had no idea what they would find, as Stoker explained:

> Some preconceived notion led me to expect a dry and parched desert; one sighted instead a bold point, covered with green and luxuriant tropical growth, from the midst of which the tops of houses peeped out to give an impression of most extreme cosiness. A group of aborigines clustered on the point gazing at what to them must have been a weird sight – these strange looking craft ploughing along over the water.[14]

A local reporter was there to observe the arrival, and the story he filed appeared in newspapers around the country:

SUBMARINES.
WARM WELCOME AT PORT DARWIN.
GREETED BY BLACKS.
DARWIN, Tuesday.

The first flag in Australia to salute the cruiser *Sydney* and the two submarines was at the aboriginal compound, at Calin [Kahlin] Beach.

> The flag was made entirely by aboriginal girls and is a beautiful piece of work. The aboriginals were greatly excited, and stood along the edge of the cliff from daylight looking out to sea, and when the vessels hove in sight, they shouted 'Yacka!' and threw their spears in the air.
>
> As the cruiser *Sydney* steamed past with the submarines following, they were in transports of merriment, shouting 'Big feller come up, two feller young; one follow up behind; all same emu . . .'[15]

Darwin had been called Palmerston until the name was changed in 1911, when South Australia handed over the Northern Territory to the Commonwealth with a sigh of relief, happy to be rid of the cost burden. That year a census counted the territory's non-Aboriginal population at 3271, of which there were just 598 women. There might have been 50,000 Indigenous people; nobody really knew or much cared.

Darwin was still a raw frontier settlement in 1914, with a white population largely made up of public servants busily administering each other, meatworkers at the local Vesteys abattoir, and a few technicians employed on the Overland telegraph line. There were bloodhouse pubs for the bare-knuckle miners, cattlemen and bushies who would drift in and out of town from 'down the Track', while the notorious Fanny Bay Gaol had a useful gallows and a 'native section'. John Marsland went ashore as soon as leave was granted, and his account paints an intriguing picture:

> It seemed obvious that we were in for a good reception, for we had to pass under an archway which bore the words 'Australia Welcomes Her Defenders' and we very bravely passed under for only a little further on was an hotel where practically everyone replenished their thirst for it was still pretty warm . . .
>
> Having found some good pals, we had a wander around the place and strolled into Chinatown, where we came across Chinese, Japanese and Malays, in fact I was surprised for I thought we had seen the last of Asiatics when we left Batavia. I also noticed that the children could speak good English, although of Chinese parents.

> Passing down the main and only street we came to a Chinese Joss House which we entered and found to contain Idols and all kinds of wooden banners that are carried through the streets on special occasions, some of the carvings were very artistic, there was also Sandalwood smouldering away, the ashes falling into large engraved brass urns...[16]

For the officers that evening, there was the inevitable formal dinner of welcome laid on by the Northern Territory Civil Service Association in the Town Hall – best white uniforms, windy speeches, many toasts. *The Northern Territory Times and Gazette* reported that Colonel H.V. Francis occupied the chair and that the floral decorations had been tastefully arranged by Mrs Francis.

> An appropriate vocal item, 'The death of Nelson,' was contributed by Mr. A.T. Hutchison and was heartily applauded... in the unavoidable absence of Mr. M. D. Andrews, Lieut. Stoker contributed a vocal number, playing his own accompaniment, and was most loudly encored, compelling a response.[17]

Replying to the toast to the Royal Australian Navy, Captain Glossop, another Englishman, offered some starchy condescension, also well reported around the country:

> I am being asked continually how the Australian navy is being run and I invariably reply that everything is being done as it is done in the Imperial navy.
>
> Again, people ask what I think of Australian sailors. 'Are they all right?' I reply 'Yes,' as soon as they understand what discipline is.
>
> Australians are not used to the same standard of discipline which exists in the Old Country. I find that when there is any hard work to be done they rush it: but they do not like dull routine. They like the big jobs, and it takes them a long time to understand that the small jobs are also essential.

The newspapers noted that Lieutenant Commander Besant, 'replying on behalf of the submarine service', said: 'We left England on March 2, and have covered 10,500 miles, creating a record for this type of vessel; and as we still feel capable of doing many more miles, I can assure you the money in these vessels has been well executed.'[18]

As it so often happens, the sailors probably had a better time of it. John Marsland and some mates wandered into the bush, 'where we came across numerous kinds of birds and snakes and different species of flies'. There was more entertainment laid on for them the next day:

> It was a splendid afternoon, and at 2 o'clock the Sports commenced with a pillow fight across a bar and it was very laughable, some of the Sailors sticking it out for quite a long time. There were also races for the Blacks, who are very good runners. There was a great attraction in one part of the field so I went over with my friends and found it was a bar, we remained quite a long time, no money was required, the best part of the programme when you are dry.
>
> The Sports over, we went and had a jolly good Tea, after which we returned to the Sports field again to wait for the concert, which turned out to be a perfect success. After the concert the Blacks gave a show which included a dance called a Crobberee [sic], a very strange dance, men and women sit on the grass, the men blow through a large bamboo stem whilst the women clap their hands and make a weird noise . . . eventually some of the Sailors got mixed up in it and made it a little livelier.[19]

Perhaps it was the Irish in him, the instinctive detachment of an outsider in the grand imperial scheme of things, but Harry Stoker was troubled by what he saw in Darwin:

> Amongst the numerous questions the Commonwealth must solve, that of the Northern Territory may well prove the most difficult. In its successful solution lie results of far-reaching importance, not only to Australia but to the whole British Empire. Vast spaces of tropical and semi-tropical land are held by the white man in a climate which makes it impossible for him to work it to the same producing power as could be done by the black or yellow man. Is the white man justified in holding this land, empty, to the exclusion of teeming millions of blacks and yellows, overcrowded in their own countries . . . ?

> [I]t follows that I must feel that the White Australia Policy is not a good policy because it is not based on good ethics . . .[20]

The Torres Strait gave the submarines another unpleasant time, big seas and winds sending spray over the bridge for a couple of days. They paused at Thursday Island for a boat to bring out welcome mail, which had magically arrived there from home, although the weather was still nasty and making life difficult for Harry Kinder in *AE2*:

> Just before leaving Thursday Island some of us had done some washing and tied it along the handrails to dry. Rough weather prevented us getting it in as the captain thought we might get washed over the side. So we had to watch our gear getting carried away as the waves caught them. My hammock managed to carry away the wireless aerial. As it was the signalman's job to repair and look after it, he said some nasty things about people washing hammocks. As it was about the fourth time it had been carried away during the trip you couldn't blame him for blowing off.[21]

Then it was down into the Barrier Reef for their next stop, Cairns. If anything, the welcome there was more exuberant and elaborate than in Darwin, with a band playing and marches through the streets, families and schoolchildren from far and wide brought into town by train and bus for the occasion. The cruiser – although not the submarines – was opened for inspection, and there was yet another speechifying civic reception from the mayor. A big crowd lining the foreshore went away disappointed when they were told the boats were not going to dive for them. The Citizens' Entertainment Committee took a party of 100 sailors to see the majestic waters of a local attraction, the Barron Falls, and other men went horse riding and sulky driving. Some just hit the town, with Glossop primly noting later in his 'Report of Proceedings' there had been too much venereal disease after Singapore and that 'amongst the younger stokers an epidemic of drink had set in'.[22]

One Jack Tar, who was ashore on Friday night, suffering from an exuberance of spirits, went through a chemist's window through his steering gear being disabled.

He was arrested and brought before the court next day. The window trouble was settled out of court, but on charges of drunkenness and obscene language he was given over to the ships' officers to deal with . . .[23]

The last days of any naval passage are always the longest, especially if you are coming home. The ship always seems to go more slowly and the hours drag by as if they will never end, as if you will never reach port. For the Australians, there was the growing excitement of an extended leave, of rejoining family and friends after so long away. Harry Kinder had been absent for four years, and he was not the only one who had left a boy and was returning a man.

The British were keen to see the new country they had chosen for a home, if only a temporary one. And all had been planned. They were due to arrive in Sydney at 2 p.m. on Saturday, 23 May, to be welcomed by flotillas of private yachts and pleasure boats, and by the destroyer *Parramatta*, which was to meet them off the Heads and escort them up the harbour. Filthy weather thwarted them again. Driving rain, high winds, a fierce hailstorm and pounding seas forced them to shelter in Moreton Bay, off Brisbane, for a night. A day late, they entered Sydney Harbour at 6 a.m. on Sunday, 24 May, the sunrise barely breaking through the banks of grey cloud.

There was no doubt it had been an epic journey. Historic. No submarine had ever been so far south. They had left Portsmouth eighty-three days earlier, spending sixty of those days at sea, covering 21,000 kilometres, of which 9000 were under their own power. There had been engine problems but all of them manageable at sea – a thumbs-up for the 'heavy oil' diesels, as they were called. And *AE2*'s faulty replacement propeller – the one with the crack – had actually lasted the distance. The men had arrived fit and healthy. When they tied up alongside at Garden Island and the command 'finished with main engines' came down, they had every reason to be pleased with themselves, from the captain to the most junior stoker.

Sydney, though, was otherwise occupied. It was Empire Day, an occasion fervently celebrated with parades and picnics and concerts and church services and lots of Union Jacks; a fine oil painting of Captain Robert Falcon Scott, who had perished in the Antarctic in 1912, was to be presented to Randwick School. So there was no welcoming fleet, and only a small crowd went down to Garden Island to see the new arrivals. But the newspapers sent reporters, although the man from the *Sydney Morning Herald* was disappointed to discover that he would not be allowed on board:

> A submarine is a deadly thing. A battleship may ride in majesty on the waves, and in a moment be torn by a torpedo hurled by the stealthy, invisible foe beneath the water.
>
> You may see everything else around you and yet miss the submarine. It is because this type of vessel is so valuable in time of war that such pains are taken to guard its secrets.
>
> For it is full of secrets. Nine hundred and ninety-nine men might go all over a submarine and come out none the wiser; but the thousandth – it is to guard against the knowledge, the cleverness of the thousandth that the Admiralty allows no one except the officers and crew to board a submarine.
>
> That is the practice followed at home; it will be the practice out here. It is said that the only civilian in the British Empire who has seen the inside of a submarine is Mr. Winston Churchill, First Lord of the Admiralty. The rule is that none but naval and army officers shall be allowed on board.[24]

The reporter from *The Sun* let his imagination off the leash in a story headlined 'War in a Submarine. Life Under Water. "Captain Nemos" of Today':

> When submarines are slipping about beneath the surface in time of manouevre the monotony of mere voyaging vanishes. Then submarine work is 'great fun.'
>
> The periscope is pushed up above the waves, and a hurried survey of the silent world is taken. The vessel does not bob up and down like a cork in a bucket but the adjustable mast which carries the periscope can be extended at will. The submarine in a naval

engagement is like a little boy from Topsy-Turveyland. It must be heard and not seen.

It must not be heard until the message of death strikes home when the racing torpedo finds its mark. Silent and deadly it goes about its work.[25]

Sydney offered its formal greetings at a Town Hall reception on Tuesday, 26 May, given by the Lord Mayor and attended by the commander of the Australian Fleet, Rear Admiral Sir George Patey, and the Anglican archbishop. Tom Besant gave what had by now become his set-piece speech about the virtues of submarines, the untiring dedication of their crews and what a valuable addition they were to the RAN; the usual toasts were drunk and that was that.

The two boats were sent off to the Cockatoo Island dockyard in Sydney Harbour for a thorough going-over. The Navy Office in Melbourne ordered a metallurgist's examination of a piece of one of the faulty propellers from *AE2*, which found that it had been cast from poor-quality bronze – too much iron, not enough zinc – and so began a lengthy but ultimately futile attempt to extract financial compensation from Vickers.

Lieutenant Stoker, philanderer and lover of life, set out to see what Sydney had to offer. Sadly, the wealthy man with the polo ponies he had come all this way to see had apparently fallen on hard times, lost his money and gone mad, but there were other attractions. There were charming and delightful people to meet, hospitable gentleman's clubs, first-class golf courses and tennis courts, race meetings, and surf bathing at Manly. Sydney was the most attractive city to live in he had ever seen, he wrote.

> Look from one of the surrounding hills on Sydney Harbour on a clear moonlit evening, when the deep shadows of the numerous bays are seemingly pin-pricked with light here and there from the houses on the sweeping curves of the shore; watch the reflection on the water of the well-lit ferries moving from side to side and island to island carrying, in your imagination, a happy cargo of seekers of well-earned pleasure after the day of toil – and then you will see to my mind as pretty a sight as the eye can desire.[26]

Exactly five weeks from the day *AE1* and *AE2* slipped through Sydney Heads, there was a shooting in the faraway Balkans. On Sunday, 28 June 1914, a Serbian revolutionary, nineteen-year-old Gavrilo Princip, assassinated Archduke Franz Ferdinand of Austria, the heir presumptive to the throne of the Austro-Hungarian Empire, and his wife, Sophie, Duchess of Hohenberg, as they drove in state through Sarajevo, the provincial capital of Bosnia-Herzegovina.

As Franz Ferdinand lay dying in the car, he kept repeating his last words: 'It is nothing.'

4
THE UNTHINKABLE

It was everything. Gavrilo Princip's two gunshots ignited a conflagration. Millions would die. Cities, towns and farms would be laid to ruin and waste. Four empires – Russian, German, Austro-Hungarian and Ottoman – would tremble and fall. Bolshevism would seize Russia, and in turn Nazism would ravage Germany and Europe. In the twenty-first century, we are confronted by the consequences still.

Australian newspapers covered the outrage in colourful detail. Archdukes were not murdered every day, even Austro-Hungarian ones, and – better still – there was a pleasing local angle. His Imperial and Royal Highness[1] had visited Australia in 1893 and been taken kangaroo shooting beyond the Blue Mountains, out of Sydney. His host, Mr Frank Mack of Narromine, recalled for the *Sydney Morning Herald*: 'He was a splendid shot, and active and energetic – he would walk about all day on these expeditions. I should have said that as a man he was rather austere, but one had little chance of judging.'[2]

That done, everyone got on with life. In Europe, though, the tangled web of alliances, treaties and guarantees erected by nations explicitly to prevent war, or at least to keep them out of it, began to ensnare them. Austria-Hungary vowed revenge upon Serbia and declared war. Russia, a Serbian ally and protector, ordered a general mobilisation. Germany demanded that Russia send its army back to barracks, and the impetuous Kaiser Wilhelm appeared on the balcony of the Berlin Palace to bluster: 'A fateful hour has fallen for Germany. Envious peoples everywhere are compelling us to our just defence. The sword has been forced into our hands...'³

France, which had an alliance with Russia, began to mobilise her armies too. Intent on striking first, Germany declared war on France and marched into first Luxembourg, then Belgium. Britain, because of her alliance with France, the *Entente Cordiale*, and wishing to guarantee the sovereignty of Belgium, was dragged to the precipice.

On the afternoon of Tuesday, 4 August, the government in London sent an ultimatum to Berlin demanding that Germany withdraw her armies. There was no answer. That evening, Winston Churchill, the First Lord of the Admiralty, was at his office in Whitehall, as he later recalled:

> It was 11 o'clock at night – 12 by German time – when the ultimatum expired. The windows of the Admiralty were thrown wide open in the warm night air. Under the roof from which Nelson had received his orders were gathered a small group of admirals and captains and a cluster of clerks, pencil in hand, waiting. Along the Mall from the direction of the Palace the sound of an immense concourse singing 'God save the King' floated in. On this deep wave there broke the chimes of Big Ben; and, as the first stroke of the hour boomed out, a rustle of movement swept across the room. The war telegram, which meant 'Commence hostilities against Germany,' was flashed to the ships and establishments under the White Ensign all over the world.[4]

That meant that Australia was also at war. There was no question about it. Prime Minister Joseph Cook issued a 'message' to the nation:

> We have just to sit tight now and see the thing through. Whatever the difficulty and whatever the cost we must be steadfast in our determination. Our resources are great and the British spirit is not dead.
>
> We owe it to those who have gone before to preserve the great fabric of British freedom and hand it on to our children. Our ancestral home is the repository of the great liberties, the great

traditions and the great pieties, and on our very lives we must cherish them. Our duty is quite clear, namely, to gird up our loins and remember that we are Britons.[5]

Harry Stoker heard the news in Sydney that Sunday as he was sitting down to lunch in the mess with a group of fellow officers. An engineer lieutenant walked in, announced that war had been declared and, with insouciant flair, ordered a gin and bitters. Stoker feared that he was going to miss out:

> Since joining the Navy we had believed that the sole reason for our existence and main demand on our efficiency was that one day we would fight the Germans. The day had dawned to find us in Australia, thousands of miles from the main scene of naval activity. It seemed cruel luck. The prospect of our ever getting a chance at the enemy seemed utterly remote, whilst our brethren in the North Sea would, in our imagination, be banging their torpedoes into Dreadnoughts and things every odd hour of the day. We cursed the moment in which we had been lent to the Australian Navy. Our self pity was extreme.[6]

The enemy was actually much nearer. Germany's East Asia Squadron posed a distinct threat to Australia's communications at sea and, indeed, to Australia itself. There were five ships: the flagship SMS *Scharnhorst*, an armoured cruiser of 13,000 tonnes; her sister ship *Gneisenau*; and the light cruisers *Emden*, *Nürnberg* and *Leipzig*. (SMS stands for *Seiner Majestäts Schiff*: His Majesty's Ship.)

They were a formidable force based in northern China, but with coaling stations scattered through Germany's Pacific colonies, they could range far and wide. Their commander, *Vizeadmiral* Maximilian von Spee, was not one of those bull-necked, monocled Prussian sycophants who surrounded the Kaiser, but an aristocrat born in Denmark and raised in the Rhineland. Mild of manner, he was an astute and experienced naval officer, austere but thoroughly professional. His two sons were serving in the squadron with him.

When war came, the RAN was already at sea, heading north from Sydney, hoping to find Spee and bring him to battle.

Direction finding by wireless was in its infancy, little more than guesswork, but intercepted German signals suggested that the East Asia Squadron was somewhere near the Solomon Islands. It was possible that Spee was making for Rabaul, the capital of German New Guinea, on the northern tip of the island of New Britain (or, as it then was, *Neupommern*), a part of the Bismarck Archipelago north-east of mainland New Guinea.

As he approached the Coral Sea, the fleet commander, Rear Admiral Sir George Patey, in his flagship, the battlecruiser *Australia*, had with him the cruiser *Sydney* and the destroyers *Warrego*, *Yarra* and *Parramatta*. The submarines were still not ready for sea.

Patey had declined the offer of the job in Australia at first, after discovering he would be not a commander-in-chief but a mere rear admiral commanding, and without an official residence – a lesser form of life altogether. Telegrams flashed back and forth between Melbourne and London and the offer was sugared with the promise of Admiralty House in Sydney for his family, active pay of £1095 and 'Table Money' of £1642/10/-.[7] There was added cream when George V knighted him not at Buckingham Palace, as usual, but on his own quarterdeck before *Australia* sailed from Portsmouth. It was a mark of royal favour not seen in the navy since Elizabeth I had tapped a gilded sword on the shoulders of Francis Drake on board *Golden Hind* at Deptford on the Thames in 1581.

Genial and well-liked and a social lion in Sydney, Patey was not perhaps in the First XI of British admirals, but he had sound judgement and no lack of energy. His plan was to spring a surprise night raid with the three destroyers in the hope of catching the Germans at anchor and asleep, and then to look for a wireless station which was known to be somewhere there too. *Australia* and *Sydney* would hold back a little out to sea to clean up, if that were needed. The destination was Blanche Bay, which cuts into the top end of New Britain in the shape of a sickle or half-moon. Rabaul sits on the bay to the north, at a small harbour then known as Simpsonhafen.

Late on the cloudy, dark and windy night of 11 August, in oppressive heat, the destroyers made ready. 'Put on war paint, drank a bottle of fizz to celebrate the first action of the Australian Navy, made wills and nailed several flags to the mast,' wrote Alec Doyle, *Parramatta*'s Australian-born engineer lieutenant. 'Thrills all down the backbone and up again.'[8]

Shortly before midnight, nerves taut, they crept into the bay, eerily lit by a fire burning on the North Daughter, one of the volcanic peaks that dominate Rabaul. Lieutenant Gerald Hill, one of *Yarra*'s watchkeepers, thought the bushfire was 'like a flow of molten lava, while the adjacent sea was all encrimsoned. One might have been gazing through the very portals of hell itself.'[9]

They found nothing. Simpsonhafen was empty. A landing party of seamen, under a lieutenant, went ashore the next morning and, unable to find any wireless station, had to be content with smashing up the local *Reichspost* office. They sailed again that afternoon.

It was the first of a string of disappointments for Patey, who, increasingly exasperated, would find himself chasing hither and thither at the whim of an Admiralty in London which had – at best – an uncertain grasp of geography and strategy in the Pacific. He had no choice. It had been agreed that Australia would hand operational control of the RAN to the Admiralty in the event of war, and this had been signed and delivered. On the very first day of the war, after a meeting in London of the Committee of Imperial Defence, the colonial secretary, Lewis Harcourt, had fired off a telegram to the governor-general in Australia to give a not-so-gentle nudge:

> If your Ministers desire and feel themselves able to seize German wireless stations at Yap in Marshall Islands, Nauru on Pleasant Island, and New Guinea, we should feel that this was a great and urgent Imperial service. You will, however, realise that any territory now occupied must be at the disposal of the Imperial Government for purposes of an ultimate settlement at conclusion of the war. Other Dominions are acting in similar way on the same understanding, in particular, suggestion is being made to New Zealand in regard to Samoa.[10]

Harcourt's geography was off. Yap is in the Caroline Islands, 3000 kilometres to the west of the Marshalls. In the coming months,

London's ignorance of the Pacific, from the Admiralty down, would prove costly in ships and lives to the point of culpable folly. But the message was clear enough. The priority would be the wireless stations and capture of the German colonies, not Spee and his squadron. Get cracking. The station at German Samoa would be next.

The last weeks of August, then, saw Patey head eastwards via Nauru and Fiji to support a hastily assembled New Zealand expeditionary force landing at Samoa. He arrived at Apia on the morning of 30 August, his ships at action stations, his guns trained, but not really expecting to find Spee. And nor did he. *Australia's* off-watch sailors sunbathed on the upper deck until, after three hours of elaborately courteous surrender negotiations with the German governor, the admiral sent the Kiwis ashore. The wireless station was duly captured, the governor duly taken prisoner and the Union Jack duly hoisted over the Apia courthouse with not a shot fired. The Australians steamed away again the next morning, disappointed.

The admiral wrote of his frustration to his sister in England:

> The German cruisers have disappeared entirely for the present. I believe they are either hiding away amongst some of the more distant Pacific islands, or they may be on their way across to America. Anyhow, they have done no harm to our trade as yet, but I wish we could run them to earth and have done with them, but it is almost impossible with a big place like the Pacific and with so few ships to do it.[11]

In fact, as Patey suspected, the East Asia Squadron had been far to the north of the equator, well beyond reach. At Pagan, in the Marshall Islands, on 13 August, Spee detached the little cruiser *Emden* to become a lone wolf commerce raider in the Indian Ocean. The German admiral had no intention of tangling with Patey.

The RAN's acquisition of its modern and powerful battle-cruiser had completely changed the balance of power in the Pacific, so much so that Spee, in a letter to his wife, wrote: 'The English Australian Squadron has as flagship the "Australia", which alone for the Cruiser Squadron is such a superior opponent, that it must be avoided. In both situations the presence of torpedo boats makes the whole situation more difficult...'

It was an accurate assessment. *Australia* – bigger, faster and more heavily gunned – could in theory stand off at her leisure while she pounded the German cruisers to pieces. There was but one course open to the East Asia Squadron: to range across the Pacific to South America to attack British trade there. And then, perhaps, to try to return home to Germany. On 23 August, Spee ordered his squadron to leave the Marshalls on a course east sou'east for Chile.

AE1 and *AE2* had no part in any of this charging about the Pacific. They remained in Sydney completing their overhaul, the crews largely taking it easy. Tom Besant had some good news, though. He was getting an extra officer for *AE1* to share the load of watchkeeping and navigating. It would make things still more cramped in the tiny wardroom and officers' sleeping quarters, but that was a small price to pay for the luxury of having a third hand. Lieutenant the Honourable Leopold Florence Scarlett arrived on 10 August.

Scarlett was another Englishman, twenty-five, the son of an officer in the Scots Guards. The 'Honourable' prefix indicated a minor twig of the aristocracy, a kinsman of Baron Abinger. More useful, he was a qualified submariner. He had joined the Royal Navy in 1904, done the usual round of battleships as a midshipman and sub-lieutenant and begun his first submarine instruction course in 1910. He was in submarines in Gibraltar in 1911, where he met and befriended Harry Stoker, but in 1912 he was diagnosed with tuberculosis and eventually invalided out of the navy.

Hoping to recover his health in a better climate, in 1913 Scarlett went to Brisbane, where his brother, Hugh, was the aide-de-camp to the governor of Queensland. He worked on cattle properties near Toowoomba for a while, and when the war came he decided to offer his services. He passed a medical examination and he was in, as a lieutenant in the RAN. Harry Stoker had hoped to get him for *AE1*, but Tom Besant pulled rank, so *AE2* it was.

The drive to seize the German colonies and silence the wireless stations gathered momentum. Beginning virtually from scratch in the second week of the war, in what would be an epic achievement of organisation and logistics, the Army and the RAN began to bring together the Australian Naval and Military Expeditionary Force (ANAMEF). Its aim was to descend upon Rabaul again, to find the wireless station that was most certainly there somewhere, and to take German New Guinea in the name of the King.

The khaki contingent would be commanded by Colonel William Holmes, a militia officer. In civilian life he was the secretary of the Sydney Metropolitan Board of Water Supply and Sewerage, but he was also a Boer War veteran, where he had been awarded the Distinguished Service Order and a Mention in Despatches, and he fell to his new task with a will. From 10 August, with whirlwind efficiency, Holmes recruited an infantry battalion of 1000 men in Sydney, including two machine-gun sections, a signals section and a medical detachment, eager volunteers all. They were bank clerks, teachers, blacksmiths, wharf labourers, shop assistants, butchers, bushies, all raring to have a crack at the Kaiser. In the space of a week he had them medically examined, formally enlisted, uniformed, armed and drilled, with officers appointed, and all encamped under canvas at the Sydney Showground waiting to embark. The RAN contributed a landing party of another 500 men, mostly reservists, some drawn from interstate. Patey would have most of the fleet with him and be the overall commander.

The troopship HMAS *Berrima*, a hastily converted P&O passenger steamer, sailed from Sydney with this motley crew on 19 August. After striking some dirty weather off the Queensland coast, which saw the rails lined with retching men in the miseries of seasickness, *Berrima* dropped anchor at Palm Island, off the coast north of Townsville, on 22 August. Holmes exercised his troops there for ten days, the soldiers in heavy woollen uniforms stumbling around in the mangrove swamps and the heat and the flies while they waited for their naval escort to arrive.

The submarines sailed from Sydney on 28 August, the ships' companies with no idea where they were going until they cleared the Heads and set a course up the coast. Then the two captains revealed that they were off to war. Finally it was happening. Tom Besant had written home to Ladbroke Grove before they left:

H.M.A.S 'A.E.1.'
Sydney
28.8.14

My Dear Father,
   The submarines are at last off for the north more than that I am unable to say.
   In the event of my not coming back, I should like my worldly goods, such as they are, divided up amongst the brothers and sisters. I have a small bank account at the National and Provincial Bank of England 208 Piccadilly, who also hold some share certificates of mine.
   I also have an account with the Australian Bank of Commerce Sydney where there is enough money to clear all my bills and leave a good bit over. As usual there is a lot to do at the last moment, so I must end up. Give my love to Auntie Doisie and the remainder of the family.
   Your affectionate son,
   T. Fleming Besant[12]

Two surface vessels accompanied them like sheepdogs, the little gunboat HMAS *Protector* and another hurriedly requisitioned merchant vessel, HMAS *Upolu*, which had been set up as a submarine tender but would eventually prove more of a nuisance than anything else. A newly recruited naval doctor on board *Upolu*, Fred Kenny, thought she was 'a cranky, rusty old tub – always something going wrong with her – the Cook's mate says she frightens the engineers & firemen – Fine weather she's all right but when she gets her tail out & races one wonders how things hold together'.[13]

The original plan was for them to all go to Port Moresby, then rendezvous with the rest of the fleet, but *Protector* was so slow and *Upolu* so afflicted by engine troubles that they were ordered direct to Rabaul, at a stately six knots.

Patey brought his invasion fleet together on 9 September, off Rossel Island, in the Louisiade Archipelago, to the south-east of

New Guinea. It was a formidable force: *Australia*, the cruisers *Sydney* and *Encounter*, and the destroyers *Warrego*, *Yarra* and *Parramatta* – more than enough to deal with Spee's squadron, should he turn up. *Berrima* was there with her contingent of soldiers and sailors, and there was a storeship, SS *Aorangi*, and three colliers and an oiler for refuelling. A hospital ship, HMAS *Grantala*, another former passenger steamer, had been hastily equipped with wards, an operating theatre and a staff of surgeons and nurses, another miracle of organisation.

The admiral called a conference with Holmes and his ships' captains and outlined his plan of attack. It was simple enough. *Sydney* and the destroyers would go ahead to reconnoitre Blanche Bay. If the coast was clear – that is, if there were no enemy ships and no mines had been laid – the soldiers from *Berrima* would be put ashore to take Rabaul at the north of the bay. Two naval landing parties, of twenty-five men each, would land at the southern end of the bay, at the settlements of Herbertshöhe and Kabakaul, to begin the hunt for the wireless station.

Hubris reigned. The colonial Germans were expected to put up little or no resistance. Like a blast of bugles, Colonel Holmes wrote to his superiors back in Melbourne:

> [A]lthough the work on which I am engaged is of great importance to the Empire and will be of historical value in changing, if ever so little, the face of the map, it will, as far as I can see, be carried out without a shot being fired, which will be a keen disappointment to many with me who, like young foxhounds, would be all the better as soldiers if they were blooded.[14]

At first all went to plan. *Sydney* and the destroyers steamed into Blanche Bay at 3.30 a.m. on 11 September and found nothing of the enemy. *Berrima*, with Holmes and his soldiers on board, waited in the bay, offshore. The sailors landed in their two groups at 7 a.m. The Herbertshöhe party was led by *Sydney*'s first lieutenant, Lieutenant Commander John Finlayson, who carried with him a briskly elegant letter from Patey, in both English and German, to be delivered to the governor, Dr Eduard Haber:

HMAS Australia,
At Simpsonshafen, New Britain
11th September, 1914
Your Excellency,

I have the honour to inform you that I have arrived at Simpsonshafen with the intention of occupying Herbertshohe, Rabaul, and the Island of New Britain.

I will point out to Your Excellency that the force at my command is so large as to render useless any opposition on your part, and such resistance can only result in unnecessary bloodshed.

With regard to this, I hereby inform Your Excellency that I shall consider further communications by you with your Naval Forces, by means of your wireless telegraphy, as an hostile act. Such communications must cease immediately.

I therefore desire that the town of Rabaul and the Dependencies under your control should be surrendered to me forthwith.

An answer should be delivered to the bearer without delay.

If you do not intend to offer resistance, you should so inform me, and give me assurance with regard to any submarine mines that may have been laid in the harbours.

Your Excellency will also be good enough to state when you will interview me or my representative with the object of transferring control.

It is desirable in the interests of yourself and of the inhabitants that this should be arranged as soon as possible.

I have the honour to be,
Sir,
Your Excellency's obedient servant,
GEORGE E. PATEY
Rear-Admiral Commanding H.M. Australian Fleet[15]

Things began to unravel from this point. The governor was nowhere to be found. Later, they would discover he had taken refuge at Toma, an inland hill resort. Finlayson handed the letter to a German settler who said he would deliver it, then finished the business by hauling down the red, white and black German flag at the district officer's residence and running up the Union Jack. Not a shot was fired. So far, so good.

A little further down the coast, at Kabakaul, Lieutenant Rowland Bowen, an Australian-born naval officer from Petrie, near Brisbane, landed his group on a wooden jetty. Cautiously, with pistols drawn and rifles cocked, they entered a small bungalow to find a Chinese cook and some New Guineans cowering in fear. The cook told Bowen the German occupants had fled up the road to the wireless station at a place inland called Bita Paka. Bowen and his men set off, taking the terrified man along as a guide.

The road was narrow, and grey with thick dust, winding between tall palms and reeking, tangled jungle. The sun burned down; the heat was oppressive. From around a bend they heard the crack of rifle fire, as Bowen recounted to a *Sydney Morning Herald* reporter travelling in *Berrima*:

> We hadn't advanced a mile before the natives were firing on us continually from the trees. It is devilish country to fight in, much worse than the South African guerrilla warfare; for while the road is clear enough, on each side is a jungle of thorny palms, cocoanuts, long grass, and great hooked lawyer vines impossible to see through for a yard ahead, and exceedingly difficult to penetrate. I ordered my men to advance by slipping in and out of the undergrowth beside the road, a slow business. I suppose it took us about two hours to do a mile and a half.
>
> Well, my right flank got separated. They had reached a point where it was impossible to go further, and they had to come back and around to the left to reach me, I being really in this way ahead of part of my own fire.
>
> They brought me a German, whom they had wounded and captured. I put him in a pit in front of me, and ordered him to call out to the others ahead to surrender, and that we had a large force.
>
> There is nothing like bluff. He hesitated for a moment. Then, seeing that I was going to shoot him if he refused, he yelled out to his crowd to surrender, as it was hopeless.[16]

So much for Colonel Holmes's bombastic optimism. The Australians had naively underestimated the enemy. In fact, the Germans had prepared with a careful, dogged determination to resist in the name of the Fatherland. There were only two regular army officers at Rabaul, commanding a militia of some sixty clerks, traders and planters and the like. Beneath them were perhaps 250 New Guineans, police or soldiers of a sort, bare-chested and bare-footed. They had no machine guns or artillery, just officers' pistols and standard Mauser rifles. But they had laid their defences well. Two ambush trenches had been dug along the road to the wireless station, and the Australians found spikes hammered into the trunks of tall trees that might have been climbed as lookout posts. The invaders would have to fight their way along the uphill ten kilometres or so.

It took them most of the day, in fits and starts, some of them violent and bloody. Some Germans surrendered but others did not, and their New Guinean troops fought well. Bowen himself was grazed by a bullet to the back of his head and, covered in blood, thought for a while that he was dying. His second-in-command, Midshipman Reg Buller, dragged him to safety and sent for reinforcements.

The first Australian casualty was Able Seaman Billy Williams, from Northcote in suburban Melbourne, twenty-nine years old and one of the reservists; he was hit by a bullet in the chest. A mate carried him back down the track to an army doctor who had come ashore with them, Captain Brian Pockley, a recent graduate from Sydney University. Pockley bandaged him up as best he could and had him sent back to *Berrima*, but he was shot himself only a little later, a bullet hitting him in the stomach and shattering his backbone. Both men died in *Berrima*'s hospital ward that day, the first Australians killed in this war.

Pockley's friend Lieutenant Alec Doyle noted in his diary:

> He lived some time and was trying to give orders to his stewards to look after the other wounded, as he knew he was done. It was a damned fine finish. I hope the rest of us may only do as well. I wish I could have been with him.[17]

More men died in the heat and the dust that afternoon and early evening, all of them sailors: Lieutenant Commander Charles

Elwell, Stoker John Courtney, Signalman Robert Moffat and Able Seaman Harold Street. Elwell, a Royal Navy officer transferred to the RAN, was shot and killed as he led a bayonet charge on the second trench, brandishing a sword. Gus Shea, an able seaman from *Yarra*, described Elwell's death in a letter home to Moonee Ponds, in Melbourne:

> Elwell gave the order: 'Fix swords, charge!' and he got out on the road and was shot dead. The crowd we were fighting surrendered fast when we were going to wipe them out. After the trench surrendered we had to carry our dead and wounded back. I with 4 others had to carry a Naval Reserve man about two miles who was shot in two places. As soon as he was hit he sang out for his mother. It is terrible to hear the wounded scream. I don't want to hear any more.[18]

That reservist was Signalman Moffat, who died of his wounds. His mother, Iris, was listed as his next of kin, at their home in Kensington, Sydney. Able Seaman Timothy Sullivan, who had fought as a soldier in the Boer War, was hit by nine bullets in the jaw and chest but survived, and told his story in a letter to a clergyman friend:

> One young chap, Harry Street, belonging to South Australia, died across my legs about 9 p.m., for I was one of the wounded in that fight. We were shot about 4 p.m. and lay in the bush till nearly 11 p.m., and having advanced so quickly we were practically cut off from the remainder of our company, and so were unable to receive any attention.
>
> I don't wish to boast, sir, as you know this is not my first campaign, but really, South Australia has reason to be proud of her boys for they bore the brunt of the fighting. I especially admired the conduct of the young lads, who had only just come out of their cadet training. In the forced march, with a temperature over 100, not one fell out, and when it came to fighting. I can assure you, sir, they never wavered, and every time those lads fired, well, it meant a native or a German taking a long journey.[19]

The fighting – sharp skirmishing, really – continued on and off until nightfall, but the Australians eventually prevailed. As the dark descended, the wireless station was taken without further loss. Its equipment was still intact, although the two masts had been demolished. It was sheer luck that more had not been killed. Landmines filled with dynamite and shrapnel had been dug into the Bita Paka Road in two places, and were cleverly concealed, but the man who was to have detonated them had come down with malaria and no one had thought to replace him.

German and New Guinean prisoners were rounded up. At least one German had been killed, and an unknown number of New Guineans. The officer who led the final attack, Lieutenant Tom Bond, another reservist, would be awarded the blue and scarlet ribbon and the silver gilt cross of the Distinguished Service Order, the first Australian decoration of the war.

In the flagship, Admiral Patey was growing more and more irritated. The German governor had been playing cat and mouse with him, sending evasive replies from his outpost at Toma, stalling for time. Patey put Holmes's soldiers from *Berrima* ashore at Rabaul, entirely unhindered, where they began some enthusiastic looting, described by Private Ambrose O'Hare:

> Lots got some good things, the men entering houses as the Germans had all fled ... guns and revolvers, clothes, money, medals, swords and all sorts of things were taken by the troops, one chap showing me a nice lot of medals, one being the Iron Cross, another having a large gold medal. Chickens and ducks, pigs etc, were being cooked in all sorts of ways ... .[20]

The next day, Sunday, 13 September, the Australian Naval and Military Expedition Force formally claimed Rabaul in the name of King George, with as much imperial pomp and swagger as if they had taken Berlin itself. The troops marched to the centre of town, to a grassy square fringed by flaming hibiscus and scented by frangipani, a light breeze blowing through the palms. They drew up in ranks around a flagstaff. The *Sydney Morning Herald*'s correspondent, Fred Burnell, was there, digging deep for purple prose:

> The population had previously been warned of the ceremony about to take place and, whether reluctantly or not, everyone was

present, from the Burgomaster and other notables in spotless ducks, down to the natives, looking highly picturesque with their red loin cloths and rich black skins. Chinese smirked amiably in the crowd, urbane Japanese rubbed their hands with evident satisfaction, while not a few Japanese women were to be seen in full array of kimonos, bright obis and butterfly-tinted paper parasols. Even a sprinkling of Malays, heavy-lipped and lustrous-eyed, watched with keen curiosity the progress of events.[21]

Holmes arrived exactly at 3 p.m., in khaki uniform, polished Sam Browne belt and jackboots, sword and medals. Then Patey in formal whites, epaulettes gleaming gold, also with sword and medals, to the thump and blast of general salutes from *Australia*'s band. The Union Jack was run up the flagpole, the warships in Blanche Bay thundered out a twenty-one-gun salute and everyone – excepting the silent, sullen Germans – joined in a lusty chorus of 'God Save the King', to the *Herald* man's ecstatic delight:

> One has heard the old, familiar, hackneyed tune vulgarized by the reek of public dinners, and rendered momentarily even petty in one's estimation by its obtrusion at petty affairs; but until one has heard it echoing from the lips of a body of men, unconquerable in death, as at the sinking of the Birkenhead, or triumphant upon an enemy's soil, even in so comparatively small an instance as here at Rabaul, one may safely be said never truly to have heard it at all. It is indescribable. Let that suffice.[22]

The Brigade Major, Frank Heritage, read a proclamation in suitably florid English, which was later helpfully translated into pidgin English:

> All Boys belongina all place, you savvy Big Feller Master he come now; he new feller Master, he strong feller too much, you look him all ship stop place ... You look him new feller flag, you savvy him, he belong British English; he more better than other feller ... no more 'Um Kaiser, God save 'Um King.[23]

Fred Kenny, the surgeon in *Upolu*, had offered himself to the navy at the start of the war. A man in his mid-fifties from the New

England district of New South Wales, he enjoyed the company of the younger submarine officers, making particular friends with Tom Besant and Leopold Scarlett. The naval and military life intrigued him. He was an acute observer, and he kept a diary in the form of letters to his wife, both tender and informative, page after page. The ritual he had witnessed on that parade ground was familiar enough in the gilded theatre of empire but it was not one many Australians had seen, yet alone brought into being by their own force of arms:

> Kiss the children – I'm always thinking about you & the peaceful Glen Innes home – The contrast to all this grim armament is striking but this armament is the sole precursor & the bedrock mainstay of peaceful homes thro our empire – There is but one feeling here & that is that Germany has got to be thoroughly thrashed – at any cost – as one old sailor said when we hoisted the white ensign on our little launch 'That'll take a lot of hauling down Sir.'[24]

Like all the Australians that day, Kenny was thrilled and exultant, carried on a wave of patriotic fervour:

> There is one thing I do hope will happen & it is this – that we stick to all German New Guinea & to all these German Islands – This is a superb harbor & a 300 mile island & lots of real good land – Let Australia have it – never yield save to force – All this side of the Pacific should be ours & our flag should fly – All I've seen reminds me of North Qld – There are fertile patches for sugar – bananas – Citrus fruits & Coco plantations – there are fine plantations to be seen all round – The Union Jack stands for freedom, justice & fair play & colonists of any race will prosper under us – This may sound high falutin' but I feel & we all feel very strongly that 'this bit of the world belongs to us' & we want peace & plenty in it.[25]

That same Sunday morning, Billy Williams' widowed mother was not at home when the telegram boy knocked on the door of her little clapboard cottage at 36 Beavers Road, next to the railway line at Northcote in Melbourne. His married sister, Mrs Martin Anthonsen, opened the envelope and read:

We regret to have to inform you of the report from the officer commanding the Australian Expeditionary Force that your son, William G.V. Williams, A.B., has been killed in action while fighting against German forces in the Pacific.

The Minister for Defence and the Commonwealth Naval Department offer their deepest sympathy.[26]

The newspapers reported that Mrs Anthonson was overcome with grief but managed to say, 'It is a great honour for him to go in that way, and father would have been proud of him' – a quote that suggests a bit of well-meant journalistic creativity.[27] The local lodge of the Protestant Alliance Friendly Society, of which Billy had been a member, sent their condolences and donated £2/2/- to a patriotic fund in his name. When his workmates arrived on Monday morning at the Melbourne Electricity Supply Company, the news of his death was on the noticeboard, and they stood bareheaded and silent in his memory as the works siren blared a farewell.

Charles Elwell, the first Australian naval officer to die in this war, had been the gunnery instructor at the Naval College in its first year at Geelong, where his passing was solemnly remembered. As a boy he had been at the King's School, Parramatta. 'The old school now adds another to the distinguished list of heroes on its records who have fought and died for the Empire,' said the *Sydney Morning Herald*.[28]

At Rabaul, Governor Haber had still not appeared. Patey resolved to use force, if necessary, to blast him out. The day after the ceremony, Monday, 14 September, four mixed companies of soldiers and the naval reservists set off from Herbertshöhe before dawn with a machine gun and, remarkably, a twelve-pound naval gun on wheels, which had to be pushed and towed uphill along a rough jungle track towards Toma. As they laboured forward, they heard the whoosh of shells overhead. *Encounter* was bombarding the ridge with her six-inch guns, a very satisfying forty-eight rounds in all, splendid puffs of grey smoke rising above the jungle green.

Reaching the ridge themselves, the men on foot saw a trench with some New Guineans in it and set up their twelve-pounder, firing a few shots that killed some and sent others fleeing. Eventually a German officer appeared on horseback, carrying a white flag of surrender. His Excellency the Governor would appear at Herbertshöhe the next day to discuss terms.

―

The submarines and their escorts had finally reached Rabaul on Friday, 11 September; the crews were glad to be there after the tedium of their plodding trip north. The admiral called Tom Besant to a meeting the next day and said he wanted the boats out on patrol with a destroyer, taking turns. Besant said he needed to fix some minor problems with the engines of *AE1* and so it was *AE2* that set out on the first patrol on Sunday, 13 September, the day of the flag raising. It was uneventful. They cruised in St George's Channel, which separates New Britain from the next big island in the Bismarck Archipelago, New Ireland (or Neumecklenburg, as it was then), and returned to Blanche Bay at sunset.

AE1's mechanical troubles had not been properly fixed – her starboard main motor was still not working – but she left Simpsonhafen the next morning, 14 September, at 7 a.m. Fred Kenny watched her go, waving to his friends Besant and Scarlett on her bridge as she headed down Blanche Bay. She joined *Parramatta* off Herbertshöhe and the two of them, with the destroyer in the lead, then moved out into the channel and on a course towards Cape Gazelle, on the eastern tip of New Britain. There they exchanged signals, or perhaps spoke by megaphone. Besant asked *Parramatta*'s captain, Lieutenant Bill Warren, what the destroyer's orders were. Warren replied that he would search to the south and return to Herbertshöhe by 5.30 p.m. *AE1* turned away to the north-east, and they soon lost sight of each other.

It was a hazy day, with visibility gradually getting worse, although the seas were smooth, and the two did not see each other again until 2.30 that afternoon. They remained more or less in company for an hour, with the haze becoming ever thicker, until *AE1* slipped out of sight once more, at around 3.20 p.m. Warren watched her low, grey silhouette slowly disappearing into the murk to the north, which he thought was odd. They were supposed to have stayed south, but Besant was the senior of the two and it was not Warren's place to question him.

He kept a lookout for a while, cruising along inshore, but he did not find *AE1* and assumed that she must have headed home. He returned to Blanche Bay himself and anchored off Herbertshöhe later than usual, at 7 p.m.

At Simpsonhafen, they were waiting for *AE1* to come in. Harry Kinder was there:

> After tea the AE2 crew was sitting around on deck. Towards six o'clock some of us went onto the parent ship [*Upolu*] as it was the custom for any crews of boats lying in harbour to watch any submarines coming in off duty. As it was just on six, everyone was watching a point a mile or more away where we would get the first sight of AE1.
>
> Six o'clock had gone and no sign. We guessed that something had happened but no-one liked to voice an opinion as to what it was...[29]

Surgeon Kenny was waiting as well, planning to have dinner with Besant and Scarlett. When they didn't turn up, he asked *Upolu*'s stewards to keep their meals hot.

In the flagship, Admiral Patey was becoming more concerned. The tropical night was descending and *AE1* was well overdue. He signalled the submarine by wireless several times, but there was no reply. He sent a query to Warren in *Parramatta*, who could offer no explanation, and he talked with Harry Stoker, who was equally worried.

At 8 p.m. he acted. He ordered *Parramatta* and *Yarra* to begin a search, instructing them to burn their navigation lights and searchlights to be as visible as possible. There was always a hope the submarine might have had engine trouble and come to a halt, drifting. Or perhaps she had run aground and could not free herself. But then why had she not signalled for help, or answered the admiral's signals? Surely it could not be the enemy. The only German vessel of any size was a small government steamer.

No one that night dared to think the unthinkable: that *AE1* and the thirty-five souls on board were lost.

5
GOODBYE TO *AE1*

Parramatta and *Yarra* stayed out all that long night, cruising slowly back and forth, lights ablaze, but saw nothing. *Encounter* joined them at daylight the next morning, and then the third destroyer, *Warrego*, coming back from another mission, was sent in as well.

Patey ordered them to concentrate around the Duke of York Islands, scattered in a small group in the channel about halfway between New Britain and New Ireland. All the ships posted extra lookouts and the men off watch on deck kept their eyes peeled as well, but still nothing. Motor launches were commandeered in Rabaul and manned by sailors, who searched the coastline, all its little bays and inlets, and again not a sign. Not even a patch of oil nor flotsam on the sea.

George Patey was torn. His natural inclination was to remain on the scene directing the search, but he had orders to return to Sydney. A great troop convoy was gathering to carry the newly formed Australian Imperial Force – 20,000 men and their equipment and horses – to the war in Europe, due to leave in weeks. It would be Patey's responsibility to organise their naval escort through the Indian Ocean, a journey fraught with risk.

The little cruiser *Emden*, sent by von Spee from the East Asia Squadron, had entered the ocean through the Dutch East Indies late in August and embarked on a superbly planned and executed campaign of lone-wolf commerce raiding. By mid-September she had captured six British merchant ships, sinking five of them and then vanishing into the empty sea wastes. The Royal Navy had thrown every available ship into the hunt for her but she had eluded them, turning up next where she was least expected. Australia's military planners and government ministers feared *Emden* getting among a convoy of the flower of the nation's young volunteer soldiers.

So Admiral Patey sailed from Rabaul in *Australia* promptly at noon on 15 September, taking *Sydney* with him. *Encounter* was instructed to take charge of the search. Colonel Holmes would handle the surrender negotiations with the governor. Before he left, the admiral again called in Harry Stoker for his advice, to ask what might have happened, but *AE2*'s captain, shaken and in mourning, had little to offer. An internal explosion of some sort was possible but unlikely: wreckage would have been discovered, surely. There might have been a navigational accident: *AE1* could have hit an uncharted rock or reef, which might have torn her open. She might have done a practice dive and suffered some sort of accident. Both men ruled out the possibility of enemy action. There were simply no Germans around. The practice dive theory seemed the most likely, they agreed. *Encounter* sent an officer ashore on Duke of York Island, attempting to ask local villagers if they had seen anything, but that drew a blank.

Afternoon turned to dusk. The lights came on in Rabaul town and in the ships in Simpsonhafen, but there was no joy in them. The sun sank over the ridges and with it went all hope. *AE1* was gone. Lost with all hands, thirty-five men. Friends, shipmates.

Shaken to the marrow, Fred Kenny wrote to his wife:

> We are face to face this afternoon with a terrible tragedy – the loss of AE1 & all her crew . . .
>
> Conjecture is quite barren – It's not a German cruiser for the firing would have been heard – Naturally everyone here is very much upset –
>
> Fancy losing one of our own in such a sudden manner . . . I took to Besant & Scarlett very much – Scarlett was a handsome, curly headed young devil with a fine face & genial manner – He and I took to each other for his people have a station on the Upper Burnett . . . His people are cattle people . . .

Besant & I also came well together – a quiet, good type of English officer – We had lots in common & talked of dogs in the bush & shooting & collecting – It's wonderful how quickly men get together when messing at the same table & linked by a common cause –

Moore I didn't see much of but poor Scarlett's end is tragic – that beautiful bright cynical boy & poor Besant, thoughtful with a sweet smile & a kind voice & a lovely manner – Then there's the men – Dare devils – You should see a submarine & yet for a few shillings – sometimes but one extra per week these chaps cheerfully & willingly risk their lives – day by day – week in & week out & think nothing of it.

In an age when men were expected to conceal fear or pain or sorrow behind a stoic façade, the diaries and memoirs of the sailors of *AE2* reveal only a little of their thoughts.

Harry Kinder's entry was succinct and philosophical: 'AE2's crew was very down-hearted at the loss of AE1. Many of her crewmen were mates as both crews had been together for two or three years. It seemed a sad and terrible end, but it is the fortunes of war.'[1]

John Wheat, a young able seaman from Woy Woy, north of Sydney, kept a diary throughout the war, an articulate and engrossing account of his service life. He had joined the old Commonwealth Naval Forces as a boy of fifteen, learning the ropes in the training ship *Tingira*, moored in Sydney Harbour at Rose Bay. The loss had cast 'a great gloom', he wrote, and he went on to speculate about possible causes:

I. <u>Motor trouble</u>. One of her main electric motors being out of repair she dived & slightly over trimmed – that is had not buoyancy enough with her one remaining motor to give complete control & finally she became unmanageable & sank.

II. <u>An old enemy Tug boat</u> was found beached, having been set on fire by her crew who had decamped. This tugboat had on board a Nordenfelt gun 5 barrel which may have been used unexpectedly by some one in hiding as the AE1 lay on the surface nearby.

> III. <u>Enemy Mines</u>. This theory is hardly probable because there were no harbours which had not been thoroughly swept & searched.[2]

The tugboat theory gained some currency for a while as rumours spread: German treachery was to blame. That would be taken up in some of the more excitable newspapers back home. Harry Stoker's memoir, *Straws in the Wind*, dismissed that possibility, however, and reluctantly came to the conclusion that *AE1* must have had some accident while making a practice dive. Tom Besant, he wrote:

> was a skilful, cautious and experienced submarine commander; he had expressed the utmost satisfaction with the capabilities of his officers and crew, and also with the manner in which his boat dived; so that it must have been a strange mischance which caused their loss in ordinary practice diving.
>
> If, however, the objections were brushed aside and one accepted as fact that she dived and became out of control while diving, the end is plain to see. The sinking submarine would slip away down into the vast depths existing in those parts, rapidly filling as the increasing pressure of water outside forced its way through the hull, bring a quick and clean death to the crew, whose end might well have come even before their steel tomb had reached the ocean's bed – there to rest undisturbed by man and his investigations.
>
> If we never know the cause, the result was, alas, too quickly realised. Australia's first completed submarine had proved Australia's first warship to be lost. In her had died three skilful officers, best of good fellows and British gentlemen, and thirty-two specially selected and trained seamen and stokers.
>
> To us, their companions and jesting rivals over many a mile of sea; their friends and messmates in harbour; who had daily shared with them every interest, joy and sorrow of many months crowded with incident and adventure; who were also losing, in many cases, friends of long years standing; whose hopes and ambitions had framed no thoughts in which AE1 did not share with AE2 – our loss was a loss indeed.
>
> May their rest be peaceful.

There seemed to me to lie but a straw in the wind 'twixt *AE2*, at anchor in Rabaul harbour and her sister ship, the steel tomb, hundreds of fathoms deep.³

At home in Australia, the newspapers had been reporting a steady and encouraging stream of Allied victories and good news. 'Kaiser's Uncle Killed!' 'Crown Prince's Army Routed!' 'Terrible Despair Exists at Austria!' The reality was rather different. At Mons, in Belgium, and then on the Marne and Aisne rivers, in France, as the northern summer became autumn, the two sides were inexorably grinding each other into the static horrors of years of trench warfare. One excitable report, widely published, announced that the Russians would be in Berlin in three weeks. In truth, the Tsar's armies had been routed by the Germans at the Battle of Tannenberg in East Prussia at the end of August, a devastating defeat with 72,000 killed and their commander committing suicide.

One victory stood out, and accurately. It was the first British submarine success of the war. On 13 September, patrolling southwest of the islands of Heligoland, in the North Sea, *E9* torpedoed and sank the small German cruiser SMS *Hela*. *E9*'s captain, Lieutenant Commander Max Horton, had surfaced at dawn for 'a look around', as submariners liked to say, and sighted the German about two miles away. He quickly submerged, closed for the attack, and fired two torpedoes at a range of around 600 yards, scoring a direct hit amidships with the second, a perfect shot. Coming back to the surface, Horton was startled by some shells which fell around him from a ship he had not spotted, so he submerged again for an hour. After seeing through his periscope that *Hela* was sinking, he made to head home for Harwich, harried for a while by some other small German warships.

E9 was a sister to *AE1* and *AE2*, also built at Barrow, and Horton was an exact contemporary of Tom Besant: they had entered the training ship *Britannia* on the same day in September 1898. Arriving at Harwich, he flew the black and white skull and crossbones flag to celebrate his victory, a cheeky riposte to

Admiral Sir Arthur Wilson's famous 'damned un-English' remark about hanging submariner pirates. That flag became a submarine tradition which endures to this day.

It was almost week before the Australian people were told of the loss of *AE1*, in a brief announcement from the defence minister, Senator George Pearce, on 19 September. The Navy Office in Melbourne had needed the time to send out the telegrams to the next of kin in both Britain and Australia: to Edgar Besant, retired at his home in Ladbroke Grove; to Lord Abinger, Leo Scarlett's brother in Hampshire; to Elizabeth Messenger in Ballarat, the mother of Engine Room Artificer John Messenger; to Ellie Marsland in Southampton, the wife of Chief Engine Room Artificer John Marsland; to Beatrice Maloney, wife of Stoker Petty Officer John Maloney, in Waterloo, Sydney; to James Guild, the father of Stoker William Guild in Perth, Scotland; to Alberta Baker, mother of telegraphist Cyril Baker in Launceston, Tasmania. One went to Kaikoura, in the South Island of New Zealand, to Catherine Reardon, mother of Able Seaman John Reardon.

There were more telegrams, to Kent and Devon and Hampshire, to New South Wales and Victoria, but only thirty-four of them. Unaccountably, awfully, the name of *AE1*'s first lieutenant, Charles Moore, did not appear on the first casualty lists. Colonel Henry Moore and his wife, Annie, of Minehead in Somerset, did not officially hear of their son's death for some weeks, prompting an embarrassed personal apology from Rear Admiral Creswell, then the First Naval Member of the Navy Board:

> Sir,
>
> On behalf of the Naval Board of the Royal Australian Navy, I beg to express to yourself and to your whole family the profound regret of the Naval Board and the Australian Navy at the extremely sad loss of your son, Lieutenant Charles L. Moore RN in Submarine AE1 and our sympathy in your great sorrow.
>
> I wish also on behalf of my colleagues and myself to express to you how deeply concerned we were and how we sympathised with the added pain that must have been caused by the omission to report your son's loss . . .[4]

The defence minister and the Navy Board were each careful to stress that there had been no enemy action – that the loss was an accident, albeit one that could not be explained. The RAN wanted it known that the men's deaths would have been quick and clean:

> The weather was fine, the sea smooth, and no enemy was in the vicinity. It was thought that she must have sighted an enemy and given chase but the result of thorough search has now caused this hope to be abandoned.
>
> The water in the vicinity of the place in which she was last seen is very deep, and there is no hope of locating the wreck if she has sunk there. We may be thankful that the water is deep, as the hull of the vessel would be unable to stand the pressure, and death would be mercifully sudden.[5]

Editorial writers at the city newspapers and in the country towns struck much the same theme, of a noble death in the service of King and country, expressed by Sydney's *Daily Telegraph*:

> If she had been sunk in action, after torpedoing one of the five German cruisers that our ships have been searching the Pacific for, it might, to some ears have sounded finer.
>
> But these men died doing their best for their country, and knowing the risk they ran, and no dramatic scene could make a death of that kind more heroic.[6]

The Adelaide *Advertiser* emphasised the dangers of serving in submarines:

> The world can ill afford to lose men who show their courage by the mere fact of accepting employment aboard a species of craft which in addition to being subject to the perils to which every warship is liable has to encounter those belonging to its own construction and functions.
>
> The very helplessness of the men who are willing to risk paying with their lives what Kipling calls 'the price of Admiralty' accentuates the tragedy.[7]

In Sydney, *The Sun* published a poem in its Sunday edition of 20 September, written by the editor, Del McCay:

She faced no battle flame, she heard no German gun;
The ship without a name, the luckless AE1.
Yet were her sailors' lives no less for Empire lost,
And mothers, sweethearts, wives, must pay the bitter cost.
Australia's warships sweep the broad Pacific Main,
But one from out the deep will never rise again;
Yet we shall not forget, through all the years that run,
The fate that she has met –
Good-bye to AE1.
Pent in their iron cell, they sank beneath the wave,
Untouched by shot or shell, they drifted to the grave.
Until their painful breath at last began to fail;
Upon their way to death let pity draw the veil.
They could not strike one blow, but out of sound and sight
Of comrade or of foe they passed to endless night:
Deep down on Ocean's floor, far from the wind and sun,
They rest for evermore –
Good-bye to AE1.
A harder fate was theirs than men's who fight and die,
But still Australia cares, and will not pass them by;
When Honor's lists are read, their names will surely be
Among the gallant dead who fought to keep us free.
Their winding-sheet is steel, their sepulchre is wide;
The sea-birds scream and wheel where silently they died;
Theirs is a Monument of History, begun
When down to death they went –
Good-bye to AE1.[8]

And so the world and the war went on. Governor Haber finally went to Herbertshöhe on 15 September for a negotiation with Colonel Holmes, and two days later he signed the terms of capitulation. The remnants of the German militia – five officers, thirty-five non-commissioned officers and 110 New Guinean soldiers – marched down from Toma into Herbertshöhe on 21 September and formally laid down their arms.

Spee and his cruisers continued eastwards across the Pacific, towards Chile. On 14 September they had stopped at Samoa, hoping, in turn, to find George Patey. When that news reached the Admiralty, they feared that Spee might double back on his tracks and descend on Fiji or perhaps even New Zealand, so Patey was ordered to take *Australia* and *Sydney* back to Rabaul. On 22 September came news that the Germans had reached Tahiti, where they had lobbed a few shells into the deserted township of Papeete. This was more than 2000 kilometres east of Samoa, supporting Patey's view that they were indeed heading for South American waters, but London still thought otherwise and ordered him to base himself at Suva, Fiji. Another wild goose chase.

In company with *Sydney* and a French cruiser, *Montcalm*, which had recently joined him, Patey – newly promoted to vice admiral – reached Suva on 12 October. *Encounter* and the destroyers *Warrego* and *Parramatta* joined him there, and a few days later *AE2* and *Upolu* limped in as well, the submarine with yet another broken propeller blade and the tender plagued by her perpetual engine trouble. *Upolu* carried a spare propeller, which was put on by divers.

For the next few weeks, Patey sortied in and out of the harbour, here and there, fruitlessly and with increasing frustration. *AE2* was assigned to take turns as day guard ship, which meant pottering around close to Suva in a watchdog role and not doing very much beyond the occasional practice dive, where they discovered a couple of minor but troubling leaks.

All the ships got shore leave, the officers relaxing in the colonial splendour of the newly opened Grand Pacific Hotel, the men hitting the pubs and bars. There was cricket on a 'splendid green sward', as Surgeon Kenny described it, as well as tennis, swimming and fishing. They revelled in a tropical holiday idyll with only infrequent news of the far distant war. A few times Stoker took *AE2* out of Suva to one of the nearby smaller islands, largely to get his men away from the grog, which was beginning to take a hold of the whole fleet. Patey eventually cracked down on shore leave after an outbreak of trouble with drunken libertymen rampaging through Suva and running afoul of the local police.

Kenny found himself spending more and more time patching up the results:

> We saw one sailor man biff his officer in the launch – The officer went wallop – It was a good humoured, drunken spree but I don't wonder at the Admiral not granting leave very often. There'll be some trouble tomorrow I expect. How some of the chaps would ever get up the gangway I don't know. There was a dark rumour that one officer even was paralytic and they passed him inboard through a port hole – Well we watched all this and enjoyed it muchly . . .[9]

AE2's captain invited Kenny on one of the island trips, for lunch and then dinner:

> Haggard and I joined the submarine crew at a game of water polo – I must have stayed in ¾ of an hour – very warm and jolly with these very fine sailor men. All save H and me in bathing costumes. Then we put off and had a cocktail and sat or stood and watched the sunset. About 7 we had dinner – a very good dinner – all cooked by electricity – even the toast – then we had wine and yarned and went up on deck & finally turned in . . .[10]

Stoker himself relished the solitude, a state of mind and body not easy to achieve in a submarine.

> Some of the islands have long, slowly shelving beaches; and if on one of these, towards late afternoon, you lie as near naked as may be, basking in the rays of a not too powerful sun, and feel the waters of the rising tide, warmed to surprising heat by their passage over the hot sand, come trickling first round your toes and slowly, inch by inch, covering your whole body – then an indescribable feeling of perfect peace is with you, which must be near akin to that which passeth all understanding.[11]

At times the war news did intrude on this perfect peace, with brutal clarity. In the first week of November there were reports of Spee's stunning victory over a British squadron off Cape Coronel, on the central coast of Chile. The East Asia Squadron had reached South American waters late in October, entirely as Admiral Patey had surmised. There Spee coaled his ships for the voyage east around the storm-tossed Cape Horn, into the Atlantic and hopefully on the way home to Germany. The Royal Navy's Fourth Cruiser Squadron, based on the Falkland Islands, sailed west around the Horn and then north up the Chilean coast to meet him.

It was a hopeless mismatch. Spee had the modern and strongly-gunned *Scharnhorst* and *Gneisenau*, and the light cruisers *Dresden*, *Leipzig* and *Nürnberg*. The British commander, Rear Admiral Sir Christopher 'Kit' Cradock, had but two obsolete armoured cruisers, slow and lightly gunned: his flagship, HMS *Good Hope*, and HMS *Monmouth*. A third light cruiser, HMS *Glasgow*, was modern and fast, and there was a converted merchant liner with a few ancient guns on board, HMS *Otranto*, but an elderly battleship that was to have joined him, HMS *Canopus*, was too slow to keep up and was left behind.

The two forces met shortly before sunset on All Saints' Day, 1 November. The British ships were silhouetted against the lowering sun, and Spee's cruisers pounded them to oblivion. Cradock fought bravely, well aware that he had engaged in a hopeless contest, and within twenty minutes *Monmouth* staggered out of the battle, burning fiercely. *Good Hope* died in a tremendous explosion of white flame and shooting stars, sinking when her bows broke off and taking all 926 men with her. *Monmouth* then rolled on her side and went to the bottom with 734 of her crew, including her captain, Frank Brandt, who had escorted *AE1* and *AE2* on the first leg of their journey from Portsmouth in the cruiser *Eclipse*. *Glasgow* and *Otranto* escaped in the carnage and fled. The Germans suffered only three men lightly wounded, from shell splinters.

This defeat stunned the Royal Navy and the wider British Empire. Stoker called it a bombshell. Admiral Patey's thoughts are unrecorded, but his frustration and disgust at the Admiralty's meddling from London must have been profound. We have a glimpse of it in a scorching letter to the Colonial Office in Whitehall written a fortnight after Coronel by the governor-general in Melbourne, a Scot, Sir Ronald Munro-Ferguson:

> While reluctant to concern myself with naval strategy, I have to report a prevailing opinion that the loss of our cruisers off the

Chilean coast is the climax of a long bungle in the Pacific. As to this, as I have intimated, there is sure to be sharp discussion later on. The maxim of seeking out and destroying the enemy's ships has been ignored. Nearly a month was wasted over Samoa; after the wireless at Simpsonhafen had been destroyed the *Australia* was detained for many days in the Bismarck Archipelago; lastly, valuable time was lost cruising around Fiji. Had Admiral Patey immediately destroyed the German wireless to the north and then sought out the enemy's ships, these would not have been left unmolested for three months . . .

Admiral Patey at our interview in Sydney on 2 August was insistent on the need for an immediate and unremitting chase of the Gneisenau and Scharnhorst, and I know that he has never swerved from that view.

There is but one opinion here, viz: that H.M.A. Fleet, and the China Squadron also, has been singularly ineffective; and that to the remoteness of Admiralty control may be traced the concentration of German ships off Chile with its lamentable result . . .[12]

It was an accurate assessment. At the outbreak of war, concerted action by Patey's ships and the RN's China Squadron coming down from the north very likely would have caught the Germans in the jaws of a vice. But it was too late now. With the menace lifted from the western Pacific, *AE2* was on her way back home to Australia in early November, with *Parramatta* and *Warrego*. The Admiralty, again in its wisdom, had decided that *Australia* would be more use in the Northern Hemisphere, so Patey was heading for the Atlantic via the Panama Canal.

There were better tidings on 9 November, when HMAS *Sydney* wirelessed to the world that she had destroyed SMS *Emden*, forcing her to run ashore at the Cocos Islands in the Indian Ocean, a burning wreck. The signal from *Sydney*'s captain, John Glossop, elegantly succinct, would enter naval folklore: 'Emden beached and done for.' *Sydney* had four killed in the fight; *Emden* lost 134, but her career as a raider had been a triumph. Under her bold and resourceful captain, Karl von Müller, she had shelled the oil tanks at Madras, torpedoed a Russian cruiser in Penang Harbour and captured or sunk twenty-two merchant vessels. Running her down was the RAN's first victory at sea and so was duly celebrated, not least because it assured the safe passage of the AIF convoy towards the Suez Canal.

AE2 was refitting in Sydney when they heard of Spee's destruction a month later. At Winston Churchill's request, Jacky Fisher had returned to the Admiralty as First Sea Lord and he despatched a powerful squadron to the South Atlantic to hunt for the Germans to exact retribution for Coronel. At the Battle of the Falkland Islands on 8 December all the East Asia Squadron was sunk, save the cruiser *Dresden*, which escaped in the mayhem (only to be sunk in another encounter a few months later, in March 1915). Among the 1871 killed were Maximilian von Spee and his two sons, who went down with their ships.

Harry Stoker, characteristically, had a good word for him, a fair tribute:

> In the ports of the East I doubt if there was a more popular sailor than Admiral von Spee. His charm of manner and general character were vouched for by many English as well as people of all nations . . . he eventually died fighting his ships in the most gallant manner possible against overwhelming odds . . .[13]

The attractions of Sydney had begun to fade for Stoker. He felt the world was passing him by, that he was missing out. It was plain that the submarine had revolutionised war at sea in just a few weeks, most emphatically demonstrated when the German *U-9* torpedoed and sank three obsolete British cruisers on 22 September in less than two hours.

HMS *Aboukir*, *Hogue* and *Cressy* had been patrolling, line abreast, in filthy weather in a patch of the North Sea known as the Broad Fourteens, off the Dutch coast. The RN sardonically called them the 'Live Bait Squadron', and that they were. They should have been zigzagging as a precaution but were relying instead on the heavy seas to keep any submarine at bay, and they got it appallingly wrong. *Kapitänleutnant* Otto Weddigen of *U-9* torpedoed and sank *Aboukir* first, at 6.20 a.m. When *Hogue* went to the rescue of her crew, Weddigen sank her at 7.15 a.m., and finally *Cressy* just before eight o'clock. There were 1459 men killed, most of them reservists or retired men returned to sea for the duration. The tragedy shocked the RN and the British people to the marrow.

Stoker knew all this, and itched to join the battle. There he was, a qualified practitioner of these dark underwater arts, with a worked-up crew and a boat in good order, yet to fire a shot in anger. And with the Southern Hemisphere – or Australian waters, anyway – evidently swept clean of the enemy, he saw no prospect of action.

The inactivity began to gnaw at him and, after some thought, he took the unusual step for a junior officer of writing to the Naval Board in Melbourne to suggest that *AE2* would be of more use in either the Mediterranean or the North Sea. More remarkable still, he obtained permission to put his case personally to the defence minister, Senator George Pearce, at the government's temporary home in Melbourne.

A former carpenter, farm labourer and gold prospector, Pearce had been elected to the Senate for Western Australia at Federation and was now in his second term as defence minister in Andrew Fisher's Labor government. He was an ardent and knowledgeable naval enthusiast and he invited Stoker to meet him at Victoria's Parliament House, where the federal parliament was sitting. Stoker described the meeting in his memoir:

> The Minister was conducting a Bill through the Senate and came out to see me behind the Speaker's chair. As I made my report and request to him, Sir John Forrest[14] was speaking from the opposition front bench against the Bill and I was greatly impressed with the manner in which Mr Pearce was able to pay perfect attention to me the while he kept one ear for the criticising voice within. After the interview I went round into the House and listened to the debate. Across a table a small man was, lynx-eyed, watching the burly Sir John; with short, quick, cat-like movement of head, nervous twitching of hands, he sat ready to pounce. I was a considerable distance away, yet his personality seemed the outstanding one of the House. I asked who he might be and was told it was Mr Hughes, then Attorney-General.[15] It was not long before he became Prime Minister and I was not surprised when it occurred.[16]

Pearce and the Naval Board took a week to make up their minds. On 16 December they offered *AE2* to the Admiralty for service in the Northern Hemisphere and the answer was a grateful yes. Stoker was ordered to get his boat ready for sea forthwith. The week before Christmas he sailed from Sydney for Albany in Western Australia, to join the convoy taking the second contingent of 15,000 troops of the AIF up through the Indian Ocean to the Middle East. His depot ship this time would be *Berrima*, their old friend from Rabaul, which would tow him most of the way. With *Emden* out of the picture, *AE2* would be the only naval escort.

They left Albany on 31 December. That same day, Henry Hugh Gordon Dacre Stoker was promoted to lieutenant commander. His orders were to join the Royal Navy's fleet in the Mediterranean, where the Ottoman Empire had entered the war on the side of Germany and Austria-Hungary.

At the zenith of their power and pomp, the Ottoman Turks had ruled the Mediterranean and the Middle East in a great Islamic caliphate that reached from what are now the modern states of Algeria in the west to Turkey itself in the east, north through the Baltic states to southern Hungary and Ukraine, and south through Egypt and Saudi Arabia to the mouth of the Red Sea. The great cities of Belgrade, Damascus, Jerusalem, Baghdad, Cairo and Mecca lay under the sway of the Sublime Porte, the ancient name for the government in Constantinople.

That had been in the seventeenth century. Since then, a chaotic succession of wars, uprisings and revolutions, virtually unending, had brought the Ottomans to decline and decay, their boundaries and frontiers shrinking. By the beginning of the twentieth century, the Turkish economy was a basket case, propped up by massive loans from the major European powers, principally Britain, Germany and France. Turkey itself was commonly referred to as 'the sick man of Europe', a cruelly accurate term coined by the Russian tsar, Nicholas I.

When Europe descended into war, Turkey's allegiance was quickly in play. After a coup in 1913, the empire was effectively ruled by a gang of three, the Young Turk triumvirate or the Three Pashas, as they were known: Talaat Pasha, the interior minister; Enver Pasha, the minister of war; and Djemal Pasha, the minister of the navy. (*Pasha* was a Turkish title of honour, roughly equivalent to a British peerage.) The modern term 'fascist' had not been coined then, but it describes the trio with reasonable accuracy. Enver, the youngest at just thirty-three, dapper with a pointed, waxed moustache, corrupt and vain, saw himself as a de facto foreign minister. The elderly sultan, Mehmed V, was a figurehead without power, a rubber stamp. The American ambassador, Henry Morgenthau, a well-informed and caustic observer, regarded the trio as murderers, thugs and usurpers. Turkey, he wrote, 'consisted of merely so many inarticulate, ignorant, and poverty-ridden slaves, with a small, wicked oligarchy at the top, which was prepared to use them in the way that would best promote its private interests'.[17]

The European powers all had their irons in the Turkish fire and jostled for influence. The greater part of Russia's export trade left her ice-free Black Sea ports and passed through the Turkish waters of the Bosporus, the Sea of Marmara and then the narrow strait of the Dardanelles, which opened into the Mediterranean. It was essential to Russia to keep those waters open. Britain needed a compliant Turkey for safe access to the Suez Canal and the oil of nearby Persia. France was in alliance with Russia and also in need of Middle East oil. Germany, if she went to war with Russia, wanted Turkey as a useful ally on Russia's southern flank and was building a Berlin–Baghdad railway for access to oil and its colonial empire.

The Germans pursued the contest with impressively large investment 'loans' – the word 'bribery' suggests itself – combined with artful diplomacy and military aid orchestrated by its ambassador, Baron Hans von Wangenheim, a suave mix of geniality and brutality and a personal friend of Kaiser Wilhelm. In 1913, a German military mission set up shop in Constantinople to modernise the Turkish army, led by a general, Otto Liman von Sanders.

This German ascendancy was helped along by a startling episode of British ineptitude. Vickers at Barrow had been building two modern battleships for the Turkish navy, *Reşadiye* and

Sultan Osman. With war approaching, the First Lord, Winston Churchill, persuaded the cabinet that Britain should seize them for the Royal Navy, and on 2 August 1914 an army battalion with fixed bayonets marched on board and took possession. Their Turkish crews were rounded up and sent packing, and the ships were quickly commissioned as HMS *Agincourt* and HMS *Erin*. All Turkey was outraged. It was an insulting betrayal, not least because the money to buy the two had been raised by public subscription as a matter of national pride, with contributions big and small from every town and village.

Any lingering pro-British sentiment in Turkey evaporated. That same day, the German and Ottoman empires concluded a secret treaty which bound the Turks to go to war if Germany declared war on Russia. Item 3 of the treaty stated:

> In case of war, Germany will leave her military mission at the disposal of Turkey. The latter, for her part, assures the said military mission an effective influence on the general conduct of the army, in accordance with the understanding arrived at directly between His Excellency the Minister of War and His Excellency the Chief of the Military Mission.[18]

The Germans had won. Turkey was in their clutches. Ambassador Morgenthau had no idea the treaty existed, but he could see the results in Constantinople, not least in the imposing person of Colmar Freiherr von der Goltz, a bug-eyed, bullnecked Prussian field marshal who had trained the Turkish army:

> German officers were rushing through the streets every day in huge automobiles, all requisitioned from the civilian population; they filled all the restaurants and amusement places at night, and celebrated their joy in the situation by consuming large quantities of champagne – also requisitioned. A particularly spectacular and noisy figure was that of Von der Goltz Pasha. He was constantly making a kind of viceregal progress through the streets in a huge and madly dashing automobile, on both sides of which flaring German eagles were painted. A trumpeter on the front seat would blow loud, defiant blasts as the conveyance rushed along, and woe

to any one, Turk or non-Turk, who happened to get in the way! The Germans made no attempt to conceal their conviction that they owned this town.[19]

Britain, though, had not yet finished with blunder and failure. Alive to the seizure of the Turkish battleships, the Germans decided to send two of their own warships to Turkey. They had the battlecruiser *Goeben* and the light cruiser *Breslau* already in the Mediterranean, and on 4 August, the day the war in Europe began, their commander, *Konteradmiral* Wilhelm Souchon, was ordered to make for Constantinople. A Royal Navy cruiser and destroyer squadron gave chase and caught up with them on 7 August as they were heading for the Dardanelles, but through a misunderstanding of ambiguous orders the British admiral reluctantly declined to give battle and retired. It was a catastrophic mistake, brought on by confusion and bungle both at the Admiralty and at sea.

By international agreement, the Dardanelles were closed to warships but the ostensibly neutral Turks opened the straits for the Germans and on 11 August *Goeben* and *Breslau* were given a rapturous welcome in Constantinople. In a charade staged for world public consumption, the red and white Turkish flag was run up and the ships were commissioned into the Turkish navy as *Yavuz Sultan Selim* and *Midilli*, but they kept their German commanders and crews, who, ludicrously, exchanged their Imperial German Navy caps for the Turkish fez. To add arrogant insult to injury, in one blatant piece of provocation, *Goeben* dropped anchor in front of the Russian embassy, the band playing and the crew lined up on deck lustily singing '*Deutschland über Alles*', '*Die Wacht am Rhein*' and other martial anthems as they ostentatiously doffed their fezzes and donned their caps in full view of the Tsar's diplomats.

Worse was to come, much worse. On 29 October, with the approval of Enver Pasha, Admiral Souchon – by now officially the commander-in-chief of the Turkish Navy – led his ships into the Black Sea. There, unprovoked, they bombarded Russian ports, including Odessa, Sebastopol and Yalta, sinking a Russian gunboat and damaging shore installations, oil tanks and granaries. It was a deliberate act of war, with exactly the consequences that Germany was striving for. 'I have thrown the Turks into the powder keg,' Souchon wrote to his wife.[20] Turkey and Russia declared war upon each other. *Goeben*, Churchill later wrote, had carried with her 'for the peoples of the East and Middle East more slaughter, more misery and more ruin than has ever before been borne within the compass of a ship'.[21]

Churchill, though, was not done either. Far from it. Without any bothersome declaration of war, impetuous and pugnacious as ever, he orchestrated what was politely called a British and French 'demonstration' against the Turks. On 3 November, two British battlecruisers, HMS *Indomitable* and HMS *Indefatigable*, and two French battleships, *Vérité* and *Suffren*, appeared off the entrance to the Dardanelles to bombard Turkish forts and gun batteries for a brisk thirty minutes. They fired on the outer forts at Seddülbahir and Cape Helles on Gallipoli and Kum Kale on the Asiatic shore. The forts were damaged, an ammunition dump blew up and eighty-six Turks were killed. 'It is a good thing to give a prompt blow,' the First Lord wrote to Jacky Fisher.[22]

It was also a spectacular telegraphed punch. There could hardly have been a more obvious indication of the Allies' military thinking. The Turks and their German advisers took the hint and rushed to strengthen their defences on the Gallipoli Peninsula and in the Dardanelles waterway, installing new gun batteries, better telephone communications and searchlights, and doubling the size of the minefields in the strait itself. They were ready in a matter of months.

All that remained now were the formalities. On 5 November Britain and France declared war on Turkey. On 11 November Turkey declared war on Britain and France and imposed conscription for all males between twenty and forty-five. On 13 November a reluctant Mehmed V, in his role as the Caliph of Islam, formally called for a *jihad* against Britain, France, Russia, Serbia and Montenegro. It was stirring stuff:

> Oh, Moslems! Ye who are smitten with happiness and are on the verge of sacrificing your life and your goods for the cause of right, and of braving perils, gather now around the Imperial throne,

obey the commands of the Almighty, who, in the Koran, promises us bliss in this and in the next world; embrace ye the foot of the Caliph's throne and know ye that the state is at war with Russia, England, France, and their Allies, and that these are the enemies of Islam. The Chief of the believers, the Caliph, invites you all as Moslems to join in the Holy War![23]

It was a submarine that drew first blood. At 3.30 in the morning of 13 December, Lieutenant Norman Holbrook took HMS *B11* into the Dardanelles to seek and destroy. He ran submerged along the western side of the strait, where it was known the currents were not so strong, surfacing every two hours to fix his position and to gulp some fresh air, coolly aware that he would have to thread his way through the minefields. *B11* was almost obsolete, having been commissioned in 1906: barely 300 tonnes, with a single petrol engine, just two bow torpedo tubes and a fixed, non-retracting periscope, it could travel at twelve knots on the surface and seven knots submerged, at best. The crew was just two officers and thirteen men.

After five hours they reached the minefield, five rows of mines stretching out from Kephez Point on the eastern shore. They went through it submerged, hardly daring to breathe, waiting to hear the scrape of mine mooring wires on the hull. When he believed he was well clear, Holbrook came to periscope depth in broad daylight and found he could see the town of Çannakale well up the strait and, in a nearby bay, a Turkish battleship. Still undiscovered, he lined up for a shot and fired one torpedo. It struck home, perfectly. *Mesudiye*, an elderly ironclad, slowly began to list and founder but managed to fire a few shells before she rolled.

B11 now had to escape, so it was back through the minefield again. With a damaged compass, working by dead reckoning and the occasional glimpse through his periscope, Holbrook took her scraping and bumping along the bottom, the air in the submarine becoming ever fouler. Each time he came to periscope depth he drew fire from searching Turkish patrol boats. It was eight hours before he could surface in the open sea off Cape Helles.

The exploit brought Lieutenant Holbrook the Victoria Cross, the first of the war for the navy and the first ever for a submariner, and with it came enduring fame throughout the British Empire. The good folk of Germanton, in southern New South Wales, voted to change the name of their little village to Holbrook; a scale model of *B11* is on display there today.

As 1914 drew to a close, the stage was set and the actors were taking their place in the wings for the tragedy of Gallipoli.

6

GENERALLY RUN AMUCK

'You will be home before the leaves have fallen from the trees,' the Kaiser told his troops as they marched off to war in August 1914. *Der oberste Kriegsherr*, the Supreme Warlord, was not alone in his cheery optimism. There were many on the Allied side, too, who believed it would be over in months.

By 1915, those hopes had been ground into the mud and the blood of the trenches in France and the mass slaughter on the Russian front. New Year's Day itself began badly for the Allies. Before dawn, the submarine again took its toll when *U-24* torpedoed and sank the pre-dreadnought battleship HMS *Formidable* in the English Channel, with 547 men lost.

In Whitehall and at Westminster an idea began to form, slowly at first, that taking Turkey out of the war might be the solution to a great many problems, and a relatively easy solution at that. On 2 January, the Russian commander-in-chief, the Grand Duke Nicholas, formally asked Britain and France to make 'a demonstration' against the Turks, to take the pressure off his armies in the Caucasus. It was an attractive proposal, something that might break the stalemate on the Western Front, and three days later the British Secretary of State for War, Field Marshal Lord Kitchener, told the War Council that 'the Dardanelles appeared to be the most suitable objective, as an attack here could be made in cooperation with the Fleet'.[1]

The idea began to gather steam. At the Admiralty, Winston Churchill seized it with his usual gusto, his love of the grand gesture and the bold stroke, and on 13 January the War Council met again. The prime minister, Henry Asquith, his senior cabinet and their military and naval advisers spent a draining day pondering what to do in France, growing ever more despondent. As evening fell, the First Lord played his hand. The Royal Navy would force the Dardanelles! Plans had been discussed. There would be no need to bring in the army, no need to take troops from the fight in France. Three modern battleships, including the brand-new *Queen Elizabeth*, and twelve older battleships would reduce the Turkish forts and guns on either side of the Dardanelles Strait, steam into the Sea of Marmara, destroy *Goeben* and appear off Constantinople. There would be panic in the Turkish capital, perhaps even a coup d'état, the government would fall . . .

The War Council's secretary, Colonel Maurice Hankey, recorded the moment:

> The idea caught on at once. The whole atmosphere changed. Fatigue was forgotten. The War Council turned eagerly from the dreary vista of a 'slogging match' on the Western Front to brighter prospects, as they seemed, in the Mediterranean. The Navy, in whom everyone had implicit confidence and whose opportunities so far had been few and far between, was to come into the front line . . . Churchill unfolded his plans with the skill that might be expected of him, lucidly but quietly and without exaggerated optimism.[2][3]

Jacky Fisher was at the meeting, as First Sea Lord the government's principal naval adviser. He had his doubts but, out of loyalty to Churchill, he remained silent. Planning for the operation gathered momentum. As it did, Fisher's opposition deepened. A week later he wrote to his friend Admiral Sir John Jellicoe, Commander-in-Chief of the Home Fleet: 'I just abominate the Dardanelles operation, unless a great change is made and it is settled to be made a military operation, with 200,000 men in conjunction with the Fleet. I believe that Kitchener is coming now to this sane view of the matter.'[3]

Kitchener was not coming to this sane view – quite the opposite. There would be no need for the army, no need for a land invasion.

Planning rolled along with increasing optimism. Hopes took wing. The Turk would be taught a lesson. Ministers began to discuss how a defeated Turkey would be carved up and distributed in parcels. Britain would take Egypt, France could have Syria and the Levant, there would be something for Italy and Greece, perhaps the Jews could have Jerusalem, Russia might even be given Constantinople.

Towards the end of January, Jacky Fisher threatened his resignation, but at seventy-four he was weary, his resolve fading, and he was no longer any match for the 41-year-old First Lord. Churchill and Prime Minister Asquith talked him out of quitting. On 23 January the War Council gave the green light.

AE2's long voyage north-west up the Indian Ocean had nothing of the interest or enjoyment of the trip out from Portsmouth. Harry Stoker found it infinitely more unpleasant. The weather was fair but in a way that made things worse, only adding to the boredom and monotony of being towed by *Berrima* at what seemed little more than walking pace. From sunrise to sunset, the days dragged by, the cramped interior of the boat growing ever more uncomfortably hot as they approached the equator.

There were two blessings, though. Another officer had joined them: John Cary, twenty-three years old and only newly promoted to lieutenant. He was also an Irishman, from Donegal, and an RN officer on loan to the RAN, where he had been in the little survey vessel *Fantome*. A third hand would ease the burden on the captain and the first lieutenant. The second blessing, perhaps even more useful, was the arrival of a telegraphist. Bill Falconer, also twenty-three, from Richmond in Melbourne, had joined the navy before the war, in 1912. 'Sparks', as he was invariably known, was fully trained in the use of *AE2*'s Marconi wireless set and in the arcane mysteries and skills of Morse code.

They touched at Columbo on 14 January for just two days in harbour, and then it was off again to the Red Sea, Aden, Suez and the canal, which they reached not quite two weeks later. There life quickened when they heard that the Turkish army had been moving towards the canal from across the Sinai Desert and was now only a few kilometres to the east, with an attack expected any day. Stoker took the precaution of having the bridge barricaded with sandbags and then went through the canal at speed, the White Ensign flying, to the cooees of the Australian troops and the cheers of the New Zealand and British troops stationed on the east bank.

There was a surprise waiting at Port Said, at the head of the canal, and it was bad news for the Englishmen on board, who had been hoping, perhaps, to return to 'Pompey' – the sailors' ancient name for Portsmouth. *AE2* was given orders to join the British Mediterranean Fleet off the Dardanelles. They set a course northwest for the island of Tenedos, in the Aegean Sea, at the mouth of the strait, a trip which should have been an easy run of just a few days but which took five when the weather turned on them.

Harry Stoker was never one to complain, but this was plain awful:

> The north wind was dead ahead and blew with the force of a strong gale; a short, steep sea frequently broke clean over the top of the bridge; intermittent rain and hailstorms made one's face and eyes smart with pain in trying to peer through them; fierce white squalls lashed the surface of the waters into a seething, driving mass of foam; and the temperature had fallen to a degree of excessive discomfort after our long spell in the tropics. Of all AE2's voyages this was the most uncomfortable. The Mediterranean is not always as blue and placid as some people think. It can be grey and overcast and very rough. It gave us a hearty buffeting until we joined the Fleet...[4]

Tenedos – known as Bozcaada to the Turks – lies off the plains off Troy on the Turkish mainland. To the ancients, Apollo was its god. The hero Achilles captured Tenedos, and the Greek fleet sheltered there in the bay before sending in the Trojan horse to do its job on the city of Troy. Alexander the Great touched there too, and in its time the island had known Greeks, Romans, Venetians, Russians and Ottomans. One of the dizzying series of Balkan wars had handed Tenedos to Greece in 1912. Now it was a Greek possession and the forward base for what would become the Royal Navy's Eastern Mediterranean Squadron.

Weary and battered, *AE2* slipped into the little harbour on 5 February, to be welcomed by the handful of B-class submarines already there and doing patrols to the north and the mouth of the Dardanelles Strait. The weather was still bitter, which Harry Kinder found hard to bear:

> It was just like living in a freezing chamber in the submarine. Fortunately, we had our hammocks on board right from Australia. We went out on patrol duty every second day and, with everything so cold, our existence was anything but pleasant. It was a hard job to get bread or meat from the supply ship owing to Service red tape. Somehow, I managed to contract malaria and pneumonia and was put on the parent ship to await the hospital ship. Some Frenchmen on board kept me dosed with hot wine until I could see a dozen ships spinning around.
>
> After a few days I got so bad I was taken over to one of the battle ships. A couple of days later the Fleet started bombarding the forts on the Dardanelles. The ship I was in had to go in to close range to draw fire. All day long the whining of shells as they passed overhead and then shells exploding could be heard. Fortunately we were not hit but some came dangerously close.[5]

As the great surface fleet began to come together, *AE2* and the other submarines moved back to the island of Lemnos and its deep, wide natural harbour of Mudros, some ninety kilometres to the southwest. Winston Churchill's exalted ambitions were taking shape in steel and guns. One by one the great battleships arrived and dropped anchor, at their head the super dreadnought *Queen Elizabeth*, with her eight fifteen-inch guns; the battlecruiser *Inflexible*, of eight twelve-inch guns; then a stirring roll call of older battleships, obsolete and due for the breaker's yard but with twelve-inch guns enough for the coming bombardment of the Turkish forts: *Albion, Canopus, Cornwallis, Irresistible, Majestic, Ocean, Prince George* and *Vengeance*, plus the ten-inch ships *Triumph* and *Swiftsure*. The French sent four of their pre-dreadnoughts as well: *Bouvet, Charlemagne, Gaulois* and *Suffren*, and around them were arrayed squadrons of cruisers, destroyers, five submarines, including *AE2*, and a fleet of merchant fishing trawlers converted into temporary minesweepers.

Their commander was Vice Admiral Sackville Carden, a greying, desiccated officer who had been Admiral Superintendent of the Malta dockyard, the sort of job you got before due retirement at the end of a dull but worthy career. His appointment surprised the RN. 'Who expected Carden to be in command of a big fleet?' Fisher would write to his friend Jellicoe. 'He was made Admiral Superintendent of Malta to shelve him!'[6] Carden's chief of staff was the firebrand Roger Keyes, who had been Commodore of Submarines before the war and the man who had farewelled the Australian boats when they left Portsmouth for Australia.

The plans were thorough and grand, pregnant with optimism. The forts on either side of the Dardanelles would be obliterated in the great bombardment. The minefields in the strait would be swept, clearing the way for the fleet to pass through and into the Sea of Marmara, when it would appear off Constantinople. Ideally it should take no more than a week.

The guns opened up at exactly 9.51 on the morning of 19 February, in glorious sunshine with smooth seas, when *Cornwallis* fired the first salvo at a battery on the southern shore. For the rest of the day, the great ships wheeled and thundered in slow and deliberate array, a magnificent sight of great, orange spears of flame from the gun muzzles, their upper decks wreathed in clouds of black and grey smoke. The cliffs and valleys above the Dardanelles Strait blossomed with the smoke and dust from their bursting shells. They kept a distance at first, but when there was no initial reply from the defenders they moved closer to the two coasts. In the afternoon, some of the Turkish forts began to return the fire. The squadron retired as daylight faded, Carden intending to resume the onslaught the next day.

The weather beat him. For five frustrating days, gales of heavy rain and thunderstorms whipped up big seas with falls of sleet and snow, and the ships withdrew to sit it out at Mudros. From then the grand naval strategy began to come inexorably undone. The Turks seized the reprieve to repair what damage they could and to strengthen the undamaged defences. In London, the War Council and its military planners began to flop this way and that. Perhaps the army might be needed after all, although men still could not be taken from France. The day after the bombardment, 20 February, Kitchener ordered the Australian and New Zealand army divisions in Egypt to ready themselves for the Dardanelles.

The battleships returned on 25 February when the weather cleared, and the bombardment continued on and off for the next few days. Demolition squads were put ashore to blow up guns in the abandoned outer forts and the makeshift minesweepers began clearing, first by daylight then at night. But the Turks began shooting back with the aid of powerful searchlights and the minesweeping operation began to falter as the civilian crews, most of them hastily trained fishermen, lost their nerve and fled under fire, to the fury of Commodore Keyes. As was his habit, Churchill in London kept up a steady volley of intrusive advice and nagging questions to Carden, and eventually the admiral collapsed under the strain of it all. The doctors diagnosed a stomach ulcer and nervous exhaustion, and by 17 March he had resigned and was on his way home to Britain in a cruiser. His successor would be his second-in-command, John de Robeck, who was hastily appointed an acting vice admiral as he hoisted his flag in *Queen Elizabeth*.

On her patrols, *AE2* had a grandstand view of the bombardment, but with no role to play beyond simply being there, Harry Stoker began to ponder what else he might do. With careful navigation it should be possible, he thought, for a submarine to pass through what was left of the minefields in the Dardanelles Strait and to enter the Sea of Marmara, where it could play havoc with enemy shipping.

He had a friend on the admiral's staff, Lieutenant Commander Charles Brodie, a submariner himself and an old mate from the days of wine, waltzing and women in pre-war Malta. The two had hit it off well. 'Stoker was a natural leader,' Brodie thought, 'spreading confidence as well as gaiety in whatever company, and his crew knew well the skill and determination behind his slightly jaunty manner.'[7] He told Stoker to put his ideas in a letter and promised to deliver it to the admiral.

Stoker spent some time at sea composing his missive, as he later recalled:

It seemed to me a good letter, an extraordinarily good letter. The arguments were worded with care and cunning and really looked most convincing. My letter would be sent over to the Flagship immediately we reached harbour that night. It would surely bring some result. I was most distinctly self-satisfied and pleased with myself.

And so the gods were annoyed.[8]

They were indeed. They put him on the rocks. It was pitch dark and starless when he entered Mudros Harbour that evening, unaware that a familiar navigation light on Sangrada Point had been extinguished. He saw a light ahead and assumed it was the one he wanted but it was not, and he missed a turn to starboard. With shocking suddenness a black shape loomed up before him, dead ahead – it was the point! – and he saw some breakers crashing silvery-white below it, a captain's nightmare. He shouted for hard a'starboard and full astern but it was too late: the boat crunched onto the rocks at the foot of the point with a horrible, grinding shudder, wedged fast by the bow. Working the engines and rudder did nothing. She was aground, helpless, unmoving.

Rescuers arrived, and quickly. With wounding irony, the first boat on the scene carried his friend Brodie, who he had hoped would impress the admiral with his navigational skills. Fat chance now. Then came a nearby French destroyer, *Chelmer*, who went in as close as she dared, turned on her searchlights and sent over steel hawsers for a tow. For three desperate hours they struggled, *AE2* bumping and lurching and scraping in the swell rolling in from the harbour entrance, but she would not move and both hawsers failed under the hammering. Stoker feared more and more that his command might be a total loss.

Eventually, when it seemed that no more could be done, the gods relented and gave up their sport. Well after midnight, a change in the wind calmed the seas a little and shifted the submarine just enough for her to be gingerly eased off, stern first, under her own engines into deeper water. They limped back to the anchorage exhausted, wrung out but afloat.

The next day revealed that the rudder, propellers and engines were undamaged, and *AE2* was sent under her own power to Malta for dockyard repairs to her battered, leaky hull. It took four anxious days to get there.

Field Marshal Horatio Herbert Kitchener, 1st Earl Kitchener of Khartoum and colonial war hero, was idolised by the British public. The recruiting posters bearing his iconic, fiercely-moustachioed face and pointing finger – 'Your Country Needs YOU' – were stuck up in every railway station, bookstall and pub from Scotland to Cornwall.

In his role as His Majesty's Secretary of State for War, though, his political cabinet colleagues found him tediously arrogant, insufferably certain of his own rectitude. Yet his prestige was such that his word in military matters was law and few dared cross him. On Friday, 10 March he summoned another colonial old campaigner, General Sir Ian Hamilton, to his room in the War Office in Whitehall, and told him, matter-of-factly, 'We are sending a military force to support the Fleet now at the Dardanelles, and you are to have Command.'[9]

Hamilton was also a writer and a diarist, and a good one. His *Gallipoli Diary* is fascinating reading. The two discussed how many troops would be sent and settled on a 'grand total' of about 80,000, including 30,000 Australians and New Zealanders, 'probably panning out at some 50,000 rifles in the firing line'.[10] Kitchener rose from his desk and paced the floor, talking volubly. Their conversation is remarkable for its hubris, its airy dismissal of the enemy, which sowed the seeds of the disaster to come.

'I hope you will not have to land at all; if you do have to land, why then the powerful Fleet at your back will be the prime factor in your choice of time and place,' Kitchener said.[11]

Hamilton had a suggestion, worth repeating in full:

> I asked K[itchener] if he would not move the Admiralty to work a submarine or two up the Straits at once so as to prevent reinforcements and supplies coming down by sea from Constantinople.

By now the Turks must be on the alert and it was commonsense to suppose they would be sending some sort of help to their Forts. However things might pan out we could not be going wrong if we made the Marmara unhealthy for the Turkish ships. Lord K. thereupon made the remark that if we could get one submarine into the Marmara the defences of the Dardanelles would collapse. 'Supposing,' he said, 'one submarine pops up opposite the town of Gallipoli and waves a Union Jack three times, the whole Turkish garrison on the Peninsula will take to their heels and make a bee line for Bulair.'[12]

Just one submarine should do it, then. They talked for an hour and a half, each man bowling up his thoughts for the other to examine, Kitchener oracular as ever:

> The best would be if we did not land a man until the Turks had come to terms. Once the Fleet got through the Dardanelles, Constantinople could not hold out. Modern Constantinople could not last a week if blockaded by sea and land. That was a sure thing; a thing whereon he could speak with full confidence. The Fleet could lie off out of sight and range of the Turks and with their guns would dominate the railways and, if necessary, burn the place to ashes.[13]

Hamilton wasted no time. He was off and away the next morning in a train for the crossing to France, farewelled at London's Charing Cross Station by his old friend Winston Churchill. He had with him a small textbook on the Turkish army and two tourist guides. By 17 March he was on board the flagship *Queen Elizabeth* – 'that lovely sea monster' – at Tenedos. There he learned that the fleet would attack again the next day.

Thursday, 18 March began in a glorious Aegean sunrise, cloudless with a warm and gentle southerly breeze and calm seas, promising a perfect day. Admiral de Robeck had issued his final operational orders the night before. At 8.30 a.m., minesweepers, which had crept into the strait by dark, reported that all was clear.

The battleships – twelve British and four French – began to enter the strait from 10.30 a.m. in three lines abreast, first 'A' then 'B' and then 'C', led by *Queen Elizabeth* with *Agamemnon, Lord Nelson* and the battlecruiser *Inflexible* in line 'A'. Destroyers went with them. The plan was for 'A' to silence the forts on both shores, north and south, with a long-range bombardment. Line 'B' would then move in closer to mop up, and line 'C' would be held in reserve.

Queen Elizabeth opened fire at 11.25, and for the next six hours the fighting raged in a cannonade of flame and smoke and howling, exploding shells. The forts replied with a vengeance and each side began to make its mark. Some of the Turkish gun batteries were blown to ruins but others were not. Well-concealed howitzers – guns that fired a high, plunging shell – struck back, and shortly after noon both *Agamemnon* and *Inflexible* were heavily hit. *Inflexible*'s fire control platform, high on her foremast, was shattered by shrapnel; the men there were roasted alive. The angry morning wore on.

At around 2 p.m. the battle turned, as surely as a gate on a hinge. *Gaulois*, one of the French ships, had been badly hit from the shore and was leaving the strait with a list to starboard and heavily down by the bow, accompanied by *Bouvet*. Watchers saw two explosions and a column of red and black smoke shoot from *Bouvet*, and within two minutes – appallingly, incredibly – she rolled over and sank in a hiss of steam and boiling sea. Nobody was sure whether it was a mine or a torpedo fired from the shoreline. The destroyers rescued just seventy-five of her crew of 718.

Worse was to come. At 4 p.m. *Inflexible* struck a mine near the southern or Asian shore, which tore a hole in her bow and drowned twenty-nine men. Her gunnery officer, Commander Rudolf Verner, burned in the foretop fire, died nobly. 'Tell my people that I played the game and stuck it out,' he whispered.[14] She limped back to Tenedos. Fifteen minutes later *Irresistible* also hit a mine, which flooded the starboard engine room so quickly that only three of the men there were able to escape. Under the pressure of the water, the midship bulkhead buckled, the port engine room flooded in its turn and the engines were completely disabled. With Turkish shells raining on her decks, she had to be abandoned and left adrift. When de Robeck saw this, he hoisted the signal for a 'general recall' and the ships turned to head back out to sea. The elderly *Ocean* had gone to the rescue of *Irresistible* but as the sun began to set she too was holed by yet another mine and her crew taken off by destroyers. She drifted off as well.

It was all over by dark, the ships withdrawn back to Tenedos. That beautiful, sunlit weather had shone upon a shattering defeat. 'We have had a disastrous day,' de Robeck wrote.[15] Much later, it was learned that the Turks had laid a new line of mines by night along the Asian shore, which the minesweepers had not discovered. The fleet had blundered into them. In the dead of night, Commodore Keyes went back to the straits in a destroyer to see what had become of *Irresistible* and *Ocean*, but they had both vanished, sunk. Deep in gloom, the Admiral told Keyes that he expected to be dismissed. The French admiral, Émile Guépratte, was *désolé*. In addition to the loss of the *Bouvet* and her ship's company, *Gaulois* and *Suffren* were both badly damaged; only *Charlemagne* remained in fighting trim.

Sir Ian Hamilton had watched the horrors unfold and the next day he cabled Kitchener in London:

> I am being most reluctantly driven to the conclusion that the Straits are not likely to be forced by battleships as at one time seemed probable and that, if my troops are to take part, it will not take the subsidiary form anticipated. The Army's part will be more than mere landings of parties to destroy Forts, it must be a deliberate and progressive military operation carried out at full strength so as to open a passage for the Navy.[16]

The campaign would be turned on its head. The original aim had been for the army to go in to clean up after the RN had sent the Turks tumbling back to Constantinople and beyond. Now the army would land in strength, with the navy in a supporting role. Victory would arise from the ashes of defeat. With Kitchener's approval, Hamilton went to Cairo and began to muster his divisions, including the Australians and New Zealanders.

Busily collecting intelligence, Ambassador Morgenthau at Constantinople had visited the forts and spoken with their German and Turkish defenders. He concluded that another day's bombardment would have seen the British through. The Turkish guns were almost out of ammunition. The most powerful fort on the Asiatic side had just seventeen armour-piercing shells left, he discovered, while on the European side the main fort had precisely ten. The troops at all the fortifications had their orders to man the guns until the last shell had been fired and then abandon them.

Prodded by the ever-insistent, ever-annoying Churchill in London, de Robeck pondered another attempt. The First Lord cabled him on 23 March, urging him to try once more to 'dominate the forts at the Narrows and sweep the minefield and then batter the forts at close range, taking your time, using your aeroplanes and also your improved methods of guarding against mines'. It was gratuitous advice from a distance, to the point of insult. Churchill had begun a lifelong habit of instructing admirals in their business, interfering in naval operational matters way beyond his competence.

The weather turned and solved the difficulty. Day after day brought strong north-westerly gales: with the forts shrouded in cloud and rain, visibility was impossibly low for a bombardment. Granted this reprieve by Allah himself, the Turks and their German commanders and advisers threw themselves into renewing their defences and replenishing their stocks of ammunition on the Gallipoli Peninsula. Soon de Robeck came to the view that the army would have to land first, and he told Churchill so.

In Malta, a naval Court of Enquiry gave Harry Stoker a light rap on the knuckles for the grounding at Mudros; he should have reduced speed and altered course to port earlier, it found. More concerning was the arrival of three new E-class boats from Britain – HMS *E11*, *E14* and *E15* – whose captains were all senior to him and therefore might be expected to get a crack at the Dardanelles before he could. Martin Nasmith of *E11* was particularly said to be a man to watch. Stoker fretted when *E14* and *E15* left for Mudros, although there was some consolation in having the Malta dockyard fit jumping wire and other new gear around *AE2*'s hydroplanes, propellers and rudder to deflect mine mooring wires, at Nasmith's suggestion.

As impulsive as ever, and thirsting for action, Commodore Keyes called the submarine commanding officers to a meeting in *Queen Elizabeth* on 14 April. Harry Stoker and *AE2* were still in Malta, with Nasmith. Keyes had one question to the others: could a submarine penetrate the Dardanelles and force its way through into the Sea of Marmara?

Stoker's friend Charles Brodie was there, with Commander Fred Somerville, the captain of the submarine tender *Adamant*, and Lieutenant Commanders Edward Boyle of *E14* and Theodore Brodie of *E15*. Charles and Theodore Brodie were identical twins, thirty-one years old. The RN had given them nicknames: Charles was 'Warhead' and Theodore was 'Dummy Head'.

Keyes put his question to each man in turn. Somerville, the most senior and experienced, said he thought it could not be done. So did Boyle. Only Dummy Head thought it was possible. With Keyes' blessing, he sailed two days later. Winston Churchill cabled him a personal message: 'I wish you God speed in your gallant enterprise.'

E15 was about fifteen kilometres into the strait on 17 April when she was suddenly caught in a violent, swirling current and flung upwards to the surface near Kephez Point, running aground beneath the guns of a fort on the southern shore. The boat's telegraphist, Alfred May, wrote:

> Everything going well until about 7am when we struck and, despite all that could be done, we were soon high and dry. The Turkish batteries then opened fire on us one large shell entering our conning tower and killing the captain as he was going on the bridge. Several shells came through the boat, one entering the engines and bursting several oil pipes, thick smoke began to come from aft, but we could not see what had happened there.
>
> The men then began to go up the conning tower and through the shell hole and take to the water. The boat was about three-quarters of a mile from the shore and this distance we had to swim.

Several men would not attempt it and I think it was because of this that so many were injured.[17]

Theodore Brodie was decapitated. Six of the crew died from chlorine gas poisoning when sea water flooded the boat's damaged batteries. The rest were taken prisoner.

For two days the navy tried to destroy *E15* to stop the Turks salvaging her. The little submarine *B6*, with a heartsick Charles Brodie on board, fired a torpedo at her but it did not run properly and missed. Two destroyers attempted to find her by night but failed in the dark, and *B11* could not see her again the next morning in the fog. The battleships *Triumph* and *Majestic* were driven off by the shore batteries, and an attempt to bomb her by Royal Naval Air Service seaplanes also scored no hits. She was finally torpedoed in a daring raid by two picket boats from the battleships. Theodore Brodie was buried on the beach with full military honours. Another Turkish victory. Until war's end, Charles clung to the hope that his twin had survived and was a prisoner.

AE2 returned to Mudros on 21 April, the crew amazed to see the armada that had assembled in their absence. The harbour was crammed with battleships, cruisers and destroyers and what seemed like score after score of transport ships, big and small, all loaded with troops. The rumour went around that the invasion, the landing of the army, was scheduled in a few days.

Out of the blue, Harry Stoker was ordered to report to the flagship. Keyes met him at the side and escorted him in to see Admiral de Robeck. Charles Brodie had kept his promise and delivered Stoker's letter, which explained how he would make the most of his batteries, with details of distances and proposed courses, depths and speeds, and ending with the phrase that 'given skillful navigation the passage is feasible'.[18]

Greying and avuncular but tired and drawn, Admiral de Robeck greeted Stoker courteously. Stoker found him to be 'kindness itself'.

> Without belittling the difficulties he simply asked how we proposed to overcome them. He found it difficult himself to

believe the feat was possible, but its military value was so great it must be tried. If we got through the other boats would immediately be sent to follow. Finally, wishing us luck he concluded: 'If you succeed there is no calculating the result it will cause, and it may well be that you will have done more to finish the war than any other act accomplished.'[19]

He returned to the boat with those farewell words ringing in his head.

AE2 left Mudros for Tenedos within the hour, and there they took in more supplies, a lot of them, including a large White Ensign big enough for a battleship. The crew realised then that something was up – no ordinary patrol, this – and eventually the captain informed them. They were all too well aware of the disaster of *E15* and were not surprised to learn that they would be next in the cauldron. John Wheat had guessed it would be the strait:

> We then had sufficient food to last us for a month to 6 weeks. We then knew that we were leaving that night at 1.30 a.m. to make a passage through the Dardanelles. An honour for the small young Aust. Fleet. We were all greatly excited and I think the majority of us had very little sleep that night: no boat had up till this time been through the Dardanelles and we did not know what dangers awaited us in the way of mines and nets etc . . .[20]

Harry Kinder shared the excitement, the anticipation of going in harm's way:

> Just before 12 the watch keeper called all hands. The engines were soon opened out and ready. The crew was a bit fed up with the starting hour but were quite unconcerned about the dangers we were about to face. Some of the remarks about the war would not stand repeating here. In casting off we wondered when we were likely to return, if ever.

Stoker told his men that if anyone wished to leave the boat now, they could. Nobody did. Instead, they sat down and wrote letters for home. Like many of them, Stoker Charlie Suckling, a 22-year-old from Perth, Western Australia, had stoically considered the possibility that he might be killed. 'All hands in AE2 knew that the chances were in favour of tomorrow bringing our own death,' he noted. 'So most of us had letters to write. Mine were sent under cover to my grandfather in London with instructions to post them if we were lost.'[21]

The Dardanelles Strait is shaped like a lazy letter 'S' running south-west to north-east, and about sixty-six kilometres long, with a current spilling out from the Sea of Marmara into the Aegean at up to five knots. The average depth is 180 feet, or fifty-five metres, although this varies considerably. The most difficult section for the boat to navigate would be the Narrows, which are about twenty-three kilometres upstream from the southern entrance and where the waterway is a bare 1.5 kilometres wide. The lower part of the strait, about two-thirds of it, was free of mines. The upper third was heavily mined in lateral rows from north to south. Naturally, the Narrows were heavily fortified.

In theory, *AE2* could travel some eighty kilometres underwater on her batteries, but this would be against the current, which would slow her considerably. She would also have to negotiate the minefields with infinite care, underwater. But there was no chance of doing the entire passage submerged. She would have to travel on the surface by night for as long as possible. But even that was fraught with danger, for it meant running the gauntlet of powerful searchlights set up on either shore.

Harry Stoker had thought it through in detail:

> It was after midnight when we made our way to the Dardanelles entrance. A lovely night, clear and calm, with a fair-sized moon and myriad stars casting their ghostly light on the smooth water.
>
> Our plan was to enter the Strait after the moon had set, and proceed slowly along the surface – slowly so that our wash, showing white in the darkness, would not attract attention from the shore; and on the surface so as to conserve electric power. We hoped in this manner to complete some miles without being discovered by the enemy. Then, at break of day, we would dive.
>
> As we arrived abreast the entrance the moon had still a small distance to go before dipping into her silvery path. By the side

of the black and sinister-looking destroyers we waited, while the perfect stillness of the night seemed to accentuate the tension of the moment. And then the moon, in an apparent effort to shorten our suspense, hastened her laggard steps, touched the horizon, and was gone.

In the darkness we crept away from the destroyers . . .[22]

Only the captain and a lookout were on the bridge, eyes peeled. Everyone else was poised to jump to diving stations in an instant. *AE2* crept forward at seven knots, a grey ghost in the night, Stoker almost whispering his helm orders to the coxswain below. 'Starboard ten . . . midships . . . port twenty . . .' Soon he shut down one engine, to lessen the noise from the exhaust. The searchlights ahead were sweeping the water, back and forth, up and down, sinister and menacing. Surely they must be discovered, and then all hell would break loose.

Then a stroke of good fortune. The first searchlight dimmed and went out, leaving them to the inky dark. It seemed almost too good to be true when the second searchlight, at Kephez Point on the southern shore, was also switched off, allowing them to move with a new confidence, further on the surface than Stoker had thought possible.

Too soon. The Kephez light suddenly switched on again, a long, white cone probing and searching, and they were now almost beneath it. Stoker gave the order to dive, sending the bridge lookout tumbling down the ladder before him and slamming the conning tower hatch closed. The ballast tanks flooded and the submarine began to nose below the surface – agonisingly slowly, it seemed. Then disaster struck, as Harry Kinder recorded:

> I had just reached my station when I heard the coxswain start working the for'ard hydroplane in electrical instead of hand gear. Evidently, his thoughts were elsewhere. I had no time to warn him that the hydroplane locking block was still in.
>
> One of the knuckle joints on the driving shaft snapped. This block is a 4 inch square piece of steel which prevents the hydroplane from moving in a rough sea or when running on engine power. The slightest incline would drive the boat under and then

there would be another submarine disaster. What the captain said when he heard the extent of the damage would fill a book but I doubt if it would be readable.[23]

There was nothing for it. They could not continue the dive and the fault could not be repaired at sea. They would have to abandon their mission, surface and make a run for it at full speed on the diesels, hoping to evade discovery and get back to the entrance before the break of dawn. Happily, the current would sweep them along.

Stoker gave the orders and, as the boat rose again, he returned to the bridge. The searchlight, still probing, receded astern into the distance as the night lightened and the morning grew first grey and then palest pink, to Kinder's relief:

> I was on watch and every minute expected to hear a shell burst overhead as we had several forts to pass. The only thing that saved us was the fog hanging on the surface of the water between first light and sunrise. It was just sufficient to shade the boat.[24]

They would all say later that *AE2* had never travelled so fast. As the sun rose, she reached the destroyers on station at the mouth of the strait, and at 8 a.m. they were in Tenedos again, where work began immediately on the driving shaft. The sense of anticlimax was bitter, almost palpable. So near and yet so far.

It took almost four hours to fit a replacement part, and it wasn't until well after noon that the captain took them out again for a test dive. It went well enough, and towards dusk *Queen Elizabeth* arrived. It was 24 April, the eve of the landing, but the admiral found time to summon Stoker again.

'It was very bad luck,' de Robeck told him. 'You did well to get so far. Try again tomorrow. If you succeed in getting through there is nothing we will not do for you.'[25] Once he reached the Sea of Marmara, he should act at his own discretion. It was an extraordinary vote of confidence, a blank cheque. Commodore Keyes escorted Stoker out onto the flagship's upper deck to return to the submarine and added one last verbal order: he was to make sure to sink any ships laying mines. 'In fact,' the Commodore added, 'generally run amuck at the Narrows. If you get there.'[26]

That sally was typical Keyes, impromptu and theatrical, with little regard for the consequences. It was an order that would sit heavily on Stoker's mind in the coming days.

AE2 weighed anchor after midnight and set off once more. It was darker this time, the moon frequently hidden behind heavy cloud. By 2 a.m. they were at the mouth of the Dardanelles Strait again, passing the destroyers on guard there. It was Sunday, 25 April. The invasion was about to begin. The army that General Hamilton had gathered was poised to storm ashore on the beaches of the Gallipoli Peninsula.

7
ABANDON SHIP!

The moon had set when *AE2* slipped in through the entrance to the Dardanelles on the surface as planned, at 2.30 a.m. For Harry Stoker and the bridge lookout with him, all was dark, inky dark, save for the menace of three bright white searchlights sweeping the waters ahead to starboard, on the southern shore. They carried on at eight knots, trimmed down, ready to dive. The weather was calm and the seas still; the only sound was the gentle wash of the bow wave and the thrum of the diesels. After a while, Stoker stopped one engine and they crept ahead on the other, edging closer to the northern shore, away from the lights.

Whoosh – bang! A shell. After about two hours they had been spotted. A gun had fired at them from somewhere on that northern side, the first enemy shot at *AE2* in the war. It missed, by a good distance. Stoker dived the boat, taking her down to about twenty to twenty-five metres. Very soon they would encounter the first row of mines.

The Gallipoli invasion began at that same time, before dawn. The British landed at Cape Helles, on the Gallipoli Peninsula at the mouth of the strait. The French made a diversionary landing at Kum Kale, on the Asiatic shore. The Australians were to take Gaba Tepe, a shingled beach on the Aegean coast. The first wave of men waded ashore into a withering fire from the cliffs above. Some were cut down before they even left the landing boats, or drowned as they stepped into deep water and were weighed down by their heavy packs. On the beach they searched for the landmarks they had been told to expect and could not find them. In the dark, most of them had been put ashore too far to the north. As the Australian official history told it:

> The boats of the 11th Battalion hit the shore 200 or 300 yards north of the point of Ari Burnu. Those of the 9th struck the point itself or its southern shoulder, and some of the 10th landed just south of it. From every boat the men doubled across the sand and took breath under the bank, whither also the wounded from the boats were hauled.
>
> Many were fixing their bayonets as they ran across the shingle. In other cases the officers or sergeants, as they and their men lay under the bank, gave the orders to strip packs – load the magazines with five or ten rounds – close the cut-off – pull back safety catches. No shots were to be fired till daylight.
>
> Anyone who depended upon a set plan for the next move was completely bewildered. It had been hoped that the halt under the sandy bank would be long enough to allow all the companies to land, form, and carry out an organised attack across the open against the first ridge. But there was no open.
>
> Officers thought that the knoll of Ari Burnu was Gaba Tepe itself. A high rugged slope pressed down onto to the beach. A fierce rifle-fire swept over the men. They had been landed in the dark on an utterly different coast, and were lying in little parties of boatloads and platoons out of sight of most of their comrades, their clothes heavy with water, and their rifles choked with sand.[1]

It was a disaster from the first hour, the opening chapter of what would become a litany of death and defiance, folly and failure. By 8 a.m. some 8000 men had landed and still the boats kept bringing more. The Australians had no choice but to fight onwards and upwards, towards the Turkish battalions dug in above them. The killing and the dying swelled.

Harry Stoker would now have to find his way by periscope and dead reckoning – guesswork, really – and he brought the boat up to periscope depth, about six metres, for the submarine captain's customary 'look around'. Dawn was beginning to break over the hills on the northern shore and he knew that he was approaching the first line of the first minefield.

He took *AE2* down to twenty metres again and began to thread his way through the mooring wires that held the mines in place. This was a passage of acute peril. If one of those wires were somehow to snag on the exterior of the submarine, it could drag the mine down onto the hull and blow them all to pieces. There was dead silence inside the boat, not a word spoken save for the coxswain occasionally calling the depth. Men began to sweat, gripped by fear, barely daring to move, to breathe. Harry Kinder waited . . .

> Shortly after 6am we hit the first wire and it was enough to stop one's heart beating to hear it sliding over the steel deck . . . it makes you hold your breath when the wires keep hitting the boat. I wondered if one of the mines had AE2 written on it. Several times we hit the mooring chains and as they dragged along the sides they made you think of the ghost stories you heard as a kid . . .[2]

The captain held them all, carried them all, as he had to do. He had their trust, their loyalty. As Charlie Suckling put it: 'Lieutenant Commander Stoker was a man absolutely loved by his crew, and there was not one of us who was not willing to go anywhere he cared to take us.'[3]

It was the nature of the job that Stoker had to conceal his own fears, to radiate calm and competence no matter what his private ghosts were whispering. The worst moments, as he described, came when he had to rise in the middle of the minefield to periscope depth to get his bearings.

> For nearly an hour the ensuing experiences provided feelings difficult to describe. The rappings and scrapings on the hull of the boat by the mooring wires of the mines, held taut by the buoyancy

of the mines themselves overhead, seemed most damnably continuous. Choose a wrong moment to rise for observation through the periscope and you choose a moment to hit a mine – so choose as few of these moments as possible.

Feel as safe as you care to when well submerged and do not think of the result should one of the wires, catching on a projection of the boat's side, drag its mine, with a bang, down on top of you.

On two occasions something hard – much harder than the wires – hit the bows and rattled away astern; were they mines which failed to explode? And once some object seemed to catch up forward and remained knocking insistently for several minutes, before it broke away and followed the rest of our enemies astern.[4]

After about half an hour, his third glimpse through the periscope showed Stoker that he had passed through the minefield more quickly than he had expected: they were now almost at the Narrows, off the township of Chanak (Çanakkale), on the southern or Asiatic shore. The tension eased. But the periscope and the wake it trailed were sighted from both shores, and the water around *AE2* was quickly whipped to a white froth by shells and bullets. Spent bullets, their force depleted, sank and rattled onto the hull like hailstones.

Through the periscope Stoker could see what looked like the hulk of a large ship anchored off to starboard, and then, suddenly hurrying out from behind it, a small, grey, two-funnelled cruiser. She was about 400 yards away, a perfect target. And perhaps she was laying mines. Levelly, calmly, he gave the orders: 'Ready the bow tube!'

Geoff Haggard, the first lieutenant, gave the responses: 'Bow tube ready; outer door shut, sir.'

'Open the outer door . . .'

The little cruiser loomed closer. Stoker was glued to the periscope, keeping her in his sights. 'Stand by, bow tube . . .'

'Bow tube standing by, sir.'

'Put me on my periscope angle . . . stand by . . . stand by . . . Fire!'

'Bow tube fired, sir!'

From the Torpedo Gunner's Mate, Petty Officer Cecil Bray: 'Shut the outer door. Time to run thirty seconds . . . stand by bang!'

The torpedo sped towards its prey but there was no time to watch it. The hunter now became the hunted. A destroyer was heading straight for them.

Stoker took the boat down to twenty metres, everyone holding their breath again as they heard the *whump-whump-whump* of the destroyer's propeller pass above them. At that same moment there was indeed a bang, a very satisfying one, and the cruiser slumped and slowly began to go down. She was not much of a prize, perhaps 600 or 700 tonnes, but not to be sneezed at either. First round to the Australians. Stoker altered course a point to starboard to avoid her sinking hull.[5]

The next few hours – in fact, the rest of the day – would be a contest of wits. Skill and chance would play a part, and so would luck, good and bad. After a few minutes Stoker altered back to port for the course that would take him out of the Dardanelles Strait and ordered periscope depth again to get his bearings. *AE2* was coming up when there was a shocking, sickening jolt as she struck something – a bank of rock, perhaps – and then lurched upwards to a depth of just three metres. For some reason the gyro-compass had gone haywire, giving wildly inaccurate bearings, and instead of being where he expected – in the centre of the strait – he was at its very edge, and unmoving. Worse, the conning tower was sticking out of the water.

Through the periscope Stoker could see a fort on the eastern shore almost towering over him. As he looked, transfixed, one of its guns fired, seemingly so close that he involuntarily jumped back from the eyepiece. God, was this it? Were they going to end up like Dummy Head Brodie and *E15*?

They could hear shells splashing around them as the captain worked the rudder and the engines to free the boat; miraculously, there was not one hit. After an eternity, *AE2* slipped off the bank to a safe depth of twenty metres, although the current then swung her around so she was heading back down the strait the way she had come. Stoker turned her again, on her port motor and with the helm hard a'port, her head swinging rapidly.

And she grounded again. This time on the opposite shore, and she slid upwards to an even more horrifying depth of only eight feet – less than three metres. Once again she was beneath a fort, although so close that the guns could not depress enough to reach her. But a gunboat and a couple of destroyers in the distance started shooting and heading towards her.

The bow was angled down, though, and Stoker took a desperate gamble that if he went forward she would move. He was right. Luck of the Irish. He ordered full speed ahead; she lurched off the bank and he took her down to twenty-five metres. John Wheat would write in his diary that night:

> During all this the Captain remained extremely cool, for all depended on him at this stage. It is due to his coolness that I am now writing this account. Nobody knows what a terrible strain it is on the nerves to undergo anything like this, especially the Captain, as all depends on him.[6]

Discipline and training kept them going, even at moments of gnawing fear. That and a certain fatalism – the thought that the future was out of your hands, that you could only push on. After that second grounding, *AE2* was back on track again. With Chanak out of sight astern, they were heading around their next landmark, Nagara Point, a jutting spit on the Asiatic shore that had been Abydos in antiquity, where the lovers Hero and Leander met their deaths.

The water was calm, so still that the periscope was immediately seen when Stoker raised it and there was more firing from small warships nearby. The hunt was truly on. Down they went to twenty-seven metres, still edging ahead until another periscope glimpse revealed a new peril: two tugs were approaching in line abreast, with a heavy wire cable looped underwater from one to the other. Sonar was unknown at this time; there was no way of finding a fully submerged submarine beyond probing or dragging for it. The tugs and the cable were doing just that. Stoker turned ninety degrees and headed for the Asiatic shore, where he decided to sit it out on the bottom at twenty-five metres. They would wait. And wait.

At around 9 a.m., some sort of vessel passed above them, dragging something – a weighted cable, perhaps – which gave them a frightening thump on the hull. Stoker decided to move yet again, but when he tried to he found that trim had been lost, that some of his ballast tanks were leaking and that the submarine was plunging below thirty metres, dangerously deeper than she had been designed for. Men at their stations who could see the two depth gauges watched in frozen fright as the needles hit their stops, praying that the hiss of air filling the tanks would get them back up again. It did. Slowly, slowly it did.

The captain brought her back to twenty-five metres, found bottom again and decided to wait it out, urging the crew to get some breakfast and, if they could, some sleep. In the late morning, it being a Sunday, he held a church service 'to be solemnly, orderly and reverently performed', as the navy's Articles of War prescribed. Harry Kinder kept busy at his diary:

> Before 11 o'clock we were called and fell in for morning prayers. I dare say it was the first time prayers were read on the bottom of the sea . . .
>
> The captain decided to wait for darkness. As it was, a certain amount of air had to be released to reflood the tanks and the disturbance it made on the surface must have been noticed by some passing boat. A destroyer started dragging for us shortly afterwards. At about quarter hour intervals we could hear her coming, the churning of her propellers drawing closer and closer. As she passed overhead within a few feet of us, her machinery could be heard working. We could hear the stokers opening the furnace door and shovelling coal into the fires. The swish of the towing wire as it cut through the water could be heard quite plainly.
>
> There was no more sleep for us as it got on our nerves to hear the boat persistently going backwards and forwards. Once the drag hit the boat and for one awful moment we waited anxiously to see if the destroyer would stop but when we heard her continue on her way we knew the drag had not caught. If the drag had held it would have been the end of AE2 and her crew as a depth charge would most likely have been our fate.

It was a great relief to hear the destroyer steam further away but our suspense was increased as the Turks might have noticed the jar on the rope. Each time she came over, our crew would stop talking as it seemed as though they must hear us. It was a proper game of hide and seek and in deadly earnest.[7]

With black humour, the captain christened their tormentor 'Percival'.

Percival passed and repassed at steady intervals. Some of the crew – lucky creatures – succeeded in going to sleep. Attempted jokes as to Percival's reappearance fell mighty flat. As the day wore on, lying in my bunk, I will most unashamedly confess to a feeling of quivering funk each time he passed overhead.[8]

Night fell and eventually the destroyer came over no more. The air in the submarine was foul now, heavy and sickening, reeking with the stench of sweat, urine and shit. Condensation slimed and dripped. At last, at 8.45 p.m., Stoker brought *AE2* to the surface and found a gleaming moonlit night. That was a concern, but there were no ships in sight and the land they could see to starboard was marshy and apparently uninhabited; with luck they could rest undisturbed, refresh the air in the boat and charge the batteries.

In the distance they could hear the thunder of the guns on land, but they had more immediate concerns. John Wheat – like all of them – was busting for clean air and a cigarette:

Immediately the conning tower lid was opened, a thick white mist rose off everything, owing to the bad air, for we had then been submerged 18 hours. As luck would have it nothing was in sight, so we immediately started our engines to charge our batteries. It was delightful to breathe some fresh air again and have a smoke. We were not allowed to smoke on the bridge as the smallest light would give us away to the enemy, so we had to smoke inside the boat at the bottom of the conning tower. It was not too bad as the Diesel engines were drawing fresh air down and aft to where they were situated in the boat, but slightly forward of the conning tower the air was so bad that a match would not burn for a fraction of a second.[9]

With the diesels gently rumbling and the batteries charging, Harry Stoker decided to let his superiors know where they were. He sent for the telegraphist, Bill Falconer, and dictated a signal: a few brief lines giving their position, that they were through the most difficult part of the strait and poised to enter the Sea of Marmara the next morning.

At the Marconi set, Falconer began to work the key, tapping out the dits and dahs of Morse code. They knew that a destroyer, HMS *Jed*, had been positioned at the mouth of the strait with orders to keep a wireless watch for them, to listen for any messages, acknowledge them and then pass them back to the fleet. Falconer finished tapping and waited. There was no reply. He sent the message again. Still no reply. Stoker and the men on the bridge and the casing saw blue and purple sparks crackling from the damp wireless aerials as Falconer kept transmitting, repeating the message over and over again, but no acknowledgement came.

It was depressing, disheartening, but there it was. Exhausted, the captain turned in for some sleep.

At Gaba Tepe, the slaughter had grown more intense, more bloody, and the confusion and chaos more impenetrable as the day wore on. Instead of the relatively easy country the Australians had expected, they found they had to fight their way through gullies and upwards over crags and jagged ridges, under a storm of Turkish fire from the heights. The New Zealanders were striking the same trouble. And the Turkish guns were blasting the beach, where the corpses and the wounded were now piling up in their hundreds. One Australian soldier described the waking nightmare:

> There was no rest, no lull, while the rotting dead lay all around us, never a pause in the whole of that long day that started at the crack of dawn. How we longed for nightfall! How we prayed for this ghastly day to end! How we yearned for the sight of the first dark shadow.[10]

Of 16,000 men who landed on that first day, the bleak estimate was that more than 2000 were killed or injured by nightfall.

A light drizzle was falling when the British officer commanding the Anzacs, Lieutenant General William Birdwood, came ashore a little after 10 p.m. In a dugout lit only by two flickering candles, and after talking with his commanders on the spot, Major Generals William Bridges and Alexander Godley, Birdwood dictated a letter to Sir Ian Hamilton and had it sent to the flagship.

Asleep and dreaming in his cabin, Hamilton was woken after midnight by his chief of staff. 'Sir Ian,' the officer said, 'you've got to come right along – a question of life and death – you must settle it!'[11]

Throwing on a greatcoat over his pyjamas, Hamilton went to the admiral's dining cabin, where he found a knot of navy and army officers gathered around the table, including de Robeck, Keyes and Rear Admiral Cecil Thursby, who had been in charge of the transports and boats landing the Anzacs on the beach. 'A cold hand clutched my heart as I scanned their faces,'[12] Hamilton later wrote. They watched in grim silence as he read Birdwood's letter:

> Both my divisional generals and brigadiers have represented to me that they fear their men are thoroughly demoralised by shrapnel-fire to which they have been subjected all day after exhaustion and gallant work in the morning. Numbers have dribbled back from firing line and cannot be collected in this difficult country . . .
>
> If troops are subjected to shellfire again tomorrow morning there is likely to be a fiasco as I have no fresh troops with which to replace those in the firing line. I know my representation is most serious but if we are to re-embark it must be at once.[13]

Birdwood was considering evacuation. Leaving, quitting, after less than twenty-four hours. Playing for time while he pondered this letter and all that it meant, Hamilton asked a few questions around the table. Admiral Thursby, shaken to the core, told him it would take the best part of three days to get the men back off the beaches; many boats had been smashed or sunk and the transports dispersed.

As another silence fell, the cabin door opened and a naval officer appeared holding a slip of paper. It was Charles Brodie, who gestured to Keyes that he should come outside. Furious at the interruption, the commodore waved him away, but Brodie insisted. Keyes stood and left the room.

Only minutes before, Brodie had been handed a signal: 'From AE2 for C-in-C,' it began. It was the message that Stoker had been trying to send that evening, which telegraphist Bill Falconer had so doggedly tapped out time and again, that *AE2* had breached the Dardanelles defences and sunk a gunboat. Finally the message had been received by the destroyer and passed on; it was a little garbled, but clear enough.

Exultant, Keyes rushed back to the meeting. 'It's an omen!' he exclaimed. 'An Australian submarine has done the finest feat in submarine history and is going to torpedo all the ships bringing reinforcements, supplies and ammunition into Gallipoli.'[14] The mood around the table brightened visibly.

Hamilton picked up his fountain pen, as he later described:

> Without another word, all keeping silence, I wrote Birdwood as follows:—
>
> 'Your news is indeed serious. But there is nothing for it but to dig yourselves right in and stick it out. It would take at least two days to re-embark you as Admiral Thursby will explain to you. Meanwhile, the Australian submarine has got up through the Narrows and has torpedoed a gunboat at Chunuk. Hunter-Weston despite his heavy losses will be advancing to-morrow which should divert pressure from you. Make a personal appeal to your men and Godley's to make a supreme effort to hold their ground . . .
>
> 'P.S. You have got through the difficult business, now you have only to dig, dig, dig, until you are safe . . .'
>
> The men from Gaba Tepe made off with this letter; not the men who came down here at all, but new men carrying a clear order. Be the upshot what it may, I shall never repent that order. Better to die like heroes on the enemy's ground than be butchered like sheep on the beaches like the runaway Persians at Marathon.[15]

Keyes stepped back out again to see Brodie. 'It's done the trick,' he beamed. Hamilton would maintain later that he had already made up his mind that there would be no evacuation. But it is clear from Keyes' reaction, and from that of all those around the table, that *AE2*'s success had underpinned the decision, had bolstered their morale, had offered hope. The next day, Keyes ordered *E14* into the Dardanelles, to follow in the Australians' wake.

It is a heavy irony that the diggers, the heroes in the ravines and on the ridges, never got to see Hamilton's stirring call to arms. It never reached them. They were otherwise occupied, fighting and dying.

―

The morning of 26 April, darkest before the dawn, found *AE2* on the surface almost at the head of the Dardanelles and heading for the Sea of Marmara, in water as clear and still as a mirror. Stoker dived the boat when the sky began to grey and the cook, Lionel Churcher, got breakfast together for a crew that had only slept in snatches. Through the periscope, the captain soon saw two warships approaching him on a parallel and opposite course.

He lowered the periscope to avoid its wash giving them away, and by guesswork manoeuvred himself into a firing position. Another quick glimpse showed what looked like a dark grey wall of warship at 500 yards. Stoker recalled:

> The bearing for firing the port torpedo was on. The ship dodged, the torpedo passed ahead of her; and then, looking round, I found to my disgust I had fired at the smaller of the two ships, a cruiser. The other, a battleship – either the Barbarossa or Turgood Reis – was following but it was now too late to bring any of the other tubes to bear with good chance of the torpedo hitting. We had lost a glorious chance, and through my fault alone . . . sick at heart, we dived on along our course, forming the resolve to find a quiet spot for rest before carrying out another attack.[16]

By 7 a.m. they were off the town of Gallipoli itself on the European shore, its little white houses gleaming in the sun, and there were fishing boats aplenty but nothing else to get excited about. *AE2* dived and made its way into the Sea of Marmara. They had made the passage and reached their objective.

The early afternoon revealed a cluster of four ships zigzagging independently, but Stoker, believing they might be merchant vessels, decided at first not to fire at them. When one of them shot at his periscope, he fired a torpedo in return but there was no hit. Either it missed or it just didn't run – another disappointment. The late afternoon provided better sport when they sighted another fishing fleet and sailed through it on the surface with the outsized White Ensign flying, coming so close to a few of the boats that they could see the fishermen on deck with their hands in the air, pleading not to be attacked. It would help to spread alarm and confusion, Stoker thought.

The night brought a full moon, a hunter's moon, for every time they rose to try to charge the batteries, they were pursued by gunboats of one sort or another and they would have to dive again and sit on the bottom to shake them off. Harry Kinder dreaded the nights:

> When the boat is lying on the bottom with only a pilot light on, one begins to imagine all sorts of things happening to the boat. Perhaps it would not be able to rise again with the crew caught like rats in a trap with no hope of escape.
>
> If you let your imagination run too long you can feel your hair rising. Even the heavy breathing of your mates who are more fortunate and able to sleep does not dispel this horrid feeling. Sometimes the sound of a voice is a welcome sound. I think that most of the crew was affected this way although some would never own up to the fact. It was surprising how soon everyone was awake and ready to talk as soon as anyone spoke.[17]

This would be the pattern of their next few days. The Sea of Marmara seemed curiously empty of shipping, perhaps because of their presence – in which case they were doing something of the job they had been sent for, disrupting supplies to the Turkish army on the Gallipoli Peninsula. But it was hardly rewarding, and there was no shortage of small warships searching for them, which meant keeping their head down.

The next three torpedo firings were disheartening too. On one, with a destroyer in sight, the torpedo engine failed to start and the damn thing rose to the surface and floated there as if it were mocking them. Two others missed the small warships they were aimed at – perhaps more motor faults. On 29 April Stoker decided to search for greener pastures and, with the horizon empty, set a course on the surface for Constantinople itself.

He was on the bridge in the late-afternoon sun when there was a puzzled cry from a lookout: 'Something ahead to port, sir. Looks like a periscope . . .'

The captain peered through his binoculars. It was indeed a periscope. They watched in growing amazement as a submarine rose 180 metres off the port bow: a familiar shape, a twin to themselves, grey and streaming water as first the conning tower and then the hull emerged, the white painted number on her bow unmistakable. It was *E14*.

The chance of a meeting like this must have been immeasurably small, but there they were, in the Bay of Artaki, on the Marmara's wide southern shore. It was a cheerful, happy encounter. Friendly faces. The two captains hailed each other with tin megaphones, Stoker recounting the sorry story of his dud torpedoes, Edward Boyle telling Stoker that his wireless messages had got through to the fleet. Stoker was all for the two of them heading on to Constantinople there and then, but Boyle wanted to wireless Admiral Hamilton first; as he was the senior of the two, his view prevailed. Boyle asked Stoker – politely, but in fact it was an order – to meet him at the same location at 10 a.m. the next day. They farewelled each other and *E14* drew away into the evening. *AE2* rested that night on the bottom, north of Marmara Island.

The next morning, *AE2* arrived for the rendezvous at precisely 10 a.m. and they thought they got a glimpse of *E14* in the distance. That glimpse vanished as quickly as it appeared, for there was a small torpedo boat on the horizon, approaching from the west – a sight all too common now. Stoker dived to avoid it.

All was well until, about half an hour later, *AE2* suddenly lunged for the surface. One minute she was underwater in perfect trim, at a depth of about fifteen metres. The next, inexplicably, she shot upwards, her nose leaping out of the sea, breaching like some playful porpoise. There was no explanation for it. A swirling current or a sudden change in water temperature or salinity can affect a submarine's buoyancy in an instant, but this leap was beyond that, surely. Shocked, the captain called for the for'ard ballast tanks to be flooded; the men at the pumps threw open the valves, while at the after-planes the coxswain, Charlie Vaughan, wrestled with his control wheel, the motor whirring.

Nothing happened. The boat would not dive. Stoker ordered full ahead, both to get maximum thrust on the planes but still she kept rising. And the torpedo boat, drawing ever closer, opened fire.

A light morning mist was beginning to lift from Gallipoli Bay when the aircraft came over. Single-engine biplanes they were, silvery Sopwith Schneider floatplanes from the seaplane tender HMS *Ark Royal*. Ali Riza was up early savouring the dawn from the deck of the torpedo boat *Sultanhisar*, his first command. He could clearly make out the red, white and blue British markings on the fuselages and tails; one flew so low and so close that he could see the goggled face of the pilot in the cockpit.

They were attacking the Gallipoli township, concentrating on the biggest building, the flour mill – Riza could hear the explosions and see rising smoke. Then one flew towards his boat and dropped a small bomb, which exploded harmlessly in the water nearby. Job done, and with engines droning, they disappeared over the hills behind the town.

Riza was in no mood to be trifled with. His regular job each day was to ferry the army commander, *Generalleutnant* Otto Liman von Sanders, to and from Maidos, down the strait near the battlefront. Arrogant German that he was, von Sanders had abused Riza the day before, sneering that he was an irresponsible Turk, and the insult was still raw. Riza had been appalled by the fighting near Maidos, on his home soil; just a few days earlier he had narrowly avoided a torpedo fired at *Sultanhisar* by an unseen enemy submarine. This Friday, the last day of April, the air attack angered him too – the impudence of it! At thirty-one and heavily moustachioed in the Turkish custom, he had once been pro-British, but he was now burning with the patriotic fervour of a naval officer whose lands, skies and waters have been violated. His blood was up and he was spoiling for a fight.

Perhaps because of von Sanders, Riza had suddenly been recalled from Gallipoli to Constantinople, to leave this morning. Against orders, he decided to take a longer route south-east that would bring him past Artaki Bay, for there were reports that a submarine had been seen there.

Sultanhisar was tiny. French-built, she displaced a bare 88 tonnes, but she carried three torpedo tubes and a pair of quick-firing 37-millimetre guns, and she could turn on a speedy twenty-six knots, enough to outpace any submarine. Her crew of twenty-three was well trained and so was their captain. Riza had studied his trade under the British naval mission in Constantinople before the war. The sun was rising above the Anatolian hills as he got underway, and in a few uneventful hours he was in the bay, on a calm sea.

The signalman saw the submarine first, a silhouette in the mist off Ari Burnu Point. It was just after 10 a.m. Riza rang for full speed and thick black coal smoke began pouring from the boat's stumpy funnels as she surged forward. She was 'nearly skipping over the sea', Riza recalled.[18] The submarine dived, leaving behind a smear of oil on the surface of the sea and Captain Riza was cheated of his prey – until a periscope appeared!

Sultanhisar got away two shots from her starboard gun before the submarine vanished again, Riza mistakenly thinking he had scored a hit. Then, when it seemed they had lost their quarry once more, the submarine suddenly broke water, bow first, some 1500 metres away. The guns opened fire again.

On board *AE2*, they did not notice the shooting. They were too intent on trying to get her down again, and eventually, with her for'ard tanks flooded, she slipped back underwater, bow first. Stoker ordered a depth of fifty feet (fifteen metres), but now she seemed to have a mind of her own, and she kept going, down and down. All eyes were on the captain, who later recalled:

> [D]own by the bows she went to 60 and then 70 feet, and was obviously quite out of control. Water ballast was expelled as quickly

> as possible, yet down and down she went – 80, 90 and 100 feet. Here was the limit of our gauges; when that depth was passed she was still sinking rapidly. We could not tell to what depths she was reaching...[19]

This was terrifying, the end in sight. E-class boats were not designed to go below 100 feet (thirty metres). Too deep and the water pressure would crush her – and all in her, flesh and bones.

At his station, Harry Kinder could see one of the depth gauges as he struggled to keep his footing:

> It was impossible to stand on the deck. The crew had to get their feet on some of the side fixtures with their backs against the decks to carry out the orders. To make matters worse, everything moveable in the boat started to slide and roll to the bows. Some of the heavier things such as boxes of spanners took some dodging and it sounded like bedlam let loose.
>
> It was hard to hear the orders above the noise of breaking crockery, rolling mess tins and the rest of the moving articles. The main diving gauges had got beyond registering the depth. Orders were carried out with great difficulty owing to the awful angle of the boat.
>
> The main motors had been reversed at full speed and all the ballast tanks blown to try and stop the boat from going to the bottom.
>
> The air pressure when blowing the tanks showed the boat to be down 175ft although we were in 240 ft of water by the reading on the chart. It was impossible to take the boat to the bottom (even if the hull could have withstood the pressure of 120lbs to the square inch) as the angle at which the boat was sinking would have driven her bows into the mud making it practically impossible to rise again.
>
> On the other hand, the Turks were waiting on top. So it was a case of between the devil and the deep blue sea with one of them to win...[20]

When it seemed that all was lost, that death was close, there was a cry from the coxswain: 'She's coming up, sir!' The needle on the depth gauge began to quiver and, with her speed in reverse increasing, once again *AE2* jumped to the surface and stayed there.

The Turks were indeed waiting. Seizing his moment, Ali Riza fired a torpedo. It failed to move, remaining obstinately in its tube. He fired a second, which launched successfully, and he and his crew watched its white trail heading for the submarine:

> My sailors were waiting next to the lifeboats. Sultanhisar was running towards the submarine like a tiger running after its prey. The end of this pursuit was coming near. We were waiting with great hope and inner joy.
>
> However, the torpedo went past the conning tower of the submarine. This miss crushed our spirits. We had fallen into a terrible position. Our last hope was also lost. The impact of the remaining guns was negligible. It seemed we had totally lost the enemy ship.[21]

The men in *AE2* never saw the torpedo. They were too busy trying to get under again. Finally she dived, reluctantly at first, but then she reprised the same wilful act, plunging to the bottom, out of control, even faster than before. Stoker feared this was the end:

> Full speed astern again ... a thousand years passed – well, this time we were gone for ever. In Heaven's name, what depth were we at? Why did not the sides of the boat cave in under pressure and finish it?
>
> And then, once again that fateful needle jumped back from its limit mark and AE2 rushed stern first to the surface.[22]

Sultanhisar's guns opened fire and scored three hits, one after the other, in the engine room, leaving the submarine holed and open to the sea. She could no longer dive. She was finished, dying at the end of her last act. In the control room, standing by the periscope, Stoker looked around him at the wreckage of their lives, at the faces of the men watching him intently, and gave his last order as the commanding officer of His Majesty's Australian Submarine *AE2*: 'Up you go. Abandon ship.'

They grabbed what few possessions they could quickly lay their hands on and began to scramble up on deck. Stoker and

Geoff Haggard, the first lieutenant, remained below and began to work the Kingston valves that would admit the sea in to drown her, to send her down for the last time. Stoker seized his briefcase from the wardroom; it had some money in it, he remembered. Harry Kinder waited stoically:

> My turn didn't come till near the last. I spent my last few minutes looking around the boat. The clock said five minutes to twelve, a time which made me think of the rabbit pie in the oven. By this time pie and oven would be all mixed up with the engines. I went to my ditty box and got 16/- and a photograph of my wife. I thought the money might come in handy. I was sorry I had paid in a few pounds to the canteen the night before we left.
>
> AE2 looked a proper wreck with everything in disorder. The captain had been collecting the ship's papers and destroying charts. The last thing I noticed was the charge of gun cotton which was kept handy under the diving gauges to blow the boat up. This would prevent her from falling into enemy hands. I often wonder (if the boat had remained on the bottom) whether the captain would have been game enough to have used the charge and blown the boat and crew to their final resting place. I think he would have.
>
> At last my turn came. I had kept one eye on the depth gauge to make sure that the boat was not sinking and with one last look around, came up on deck to start a new life in an unknown country. It was like leaving home.[23]

The third hand, Lieutenant Cary, was on the bridge watching her get lower in the water, judging the moment, and he yelled down the hatch for Stoker and Haggard to come up. When Stoker reached the deck – the last to leave, as was right and proper – most of the crew were already in the water, in life jackets. The remaining six men jumped for it – one dived as neatly as if he were at a swimming pool. Then she went under, in a swirl and a bubbling froth of white water, down to her sea grave. Stoker noted the position: some seven kilometres north of a small peninsula on the Turkish mainland known as Karaburun Point.

She disappeared 'like a big wounded fish', thought Harry Kinder. 'I felt sorry to see AE2 come to such an end but she had died fighting.'²⁴ In the water, he noticed that Geoff Haggard was floating in a lifejacket and nonchalantly smoking a cigar.

AE2 had travelled 56,400 kilometres in peace and at war, farther than any submarine had ever been. She had done what many thought could not be done: forcing the Dardanelles was a strategic blow that dramatically altered the conduct and character of the Gallipoli campaign. Seriously alarmed by her sudden, dramatic appearance and by the submarines that followed her into the Sea of Marmara, the Turks largely abandoned their sea supply lanes from the mainland to the Gallipoli Peninsula and back. They were forced to replenish their army with weapons, ammunition and fresh troops by the much longer and considerably less efficient overland route. Their wounded soldiers, too, had to be withdrawn by land, not sea. In that sense, Commodore Keyes' order to 'run amuck' had been obeyed to good effect.

Yet the cold light of hindsight, shining astern through the fog of war, also reveals a grim consequence. Turkey's supply difficulties in fact prolonged the campaign by many months, creating a protracted struggle of attrition that only delayed the inevitable Ottoman victory, at untold cost in lives and treasure on both sides.

As for *AE2*'s crew, in Stoker's words:

> No captain has ever been more proud of the men under his command than I was whilst commanding, in my good fortune, that Australian submarine . . .
>
> [H]ard work, privation, discomfort, dangers, were their companions during practically the whole of *AE2*'s short life. And if that were not enough, they entered, at her death, on a new life which was not a life, but a sorry existence. Good comrades, loyal servants and brave men: the straws in the wind led them to captivity.²⁵

They left her lying in her deep grave, for the sea and the twentieth century to wash over her.

8
ARRIVAL AT PRISONER AVENUE

Ali Riza ordered lifebuoys to be thrown overboard and lowered a boat, which picked up Harry Stoker and a few men who could not swim. Within minutes they were on board *Sultanhisar*, all thirty-two of them, dripping wet and dejected but not a man injured, not a life lost. Riza later described the meeting of the two captains:

> 'Captain Ali Riza.' And I extended my hand. He firmly shook my hand and responded:
> 'Captain Stoker,' he said.
> I was looking at his face with interest.
> I said:
> 'Never mind!'
> 'Thank you,' he said.
> I felt the need to console him.
> I said:
> 'Things like this happen in war. However I was not expecting to get into a battle with a British submarine in our own backyard.'
> If my words made him even more emotional I do not know. He felt the need to lean against the rail surrounding the deck . . .[1]

Turkish sailors took the Allied crew's wet clothing down to the engine room to be dried and offered them cigarettes as they stood about on deck stark naked. They were taken first to Gallipoli, where Riza tied up alongside a hospital ship, which had just arrived with wounded from the fighting. He ordered his prisoners to line up on deck and they were inspected by none other than General Liman von Sanders himself, who stared at them for a few minutes as if they were cattle at market and said nothing, then spun on his jackbooted heel and left.

According to Charlie Suckling:

> I have often wondered what he must have thought of us, we certainly were a nondescript lot, most of us in nothing but trousers and singlets, and coming from a Service that is renowned all over the world for its smartness I am afraid we did not create a very good impression.[2]

They were fed that evening, their first meal in captivity:

> [T]wo small loaves of bread each, two big dishes of stew having a very strong taste of garlic, two dishes of a kind of salad, and some sort of green stuff with oil. This had a horrible greasy bitter taste. After this we had two dishes of a kind of sweet bran mash.[3]

For men used to meat and potatoes, or rabbit pie at best, it was hard to swallow. They left for Constantinople in *Sultanhisar* that night, arriving the next morning as the rising sun lit up the waters of the Golden Horn and the domes of the city's mosques.

For the next three years and a few months more, they would be 'guests of the Sultan', as they sometimes referred to themselves in moods of morbid humour. Their lives would be a dystopia of misery, of back-breaking labour, of hunger and disease, of loneliness and despair. There would be sporadic episodes of brutal punishment, of torture and of sexual depravity, inflicted upon them. Four of *AE2*'s crew would die in captivity. The urge to survive and a thread of mateship, slender but unbreakable, held them together.

In the first few days the men were quartered in an army barracks. Their uniforms were taken and they were given rough Turkish clothing, unwashed and crawling with lice, to be topped by red fezzes all the wrong size, which caused a certain wry hilarity. The three officers insisted on keeping their uniform caps and were soon separated from the men. Their heads were roughly shaved. There was nowhere to bathe or wash. By day, groups were taken for questioning. By night, stretched out on the hard wooden floor and tormented by bedbugs and legions of lice, they were awoken every few hours to be counted by the guards.

Harry Stoker was interviewed several times. When he offered nothing to satisfy his interrogators, he was taken before the war minister himself, the swaggering Young Turk psychopath Enver Pasha. (Famously, Enver had three large portraits on his office wall: himself in the centre, flanked by Napoleon and Frederick the Great.) Giving nothing to him either, Stoker was ordered into solitary confinement for a week.

On 8 May, a Saturday, they were herded onto a train, which, after two days, emptied them into the town of Afion Kara Hissar. The name, literally translated, meant 'Opium Black Castle', and it would become synonymous with the squalor of their existence. Afion sat in mountainous country in western Turkey, some 400 kilometres to the south-east of Constantinople, its narrow, snow-covered streets and drab, timbered buildings sprawling beneath a barren stone crag of forbidding ugliness. Atop the crag sat the castle itself, which dated back a millennium BC, its ruined battlements like a row of broken teeth. It was surrounded by opium poppy fields and marble quarries.

There was no prison camp, no huts hemmed in by barbed wire and watchtowers. Instead, the officers and men were put into tumbledown wooden houses, which, they would learn later, had belonged to Armenian families forced into exile or possibly just murdered. The Armenian genocide had begun just weeks before. A mostly Christian ethnic minority, usefully scapegoated by the Young Turks for the economic and military ills which had afflicted the Ottoman Empire, the Armenians fell victim to one of the century's great atrocities, in which an estimated one million of them would be slaughtered in mass shootings, drownings or on forced route marches through the desert.

AE2's crew would learn and see more of this in the years ahead. For now, they were crammed into one room in the first house they stayed in, with the inevitable lice and vermin for company and no glass in the two windows, just iron bars. Charlie Suckling shivered in the cold:

> As the ground outside was still covered with snow the temperature inside was very little above freezing and we had very little clothes and were by this time half starved, so we had a rather terrible time. Sleep was impossible, all we could do was run around the room until we were exhausted and then lay in heaps on the floor until the cold started us moving again.[4]

They were taken to another, bigger building a few days later, a former school, where there was at least one pleasant surprise: the survivors of *E15* were there. There were French and Russian prisoners as well. They were now in two rooms – John Wheat guessed each measured twenty-two by fifteen feet (6.7 by 4.5 metres) – which they shared with *E15* men, being allowed out only to go to the toilet escorted by a guard armed with a rifle and bayonet.

> Our food consisted of a two pound loaf of bread a day, a dish of boiled wheat between ten men in the morning and in the afternoon a dish of cabbage or potato soup with olive oil . . .
>
> [W]e had no way of washing our clothes or even our bodies. To break the monotony someone suggested we start a competition to see who could catch the most lice off their own clothes. The record catch for one man was 250 in a day.[5]

After a week of this confinement, doing nothing, they were sent out to work on local roads, breaking rocks from 6.30 in the morning until they returned exhausted to their rooms at 6.30 in the evening. At last the snow had gone, to be replaced in time by a scorching summer. Wrote Harry Kinder:

> On arrival at 'Prisoner Avenue' as we called it afterwards, we either got a pick, a shovel or a rickety old wheelbarrow and a few knapping hammers.
>
> The Turkish engineer, with the usual promises, said that if we worked well we would be given eight piastres a day. (About 1s.4d.) At the end of the month the commandant lined us up and told us that we should have all been shot when we were captured. Evidently, our work didn't please him. To make matters worse we heard a rumour that the Commandant was swelling his bank account at our expense, so like good Australians we went on strike.

> When we had been working, we had to wheel each barrow about 200 yards backwards and forwards all day long in the blazing sun. At first, when we went out after being kept inside for so long we got sun-burned. Blisters and big sores formed and the fezzes were no protection from the sun. I was wearing a pair of Maltese sandals and the hot sand burnt and blistered my feet so that I could hardly walk. Some of the men didn't have any shoes.
>
> The road we were supposed to be building was just on the outskirts of town and close to a putrid water hole over which millions of flies hovered. The stench was terrible. All day it was just one long battle with the flies. The town's rubbish and offal was carted out and dumped at the end of the road we were making and we had to cover it. Each cart load brought a few more odours and thousands more flies. It was a great wonder we didn't all go down with fever.[6]

The officers fared better. Their food was similar, but their houses were not so cramped, although they were equally squalid, sleeping eight to a room on thin mattresses on the filthy floor. But they did not have to work, for the Hague Convention said officers could not be made to, and the Turks observed this. Harry Stoker struck up a friendship with a fellow Irishman, the ginger-haired, whimsical Geoffrey Fitzgerald, a lieutenant from *E15*.

News of the loss of *AE2* was slow to reach Australia. The Turks themselves did not mention it until a brief announcement on 12 May, made via Berlin, in which they claimed, entirely accurately, that the submarine had been sunk and that thirty-two men had been taken prisoner. Australian newspapers reported this in a couple of paragraphs, with the rider that there had been no confirmation from the Admiralty in London. It was not until 18 May that the Admiralty conceded in a cable to the Australian government that *AE2* was no more; yet they managed to get the numbers wrong. The defence minister, George Pearce, read the cable to the Senate on 20 May:

> No communication having been received from submarine AE2 since 26th April, her loss must be presumed. From a report

received through diplomatic channels at Athens it would appear that three officers and seventeen men were taken prisoners out of a total of three officers and twenty-eight men. Every effort is being made to ascertain further 'particulars' of the survivors.

Board of Admiralty desire to record their deep regret at the loss of this vessel with so many of her gallant crew, after a memorable feat of arms, and congratulate the Commonwealth on the high qualities of their officers and seamen.[7]

Pearce added only that he was sure the honourable senators would share the sentiments of the message. And that was it. He made no acknowledgement of the naval feat of penetrating the Dardanelles. He was much more excited by the news from the army, that the Australian commanding general at Gallipoli, William Bridges, had been shot and wounded by a sniper, declaiming absurdly that:

> I think we can claim, without any boastfulness, that the landing of that Army and its subsequent operations will stand out alongside the feat of Wolfe on the Plains of Abraham, that as time goes past and we are able to look at the thing in proper perspective, it will be one of the great battle stories of the British Empire, and the name of Major-General Bridges and his command will always be associated with it.[8]

In fact, Billy Bridges had been one of those who had recommended withdrawal on that fateful first night.

The Admiralty's error in the number of men recovered aroused fear and heartache in families in both Britain and Australia. It was not corrected for another month, until, on 21 June, the newspapers reported:

> A cable communication has been received by the Navy Office, Melbourne, from the Commonwealth naval representative in London, stating that Lieut.-Commander H. H. Stoker had reported by a letter dated May 15 that all officers and men late of the submarine AE2, now prisoners of war in Turkey, were in good health.[9]

That eased the anxiety a good deal, and after a month or two some letters from the prisoners began to trickle home. The prison officials permitted only one letter a week, of four sentences, and they were strictly censored. This article from Alice Nichols, the mother of 22-year-old Able Seaman Alex Nichols, appeared in the Brisbane *Courier* in late September.

> LETTERS WANTED.
> AN AUSTRALIAN PRISONER.
> ONE OF THE AE2 BOYS.
>
> Mrs. Nichols, Berry-street, writes:- I have received a letter from my son, A.C. Nichols, who is a prisoner of war in Turkey. He pleads for 'letters from everybody.'
>
> His address is: 'Prisoner de guerre, á Constantinople. A.C. Nichols, Australian naval prisoner, c/o Admiralty, London' His letter dated July 4 says: 'Things are no different, but we cannot grumble about the treatment we are receiving from the Turks. They are really good to us, and I shall never again have a bad opinion of the average Turk. I suppose we shall be here a couple of months yet, but I do not worry, as God rules our destiny, and when He wills it we shall be glad to get away. Let my friends know that I am quite all right.'[10]

After a few months, letters did begin to come and go, and parcels of food and clothing were sent via the International Red Cross at Geneva. It was spasmodic, and sometimes the packages had been opened and filleted of anything of any value, but contact was made. There were occasional visits from officials of the American embassy, the protecting power representing British interests in Turkey, who took the responsibility seriously and distributed small but much-appreciated sums of money and did their best through diplomatic channels to act on complaints of mistreatment. Some Turkish prison officials behaved decently, even sympathetically; others were vicious and sadistic.

Harry Stoker and his friend Geoffrey Fitzgerald were suddenly sent to Constantinople in October 1915, a surprise which lifted their spirits and led them to think, optimistically, that an early release might be on the cards. It was not. When they arrived, they were told that Turkish prisoners of war in Egypt had been cruelly mistreated by the British. His Excellency Enver Pasha himself had ordered that two British prisoners would be placed in solitary confinement in reprisal.

Stoker and Fitzgerald protested in vain: their belongings were confiscated, and they were thrown into two black, stinking and infested cells, just ten feet square, water sloshing on the floors. The only furniture, dimly visible in the dark, was a wooden bed and a small table. They were told they should write letters to the British government explaining the situation, which they did, Stoker adding one to the American ambassador for good measure.

For twenty-five days the Irishmen endured this solitary hell, their cells far apart. The food was filthy but they struggled to swallow it because there was nothing else. Lice and bedbugs swarmed over them. Stoker scratched a calendar on the wall, and to keep himself sane he befriended a rat that shared the cell with him, naming it Archibald and holding long conversations with it. For exercise he would pace the floor, around and around, dreaming of halcyon days of sunshine, wine and roses. Hallucinating, he talked to his bed, to the floor, to the walls. He knew he was losing weight, alarmingly so. Halfway through this nightmare, some relief came from the ever-diligent American ambassador, Henry Morgenthau, as Stoker later described:

> One night an interpreter arrived carrying a large bundle. It contained, to my bewilderment, two excellent rugs, a pillow, sponge, toothbrush and powder, socks, slippers, handkerchiefs and last – wondrous link with civilisation – some pyjamas.
>
> Whence were these good things, I asked the interpreter? He did not know. But I did – and here hope rose in an almost stifling manner – for they <u>must</u> have come from the American Embassy! If that was so it meant the Ambassador knew of our state, that he would be working for us, that release must be at hand! I spent the happiest night since reprisals had started.[11]

On 5 November, Stoker and Fitzgerald were released as abruptly as they had been imprisoned, in an almost impossibly surreal fantasy. Bathed and shaved and handed five English pounds by the prison commandant – who apologised profusely for their unfortunate detention – they were then escorted, bewildered, to Constantinople's most luxurious hotel, the Pera Palace. Ambassador Morgenthau had worked his magic yet again, obtaining an audience with Enver Pasha to appeal for clemency:

> I now proposed that Enver should give them a vacation of eight days in Constantinople. He entered into the spirit of the occasion and the men were released. They certainly presented a sorry sight; they had spent twenty-five days in the dungeon, with no chance to bathe or to shave, with no change of linen or any of the decencies of life. But Mr. Philip took charge, furnished them the necessaries, and in a brief period we had before us two young and handsome British naval officers. Their eight days' freedom turned out to be a triumphal procession . . .[12]

For almost a week they luxuriated in the gilded and marbled splendour of the Pera Palace, a pleasure dome built as the terminal for the passengers of the *Orient Express*: crisp linen sheets on plump beds, hot baths, champagne! The ambassador and Hoffman Philip, the counsellor at the American embassy, laid on lunches, dinners and shopping excursions, carriages and automobiles, and – bliss – a visit to the American Girls' College, where they could talk with young women and, later, attend a church service.

This idyll ended as suddenly as it had begun. After a week they woke in their hotel rooms to find military police ready to bundle them back on a train to Afion.

Morgenthau, though, had one more card to play. Fitzgerald was engaged to marry the daughter of the British minister to the Vatican. In concert with the Vatican's apostolic delegate to Turkey, Monsignor Angelo Dolci, the ambassador successfully arranged with Enver Pasha for his repatriation on humanitarian grounds. Morgenthau tried something similar for Harry Stoker but failed. Stoker was devastated when his friend Fitz left.

The Gallipoli campaign had disintegrated in defeat and retreat at the end of the old year, 1915, with Hamilton dismissed that October and the Anzacs taken safely off the beaches in a brilliantly staged withdrawal by night in December. It had all been in vain. The Australians left behind 8709 dead, with 19,441 wounded. The Kiwis lost 2701 dead – a quarter of their number – with 4752 casualties. British losses were still more appalling at 73,485, including 21,255 dead.

The next year, though, would be the cruellest yet, with another British disaster at Kut-al-Amara, on the River Tigris south of Baghdad, in April, almost exactly twelve months after the Gallipoli landing. Hunger, disease and incompetent leadership forced the surrender of a British and Indian garrison besieged there by the Turks, with some 13,000 men captured. Most were sent on a forced route march through the Syrian desert and into Turkey, uncounted thousands of them dying on the way from exhaustion, hunger, thirst, disease and the homicidal brutality of their Turkish, Arab and Kurdish guards, who whipped them along like cattle. It was a death march of some two months. *AE2* men saw some of the survivors arrive at Afion, skeletal figures near naked, starving and burnt black, some of them insane. The two British medical officers there were refused permission to treat them.

By the middle of 1916, a network of camps was spread across Turkey. At the end of the war there were some 16,000 British and Indian colonial prisoners in the country, perhaps a quarter that number of French, and countless Russians. At Afion, the prisoners were moved into what had been an Armenian church and school before every Armenian in the town was either murdered or forced into exile. Harry Kinder recorded it:

> Our coxswain had been taken up to see this school but the stench was so bad he did not go right up to it. Shortly before, about 300 Armenians had been massacred in the church and their bodies heaped up in a narrow alley between the church and wall. Some of the prisoners had to go and clean up, throwing the bodies down a well. Bloodstains still showed on the woodwork inside after the prisoners took it over. Later, some 200 children of the massacred

parents were still attending the school but shortly after they disappeared and, by all accounts, followed their parents' fate.[13]

Some of the sailors were sent to Belemedik, high in the Taurus Mountains in central Turkey, and a staging point for the building of the Berlin–Baghdad railway. There they worked exhausting hours in wintry cold and snow, breaking rocks, wheeling loads of stone and tunnelling, though the camp itself, rows of wooden huts, was regarded as not too bad. The commandant was a Turkish naval officer who had worked under the British and treated his prisoners reasonably well, and the German engineers were sometimes even friendly. The men were paid for their work in piastres, and they were able to buy food and clothing at extortionate prices in ramshackle local stores, and alcohol too, the fiery local brandy known as raki, which led to drunken brawls between the prisoners.

Sex was also available. Corporal George Kerr of the Australian 14th Battalion, captured at Gallipoli, took note in his diary:

> There is a woman in the town who does it. There are several for that matter. A woman named Mme Sophia and her daughter are not very sensitive about taking money, only the daughter wants too much. Johnny was with Mme Sophie for a dollar yesterday but he tells me he was with a girl of about 19. That would be her daughter, who would want more than that ... in reference to the foregoing, I must say that we never expected to get so much liquor in the town, nor did we dream that any of us would be able to sleep with a woman.[14]

But disease swept Belemedik in the chilly autumn of 1916 and men began to die.

The first *AE2* man to go was the chief stoker, Charlie Varcoe, a Cornishman who had been with the boat since Barrow. At the age of thirty-seven, he succumbed to meningitis, his passing carefully noted in the sombre little diary kept by one of his fellow stokers, Petty Officer Herbert Brown. There was no chaplain to do the honours, only a sailor from one of the British submarines: 'On the 18th of September at 7.30 a.m. Charles Varcoe, Chief Stoker of A.E.2 Submarine died in Hospital at Belemedik and was buried at Belemedik at 5 p.m. as many Naval & Military Prisoners as possible attending the Funeral E.R.A. McLean Conducting the burial Service.'[15]

'McLean' was Chief ERA Herbert Macklin, from the submarine HMS *E7*, which had surrendered after becoming trapped in nets on its second mission into the Dardanelles in September 1915. Charlie's friends dug his grave in a small, overgrown Armenian Christian cemetery nearby, surrounded it with a rough picket fence and placed a rough-hewn wooden cross with his name carved on it.

A fatal scourge of typhus and malaria descended upon Belemedik a few weeks later. There was a prison hospital in name, a primitive hut in charge of a German doctor known to the men as 'the Swine', but without medicines it served only as a last staging post for the dying, somewhere to bundle them out of the way. The epidemic killed hundreds, including three more *AE2* sailors, Stoker Michael 'Bill' Williams on 29 September, Petty Officer Stephen Gilbert on 9 October and Able Seaman Albert Knaggs on 22 October.

Williams's death at twenty-two was darkly mysterious, for he had been sent away from Belemedik to another camp at Bozanti, some thirty kilometres away. It was known he had been profoundly depressed by news that his brother John had been killed on Gallipoli at Lone Pine, and he had also been injured in a rockfall on the railway. It was said he succumbed to dysentery in the Bozanti hospital, but his body was never found and nobody seemed to care much, for he was not popular, being regarded as a punchy drunk and a shirker. The date given for his death was guesswork, an estimate.

For that sour, bureaucratic reason, his mother, Margaret Williams of Hamilton, Victoria, only obtained her due compensation years after the war, and then by writing in despair to Prime Minister Billy Hughes. 'Sir, I just heard my son who died a prisoner of war met with foul play, they blame the warders in the hospital and my son was buried as a Turk, which is hard on free Britishers,' she told him.[16] Four of her five sons had enlisted for the war. They were all killed.

The men who remained at Afion had to deal with another scourge: a new commandant named Maslum Bey, a fat and swarthy tyrant infamous for pilfering valuables from Red Cross parcels, for capricious bashings and more. John Still, a second lieutenant with the East Yorkshire Regiment, kept a record of him:

> Some of the British soldiers were very young, fair-haired Saxon boys from Wessex. They had seen a vast deal of cruelty, and they knew how easy it was for Maslum Bey to flog them, even to kill them, or to send them to places where they would almost certainly die. Four of these became the victims of the abominable wickedness of Maslum. Under the shadow of a raw hide whip, in the hands of Turkish non-commissioned officers, they were his victims.[17]

John Wheat noted him too:

> He and other senior Turkish officers would send for the youngest prisoners to have secret and private interviews with them on the excuse of cross examination for some trivial cause and when alone and quite at his mercy his conduct and morality was so bestial and unnatural that at length a revolt throughout the camp seemed imminent. The evils of Sodom and Gomorrah found very apt pupils amongst these Turkish officers . . .[18]

This ogre took a particular dislike to Geoff Haggard and, for no particular reason, sent him into solitary confinement. Eventually a group of British officers managed to lodge a formal complaint to Mazlum Bey's superiors and he was withdrawn from the camp.

As it happened, the commandant who replaced him, Zeir Bey, was a benign man who permitted concerts, amateur dramatics, games and sports, and allowed officers to walk in the nearby hills. Harry Stoker became a star actor in some of the theatre productions. Life improved remarkably. The French, inevitably, produced a chef who could work culinary miracles with whatever was on offer in Afion's local markets.

The idea of escaping, the allure of freedom and the longing for home were ever present but it took resolve and courage to act upon them, for the obstacles were formidable. The only feasible way of leaving Turkey was by sea, to trek overland to the southern coast on the Mediterranean, somehow find a boat there and sail it the 200 or so kilometres to the British-ruled island of Cyprus.

Stoker decided to try. His first thought was to go with his two officers from *AE2*, Haggard and John Cary, but, on reflection, he worried that reprisals might fall too heavily on the crew left behind. Two others joined him then: Lieutenant Commander the Honourable Archibald Cochrane, a twig of the Scottish nobility,[19] and the captain of *E7*, and Edward Price, an Englishman who had been first lieutenant of the ill-fated *E15*.

For weeks they made their plans, quietly gathering food and rough haversacks and a little money in piastres, and devising a route. Afion was 300 kilometres from the coast but that was as the crow flies. To reach it they would have to traverse wild, rugged country on foot, from the mountains to the sea, avoiding roads where they could, moving by night and hiding by day. As the snows began to melt that spring, they set off after midnight on 23 March 1916, prising open the rusted bars on a window of their prison house and dropping to the ground while the sentry was distracted by other prisoners. Stoker described their early progress:

> We slaved and toiled amongst the hills all night, to find, at dawn, the town was still in sight – barely eight miles away. We had thought to have covered twice that distance. If that was disheartening it was only a foretaste of the disappointments and trials ahead. From the time of gaining the mountains we were never free of them again; the best going we ever had in the first week was a ploughed field. There were rivers to cross and once a foul marsh dyke to swim. Daylight would generally find us hiding on the side of a hill or a mountain, spying out the valley below; then, at dusk, down and across the valley and up the opposite mountain – pushing on as far as possible in the dark. As we were often above or near the snow-line the cold was intense, and sleep impossible when further progress was barred. Ever present was that ghastly hunted feeling; and hunger, thirst, footsoreness and physical strain.[20]

On the fifteenth day, sitting on a mountainside, they could at last see the Mediterranean, the blessed sea, their natural element as sailors, shining a wondrous blue in the distance, with little fishing boats bobbing near the mouth of a river. It looked like their deliverance and their hopes rose, but they were nearly at the end of their tether. Their food had run out, their boots were in shreds, their beards and hair were matted and filthy, they were physically wasted – and there was still one more daunting range of hills between them and the coast. Struggling along yet another rockstrewn valley, desperate to find something – anything – to eat, they came across a goatherd's hut:

> When we told the goatherd we were German surveyors he would sell us no food. After much argument and in desperation, we told him we were escaped British officers, that we were dying of starvation and that if he did not give us food we would die at his door. Whereat food was produced. A simple, kindly old man he seemed, for he bade us stop the night in one of his huts while he killed and cut up a goat. Next morning, with our bread, yaout (sour milk), meat and goatskin, we moved off into hiding and commenced cooking the meat and drying the skin to make coverings for our feet.[21]

That evening there was a noise in the bushes near their hiding place and a squad of Turkish gendarmes burst through towards them, rifles cocked, fingers trembling on triggers. The kindly old goatherd had betrayed them.

Harry Stoker was bound with his hands behind his back and Cochrane and Price were handcuffed together. In a few days they were in Constantinople for three weeks of solitary confinement in Stoker's old prison. The Turks convened a court martial, which sentenced them to a further six months in that same jail, in a verminous cell where, to their horror, they could hear the floggings and screams of other prisoners being tortured. They saw a man bastinadoed, a torture in which the victim was strung up by his heels and caned repeatedly on the soles of his feet.

There was a curious reprieve that Christmas, a quixotic decision by their jailers to permit the three of them to attend a church service conducted by a Scottish clergyman, Dr Robert Frew, who had attached himself to the Dutch embassy, which gave him diplomatic protection. Seeing them in his congregation, Frew said nothing but quietly sent a boy to gather supplies while he continued his sermon.

> Our guards had forbidden us to speak to anyone and we filed out of our rear pew across the aisle and into the porch. There stood His Reverence, smiling all over his Scotch face; and he held a large basket, which he thrust into my arms as I marched past.
>
> That night we had cake and crackers, and biscuits and butter, and chocolate, and heaven knows what for our Christmas dinner – and plum pudding.[22]

They were not released until February 1917, when they were sent from Constantinople to another prison in the interior, Yozgad. Archibald Cochrane made a second escape in August 1918, an epic trek with seven other officers, in which they successfully seized a motorboat on the coast and reached Cyprus. Price was felled in a wave of influenza that swept the camps in October 1918. Stoker came down with it too but recovered and tended his friend in the torment of his last days.

Lieutenant Edward Price RN, submariner, died on 16 October at the age of twenty-eight, two weeks to the day before the Turkish armistice.

John Wheat and his mate Alex Nichols made their escape from Hacikiri, a small railway camp further along the line from Belemedik and about eighty kilometres from the coastal town of Mersin. They were both enterprising and intelligent young men and they had prepared carefully, befriending a Greek interpreter who spoke English and who, after some coaxing, gave them a map of the countryside marked with the location of his father's farm near Mersin, where they could shelter and get food if they needed to.

The plan was to reach the coast, build a timber raft and sail it to Cyprus, so over a few weeks they stole an axe, some nails and rope and a few other bits and pieces, and put them together with biscuits, bread and Oxo cubes from food parcels. In the evening of 12 August 1916, well after full moon, they slipped out of the camp while the sentries were diverted and began their trek across rough, hilly country, stumbling and sliding up and down cliffs and slopes and across creeks and along valleys and gullies, moving by night and hiding by day.

Their food held out for a good few days. Finding water was hard, although occasionally they would happen on a well where they could top up their bottles. The going got easier when they could move along a road or track in the direction they wanted, but there was always the risk of discovery. They skirted villages and shepherds' camps, diving into the scrub when the dogs began barking, or just brazening it out as nonchalantly as possible if they encountered a Turk coming in the other direction. The heat sapped their bodies, insects assailed them, wild dogs howled at them in the night. Nichols was bitten by a scorpion or some such, which had him in agony for a day.

Their Greek friend's map was accurate, and after two weeks they reached their objective, a beach near Mersin, which they found was patrolled by a couple of Turkish soldiers. They moved further away to a creek the Greek had recommended as a good hiding place and there, after a cleansing splash in the water and a sleep, they began to build their raft by night, cutting down saplings with the saw they had brought and lashing them together. It took them four nights, by which time their food was running out. Wrote Wheat:

> The next day we completed the raft all ready for launching that night. In the afternoon we christened the raft, naming it 'Success'. We read the service from a prayer book which we carried in a very solemn earnest way, sprinkling water on as we named it. I am afraid had we had anything better than water it should not have been wasted on the christening.
>
> About 8.30 p.m. we launched the raft on to the creek. It was very heavy and we had great difficulty in getting it down into the water. However we got it out into about three feet of water. It certainly looked a success. One of us got on it and it stood the strain but when the two of us got on it barely floated. Certainly not good enough to put to sea in. It was a huge disappointment.[23]

It was more than that. It was shattering. Despondent and at a loss, they found yet another hiding place with a view of the sea and rested there for a few days in the fanciful hope that they could signal some patrolling British warship that might come by. With their food now gone, Alex Nichols decided to risk it and walked to a nearby village, where he told an elderly man that he was a German telegraph mechanic and could he buy some food, please. He was given a glass of water and a plate of fresh figs, and then ten eggs and some thin pancakes, which he took back to John Wheat.

For another two days they waited and watched for a passing ship, but eventually they realised the futility of it and decided to move along the coast, planning to steal a boat. They had no luck with that, either. After much wrenching thought, they agreed that the game was up: their mission had failed, and they had best find their way back to the prison camp. For a couple more days they struggled on, weak from hunger, keeping to the backroads and bypassing the ancient town of Tarsus, the birthplace of Saint Paul the Apostle. A couple of incurious village women saved them one day with some grapes and figs, and they battled forward again.

By luck they happened on a Greek workman from the railway, who, when he learned they were Australians, gave them bread and cheese and offered to take them to a camp up the line where there were some British prisoners. He was as good as his word, and there they found six army sergeants, who turned out to be survivors of the Kut-al-Amara death march. The British men welcomed them with a loaf of bread each and a filling plate of stew.

> We lay down to sleep the first time for 19 days with a full stomach and a contented mind. In the morning we turned out and went down to a creek and had a good bath, after which we felt much refreshed. We had a good breakfast and dinner and in the afternoon we decided that in the evening we would push on to our own camp about seven miles distant and give ourselves up. About 6 p.m. we said goodbye to our friends and started off. All went well till within half a mile from the camp when we had to pass a sentry on the road. We were challenged and did not evidently satisfy the sentry. He took us into the village where our camp was and took us before the Commandant. He was sitting on the veranda talking to the officer of police. He immediately recognised us

and flew into such a temper that he could hardly speak. Both he and the Police Officer were cursing us which we had to stand without saying a word.

They had been away for nineteen days. They were sent on to Belemedik and put in prison on half-rations of bread and water for a week until Alex Nichols came down with an attack of malaria, retching and shivering. A Turkish army colonel took pity upon the two of them, accepting that it had actually been their duty to escape, and ordered their release. They went back to work on the railway.

For two more years John Wheat battled on, shunted from camp to camp, labouring on the railway. He came down with typhus, which covered his body in an evil black and red rash and left him delirious in hospital for three weeks. He recovered from that, and a year later caught malaria, which he also survived. Indomitable, unbeaten, his strength of character shines from his memoir.

Towards the end of 1917, he resolved to escape again, this time with another *AE2* mate, 23-year-old stoker Jim Cullen, a knockabout larrikin from Western Australia, and Harold Samson, a Victorian army private from the 14th Battalion captured at Gallipoli. Incredibly, the three of them set about building a boat at the Gelebek camp on the railway, about fifty kilometres from the coast. They stole the makings, timber and canvas, from the German construction site:

> In about three months from the time we had procured the material we had constructed a fine little canvas boat, 12 feet long 4 ft 6' wide, 2 feet 3' deep. We reckoned this would hold us easily. All the frame work we made in sections. The canvas would be the heaviest part making one man's load. The only thing we were in need of was some tar to put on the outside of the canvas, and sure enough a few days before we were ready to leave we managed to get some Stockholm tar. This was easy to put on. When we were finished we buried all the parts of the boat so that we could not be found out at the last minute and dash our hopes to the ground. We had procured a small German pocket compass with illuminated dial. We had been studying strict economy all this time, and had managed to save up some biscuits and money. The biscuits

came from occasional parcels we received, our friends giving us their biscuits when they knew we were going to attempt this escape. We decided to leave on the 29th April 1918.[24]

This they did, carrying their boat in sections. They made it within sight of the coast, but the weather and hunger beat them, cruel days and nights of torrential rain which stopped them in their tracks.

> We began to see the terrible possibility of failure. Nearly all day we discussed the situation and came to the conclusion that if the rain did not stop it would be impossible to reach the coast at our present rate of travelling. In the afternoon the rain cleared up and we had hopes of being able to continue the trip with success. We could see Tarsus in the distance and knew by our position that we would still have about 13 miles to do. We had gone about 2 miles when another terrible rain storm broke and it was not long before we were like drowned rats. We stopped for about 1 hour in the hopes of it clearing off but no such luck. It seemed as if it was going to last. We knew that with the small amount of wet biscuit we had, we could not possibly do the trip. After reaching the coast we had a 4 to 5 days trip. At sea we could not possibly stand the strain of this without food. We ate the remaining biscuit and decided that we would start back to camp before any of us became too sick to walk. Cullen had a slight attack of malaria and we did not know the minute we might all be stricken down with the same complaint.[25]

Back to camp it was. Wheat was jailed again, this time in a tiny, stinking cell with ten Turkish and Kurdish prisoners, and there he languished for a fortnight until he was discovered by one of the English prison doctors, who talked the Turks into releasing him. He was sent back to Afion, where he endured yet another bout of malaria, but had lenient treatment under a decent commandant.

In October 1918 the Ottoman Empire finally disintegrated. The straw that broke its back was a British and Australian drive into Palestine, swift and unstoppable. On 1 October the city of Damascus fell to the Desert Mounted Corps, brilliantly commanded by the Australian general Harry Chauvel. Exhausted and bankrupt, with 300,000 soldiers dead and the army hollowed out by desertions and in headlong retreat, the government in Constantinople sued for peace. On 30 October, Britain and Turkey signed an armistice on the island of Mudros, where the Gallipoli disaster had begun. The infamous Three Pashas – Talaat, Djemel and the odious Enver – fled into exile.

Rumours of an end to the war had been circulating in the prison camps for some weeks and the fall of Damascus was quickly known. Almost overnight the Turkish guards abandoned any hostility to their prisoners and became something close to affable, expressing contempt for their former German allies.

John Wheat's war was coming to its end too. With other prisoners at Afion, he was told to pack his belongings on 20 October and then put onto a train of cattle trucks, which took them to Smyrna, a port city on the Aegean which is today called Izmir. There they were quartered in the American College for ten days, with the run of the town until they were told that a hospital ship had arrived to collect them.

> Just before daybreak we were fell in [sic] by our own officers and marched to the train that was waiting for us; this train ran us down to the jetty, and it was not long before we were all aboard 3 Turkish tugs steaming merrily through the mine fields out of Smyrna harbour. About 3 pm we sighted a hospital ship in the distance. Can anybody realise our joy at this sight and especially the Australians, when this ship proved to be the Australian hospital ship 'Kanowna?' . . . The treatment we got aboard the 'Kanowna' was excellent how it cheered us up to see the bright smiling faces of the sisters on board & see an English woman, practically the first for 3½ years. The same night we left for Alexandria. On arrival there we were put into a large military camp, to await a ship for England.[26]

With tens of thousands of troops to be brought home from Europe, many of them wounded, a few ex-prisoners from Turkey were not a high priority. John Harrison Wheat would not arrive back in Australia until January 1919.

9
ENTRANCES AND EXITS

The totals of those killed in World War I, military and civilian, can never be exact or agreed. According to the Australian War Memorial, 'It is generally accepted that the First World War killed some 16 million people worldwide, of which military deaths constituted about 9.5 million. It is also estimated that around 20 million were wounded, including 8 million left permanently disabled in some way.'[1] Other estimates are higher, twenty million dead and more. If the influenza pandemic which swept the world from late 1918 is factored in, then perhaps 100 million people died.

Vast tracts of Europe were left in ruins – cities, towns, villages and farms – chiefly in France and Belgium. Russia had been seized by Lenin's Bolsheviks. Germany was ground down by economic chaos, poverty, hunger and the fires of revolution. The collapse of the Ottoman Empire bankrupted Turkey and plunged her into a series of new wars with old enemies, chiefly the Greeks, in conflicts big and small and so dizzily confusing as to defy explanation.

The survivors did what they could to get on with their lives. What we recognise today as post-traumatic stress disorder was entirely unknown. You were simply expected to shed your uniform and pick up your former life where you left off, for better or worse. Harry Stoker did not say in his memoirs how he returned home from Turkey, only that he reached England at Christmas 1918. There he found that his wife, Olive, had given birth to three children in his absence, two daughters and a son, to different fathers. He made no mention of this, either, but the shock must have been profound and he quickly sought and obtained a divorce.

After two months' leave – it hardly seems enough – Stoker returned to service with the Royal Navy in February 1919, but he found life there a very different beast to the carefree existence he had so enjoyed in the years of peace before the war. He was uncomfortable, unsettled, a state of mind perhaps exacerbated by the almost perfunctory recognition of his feat in having been the first to force the Dardanelles. He was given the Distinguished Service Order for 'gallantry in making the passage of the Dardanelles', as the citation read in *The London Gazette*,[2] and later a Mention in Despatches for his service with the RAN, but other submarine commanders, his friends and contemporaries, did rather better. Norman Holbrook of *B11*, Edward Boyle of *E14* and Martin Nasmith of *E11* were all awarded the Victoria Cross for their exploits against the Turks. Yet if Stoker felt hard done by, he never so much as hinted at it.

It was the navy itself that was getting him down. He was given command of another submarine, HMS *K9*, which should have been some sort of consolation, but the K boats had an appalling record of accidents and fatalities. Disaster hung about them. They were great lumpy things, big, fast and steam-powered, capable of a spanking twenty-four knots on the surface and eight submerged, yet they handled appallingly badly up top, where it was said they would roll on a wet carpet and nosedive into heavy seas. They were little better below, tending to lunge for the bottom when diving. It took a good thirty minutes to dive them, including time spent shutting down the boilers and retracting the stumpy twin funnels.

K13 had dived and failed to come up again when her engine room flooded on her acceptance trials in 1917 in Scotland's Gare Loch, with thirty-two men killed.

In a horrendous chain of disasters on 31 January 1918, on a cold, dark and misty night near May Island at the mouth of the Firth of Forth, no fewer than eight vessels of the RN's Grand Fleet – surface ships and K-class submarines – were involved in five separate collisions as they put to sea for exercises.

Forty ships in all left the great base at Rosyth after sunset – battleships, battlecruisers, cruisers, destroyers and nine of the K boats in two flotillas – steaming in a line some fifty kilometres long, without navigation lights, and reaching twenty knots as they headed out towards the North Sea. Night had well fallen when the submarines in the van altered course to avoid some lights coming towards them, thought to be patrolling trawlers. It was the catalyst for disaster. *K14*'s helm jammed hard over and she swept off in a circle. *K22* rammed into her, holing her bow and sending a flood of water sweeping through her. Two of *K14*'s crew were killed.

The omens were not good. *K22* was, in fact, the ill-starred old *K13*, salvaged from the bottom of the loch, restored to service and recommissioned with a new number. By unholy coincidence, this night off May Island was the anniversary of that first fatal test dive. And worse was to come in the next hour – much worse. As the two submarines limped apart, the battlecruiser *Inflexible*, following astern, rammed *K22* and bent her bow at right angles, ripping off her starboard fuel and ballast tanks before steaming on, evidently unaware.

Confusion mounted in the thickening mist. Frantic signals were sent but not received. *K3* narrowly missed *K4*. *K6* then slammed into *K4* amidships, sending her to the bottom with all her crew. *K4* was struck by *K7* as she was going down. Steaming at full speed, the cruiser HMS *Fearless* hammered into *K17* and she, too, sank in minutes. In perhaps the ultimate horror, *K7* reversed through *K17*'s survivors struggling in the water, killing an unknown number. Only nine of the crew of fifty-six survived, and one of them died later.

In just over an hour, two submarines had been sunk and three damaged, and 105 men killed, with not an enemy in sight. This catastrophe became known, with sardonic black humour, as the Battle of May Island; another grim joke was that the submarines' K stood for 'Kalamity' or 'Killer'. An enquiry was hastily convened; the captain of *Fearless* was court-martialled but exonerated; a few other officers were rapped across the knuckles but nobody was explicitly held to blame for anything. The RN was so shamed by this shambles that the documents, logs and records were sealed and not opened until 1994.

Five Australian midshipmen had been in the middle of it all in separate submarines, young men from the inaugural 1913 class of the Australian Naval College sent to training in Britain. One of them, Harry Showers, in the luckless *K22*, distinguished himself by rescuing an injured seaman struggling in a flooded compartment and then slamming shut a watertight door – quick thinking which quite likely saved the boat.

Another boy, Dick Cunningham, a nineteen-year-old from Hurstville, Sydney, was lost with *K17*. His body was never found. Nine days later, the Admiralty – hiding behind a wall of wartime secrecy – informed his family in Sydney only that their son had been 'drowned in the North Sea on a submarine on active service'. Dick's father, the principal of Hurstville Public School, wrote to the Naval Board in Melbourne asking for more information, but was eventually told that *K17* was too deep to be salvaged. End of story. It is likely the young man had been among those in the water when *K7* backed through them.

Cunningham and Showers had been best mates in that first college intake, up near the top of the class, both keen sportsmen. A contemporary photograph of Dick shows him with his officer's cap at a slightly jaunty angle, the midshipman's white patches on his collar, a shy smile on a handsome face. It is a poignant portrait of a youngster on the threshold of manhood, so fresh and clear in that timeless uniform that it might have been photographed yesterday.

Ernest Semple Cunningham – Dick was his nickname – was the first of those 1913 pioneers to die at war. Harry lived on, and in 1927 he married Dick's sister, Jean Cunningham. In World War II he served as a fighting cruiser captain in the Pacific and retired a rear admiral, dying in 1991 at the age of ninety-two, the last of that storied class to 'cross the bar', as the navy says.

Harry Stoker would have been well aware of the K boats' calamitous ill fortune, and he shared in a little of it. In 1919, misjudging a turn at Portsmouth, he smacked *K9* into the side of the monitor HMS *Terror*, although with little damage beyond considerable loss of face. A court martial cleared him of any fault but he was reprimanded by an unimpressed admiral. Towards the end of the year, Stoker was promoted to full commander but it was cold comfort. He was beginning to feel he was no longer up to the job and he asked to leave the submarine service.

> I was not happy in my new command; my methods of dealing with my officers and men did not seem to work so well as in the old days; I somehow failed to understand them, and they failed to understand me. I had never before had to use punishment as a means of obtaining the best work out of the men under my command; I had to use it now and hated doing so.
>
> With the exception of the time as prisoner I had now served continuously in submarines since 1906, and I was tired of them. So at the beginning of 1920 I applied to be sent as second in command of a battleship or a cruiser . . .[3]

He had no luck there either. The Admiralty briskly informed him there were eighty-seven commanders ahead of him on the waiting list for jobs in very few ships. He would have to cool his heels.

On the loose in London, killing time, he met by chance a celebrated actor and producer, Norman McKinnel, who had a new play under rehearsal at a West End theatre. When one of the cast dropped out, McKinnel offered Harry the part – another of those straws in the wind. With happy memories of his performances in prison plays in Turkey, he seized the chance and took to it with relish. He had been on stage for a fortnight – under an assumed name, Hew Gordon – when the Admiralty suddenly, out of the blue, informed him he had been appointed captain of the elderly cruiser HMS *Royal Arthur*, a submarine depot ship. He should join her forthwith.

One more straw in the wind. To stay or go? It would be a difficult decision to quit the navy and risk all in the uncertainties of the actor's trade, but after deep thought he did it with his ebullient Irish optimism. Certainly, he recognised, he would miss the naval life:

For the sea is a wonderful mistress, and a wonderful mother too. Few of those who go down to her withstand for long the claim she makes on their hearts. I doubt if human wives and sweethearts ever realise the strength of the rival they have to fight in winning and keeping a sailor lover. For the sea, though a woman, is straight and true; she does not lie or cheat; she has beauty and grandeur in all her myriad moods; she appeals always to the best, never to the worst, of the men who meet her; she helps a man to be a man, and never tries to undermine his strength nor play upon his weakness . . . A dangerous rival, Miladies.[4]

The bitterness of his wife's infidelity and their failed marriage still hurt him. With time, though, he cast that aside, and from that year, 1920, he built a career on stage and in films. Stoker never made it to the dizzy heights of star billing, but he found regular paying work in supporting roles, often playing a gentlemanly sort of chap with the right accent.

His memoir, *Straws in the Wind*, arrived in the bookstores in 1925, to good reviews in London and around Australia. 'A more breathlessly exciting account of perils calmly faced and bravely overcome I have never read,' wrote the reviewer in the *Sydney Mail*.[5] The author 'is to be congratulated upon having written one of the best books about submarine warfare anyone could possibly wish to read', said the *Western Mail* in Perth.[6]

Stoker's big acting break came in 1928, in a London stage production of *Journey's End*, a nail-biting thriller about trench warfare in France, which starred a 21-year-old Laurence Olivier. H.G. Stoker had a small but pivotal part as an army colonel, and his wartime background was noted by the Fleet Street newspapers. The conservative *Daily Telegraph*, holy writ for the Tory Party, lauded his performance, lamenting that he had not been properly acknowledged for his achievements in the Dardanelles:

> His claims to be given a VC were somehow forgotten, though both the next two officers who followed where he had shown the way got their VCs. The DSO which came his way much later must have been a poor consolation for the loss of the highest military honour so worthily earned.

In 1935 he played a naval captain in the film *Brown on Resolution*, in its day a box-office blockbuster of plucky British sailors and dastardly Germans up to no good in the Pacific in World War I. He was 'an interesting member of the cast', said Sydney's *Sun* newspaper, in a brisk sketch of his wartime career.[7]

His reviews were invariably favourable. According to London's *The Sketch*:

> The playgoing public is becoming accustomed to the intermittent appearances of a smallish man, very neatly dressed, who has a perpetual elevation of the eyebrows, an unaffected drawl, a tone of gentle reasoning, and a smile that only comes off when some situation in the play renders assumed gravity absolutely necessary.

Stoker was invariably to be found 'sitting condescendingly on the edge of chesterfields and raising his eyebrows to an enviable height, and trickling cold water mingled with the warm milk of human kindness down the impetuous backs of the loveliest leading ladies of the moment'.[8]

And so life treated him well in his third act. He married again in 1925, at the Savoy Chapel in Westminster, his bride a well-known Shakespearean actress, Dorothie Pidcock, himself in full naval dress uniform of cocked hat, frock coat with epaulettes, sword and medals, and although they had no children they were happy together for forty years.

World War II brought Stoker back into the Royal Navy, with the rank of acting captain, in posts ashore but nothing at sea. He was on the staff at Dover Castle in the month before the D-Day invasion of 1944, with one eye on the midget submarines to be sent across the English channel as an advance guard. After the war it was back to acting, again with comfortable success, and also as manager of the grandly gilded Apollo Theatre, in London's Shaftesbury Avenue. He appeared on stage in New York and Canada and on BBC television and radio.

In retirement Stoker threw himself with gusto into sports and London club life, becoming something of a fixture at that comfortable theatrical watering hole the Garrick Club. He played golf at the best courses around London's home counties and tennis at Wimbledon. In 1962, at the age of seventy-seven, he became – of all things – the Irish croquet champion.

Old shipmates stayed in contact, and he with them. In 1965 he replied to a letter from Cecil Bray, a chief petty officer and one of the Australians who had joined *AE2*'s commissioning crew at Barrow and survived the Turkish camps:

My dear Bray,

Your letter arrived yesterday and caused me the very greatest pleasure. It is good to know the world has gone well for you, and I am quite sure you have well deserved it. The years have treated me kindly too and I'm in almost indecent good health considering my 80th birthday was last month . . .

Of course the sad part of living so long is watching old friends die off. Nichols very kindly wrote me two very long letters last year telling what he could about all our grand chaps of AE2 – including you, of course. The sad list of deaths, too. Wheat and his wife had called on me some years ago, so I was particularly sorry to hear that he had slipped the cable. Nichols seems understandably proud of the grand progress Australia is making, and I was proud of the successes most of our chaps seem to have made of their lives after leaving the navy . . .[9]

Towards the end of his life, reflecting in tranquillity, Stoker wrote on the final page of his diary a log of events or moments that had given him 'the big thrill', or just a good laugh:

- To 'walk with kings' – and princes and princesses.
- In 1900 the practical birth of submarines, the thought of commanding one seemed thrilling.
- To win cups in lawn tennis and golf and croquet. To make centuries in cricket. To see packed stands at big Rugby matches.
- To write a book and receive laudatory reviews in London, provincial and Dominion papers.
- To act in West End stage with stars of the day, in successful plays, and on television and radio, and in films, and in New York and Canada.
- To be given a role in history books.

- To hear a song one had composed sung by the leading baritone of the day – loudly applauded.
- To be a prisoner of war of the Turks and to escape, and to be recaptured.
- To stand on the stage at a successful first night and receive cheers and applause of the audience as the author.

Not a bad list. With perfect theatrical timing, Henry Hugh Gordon Dacre Stoker died on his eighty-first birthday, 2 February 1966. Sailor and submariner, officer and captain, actor, writer, sportsman and philosopher, lover, philanderer and friend to many, he had lived his life fully and well, leaving an indelible mark on Australian naval history.

'They have their exits and their entrances, and one man in his time plays many parts . . .' Some survived their war unscathed, at least outwardly. Others were traumatised physically and mentally, afflicted for the rest of their lives. Fate dealt with them in different ways.

Chief Petty Officer Cecil Bray, *AE2*'s torpedo gunner's mate, survived his imprisonment well, even winning himself a job reference from the German railway builders, but the malaria he contracted at Belemedik remained with him for life. Unlike many, he stayed in the RAN after the war, serving in submarines again and also ashore until 1932, when he retired. He was back in uniform again in 1940 for World War II, briefly in the cruiser HMAS *Brisbane* and then ashore again. He left for the final time in 1946, lived in Sydney and died in 1965 at the age of seventy-seven.

Stoker Petty Officer Herbert Brown, one of *AE2*'s Englishmen and a prison diarist, enlisted after the war in the RAN and migrated to Australia with his wife and three children in 1919. He served for a while in the cruiser *Sydney*, left the navy in 1922 and set up an orange orchard with his wife north of Sydney.

The third hand in *AE2*, **Lieutenant John Pitt Cary**, was a trained hydrographer. After his release from prison, he resumed life in the RN and returned to Australian waters in the survey sloop HMS *Merlin*, surveying and charting the Torres Strait. He left the navy in 1935 with the rank of commander but was called back again for postings ashore in London during World War II. In 2019 his personal papers of letters and scrapbooks were discovered, quite by chance, at a council garbage tip in Dorset, in south-west England, and were sent to the Imperial War Museum in London. They included a letter from King George V welcoming him home from Turkey. Cary died in 1953, having suffered a heart attack while playing golf.

The most ardent proponent of the Gallipoli invasion, **First Lord of the Admiralty Winston Churchill**, was held chiefly responsible for its failure. Privately, he intrigued to have Lord Kitchener removed from the War Office, but he himself was sacked from the Admiralty in May 1915. With his political career derailed but his ego still in high gear, he demanded to be appointed a major general in the army but eventually went to France to command a battalion of the Royal Scots Fusiliers as a lieutenant colonel. He returned to politics in 1917 and was Minister of Munitions for the rest of the war.

Vice Admiral Sir William Rooke Creswell, who is justly recognised as the 'Father of the Royal Australian Navy', remained on the Navy Board as the government's chief naval adviser until August 1919. With the deployment of Australia's ships ceded to the British Admiralty, his wartime role was chiefly administrative. Sorrow attended him, for two of his sons died in the war. With tragic irony, his youngest boy, Lieutenant Colin Creswell, twenty-two, was lost when the RN submarine *E47* failed to return from a North Sea patrol in August 1917. Three months later, an older son, Captain Randolph Creswell, twenty-seven, was killed with the Australian Army's Camel Corps in Egypt. Also in 1917, Randolph's twin brother, Lieutenant Edmund Creswell, of the army's 2nd Pioneer Battalion, was shot in the chest at the bloody, futile Battle of Bullecourt, but survived. Sir William was promoted to vice admiral in retirement in 1922. He died of pneumonia in 1933 and was given a state funeral in Melbourne. The Royal Australian Naval College at Jervis Bay, New South Wales, is HMAS *Creswell*.

Stoker James Cullen, the larrikin escapee from *AE2*, was another malaria victim, returning to his wife Ruby at St Kilda, in Melbourne, in 1919. He signed on for the RAN again but apparently changed his mind and was given a discharge in 1920. He moved to New Zealand in the 1930s and was reputedly killed in an earthquake there in 1945.

After the armistice, **Enver Pasha** fled to Germany and then to Moscow, where he ingratiated himself with the Bolsheviks and gained the trust of Lenin. When the Muslim peoples of Central Asia rose in revolt against Bolshevik rule in 1920, Enver switched sides and – as vain as ever – proclaimed himself 'Commander-in-Chief of all the Armies of Islam, Son-in-Law of the Caliph and Representative of the Prophet'. A squadron of Red Army cavalry killed him in 1922, either by machine-gun fire or by decapitating him with a sabre – the accounts vary.

Telegraphist **William Falconer**'s persistent wireless signals reporting *AE2*'s breakthrough into the Dardanelles were a pivotal point in the Gallipoli campaign, but went unrecognised. He was recommended for a medal but the Admiralty in London controlled decorations for the RAN and rejected the nomination on the churlish grounds that it 'did not propose to take similar action' for its own people. He returned to Australia and left the navy in 1919, working for the Commonwealth Public Service. Falconer should be recognised as a true pioneer of RAN communications. He died on the eve of Anzac Day in 1968.

Ever more irascible and eccentric with age, **First Sea Lord Jacky Fisher** finally fell out with Winston Churchill over Gallipoli and resigned in May 1915, bizarrely hiding himself away in London's Charing Cross Hotel. When he was discovered, he was ordered by Prime Minister Asquith – 'in the King's name!' – to return to his post at the Admiralty. He replied with a list of demands for absolute power so absurd that the government let him go. Many people regarded him as a deserter. He died of cancer in 1920, aged seventy-nine, and was given a state funeral at Westminster Abbey.

Lieutenant Commander Geoffrey Haggard, *AE2*'s first lieutenant, was awarded the Distinguished Service Cross in 1919 and retired from the RN in 1920. A family friend, the Earl of Stradbroke, had been appointed Governor of Victoria and he took Haggard to Melbourne as his aide-de-camp. There, in 1923, he married Marjorie Syme, a daughter of the powerful newspaper baron David Syme, and he began a new and happy life as a gentleman grazier at the Syme family property at Woori Yallock, in the Yarra Valley. The Royal Navy accepted his services for World War II in October 1939. After celebratory drinks at a local pub, Haggard was walking home at night along a railway line when one of his boot heels became caught in a cattle grid by the track. An oncoming train missed him, but something – perhaps a stone – struck him in the head. He freed himself and crawled away but died in the long grass near the line. His body was found the next day.

General Sir Ian Hamilton's dismissal at Gallipoli ended his military career. Decent and honourable though he was, his leadership at the Dardanelles had been uninspiring at best in a campaign doomed to failure, and he took the blame. As a sop he was appointed to the ceremonial post of Lieutenant of the Tower of London. In the early 1930s he was an admirer of Adolf Hitler, but later changed his mind. He died in 1947.

In April 1918, the impulsive former **Commodore Submarines Roger Keyes** planned and led bold naval and commando raids on German U-boat pens in the Belgian ports of Zeebrugge and Ostend. Hailed as a triumphant British victory, they were, in fact, a lethal failure. Six hundred British soldiers and sailors were killed or wounded at Zeebrugge but almost no Germans, and the port was reopened in less than a week. A friend and favourite of Winston Churchill, Keyes returned for World War II as a full-blown Admiral of the Fleet and a peer of the realm. In 1940 he became the first director of Combined Operations but his ideas were so wildly impractical that he was quietly pushed aside a year later. He died on Boxing Day in 1945.

Stoker Petty Officer Harry Kinder returned from Turkey to Australia in poor shape, suffering malaria and kidney damage, and left the navy in 1919 with the award of a Mention in Despatches. He became a small farmer and telegraph linesman in northern New South Wales. His diary is an invaluable record. He died on Anzac Day in 1965.

The failure at Gallipoli and a shortage of munitions for the army tainted **Lord Kitchener**'s reputation as Britain's omniscient warlord – not to the British people but privately with his political and military colleagues, who grew weary of his aloof and condescending manner. He despised many of them in return. For all his public prestige as war minister, he was largely ineffectual and sometimes simply a nuisance to the cabinet. In June 1916 he set out on a military and diplomatic mission to Russia, sailing from Scapa Flow, in the Orkney Islands, on board the cruiser HMS *Hampshire*. In dirty weather on the night of 5 June, *Hampshire* struck a mine laid by a German U-boat and sank in twenty minutes. Kitchener was one of the 737 men killed or drowned. His body was not recovered.

The British tracked down and arrested the sadistic and predatory Afion commandant **Maslum Bey** after the war. 'I watch the newspapers daily to see some notice that he has been hanged, but so far I have watched in vain,' wrote one ex-prisoner.[11] In the end he was set free; he was not tried for male rape because it was feared that victims who gave public evidence against him would be stigmatised for life.

Ambassador Henry Morgenthau, every inch a diplomat, principled and exemplary in his care for the Allied prisoners of war in Turkey, resigned as US Ambassador to Constantinople in 1916. The Armenian genocide had sickened him; as he wrote in his memoirs, 'I found intolerable my further daily association with men who, however gracious and accommodating and good-natured they might have been to the American Ambassador, were still reeking with the blood of nearly a million human beings.'[10] A friend and political ally of President Woodrow Wilson, he was a US envoy at the Paris Peace Conference in 1919. He died in 1946. The distinguished American historian Barbara Tuchman was his granddaughter.

Petty Officer Alex Nichols, cheerful and high-spirited despite his ill health, married an Englishwoman, Eva Bellinger, at Portsmouth while on leave in 1919, then returned to Australia and left the navy. He signed on again for World War II, mostly in shore jobs, and was in Darwin for the Japanese bombing in 1942. He died in 1970.

Stoker Charlie Suckling, embittered by the brutality he encountered as a prisoner, returned home to Western Australia in February 1919 and was discharged from the RAN that April. In civilian life, he opened a butcher's shop with his wife, Margaret, at Fremantle. He gradually lost his eyesight and became totally blind, a condition attributed to having been bashed on the head in prison. He was, though, *AE2*'s longest-living veteran, dying in 1983 at the age of ninety-two. His memoirs are a valuable document.

The life and times of *AE2* and her men are brilliantly illuminated in **Able Seaman John Wheat**'s diaries, which have been transcribed online by the State Library of New South Wales.[12] He lives on in their pages as an exemplary sailor: bold, loyal, resourceful, intelligent, thoughtful. The RAN held him until 1920, when he was discharged at his own request, and from then his image fades a little. At some stage he joined the British India Steam Navigation Company, based in Singapore and Bombay, and he rose to become a third officer in ships of the line. In 1924 he married an English nurse, Marie Hunstone, at St Andrews Cathedral in Singapore. They returned to Australia in the 1930s, where John took up life as an oyster farmer at Lake Conjola on the New South Wales South Coast. He died in 1953.

On a chilly autumn morning in 1918, the surviving U-boats of the German navy began sailing out of the North Sea and into internment at the port of Harwich, on England's south-east coast. It was Wednesday, 20 November, less than a fortnight after the armistice. There was a heavy fog at sea, and for a while the watchers on the British ships waiting to receive their beaten enemies feared they were not going to turn up at 10 a.m., as ordered. A little behind time, they gradually began to emerge from the gloom. An officer on board a destroyer recorded the moment:

> From the north, a long line of a hull with a dome-shaped conning-tower in the centre slid across the water. No boat built in a British yard ever looked like that – the Huns had come. She was

followed by five others in straggling order. One was a large new vessel (U.135) elaborately camouflaged and mounting a 6-inch gun forward. It is impossible to describe in words the feelings of the officers and men who witnessed this amazing sight.

Try and imagine what you would feel like if you were told to go to Piccadilly at 10 a.m. and see twenty man-eating tigers walk up from Hyde Park Corner and lie down in front of the Ritz to let you cut their tails off and put their leads on and it really was so. Add to these impressions the fact that many of those present had been hunting Fritz for over four years, in which period a man who could boast, 'I have seen six Fritzes and heard them four times on my hydrophones,' was accounted favoured by the gods, and you may get an insight into what British crews felt. More boats drifted out of the fog and anchored under the guns of the British destroyers . . .[13]

The Germans had built 375 submarines for the war, far more than any of the other belligerent navies. Nearly half were lost in action: sunk by mines, depth charges or surface gunfire, a grim total of 178. More than 5000 of their men were killed.

Yet they had been a fearsomely effective weapon. U-boats sank ten battleships, eighteen cruisers and a host of smaller warships, and more than 5000 merchant vessels from big ocean liners to fishing trawlers, for a total of well over 11 million tonnes. Some 15,000 merchant seaman were killed or drowned. The value of the cargoes lost is incalculable, pushing the British economy very close to breaking point. A German U-boat commander, Lothar von Arnauld de la Perière, became the most successful submarine captain of all time, sinking 189 merchant vessels and two small warships, a total of 453,876 tonnes.

The Royal Navy had a smaller submarine fleet for the war, 156 boats in all. But it, too, lost almost half – sixty of them.

These numbers were small when measured against the carnage on land. But in just five years the submarine had radically changed the nature and execution of war at sea. New strategies and tactics had emerged, both offensive and defensive. In five years the primitive boats of the turn of the century had been superseded by submarines of ever more sophisticated technology and potent, lethal menace.

The price had been high, and there would be more to pay. The submarine was here to stay. There would be no turning back.

10

FIRST TO THE PERISHER

The victors of 1918, governments and peoples, were bent on ensuring that there could never be another Great War. The losers were in no position to ensure anything. Disarmament became the goal of nations and statesmen, to be achieved by diplomacy and treaty and, hopefully, by goodwill.

It was easy to offer platitudes, harder to achieve the result. High-minded, altruistic and annoyingly didactic, President Woodrow Wilson had handed down his '14 Points' to end the war and establish the peace in a speech to a joint session of the US Congress in January 1918. These would form the basis of the peace negotiations, despite misgivings and at times outright opposition from Britain and France – the French premier, Georges Clemenceau, is said to have exclaimed, 'The good Lord had only ten!' – and, closer to home, from the Australian prime minister, Billy Hughes.

Point 2 called for 'Absolute freedom of navigation upon the seas, outside territorial waters, alike in peace and in war, except as the seas may be closed in whole or in part by international action for the enforcement of international covenants'. Point 4 sought 'Adequate guarantees given and taken that national armaments will be reduced to the lowest point consistent with domestic safety'.

The fourteen points were accepted only in part. Britain refused to agree to the clause on freedom of navigation, concerned that it might restrict the Royal Navy in the defence of the empire. Wilson's overarching hope of establishing a League of Nations to order the world was achieved, although, perversely, a stubborn

Republican majority in Congress refused to sign up and the United States did not join.

The size and shape of the world's big navies was a thorny problem. After long months of haggling, a conference of the five major naval powers in Washington in 1922 agreed to prevent another naval arms race by limiting the numbers of capital ships each country could build or maintain. Britain and the United States were permitted the biggest navies, of equal size in battleships and aircraft carriers. The Japanese agreed – very reluctantly – to limit their number of big ships to about two-thirds the size of the British and the Americans, and those of the French and Italians were smaller again.

Significantly, there was no limit placed on the number of submarines any nation might build. Acutely conscious of the havoc the U-boats had wrought in the war, Britain had argued for a total ban on submarines, in effect seeking to abolish them altogether and forever, but none of the other powers would accept this. Submarine design and construction continued apace, in leaps and bounds. The Germans, particularly, went at it with a will – and with secrecy and duplicity.

The Treaty of Versailles, which ended the war, had slashed what was left of the German navy to a skeleton. No longer the Imperial Navy (*Kaiserlichemarine*) – it was renamed the Realm Navy (*Reichsmarine*) – it was allowed no more than 15,000 men. There could be only six pre-dreadnought battleships, six light cruisers, twelve destroyers and twelve torpedo boats. Submarines were not permitted at all. Of the 172 U-boats surrendered at the end of the war, most were scuttled or broken up by the British and French. Seven were towed to Japan, where they were closely studied.

Humiliated and resentful, the residue of Germany's naval chiefs schemed to keep the U-boat dream alive. They had built the best, the most technologically advanced and unarguably the most successful submarines of World War I, and no matter what Versailles stipulated, they had no intention of the Fatherland losing that edge. They were urged on by what was left of the once mighty German shipbuilding companies and the industrialists who ran them.

So in 1922, the same year as the Washington Naval Conference, a new company was very quietly set up at the Hague, in Holland. It was, to all intents and purposes, a Dutch enterprise with a very Dutch name – the NV *Ingenieurskantoor voor Scheepsbouw* (the Engineer Office for Shipbuilding). In fact, it was funded by the German Navy and three shipbuilders: AG Vulcan at Hamburg, Germaniawerft in Kiel and AG Weser in Bremen. IvS, as the company became known, set about putting new U-boats on the drawing boards.

It was successful. After a slow start, it designed and sold submarines to Turkey, Finland and the Soviet Union, the boats constructed in European shipyards and each new one a technological advance upon the last. IvS's final three boats, built in Finland, would be the prototype for the German Type VII U-boat of World War II, the workhorse of Adolf Hitler's navy.

With the rise of the Nazis to power in 1933, both the secrecy and Germany's adherence to the Versailles treaty were abandoned, quietly at first and then flagrantly. IvS was wound up. In 1935 an Anglo-German naval agreement effectively allowed the Germans to begin building again, although to only 35 per cent of the total tonnage of the Royal Navy. The French, who were not included, nor even consulted, were furious. The Germans informed the British that they had laid down twelve U-boats at Kiel and that more would be built.

That same year, a German World War I submariner named Karl Dönitz was given command of the three operational boats of Submarine Flotilla 1, in the newly renamed War Navy (*Kriegsmarine*). Dönitz had no love for the British. In October 1918, a month before the armistice, the boat he was commanding, *UB-68*, was sunk by two British destroyers in the Mediterranean. He survived and was held as a prisoner of war at a camp near Sheffield until 1920, time he spent developing what would become known as his *Rudeltaktik*, the idea of a 'wolf pack' of U-boats gathering and homing in to attack a convoy.

As the 1930s wore on, U-boat construction gathered speed and purpose. When war began again in September 1939, Germany possessed sixty-five U-boats, twenty-one of them at sea ready and waiting. At over 800 tonnes, with a surface speed of seventeen knots and eight below, five torpedo tubes and an 8.8-centimetre quick-firing deck gun, the Type VII U-boat was by far the most advanced submarine of any navy. By 1945, no fewer than 703 of them would have slid down the slipways. To this day, it remains the largest class of submarines ever built. In due course, first as overall U-boat commander and then Commander-in-Chief of the *Kriegsmarine*, *Großadmiral* Dönitz would become the Royal Navy's most formidable opponent in World War II.

By the mid-1930s, naval disarmament was alive in name only. The maritime powers made another stab at it in 1936, with the Second London Naval Treaty, but it secured very little. Capital ships – that is, battleships and aircraft carriers – were to be no bigger than 35,000 imperial tons, with fourteen-inch guns the most allowed. Submarines were restricted to 2000 tons.

Ominously, Italy and then Japan refused to sign it. In 1937 the Japanese launched what they called Circle Three, their third major shipbuilding program, which included the giant battleships *Yamato* and *Musashi* – at an eye-watering 70,000 imperial tons, twice the London Treaty limit, they would be by far the biggest ever built. Then came modern aircraft carriers, destroyers and a fleet of cruiser submarines well over the 2000-ton London provision. Behind the so-called bamboo curtain, the Imperial Japanese Navy was preparing for war with what it saw as its most likely foe, the United States. They set to work on midget submarines, too, boats with a two-man crew and two torpedo tubes. By their entry into the war in 1941, they had more than sixty of them.

The Italians were playing their own game with submarines large and small, intended for use chiefly in the Mediterranean. Their big boats were odd, to say the least, in a confusing array of types and classes, many with outsized conning towers and even enclosed bridges with glassed windows, features that would make them relatively easy to detect on the surface, with often fatal results. They had the largest fleet of all at the start of the war, 116 of them all up, with eighty-four boats operational.

Italy's striking achievement underwater was the human torpedo. The Italian Navy, the *Regia Marina*, had used a primitive version in World War I, successfully penetrating the harbour at Pola to sink an Austro-Hungarian battleship. In the 1930s, two visionary naval engineers at the Naval Academy at Livorno, Teseo Tesei and Elios Toschi, revived the idea. They called it the *Siluro a lenta corsa*, the slow-running torpedo, although its operators would nickname it *Il Maiale*, or 'The Pig', because it was so tricky to pilot.

It was, in effect, a mini submarine in the shape of a torpedo, a little over seven metres long and crewed by two men riding upon its back like cowboys on horses. They wore flexible rubber suits especially designed by the Pirelli tyre company, and breathed with a primitive though effective scuba respirator developed by Italian recreational spearfishermen before the war and adapted for military use, again by Pirelli. The crews were volunteers chosen for their exceptional physiques, endurance and swimming prowess. These were the very first 'frogmen', *uomini rana* in Italian.

The idea was to penetrate enemy harbours or anchorages where surface ships or conventional submarines could not go. The Pig was launched from another vessel, generally a submarine; travelling at a depth of fifteen metres, propelled by an electric motor at the glacial speed of three knots at best, it had a range of about thirteen nautical miles. On its nose was a removable warhead, which would be attached to the bottom of a target ship and detonated by a timer that, in theory, gave the two crewmen time to get away.

The Italians set up a special unit to plan and run these operations, the *Decima Flottiglia Motoscafi Armati Siluranti*, usually shortened to *Decima MAS* or, in English, the Tenth Assault Vehicle Flotilla. It was the world's first dedicated naval commando unit, employing fast motorboats as well, and it set about its work boldly and efficiently. The results would be striking and far-reaching.

In Britain, even after the striking successes of underwater warfare, there was still a shellbacked crust of conservatives at the Admiralty and in the fleet who held that submarines were a piratical sideshow. Real naval battles were still conducted on the surface and always would be, they thought. Only surface ships could service and guard the British Empire, could hold dominion over palm and pine.

Wiser heads prevailed and Britain continued to design and build submarines within the treaty limits. Men continued to train for them. And quietly, in the background, beneath a heavy cloak of secrecy, a handful of Admiralty scientists began thinking about new technology to detect submarines underwater.

The first steps had been taken in 1915, when the Admiralty set up the Board of Invention and Research, which, happily, held its early meetings in the elegant comfort of the Metropole Hotel at Trafalgar Square. Its chairman was none other than Jacky Fisher. Scientists were recruited, and in 1916 two Canadian physicists, Robert Boyle and Albert Wood, began studying ways of finding hidden submarines. By mid-1917 they had come up with a prototype, which they demonstrated to the Admiralty's Anti-Submarine Division. It used what the boffins called quartz piezoelectric crystals to transmit waves of ultrasonic sound, which would strike a solid object and then bounce back to a listening operator on board a ship. It showed promise, but the war ended before it could be put to use at sea.

Work went on, and from 1918 a team of scientists continued to refine the thing in a laboratory at Portland, in England's West Country, despite a shortage of personnel and cuts to the budget. Over time, they came to call it Asdic. Historians have often written – wrongly – that the word was an acronym from the initials of an Allied Submarine Detection Investigation Committee, but no such body ever existed. In fact, the first three letters came from the Anti-Submarine Division, and *-ic* was stuck on the end as usefully opaque shorthand for the word ultrasonic, to preserve secrecy.

The first truly workable Asdic gear was installed and successfully tested in an ancient cruiser, HMS *Antrim*, in 1920 and put into production two years later. By 1923, the RN's 6th Destroyer Flotilla was equipped with this newfangled technology, and a year later an anti-submarine warfare training school, HMS *Osprey*, was set up at Portland.

Essentially, Asdic sent out its sound signals – *ping* . . . *ping* . . . *ping* – from a transmitter in a steel dome bolted to the bottom of a ship's hull. The transmitter could be rotated through an arc of forty-five degrees, to both port and starboard. When those pings struck a solid object they would bounce back as an echo to be heard by a listening operator. The course and distance – although not the depth – of a submarine could be estimated by the time it took for the echo to return.

There were refinements and improvements over time. Asdic could discover whales, schools of smaller fish and seabed rocks just as well as it could find submarines, and it took a well-trained operator to distinguish which was what. The soundwaves could also be affected by different layers of water temperature and even, at times, by a swift flowing underwater current.

But by 1939 Asdic sets were in full production and being installed in destroyers, corvettes and anti-submarine trawlers as fast as they could be built. Without Asdic, Britain would have lost the Battle of the Atlantic and World War II.

Despite the loss of *AE1* and then *AE2*, the RAN hoped to remain in the submarine business. With World War I still underway, the Australian government sought to buy or build replacement boats in Britain but was told that nothing could be done. The shipyards were at full capacity.

They tried again in 1919 and this time the Admiralty came to the party. They offered Australia a gift of six J-class submarines and an officer to command them – none other than Commander Edward Boyle VC, the hero of *E14* in the Dardanelles. After several false starts with mechanical breakdowns and some difficulty finding crews, they left Portsmouth for Sydney that April. Harry Showers, survivor of the Battle of May Island and now a sub-lieutenant, was one of the crew of *J3*. Five of his term mates from 1913 were in the other boats.

On paper at least, the J-class boats were a leap forward from the older E-class. They were built for speed. Early in the war, the Admiralty had an intelligence report that the Germans were building submarines capable of twenty-two knots on the surface, enough to keep company with the main battle fleet, and the J-class was designed to match them. In fact, there was no truth to the report, but that was not discovered until after the war. At more than 1600 tonnes submerged, the J-class were nearly twice the size of the E-class boats, with six torpedo tubes and a crew of five officers and forty men. Remarkably, they boasted three twelve-cylinder diesel engines, which could churn out a handsome nineteen knots on the surface and two electric motors good for nine knots submerged. The RAN was delighted to get hold of them. For a while, at least.

They were plagued with breakdowns and delays on the voyage out to Australia. A few days out from Portsmouth, *J5* struck and sank a French yacht sailing at night without lights. Later she broke down in the Red Sea and had to be towed the rest of the way to Sydney. One young Australian officer in *J2*, Sub-Lieutenant Frank Larkins, was lost overboard on the way out from Singapore in the Karimata Strait between Sumatra and Borneo. Like most of the crew, Larkins had been sleeping on the upper deck in the cool night air of 20 June, in a calm sea, but it seems a small wave washed him off. His absence was reported at dawn, and all six boats searched for him for the rest of the day, but neither he nor his bedding were found. That night they held a burial service in *J2*'s control room.

It was a cruel hit. Larkins was a kid of twenty from Melbourne, and another of the cadets from the pioneer year of the Naval College, where he had been a standout as the first cadet-captain and chief captain and a rugby star, a young man sure to go places. His term mate and close friend Frank Getting had been on the homeward journey in *J1*, and he wrote to the grieving Larkins family:

> Your son was our leader in everything. At college, as you know, he was our games leader and our senior captain, and one we always looked for wherever we were. I knew him probably better than anyone else in our term, and I cannot say I have met a finer and fairer fellow.[1]

The boats arrived in Sydney with their tender, HMAS *Platypus*, on 15 July, to a rapturous welcome on the harbour. Commander

Boyle – 'tall, clean-shaven, modest and approachable, just the type that has made the British naval officer loved in every land'[2] – assured a press conference that 'submarines will play a very important part in the defence of Australia ... If it is a question of pounds, shillings and pence than Australia can get better value both for defensive and offensive purposes from submarines than from larger ships.'[3]

The lovable Commander Boyle may have come to rue those words. The J-class submarines – the 'gift boats', as they were known – were not a success. Far from it. Their dismal performance on the way out would continue for all their time in service with the RAN. Things were not helped by indecision and bungling at the Australian end, either, with dockyards in Sydney and Melbourne simply unprepared for or unable to cope with the unending demand for maintenance and repairs. Breakdown followed breakdown, and in most cases machinery and spares had to be shipped out from Britain, causing long delays in getting boats back into service. It may well have been that that the Admiralty was quietly pleased to get rid of them.

Incompetence reared its ugly head from day one. When the submarines first arrived, they found there had been no proper shore accommodation arranged for their crews, a bungle that took the naval bureaucracy months to sort out. It got worse. In early 1930 the flotilla was sent to be based in Port Phillip Bay, at the old naval college building Osborne House, in North Geelong, but nobody had thought to check the depth of the water at the pier. Absurdly, it turned out to be too shallow for *Platypus* and her charges to go alongside, so they had to anchor or swing off buoys in the bay.

An exasperated Edward Boyle wrote to the Naval Board to request:

> [a]n adequate pier to prevent the massive wastage in the transporting by boat of two hundred and eighty-five men from submarines to base for every meal and to and from work; also to enable the submarine battery cells to be transported smoothly from workshop to submarine as they are easily cracked.[4]

In truth, in the years immediately after the war, the RAN was adrift and struggling for relevance, unsure what exactly it was supposed to do. The chief political figures of the day had little idea either, and less interest. The grandest figure in the Royal Navy, Admiral of the Fleet Lord Jellicoe, had been invited to Australia in the winter of 1919 to report on a future for the RAN, and after a three-month tour of inspection he produced a report in four mammoth volumes.

Presciently, Jellicoe put his finger directly on the White Australia policy and the most likely source of danger to it: the rising sun of Japanese expansion to the south.

> [T]here is always a strong possibility of future trouble so long as the present policy of the exclusion of Japanese from Australia continues . . .
>
> [A]ny foothold of Japan in an island of the Dutch East Indies possessing a good harbour would constitute the most serious threat to Australian sea communications to the westward, and to Singapore, and is not to be thought of.
>
> It is, therefore, almost inevitable that the interests of Japan and of the British Empire will eventually clash, and the two parts of the Empire most affected are Australia and India. For this reason the potential enemy in the Pacific is taken as Japan.[5]

He recommended the creation of a great Far Eastern Imperial Fleet, centred upon a new base at Singapore, to which Australia would contribute no fewer than two battlecruisers, one aircraft carrier, eight light cruisers, one destroyer flotilla leader, twelve destroyers and a depot ship for them, eight submarines with another depot ship, one minelayer, two minesweepers and a fleet repair ship. There would also need to be new bases dotted around Australia. It would cost a whopping £4,024,600, or one pound for every man, woman and child in the country. A liveable family wage at this time was around £200 a year.

This was almost in the realm of fantasy. Everyone agreed on the general frightfulness of the Japanese and the proposal for a fleet in Singapore, but that was it. There was no way Australia could afford such a navy, nor find the people to staff it. With all the talk of disarmament in the air and the Australian economy faltering, Jellicoe's report was quietly shelved and he went off to be governor-general of New Zealand. The government tightened the RAN's belt severely for the next few years, cutting millions. Ships were mothballed and officers and men were let go by fair means or foul, so that by 1924 the navy had lost more than a quarter of its people, many the best of them.

It became ever more obvious that the J-class boats were obsolete and a draining waste of time and money. In mid-1921, three of the submarines were laid up in reserve at the Flinders Naval Depot, resting and rusting on the mud there, their batteries removed. The other three were still working but so short-handed that there were often only two officers to take them to sea, the captain and first lieutenant. Over the next few years, they too were pensioned off.

The last to go was *J7*. She sat unloved and unmoving at Flinders until 1927, when she was stripped and sold to the Melbourne Harbour Trust, and was finally and ignominiously sunk as a breakwater near the Sandringham Yacht Club.

Yet the dream of an Australian submarine service flickered on, fitfully alive.

Frank Edmund Getting passed his 'Perisher' in 1926. Known first as the Royal Navy's Periscope School and then as the Commanding Officers Qualifying Course, the Perisher got its nickname because it was notoriously tough, a white-knuckle ride: you either passed or perished. There were no second chances. If you failed, you were quietly sent back to the surface fleet, never again to set foot in a submarine. The attrition rate could be as high as a third and more of the officers who made the attempt.

Frank was the first Australian to crack it, a notable feat for the young man from Manly, on Sydney's Northern Beaches. It had been quite a journey. His father, Paul, born in Paris, had emigrated from France for a new life in Australia, where he married a Sydney girl and worked first as a police officer and then as the superintendent of the Quarantine Station on the harbour at North Head. Living in the superintendent's cottage, Frank and his elder brother, George, had grown up with a panoramic view of the harbour and its smoky ferries bustling back and forth from the city, the merchant steamers and warships coming and going, and the salt sea itself. 'Seven miles from Sydney and a thousand miles from care' was the slogan on the tourist ferries.

It was almost ordained that he would be accepted into the first year of the Naval College. Nuggetty and muscular, he made a name as a rugby forward, a rower and a boxer in an era when sporting prowess was seen as essential for the making of a good officer. During his wartime British training as a midshipman in the battlecruiser HMS *Glorious*, he had won the fleet light heavyweight championship in 1917 with a first-round technical knockout, the bout held on the quarterdeck of the battleship *Ajax* before a cheering audience that included the commander-in-chief himself, Admiral Sir David Beatty. The thrill of that win soured when Frank heard the news that his brother, serving in the army with the 5th Field Ambulance, had died of his wounds during the Battle of Passchendaele.

Frank had chosen submarines for his career path, the only man in his college term to do so, and in 1919 he was back in Britain for a course at the Torpedo School, HMS *Vernon* at Portsmouth, where he topped his class of forty-six, a knock-'em-dead achievement for an Australian. After time back home he returned to Britain in 1924 for two years as first lieutenant in two RN submarines and then, in 1926, he was selected to do the Perisher course, a mark of his superiors' confidence in him.

The Perisher was a very different beast to a boxing match. Located at the naval base at Devonport, in the west of England, it had been going since 1917, when the RN realised it needed something rather more concrete than submarine captains willy-nilly passing on their knowledge to their junior officers. Five or six aspiring young lieutenants would attend each course for a gruelling ordeal of theory and practice, four months of it.

There they would be introduced to the arcane mysteries of the 'Is-Was', an invention of the Dardanelles VC winner Martin Nasmith and whimsically so named because it told you where you Is and where you Was when you were lining up a torpedo shot.

In effect a circular slide rule hooked up to a Sperry compass repeater, it computed the mathematics of distance, courses, speeds and bearing of both moving submarine and moving target to produce the deflection angle you needed to send your torpedo where you wanted it. The thing was not foolproof, but when you mastered its use it was a giant advance on the fingers-crossed guesswork of the early days.

At Devonport, too, was the newly invented Submarine Attack Teacher, a plotting table partly electric, partly clockwork, installed in the library. Trained sailors would move little model target ships while the student peered through a periscope – 'dancing with the grey lady', they sometimes called it – and gave his helm and speed orders. It was a fine blend of science and art. The instructor, always an experienced captain, was known as 'Teacher'.

The final, nail-biting test began when you had come through the stuff ashore to take actual command of a boat at sea for a month – an exercise nicknamed 'the Cockfight' – with Teacher watching like a hawk as he threw all manner of problems, alarms, emergencies and unspeakable horrors at you. This was so arduous, so demanding, that one bad mistake might be enough to fail you even on the final day. In which case you were politely sent packing with what became the tradition of a farewell bottle of whisky. Those who passed were invited to champagne in the wardroom.

Lieutenant Getting RAN made it to the champagne celebration. His commanding officer, Commander Colin Cantlie, noted on his record that he was 'a keen and capable officer who has taken great interest in the course and has carried out good attacks. He has plenty of self confidence and initiative and has a good power of command. He should make a good and reliable Commanding Officer of a submarine.'[6]

Frank's first command, that joyous event in an officer's life, arrived in short order, the RN submarine *H29*. He drove her for only a few months, for the navy had other things in store. In February 1927, he and another young Australian officer, Lieutenant Norman Shaw, were on the night train from London to Barrow-in-Furness. Shaw had done the Perisher on the same course as Getting. At Vickers Armstrong, they would stand by the build of two new submarines for the Royal Australian Navy, with Getting to be first lieutenant of HMAS *Oxley* and Shaw to be first lieutenant of HMAS *Otway*.

These were the first two Australian boats to carry a name, not a number. One honoured the nineteenth-century explorer and former naval officer John Oxley, the man who found the site for Brisbane; the other for Cape Otway, in southern Victoria.

Portsmouth turned on a miserable day for *Oxley* and *Otway*'s departure for Australia, cold and rainy, with a sharp breeze and a heaving sea out in the English Channel. It was Wednesday, 8 February 1928. The voyage would be south into the Mediterranean, through the Suez Canal into the Indian Ocean, and on to Singapore and Batavia, the same as that taken by *AE1* and *AE2* back in 1913. This time, though, there would be no accompanying cruiser to shepherd them. *Oxley* and *Otway* would be on their own. There would be no diving, surface travel only. If all went to plan, they would meet their tender ship, HMAS *Platypus*, at Thursday Island on Anzac Day, 25 April.

That should be no problem. These new Oberon-class boats (the first to be given a name, not a letter) were the latest thing, the first post-war British design, a grand new long-range type to be known as Overseas Patrol Submarines, chalk and cheese from the old A-class. At over 1600 tonnes submerged, they were almost three times bigger than the As. With a crew of fifty-three – including five officers – and two Admiralty-designed six-cylinder diesels, they could notch up fifteen knots on the surface. Batteries gave them nine knots below. They boasted eight 21-inch torpedo tubes, six in the bow and two in the stern and, remarkably, a four-inch gun in a mounting forward of the conning tower, a gun big enough for a destroyer. More remarkable still, they were the first boats to carry Asdic.

Oxley and *Otway* were the RAN's latest attempt to get back into the submarine business after the dismal experience of the J-class boats. They had cost a handsome £716,340 for the pair.[7] The Portsmouth farewell began with visits and florid speeches from the Australian high commissioner, Major General Sir Granville Ryrie, and the Australian press and radio baron Sir Hugh Denison, who presented two silken White Ensigns as a publicity stunt for his Sydney *Sun* newspaper. The officers dined in the Blockhouse mess with the chief of the Submarine Service, Rear Admiral Henry Grace – a son of the legendary cricketer Dr W. G. Grace – in the gilded presence of the Commander-in-Chief Portsmouth, Admiral Sir Osmond de Beauvoir Brock, who had led the 1st Battlecruiser Squadron at Jutland. More speeches.

There were very likely some hangovers the next day. *Otway* was the first to slip, shortly after noon, followed five minutes later by *Oxley*, their crews out on the casing for'ard to return the cheers of RN bluejackets lining the Blockhouse shore. Sleek and purposeful, they glided out to sea with that aura of latent menace that submarines have. The depot band played 'Waltzing Matilda' and 'Auld Lang Syne' and a small ferry followed astern, thoughtfully provided by Admiral Brock to carry wives, families and friends out into the channel to wave a final goodbye. At least one man had seen it all before: the veteran Cecil Bray, torpedo gunner's mate of *AE2* and survivor of the Turkish prisoner-of-war camps, still in the RAN, was now a chief petty officer and coxswain of *Oxley*.

Frank Getting and the other Australian first lieutenant, Norm Shaw, might have had cause to feel hard done by on this day. Both had passed their Perisher, both had commanded H-class submarines for the RN, both had reason to hope they would captain these new RAN boats, yet here they were relegated to supporting roles. The Admiralty had decreed that more experienced men were needed and the RAN had agreed, and so both captains were RN officers. The senior of them was a fully fledged commander, Hugh Marrack, who had once run the old Periscope School at Devonport. Getting and Shaw were quietly assured that their time would come – Getting first, as he was a year senior to Shaw – and they submitted with good grace.

Spithead and the Isle of Wight slowly disappeared off the starboard quarter and the boats were on their own early in the afternoon and heading for the Bay of Biscay, where strong headwinds and lumpy seas kept them down to a dogged eight knots.

They arrived at Gibraltar late on the evening of 13 February and sailed again the next day, east through the Mediterranean.

Trouble struck two days from the next port of call, the fortress island of Malta. *Otway*'s warrant engineer, Alec Nairn, discovered a fracture in an engine column – not a fatal problem but certainly worrying. Nairn, a Melbourne man, was an experienced hand who knew his business. He and his artificers ran a heavy leather strap around the crack to hold it together, just in case, and the defect was reported to Commander Marrack in *Oxley*.

From there the matter snowballed. The engineers in both boats made a thorough inspection and, to some consternation, discovered that their engine columns – the heavy castings that held the engines together – were riddled with fractures, dozens of them. If one or more were to split apart, the engine could well erupt in pieces, causing untold internal damage and probably disabling the boat. Gingerly, with some of the cracks spreading and new ones appearing, they limped into Malta's Grand Harbour on 19 February, berthing alongside the depot ship HMS *Cyclops*.

Vickers, the builder, sent out engineers, as did the Admiralty, and after much haggling it was decided the engines would have to be completely stripped and rebuilt, from the ground up. This provoked a row between Vickers and the Australian government, with the company claiming it was all the fault of the submarine captains, who had driven the boats too hard at high revolutions. That excuse was scotched when identical serious fractures were discovered in a sister boat back in Britain, HMS *Oberon*.

At first the RAN and the Australian government deviously tried to portray this shambles as a 'mishap', but as the repairs dragged on and on, month after month, the truth emerged. The engine design and the Vickers build had been badly flawed, to the edge of incompetence. Both submarines were formally decommissioned and placed in reserve, with their stores and ammunition removed and the crews billeted ashore or sent home. The two British commanding officers went back to the UK, and so it was that Frank Getting, newly promoted to lieutenant commander, was appointed captain of *Oxley*. It was a signal moment: he was the first Australian to command an Australian submarine.

They finally left Malta that November, with more relatively minor though aggravating engine troubles, sickness in the crews and, worrying, a breakdown in discipline and sailors deserting at ports along the way. An able seaman was charged with attempting to punch an officer in Colombo, and five men jumped ship in Singapore. It was hardly fair but equally unsurprising that cold, driving rain and a miserable southerly gale met them when they arrived in Sydney on the evening of 4 February 1929, unwelcomed and unloved, more than a year after they had sailed from Portsmouth.

The sad truth was that nothing much improved. After yet another refit, in June that year both *Oxley* and *Otway* began working around Jervis Bay, on the South Coast of New South Wales, and later there were exercises with the new fleet flagship, the cruiser *Australia*. But the end was near. With the Great Depression looming, the Labor government of James Scullin first put both boats into mothballs and then decided to be rid of them altogether. In April 1931 they were offered as a gift to the Royal Navy, and sent back to Britain. It was over. There would be no submarine service in the RAN for another thirty-five years, long after World War II.

Frank Getting would spend the rest of his career on the surface, with a spell ashore. In June 1942, as a four-ringed captain, he took command of the heavy cruiser *Canberra*, a sister ship to *Australia*. He was in her at the fateful Battle of Savo Island, in the Solomon Islands, that August, an Allied disaster in which, by night, a Japanese force surprised and comprehensively defeated an American and Australian force of cruisers and destroyers. Four heavy cruisers were lost, including *Canberra*, and more than 1000 men died, including Captain Getting.

He was on the bridge when a line of Japanese cruisers poured shell after shell into the ship. Hit by shrapnel, he fell to the deck badly wounded, bleeding profusely from a shattered leg, but he told the ship's doctor to attend to other wounded men before him. Able Seaman Patrick Mackintosh was nearby, and told a reporter:

> I saw Captain Getting badly wounded, sitting bent up on a stool, directing the Chief Telegraphist what to do. The commander,

Commander John Walsh, was with him and was wounded in the face.

The doctors wanted to get Captain Getting down below to apply first aid to him, but he would not leave his post on the bridge. Commander Walsh stayed there with him.

At last they carried the captain down, protesting. They could see he was in a bad way.[8]

In the chaos of the night, *Canberra* was almost certainly torpedoed by an American destroyer whose captain panicked. A burning wreck, she was abandoned the next day, and the American admiral ordered her to be torpedoed and sunk.

Eighty-four Australian sailors were lost at Savo. Frank Getting died of his wounds on board an American attack transport and was buried at sea.

His widow, Hazel, spoke to the newspapers at the flat they had shared at Potts Point in Sydney. 'I am proud of Frank,' she said. 'He loved the sea, he loved his ship and he was willing, if needs be, to give his all for his country. He would not have wished to go in any other way.'[9]

11

LIFEBOAT NUMBER SEVEN

Victoria's Western District is rich pastoral country, some of Australia's finest. Ian McIntosh, born in 1919, grew up there on his family's property, Meningoort, near Camperdown, south-west of Melbourne, on land pioneered by forebears who had emigrated to Australia as free settlers in the great Scottish diaspora of the nineteenth century.

Unusually for a country boy, he developed an early interest in ships and the sea, building rafts and a canoe to paddle on the property's dams during holidays from his boarding school, Geelong Grammar. He devoured whatever books and stories of seafaring he could get his hands on. One favourite was Lieutenant William Bligh's journal of the fabled mutiny on HMS *Bounty*, with its absorbing account of his epic, 6500-kilometre journey in an open boat across the Pacific to the Portuguese island of Timor. Ian built a model of *Bounty* in tribute.

The navy beckoned. His parents put their foot down at the idea of him applying for the naval college at the tender age of thirteen but it was a losing battle. At eighteen, when he left school, he sat a famously rigorous exam for a rare Commonwealth scholarship as a cadet midshipman in the Royal Navy, and to everyone's surprise – including his own – he passed. In late 1937, Ian McIntosh packed his bags, said his farewells, and took a ship to Britain.

This was a dive into the deep end. British cadets his age had already done four years at the Royal Naval College at Dartmouth. He and a handful of other Commonwealth entrants were ensconced in an old monitor at Portsmouth, HMS *Erebus*, where they were given a three-month crash course to catch up on boatwork, seamanship, navigation, gunnery, engineering and much more, including instruction in the arcane qualities and knowledge required of a naval officer and gentleman. Then came time at sea in a training cruiser, HMS *Vindictive*, and a personal triumph when he carried off the King's Dirk, the prize for best all-round cadet. No Australian had done that before.

When war broke out, McIntosh was at the Egyptian port of Alexandria in the heavy cruiser HMS *Sussex* with the Mediterranean fleet, still a midshipman. The first wartime order he received was quaintly Nelsonian: to sharpen his cutlass in case he had to lead a boarding party.

Britain's declaration of war on Germany was but hours old when the first shots were fired. They were torpedoes. The British transatlantic liner SS *Athenia*, on passage from Glasgow to Montreal, had been stalked for three hours by the submarine *U-30*, commanded by *Oberleutnant* Fritz-Julius Lemp. At 7.40 p.m., in the early dark of Sunday, 3 September 1939, in the cold waters some 370 kilometres north-west of Northern Ireland, Lemp fired two torpedoes from his bow tubes at virtually point-blank range, and then a third. Two missed. One struck on the liner's port side and exploded in her engine room, setting her sinking slowly by the stern.

Athenia was carrying 1103 passengers, nearly half of them Jewish refugees, plus Canadians, Americans, seventy-two Britons, and a crew of 315. She took fourteen hours to go down. Her boats were lowered and nearby vessels came to the rescue, but 117 people were killed, passengers and crew, either by the initial explosion or in the chaos of taking to the boats in the dark. Twenty-eight of the dead were American citizens. After inspecting his handiwork, Lemp took *U-30* away into the night.

But if he thought he had scored a coup for his *führer*, he was mistaken. Hitler was annoyed. Anxious to keep the United States out of the war, he did not need the death of American civilians to provoke outrage in Washington, as it had done when the liner

RMS *Lusitania* was sunk by a U-boat in 1915, with 128 Americans killed. Berlin heard about the sinking first from British radio, the BBC.

When Lemp returned to Wilhelmshaven, he claimed to have thought *Athenia* was an armed merchant cruiser and thus a legitimate target, but he was hauled over the coals by the submarine chief, Karl Dönitz, and sent in disgrace to Berlin to explain himself. Dönitz ordered the U-boat's war diary to be falsified, and the crew was sworn to secrecy. The propaganda chief, that poison dwarf Joseph Goebbels, concocted a story for the *Völkischer Beobachter*, the Nazi Party's newspaper, claiming *Athenia* had been sunk on the orders of Winston Churchill, to turn world opinion against Germany. The full truth would not emerge until Dönitz was tried for war crimes at Nuremberg in 1946.

The Battle of the Atlantic had begun, the longest, most bloody, most costly campaign of the entire war. Winston Churchill, back for the second time as First Lord of the Admiralty, foresaw the nature of the conflict, the course it would take, telling the House of Commons in his inimitable manner:

> Such is the U-boat war – hard, widespread and bitter, a war of groping and drowning, a war of ambuscade and stratagem, a war of science and seamanship. All the more must we all respect the resolute spirit of the officers and men of the Mercantile Marine who put to sea with alacrity, sure that they are discharging a duty indispensable to the life of their island home.[1]

It would last until the final hours of the day of Germany's surrender, when *U-320* scuttled herself off Norway after being depth-charged by an RAF Catalina flying boat on 8 May 1945.

Britain's very existence had been at stake, and she came very close to losing it. Churchill would write, when it was over, that 'the only thing that ever really frightened me during the war was the U-boat peril'.[2]

Ian McIntosh passed his sub-lieutenant's courses with firsts in all six subjects, heard that the navy was calling for volunteers for submarines and put his hand up.

I suppose initially I didn't know very much about them, other than the people I'd met who were in them. But once you got into them they were simply magnificent things, because they had a perfectly fascinating technical type thing: you became unconsciously much more engineering-minded than the general run of officers in the surface fleet. Secondly, you all lived very, very close together. You knew each other very well indeed. And thirdly you got responsibility very young . . . so it all built up together to be a very attractive thing to be in.[3]

He was accepted, sent to a quick training course at Blockhouse – five short weeks – and was posted out to Alexandria to become that lowest form of submarine officer life, a spare fourth hand in the squadron there. After a month's leave he joined a ship to carry him south.

The SS *Britannia*, 7900 tonnes, a comfortable steamer of the Anchor Line, sailed from Liverpool on 11 March 1941, in convoy with four other liners, down the Mersey and out into the Western Approaches. At the Mersey Bar Light Vessel, an escort of three destroyers took station, one in the van, the other two out to port and starboard, with an armed merchant cruiser bringing up the rear, all at a reasonable clip of around fifteen knots.[4] *Britannia* would avoid the Mediterranean and take the long route south down the Atlantic and east around the Cape of Good Hope, then north up to Bombay. Ian would find another ship there to get him through the Suez Canal to Alexandria. Most of the 327 'passengers' were servicemen and a handful of women posted abroad, with a leavening of Indians travelling home third-class. *Britannia*'s sole weapon was an ancient four-inch gun – unpromisingly dated 1906 – mounted on the poop deck astern and manned by a party of navy sailors.

The first two weeks were a delight, idyllic. The junior naval officers organised extra lookouts for watches on the bridge, but Ian had plenty of time for the luxury of reading and writing letters, playing his collection of records on his portable gramophone and indulging his new hobby of teaching himself Italian. But for the screening destroyers and the occasional RAF Coastal Command Sunderland patrolling overhead, it might have been a holiday cruise.

After ten days, north of the equator off the coast of West Africa, the escort left them and the convoy dispersed to sail on independently. The idyll was about to end, as McIntosh would describe in a letter to his mother:

> [O]n the 25th of March at 8 o'clock, just as I was getting up to the bridge to go on watch before breakfast, the alarms went and a couple of shells landed. Being on the top part of the bridge I had a grandstand view of the proceedings. We were being attacked by a German armed merchant cruiser which was lobbing pairs of shells at us – in proper Whale Island[5] language she was firing two-gun salvos – and doing it pretty accurately as usually one landed either side of us. It was interesting to watch. We ran for it, making smoke, but she was faster than we, and it was only a matter of time, for one 4-inch gun is not much good against what she had.[6]

Kapitän zur See Otto Kähler knew his business. He had been a U-boat man in World War I and now, at the age of forty-five, he was making his mark as the captain of *Hilfskreuzer IV* (Auxiliary Cruiser IV), a 4000-tonne freighter, modern and fast, converted into a commerce raider with a crew of 350. Concealed beneath her innocuous mercantile exterior were six six-inch guns, four anti-aircraft guns, assorted machine guns and four 21-inch torpedo tubes, plus a little *Arado* float plane for scouting over the horizon. She was also known as *Thor*, after the Germanic god of storms, thunder and lightning.

The name was apt. After a rigorous workup, Kähler had taken her to sea from a Norwegian fjord in June 1940, evading the British blockade and vanishing into the vastness of the Atlantic to prey on Allied shipping wherever he might find it. In eight months *Thor* wreaked havoc, capturing and sinking eight freighters – British, Belgian, Dutch and Greek – and coming off best in two encounters with British armed merchant cruisers: he damaged one, while the other, also hard hit, turned and fled. Observing the laws of war, Kähler humanely allowed the crews of his victims time to abandon ship and took most of them on board, his holds full of prisoners. Supply vessels met him at prearranged positions to replenish his fuel, ammunition, food and stores.

When *Thor* found *Britannia*, to the west of Freetown, on the coast of Sierra Leone, the gun crews, drilled to perfection, went about their task with clinical accuracy. Their shells quickly hit home. The liner's master, Alexander Collie, ordered full speed and made smoke but soon there were fires out of control on the upper deck and the wireless aerials were brought down. The four-inch gun on the stern got away a couple of rounds, to no effect, before it was blown to pieces by an incoming six-inch shell and its crew killed or wounded.

Amid the chaos, the ear-splitting explosions, the mounting destruction, the cries of the bloodied wounded and the rising panic of some of the passengers, Ian McIntosh helped rig a makeshift wireless aerial and *Britannia* sent out an SOS – her position, with 'RRR' in Morse code to report a raider, followed by 'QQQ' to indicate an unknown surface vessel.

After that, there was nothing more to be done. At 9.20 a.m. Captain Collie struck his colours and gave the order to abandon ship. When the Union Jack came down, Otto Kähler held his fire to allow the lifeboats to be lowered. Slipping into his uniform jacket with its single sub-lieutenant's stripe and jamming his cap on his head, Ian threaded his way to his lifeboat, Number Seven, aft on the starboard quarter. The crowd there was a desperate, milling knot of fear, some passengers clutching their life's belongings in bags and bundles. The throng swelled because the opposite boat, Number Eight, had been smashed by gunfire. A couple of other boats were hanging crookedly by the falls, apparently jammed.

With difficulty, *Britannia*'s third mate and a shipwright managed to lower Number Seven. Ian McIntosh could see trouble brewing:

> I got into the boat fairly early on because it was right by the counter and there was a fairly choppy sea . . . the boat had to be borne away so it didn't smash underneath the counter, and I got people stacked in and so on, and eventually we got the last of them off the remains of the poop and I managed to shove off.[7]

I got four oars out and got some of the people to try rowing. I got bailing because there turned out to be quite a number of shrapnel holes through the boat, a wooden one. One of the Sikh passengers – he appeared to be the head man – I gave him a bailer and told him to get bailing, to get the water out. He looked at me in blank astonishment and said 'oh, but sir, we are passengers.'

I did use some fairly strong sailor's language and he bailed quite quickly after that.[8]

When Otto Kähler judged that *Britannia* had been properly abandoned, he opened fire again, pumping shells into her waterline to send her plunging down by the bow, her stern rearing. Like a wounded animal in pain, she gave a final blast on her siren as the surging sea closed over her in a great bubble and swirl. This time Kähler did not rescue survivors. His radio operators had picked up what they took to be a nearby British warship responding to the distress calls, which he had no wish to encounter, so *Thor* vanished swiftly below the horizon. It was all over well before midday.[9]

Ian McIntosh struggled to ship the heavy wooden rudder, helped by a *Britannia* sailor, and with men heaving and grunting haphazardly at the oars, the lifeboat wallowed clear. The sea was strewn with the dismal wrack of a lost ship: a detritus of corpses, makeshift rafts, empty lifebelts, a large patch of filthy, burning oil and two or three other distant lifeboats.

Time to take stock. First, a head count. There were eighty-two people – all male – crowded aboard Lifeboat Number Seven. This made it perilously overcrowded, for it was licensed to take only fifty-six. There were nineteen Europeans, service and civilian. Some of the sailors and officers, new members of the Royal Navy Volunteer Reserve, or RNVR, had literally never been to sea before. Of the others, twenty-four were paying passengers, Indian Sikhs or Goanese, and thirty-nine were Lascars, as Indian or Asian seamen were then called. Jammed together cheek by jowl, shoulder and thigh, packed like tinned sardines, they were barely able to move.

The boat itself was a lump of a thing, a typical ship's lifeboat, clinker-built (meaning the hull constructed of overlapping timber planking), open to the elements, about nine metres long and three metres in the beam. There was no engine. Technically known as a dipping lug cutter, the boat had a mast that had to be stepped or erected for'ard, to bear a small triangular foresail and a larger, four-sided mainsail. The shrapnel from *Thor*'s shells had slashed four holes in the hull, which they plugged with rags, but the water kept entering and the bailing barely kept pace.

Ian McIntosh had taken command instinctively because he knew what needed to be done – all that messing about in boats at the Naval College – but he was not the senior man. That dubious honour belonged to Frank West, an RNVR lieutenant in his late thirties. He was no sailor, though, but a firefighting expert on posting to a Fleet Air Arm station in Egypt. Thankfully, he knew it and had the good sense to defer to the Australian sub-lieutenant in matters of seamanship and much else, and the two would strike up an amicable and effective working partnership. West later described McIntosh in glowing terms:

> [W]ell over six feet tall, lithe and muscular, he had in abundance the ebullience and energy usually found in officers of his rank. Beneath his dark, straight hair, with its unruly forelock falling over a high forehead, his youthful eyes and features were already developing like those of a man used to responsibility and command. A ready smile and a twinkle in the eyes was never far distant, and he certainly had the ability to get enjoyment from life. Under this, but very near the surface, was a quiet seriousness of purpose for whatever was in hand, an already deep knowledge of the sea, and ability to get things done.[10]

Bill McVicar, *Britannia*'s third mate, a sturdy Glasgow Scot aged twenty-seven, was a more than competent seaman but had little experience in small boats. Lieutenant Frank Lyons, an RNR officer in his forties, was a retired merchant mariner. Before the war, David Purdie had been a travelling salesman for the Lea & Perrin sauce people, qualification enough for the navy to turn him into an RNVR supply assistant. Aged twenty-four, this was his first time at sea, but he would prove invaluable in the days to come.

McIntosh stayed at the helm while McVicar and Purdie shoved their way through the throng of Indians to step the mast and hoist the foresail with stays and halliards that seemed ominously decayed and fragile. West looked for provisions and found:

> Two barricoes of fresh water each holding about six gallons, 48 tins of Nestlé condensed milk and two bins of ship's biscuits . . . we had a conference to decide what rations should be issued and decided to give a third of a dipper of water each per day, at sundown, with one biscuit each. The milk is to be issued at the rate of two tins per day, one at sunrise and one to be spread on the biscuits at sundown. Each tin to be equally divided between the number in the boat . . .[11]

For a while they could see a couple of other lifeboats, but they slowly drifted apart. West arranged the people into three groups, the Lascars in the bow, the Indian paying passengers amidships and the Europeans in the stern. Many were seasick and vomiting, others shat themselves or pissed, all where they sat, for they could not move. The tropical night came quickly, the bailing kept going, organised in shifts, and Ian McIntosh remained at the helm until dawn the next day. In the pinkish light, slowly brightening, they found the other lifeboats gone and themselves alone on a sea still littered with wreckage.

The urgent need now was to fix the shrapnel holes, for the rags they had stuffed there yesterday were failing. McIntosh knew they needed 'tingles', an old sailor's word for a patch in a boat's hull. His solution was an ingenious triumph of invention in adversity. Using scissors from a first-aid box, they cut squares of cloth from a thick blanket and more square patches from an empty tin of condensed milk – the tingles – and they prised nails from a wooden box that held the condensed milk. McIntosh had the sails lowered to stop the boat and got to work:

> Two were in the bows, near the keel, each about two inches by an inch. I fought my way for'ard and then scrambled down to the

forepeak, and caulked them with a bandage until only a trickle came through. The atmosphere in the bottom of the boat was perfectly foul, the Indians having relieved themselves and been sick freely all night (a hard habit to break!) and as soon as I had done the job I was promptly sick, although I did not feel ill. Then I came aft and hearing the noise of running water found another hole, which the buoyancy tank made it impossible to reach from the inside. There was nothing to do but to repair it from the outside.[12]

Stripping off his shirt and jacket, and with David Purdie gripping his legs, McIntosh hung over the gunwales upside down in the sea, submerged to his ribcage as first he stuffed the hole with some cloth and then hammered the tingle in place with the nails and the hatchet, struggling to the surface every so often to gasp for air. He repeated the process for a couple more holes they found. It was a prodigious feat for these two young men and it worked. The boat still had to be bailed but only sporadically now, and they could ride more easily. The question now being: where to?

McIntosh had pondered this through his long watch at the tiller that first terrible night. Alone with the mantle of stars, the slap of the sea and the grunts and snores and occasional wails of his fitfully sleeping companions, he had put his mind to the future. McVicar knew the ship's position where she was sunk, the exact latitude and longitude. They were nearly 1000 kilometres west of Freetown, about eight degrees north of the equator. The natural thing to do – the obvious thing – would be to head eastwards for the African coast. Yet in his trained seaman's mind, McIntosh knew that the prevailing winds in this part of the world were the nor'east trades, blowing from exactly the wrong direction: the direction they would have to take for Africa. It would mean beating to windward – that is, sailing as close as possible to the direction the wind is coming from, by tacking a boat this way and that – a challenge even for an experienced sailor.

Making things more difficult still, McIntosh had found that the boat – horribly unwieldy – had an infuriating tendency to 'luff up', turning itself towards the wind and then lurching to a stop, the sails flapping uselessly. A competent hand at the helm could avoid that, but not this motley crew of novices and lubbers, and it had already happened a lot, particularly with Lyons at the tiller, however hard he tried. Each time, McIntosh, McVicar and Purdie had to go for'ard into the bow with an oar to heave and wrench the boat back on course again, an exhausting business.

The alternative was to head south-west across the Atlantic towards Brazil, with the wind behind them. Yet that would be a journey of around 2500 kilometres, more than twice the distance. Knowing the length of the lifeboat, McIntosh, McVicar and Lyons had estimated their speed through the water by dropping pieces of kapok from lifebelts over the bow and timing how long it took for them to pass astern. They figured they were making about four knots, give or take. In theory, if the trade wind held and if the weather and sea stayed fair, they could make Brazil in three weeks or so. Those were big ifs. And then there were the doldrums, that shifting zone around the equator, infamous for mariners, where the winds can die to nothing and sailing vessels might lie becalmed for days or even weeks. Ian weighed these risks and concluded that still it would be better to head for Brazil than to battle into the wind towards Africa. Heading south-west would also take them across regular shipping lanes, where they might be seen and rescued.

That morning, hunched in the stern sheets, the officers held a conference, with Frank West as the senior. Lyons had experience on the Brazilian coast and he backed McIntosh's view. So did McVicar. They prevailed. Brazil it would be. To make sure, for a margin of safety they would ration the drinking water, the condensed milk and ship's biscuit to last a month. And perhaps they might catch some fish.

Navigation was the next challenge. There were no charts and there was no sextant to shoot the sun at midday to obtain their position. A search produced a boat compass, which had no light and was therefore useless at night, but a passenger had a prismatic compass with a luminous dial, which did the trick. With that, and steering by the sun and stars and the feel of the wind, Ian reckoned he could keep a course west-south-west. It was the best he could do.

With both sails hoisted again, they got underway. They had barely started when one of the Indians cried out that he could see a ship.

> There was great excitement, but since it was about eight miles away I had not very high hopes. However, we did everything we could – lit a couple of flares, burned rags soaked in oil on the end of our oar, hoisted a length of blue turban at the head of the foresail, flashed with a mirror and the sun, but as I expected, it was fruitless. Everyone was most disappointed and some of the more foolish even began to accuse the ship of ignoring us after sighting us, or complained at the bad lookout they were keeping... hardly any of them had ever been to sea before and their months in the Navy would not fill one hand.[13]

A routine of sorts settled upon them, with McIntosh, McVicar, Lyons, Purdie and another man named Westgarth taking turns at the helm. Westgarth was RN, a commissioned torpedo gunner who had left his assigned lifeboat at the sinking and clambered into Lifeboat Seven despite being told it was full. Truculent and constantly complaining about his lot, he came to be despised by the rest of the Europeans, who called him 'the Rat'.

By day the sun was baking, burning, with a blinding glare from the surface of the sea, and faces and arms began to redden and blister, which made them long for the cool relief of the tropical twilight. The nights, though, were cold and they huddled together for warmth until dawn began the bitter cycle again. Frank West supervised the distribution of the rations in scrupulous detail: for each man a daily sip of water from a dipper, a smear of condensed milk in the morning and one of the hard tack ship's biscuits, which became an increasing struggle to chew and swallow as their saliva dried up. Some of the Indians began drinking sea water, despite being cautioned against it. They threw out fishing lines to trail behind the boat, with no bait but improvised spinners. There were plenty of fish to be seen at times, sometimes whole schools of them dashing and darting nearby, but not one ever fell for a hook.

The weather was fine for the first few days, with the trade wind constant and the sea benign. McVicar and Lyons sketched a rough chart on a sheet of paper offered by one of the Indian passengers and they marked their progress each day, reckoning that they were covering about 145 kilometres from noon one day to noon the next, about the speed they had estimated. On the third day they sighted another ship in the distance but again could not attract its attention. On the fourth night they saw the white masthead lights of a ship steaming away from them, an aching disappointment.

Adding to their despair, the sails and rigging kept failing. The rotten ropes were fraying under the strain and every so often one would break, bringing down a sail or, a couple of times, the mast itself. There would then be a hunt for spare lengths of rope or cord in the boat, which, praise be, they found and McVicar would attempt a repair job enough to hold things together again until the next sickening collapse. On day six, Sunday, 29 March, West attempted a church service in the morning, saying a prayer and asking his fellow Europeans to join him in a few verses of 'O God Our Help in Ages Past'. Then he set about some more practical care for his charges:

> I did some medical first aid for already our bodies were fairly well covered with salt water sores, rather like boils, mostly upon buttocks and hips. During the early days we felt considerable pain from these but as the days passed they seemed less painful despite the increased number and size. Some developed into abscesses, with holes in our bodies as large as a pigeon's egg. Our lips were swollen and cracked and some, who had failed to keep arms and legs covered, were badly sunburned. We were also by now terribly thin, just skin and bone. I think we lost all the weight we could in this first week. Our bodies were a horrible sight as we stripped off for bathing. It is hard to believe bodies could be so ugly. We looked, in fact, quite repulsive.[14]

Men began to die in the second week. The first was *Britannia*'s chief cook, one of the Indians, who either fell overboard or perhaps threw himself into the sea after midnight on the seventh morning, when Bill McVicar was on the tiller. They knew he had been drinking sea water, against all the warnings, and perhaps he had grown delirious or outright mad, they thought. He quickly disappeared in the blackness and there was no going back to search for him, for the boat was running in a strong breeze and to try to bring it about short-handed at night would have been near impossible and almost inevitably futile.

From that day the toll rose, whether from hunger, thirst, exposure or perhaps all of those, or just from a loss of hope and a fatal despair. It didn't seem to matter much. When you got down to it, a death was a death, a happening in this perilous venture that had to be managed more and more frequently, as swiftly and clinically as possible. After a few days Ian McIntosh could tell when a man was going to die: the light went from his eyes, replaced by a dull, staring sheen; his body slumped in listless, unmoving despondency until the end came and he stirred no more. There was no ritual of burial; just over the side and that was it.

> It was a pretty wretched business disposing of corpses in the morning, when a few seem to have accumulated. I will say this in the Sikhs' favour – they buried their own dead. Not so the others, they just ignored them, and Mac and I used to hunt for the corpses in the morning, when we had trimmed the sails. It sounds all very gruesome, but it had to be done, and lacked any personal element. It really was quite hard work. In fact the hardest bit of work I did on the trip was caused by one of the Indians. Right up in the forepeak he had managed to lie down underneath a thwart . . . he had died in this position and stiffened . . . there was no moving him. As it was impossible to get him out head first, the only remaining course seemed to be to take him out the other way, breaking down the panelling . . . after swearing and straining for ten minutes I bust the thing off and threw him overboard.[15]

Wally Beck and Ken Harman were the first Europeans to go, both on the fourteenth day, Sunday, 6 April. Beck was an able seaman, aged twenty-three, one of the youngsters who had never been to sea before. He simply wasted away. Sub-Lieutenant Harman, RNVR, was a relatively elderly man of forty who had been in charge of the gun crew on *Britannia*'s stern. A piece of shrapnel had smashed his kneecap. It had been dressed by *Britannia*'s surgeon before the order to abandon ship and Harman had been lowered into Lifeboat Seven, where he lay in constant, unremitting pain. He bore it courageously, helping where he could by assisting Frank West with the food rationing, grateful when they could clear some small space for him to rest, uncomplaining to the last.

West sat with both men as their lives faded, recording Wally Beck's last moments in his diary:

> He had courage beyond my powers to describe. From time to time he would speak of his parents, giving me messages for them; I was to tell them he had tried hard and done his best, that he was sorry he would not come home to them again. It was best for him to die, he told me many times, and I could not answer him. His hands gripped mine to express the words he could no longer speak as his head fell forward and the hands went limp.
>
> Our hearts were heavy and sad as we reverently committed them to the sea . . .[16]

More deaths would come, many more. Sometimes the bodies would float away. At other times, if the boat was not moving, they would bump against the hull, which West found deeply distressing. Bill McVicar developed a poisoned foot, which gave him a stabbing pain when he moved.

Through it all, the young Australian sub-lieutenant Ian McIntosh presided in command: indomitable, indestructible. Propelled by his naval training, boundless optimism and force of character, he held them all together.

> Evenings, weather permitting, provided the peace for reflection. One evening I persuaded the Sikhs to sing. One man led with a chant and the rest joined in as a chorus. I never knew whether it was secular or religious but it was soothingly beautiful. On many occasions, not shared with others, I found myself in awe of the beauty of the world; of the sea and sky; of the emerging stars building to their full glory. It was a strange trance-like state in which I felt a great love for all mankind.

Nights, too, provided the solitude to reflect. In these moments I found myself thinking of my family in Australia and, more particularly, of a beautiful blonde girl, Elizabeth, who I had met while on leave prior to sailing in Britannia. These thoughts provided me with the empowering determination to survive and drove all my efforts. Never once did I doubt that I would survive.

I was to learn later that Elizabeth, alarmed at the lack of news, had got her mother to write, on 13th April, to request news. On the 16th she received a letter from the Offices of the War Cabinet with the following:

'I regret to tell you that SS Britannia was sunk by a raider on 25th March, some 500 miles west of Sierra Leone. So far 194 survivors have been accounted for, but Sub Lieutenant Ian McIntosh is not among these. There is still some hope of a few more of the missing turning up, but I fear, owing to the lapse of time, this is improbable. I sympathise deeply with your daughter in her anxiety.'

I am glad that I did not know this at the time, but there was a certain frustration at not being able to let anyone know that I was alright and was going to survive.[17]

Another week passed, each day unrelentingly the same as the one before. But on the Tuesday of the second week, 8 April, black clouds welled up on the horizon and soon a rainstorm was upon them, sweet, beautiful rain, bucketing down for two long, drenching, glorious hours. They formed a gutter from the foot of the mainsail and collected the water to fill every tin and bucket and tank, washing their bodies and matted beards, exulting in this strange sensation of cleanliness. For the moment, their water worries were over, and that night they each drank a full tin of half water and half condensed milk with their ship's biscuit.

There were more deaths again over the next few days but Ian began to believe they had come safely through the doldrums, for the wind was now coming from the south-east, exactly as he had expected and hoped. If all their calculations had been right – and it was still a big if – a new course of south-south-west, on port tack, should bring them to the nearest point of land in a few days.

Frank Lyons, though, had developed a fever and was weakening, no longer able to take his trick at the tiller. On Easter Sunday, 13 April, they caught some more rainwater, happy again, and held an evening service with what words of the *Book of Common Prayer* they could recall, McIntosh improvising a sermon and all of them joining, voices cracked and ragged, in a familiar old Wesleyan hymn, 'Christ the Lord is Risen Today'.

Frank West, physically near the end of his tether but still hopeful, found it inspiring:

> The memory of this evening is still clear. The heat of the day giving way to a delicious coolness, the hurtful brilliance of the sun gradually easing as it sank to the horizon, the orange glow of a lovely sunset and its reflection on the water and enough wind to keep the sails full and the boat ever nearing land. Then shortly came the sudden change to night, the light giving way to dark, the sun to moon and stars; never did the Southern Cross seem so brilliant and comforting, and all was quiet and still. Surrounded by the limitless, unending sea, we felt uplifted and at peace.
>
> We were not alone.[18]

Their deliverance came two days later, as Ian wrote in his letter to his mother:

> On the Tuesday after Easter, the 15th, I smelt land. It was a wonderful strong rich smell of earth and vegetation, and hot sun after rain. Soon everyone smelt it and we were glad. Then we saw twigs and branches, more and more of them; then the water became greener and muddier. It looked as though we were near the mouth of some river. Then, at 1140, we sighted land.[19]

Land! The coast of Brazil! Lifeboat Number Seven had made it.

As they drew closer, they could make out first a low ridge, then a sandy beach. Elated, the landlubbers expected to head for it there and then, but it was a lee shore – the wind blowing from the sea to the land – and Ian could see a heavy surf running. He had no intention of risking the boat in that. With sunset drawing in, he stood out to sea again to spend the night at a safe distance, so they might search for a suitable place to land the next morning. In the dark they could see the flashing beam of a distant lighthouse.

Frank Lyons by now was delirious. Through those long night hours, West did what little he could for him, giving him frequent sips of water through lips that were cracked and bleeding and mopping his fevered body, but he grew ever weaker and at about ten o'clock the next morning he died. It was a gut-wrenching irony, as West recorded:

> He had made a great contribution to the success of the journey and it was a bitter blow to us that he should have died when we were so near the end of it. He was the last man to die and I am glad we buried him at sea. He was a sailor and rests, I hope, more peacefully in the sea than in the soil of a foreign land. Our hearts were very full as we said prayers for him and expressed our gratitude for all he had done for us.[20]

Ian McIntosh brought the boat inshore again and this time luck was with them. They saw land once more at around noon, and ran into what Ian took to be a wide, sheltered bay of still water.

> In the early afternoon we grounded some 300 yards from the water's edge where the water was, for me, thigh deep, but for others a bit deeper. Some of the men were reluctant to leave the boat and I had to throw them overboard. They, finding firm sand under their feet, made their way slowly to the beach. Bill, whose badly poisoned foot prevented him from walking, we carried ashore. Then Frank and I returned to the boat to salvage any useful items. Securing the boat's painter [rope] to a stake driven into the sand we made our way, heavily laden, back to the beach. Those who had first got ashore had found fresh water behind the beach and using dry twigs and sticks together with dried cattle dung, had got a fire going and boiled some water. There all 38 survivors enjoyed the luxury of lying out full-length with no movement to disturb us. As we lay we drank the boiled water, flavoured with some berries that birds had been seen to be eating and therefore assumed not to be poisonous. The fire was

kept burning through the night while we listened to the gentle murmur of the waves on the shore, hardly noticing the deep salt water boils that covered our bodies.[21]

Thirty-eight survivors, skin and bones, but alive. Of the eighty-two who had begun that epic journey, forty-four had died – more than half. Yet it was beyond extraordinary, surely a miracle of providence, that any had made it at all. Lifeboat Seven and its desperate, starving and dying human cargo had travelled some 2500 kilometres in twenty-three days, almost exactly the distance and span of time that the young Australian had foreseen.

The next morning McIntosh went searching:

Frank and I, accompanied by two seemingly strong ratings, set off to explore the land behind the sandhills. Shortly, we sent back the two ratings who were tiring rapidly, leaving Frank and me to continue, hoping to find fruit as well as higher ground from which to see the lie of the land. Fruit was scarce and what appeared to be higher ground proved to be merely taller mangroves. In trying to reach this higher ground, we found ourselves slithering in the thick black mud of the mangrove swamp, sinking sometimes up to our thighs. Much exhausted by this exertion, we decided to make our way slowly back to solid ground. Resting from time to time in the oppressive heat, we headed for the beach and, to ensure that we did not become lost, well to the southeast of the camp, so that we would know which way to turn to reach it. At the beach we found a substantial and deep pool in the sand. There we sat and washed off the sweat, dried mud, and blood from the numerous mosquito bites. Then, to our surprise, we discovered that the water was fresh and we drank our fill. At that moment two small native boys appeared. Smiling, they beckoned us to follow them. Leading us along the beach past the now-abandoned and cleared campsite, we came, about a mile further on, to a small settlement of five or six palm-thatched and walled fishermen's huts to which the other survivors had already been taken and fed by these kindly people. There seemed to be some twenty or thirty souls, desperately poor and leading a subsistence life on the fish they could catch and the fruits they could gather . . .

> Kindly and generous, they insisted in going out and catching more fresh fish to add to salted shrimps, melons, pawpaw, mangoes and farinha. We found the meal delicious and suffered no ill effects from a most unusual diet following a period of starvation... Neither before nor since can I remember such generosity from people with so little to spare.[22]

After a few days they were taken to the provincial capital, São Luís, on Brazil's far north coast, a little below the equator. There, with the energetic assistance of the local British consul, they were welcomed into the city's Portuguese Hospital, where, for six weeks, they were tended by its doctors and nursing nuns. Brazil was a neutral nation in the war but effectively pro-British. Photographs and details were taken, and after a while the authorities in Rio de Janeiro helpfully ruled that these unusual new arrivals were not active combatants who, by international law, should be interned, but distressed seamen who could be permitted to leave.

The Indians were sent to New York, in the care of the now recovered Bill McVicar. At the end of May, the thirteen surviving Europeans left São Luís by ship, first for Trinidad and then Bermuda, where the six officers – though not the sailors, it must be said – were feted like visiting royalty. Another Atlantic sea crossing loomed, not an enticing prospect. Fit and restored to health, and after exercising his considerable charm, Sub-Lieutenant Ian McIntosh talked his way aboard a Catalina flying boat on a delivery flight to Britain via Canada, signing on as an engineer. In a week, it landed him at Greenock, on the River Clyde in Scotland.

The navy allowed him a few weeks of survivor's leave, in which time he renewed his friendship with Elizabeth Rasmussen, the young woman who had occupied his thoughts so often in those grim watches of the night.

Slowly, life returned to something approaching normal. McIntosh began to worry that he was being left behind while other officers from his class were already at sea, their careers on the move.

12

SPECIAL AND HAZARDOUS SERVICE

In his smartest uniform, newly tailored, the young officer made his way through bombed and battered London to Northways, the headquarters of the submarine service in the Finchley Road. It was summer now, late June 1941. The Blitz had ended only a few weeks before and the scars were everywhere: the air-raid shelters dug into the parks, the burnt-out buildings boarded and barricaded.

The men on the streets were almost invariably in khaki or blue, like Ian McIntosh himself. Survivor's leave had restored him to youthful good health, had helped him regain the nearly twenty kilograms in weight he had lost in the lifeboat. He was no longer skin and bones. The uniform was neatly pressed, the single sub-lieutenant's ring bright gold on the jacket cuffs, the shoes well-polished, and all for a very good reason: McIntosh was to meet no less than the Vice Admiral of Submarines himself, the formidable Max Horton.

This was the very same Max Horton who had scored the RN's first ever submarine kill in 1914 as a young lieutenant commander, and who had returned to base at Harwich triumphantly flying the pirates' flag, the Jolly Roger, thereby starting a submarine tradition. The years had given him a reputation for ruthless efficiency and a refusal to suffer fools gladly, if at all.

The meeting was unusual, to say the least. Very junior officers like McIntosh rarely, if ever, found themselves summoned to the private presence of such gilded greatness. Horton, though, had heard of the epic Atlantic voyage and was keen to hear the story firsthand. He listened intently, asking the occasional question while the young Australian took him through it.

'Well, McIntosh,' he said at the end of it. 'You've got the first attribute required by a submariner. You've got luck.'

'Thank you, sir.'

'Which boat would you like to go to?'[1]

This, too, was remarkable. Even senior officers, commanders and captains, would not expect a choice of job, a choice of ship, and would be astonished to be offered one. The admiral was bestowing a mark of high favour. Typically, though, McIntosh had anticipated the question and had an answer ready.

'HMS *Porpoise*, please,' he said.

Porpoise was a fast and modern boat, commissioned in 1933, one of six Grampus-class submarines designed especially to lay mines. She could carry fifty of those, plus twelve torpedoes. She had already done thirteen war patrols, the last to Halifax, Nova Scotia, and back. McIntosh knew she was refitting at Troon, Scotland, on the Firth of Clyde. The deal was done. In a hectic couple of days he packed his bags, said his farewells to Elizabeth and caught the train north. He joined *Porpoise* as third hand on 15 July.

With the refit done and the workup complete, they sailed for the Mediterranean on 2 October. Ten days later they arrived at Malta. Ian McIntosh had joined the war in Mussolini's *Mare Nostrum*.

Other Australians had begun to find their way across the world to Britain and the Royal Navy, some by design, some by the roll of fate's dice.

Max Shean was in his second year of an engineering degree at the University of Western Australia when the war broke out. He kept at it into the new year, 1940, all the while conscious of 'an uneasy feeling of obligation', as he put it.[2] The retreat at Dunkirk in May and June brought that feeling into sharp focus, and a few weeks later he read a newspaper advertisement calling for young gentlemen with experience in sailing to step forward. Yachtsmen, they wanted, to be commissioned as temporary acting

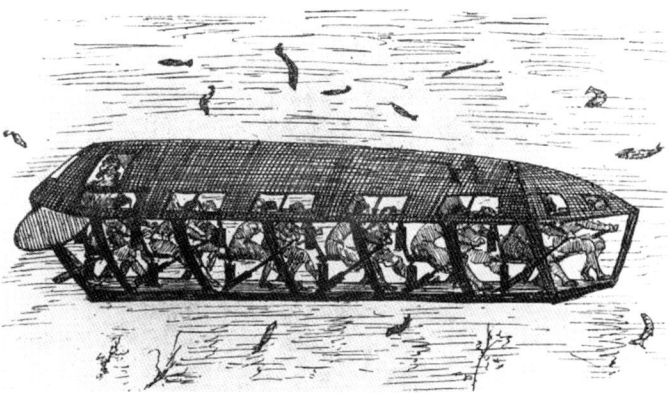

Cornelis Drebbel's first submersible, a greased leather rowboat

David Bushnell's *Turtle*, which Bushnell offered to George Washington for the revolutionary war against the British (Ullstein bild/Getty Images)

HMS *Holland 1*, the first of the Royal Navy's six Holland-class submarines, shortly after its secret launch at the Vickers Maxim shipyard at Barrow-in-Furness, Cumbria, October 1901 (Hulton Archive/Getty Images)

AE1 in Portsmouth Harbour, 1914 (Royal Australian Navy)

The last known image of *AE1*, 9 September 1914; HMAS *Australia* and *Yarra* are in the background (Royal Australian Navy)

Lieutenant Commanders Geoffrey Haggard and Harry Stoker of *AE2* in 1919 (Royal Australian Navy)

Skilled submariner officer Harry Stoker, captain of *AE2*, tasked with taking the boat on its 21,000 kilometre journey from Portsmouth to Sydney

AE2 in the Sea of Marmara by Charles Bryant, 1925, oil on canvas, 122.6 × 183 cm (AWM ART09016)

The small Turkish torpedo boat *Sultanhisar*, captained by Ali Riza, which captured *AE2* in April 1915

Top left: Captain Ali Riza of the *Sultanhisar* (Alamy)

Top right: Stoker, top row, second from the right, Geoffey Haggard, bottom right, and other prisoners in captivity in Turkey (Royal Australian Navy)

Middle Right: Afion Kara Hissar – the Opium Black Castle, site of the main Turkish PoW camp (Australian National Submarine Museum)

Bottom: Belemedik, a work camp high in the Taurus Mountains on the Berlin–Baghdad railway (State Library of Queensland)

Lieutenant Commander Frank Getting RAN, first to pass the Perisher, the Royal Navy's notoriously tough Periscope School. It got its nickname because you either passed or perished (Royal Australian Navy)

Lieutenant Max Shean by Geoffrey Mainwaring, 1958, oil on hardboard, 76.4 × 61 cm (AWM ART27531)

Ian McIntosh, the hero of Lifeboat Number Seven, seen here as a midshipman (family photo)

The European survivors of Lifeboat Seven. Ian McIntosh is in the front row, second from right

Tirpitz in her fjord (Tirpitz Museum)

HMS *Varbel*, the midget submarine base in Scotland (Royal Navy)

Lieutenant Commander Ken Hudspeth RANVR, midget submariner (Royal Australian Navy)

Lieutenant Henty Henty-Creer RNVR (family photo)

Shean and Henty-Creer, in the diving suits they called 'clammy death' (Royal Australian Navy)

An X-craft on Loch Striven (Royal Navy)

Max Shean (left) and Ian McIntosh on board HMS *Sceptre* (Royal Navy)

HMS *Bonaventure*, the midget submarine depot ship (Royal Navy)

XE Type being hoisted out of *Bonaventure* (Royal Australian Navy)

X-craft net and cable cutter at the Royal Navy Submarine Museum, Portsmouth (Geni, Wikipedia)

Max Shean's *X24* at the museum (Geni, Wikipedia)

X24's interior. The Wet and Dry compartment is through the circular door (Geni, Wikipedia)

Sub-Lieutenant Ken Briggs, who cut the cable at the mouth of the Saigon River as part of Operation Sabre (family photo)

Oxley training with army commandos, 1974 (Royal Australian Navy)

Captain Ian MacDougall, later a Vice Admiral and the first submariner to be Chief of Navy (Gary McLean/ *Sydney Morning Herald*)

Top: Oxley, departing for Gallipoli, 1990 (Royal Australian Navy)

Middle: Lieutenant Commander Terry Roach, of the *One And All* rescue (family photo)

Bottom: Sub-Lieutenant Ken Briggs and his nephew, Rear Admiral Peter Briggs (Ben Johnston, Evocative)

Ovens with 816 Squadron Seahawk, off the Western Australian coast (Royal Australian Navy)

Onslow, September 1981 (Royal Australian Navy)

Top to bottom: *Oxley, Otway, Onslow, Otama*, August 1982 (Royal Australian Navy)

Otway in December 1995. She now rests at the submarine museum in Holbrook, in country New South Wales, far from the sea, where she sits rather incongruously anchored in concrete and grass lawn (Royal Australian Navy)

Former Australian warrant officer Dave Bryant and Captain Igor Kurdin laying a wreath at the Kursk memorial service, Serafimovskoe Cemetery, St Petersburg, in September 2018

The sunken stern of *AE1* (courtesy of Paul G. Allen, Find *AE1*, ANMM and Curtin University © Navigea Ltd)

Digital 3D model of the wreck of *AE1*, port side (Curtin University HIVE from images courtesy of Paul G. Allen, Find *AE1*, ANMM and Curtin University © Curtin University)

sub-lieutenants in the Royal Australian Naval Volunteer Reserve, for training as anti-submarine specialists.

Shean fitted the bill. He had grown up messing about in boats with his father on the Swan River, in launches and sailing dinghies and camping expeditions. Lean and active – a gangling, skinny kid, really – he was also good with his hands, making model aeroplanes and, once, a model compass and sextant he designed himself. One spectacular success was a homemade diving helmet, knocked together from a four-gallon steel drum, a garden hose, a tyre pump and odd bits of timber and glass. It actually worked – unless you leaned forward, when it would flood with water.

In late June he and a university sailing mate took themselves off to the navy recruiting depot at Fremantle, where they filled out forms, sat some tests, went through some interviews and a medical exam and were sent back home to wait. In August came a letter to say that Maxwell Henry Shean had been accepted. On 28 October 1940, at the age of twenty-two, he was fitted out with a uniform bearing the single, wavy gold stripe of a volunteer sub-lieutenant, and a week later, with another eleven young men, he was at the Flinders Naval Depot in Victoria for four weeks of basic training in everything from marching, rifle and sword drill to torpedoes and seamanship.

This was the beginning of what was officially known as the Dominion Yachtsmen Scheme, a brainwave of the Admiralty in London, which was looking for potential officers in any outpost of the empire. Not all the dominions took part. The Canadians were hastily trying to build their own navy, while only a few New Zealanders were interested and fewer South Africans, but Australians dived in. It was haphazard, hit and miss. Some volunteers, presumably the more gentlemanly ones, became officers from the start, like Max. Others were taken on as ordinary sailors, with the possibility of a commission if they measured up as wardroom material down the track. Nobody seems to have counted the exact number, but around 500 Australians were taken on. The Yachties, they called themselves.

Next for Shean came weeks of grinding instruction at the navy's anti-submarine school at Rushcutters Bay, Sydney, where he dived headlong into the arts and sciences of Asdic and navigation and passed with flying colours. After two weeks' leave back in Perth, farewelling family and mates, in May 1941 he took passage for Britain in the liner *Coptic* up through the Panama Canal, arriving in Liverpool towards the end of June. Predictably, no one had heard of him or knew what to do with him, but eventually an order came to 'Report Commander Destroyers, Liverpool' and to join a ship.

> I was directed to Clarence Dock, by following the elevated railway by the Mersey River. The railway was a sad sight, having been put out of service in the Blitz. A policeman gave me further guidance: 'Just a short walk down river past the stink.' Not wishing to stick my neck out with a constable any more than with a gunnery instructor, I contained my curiosity and marched off towards the sea, sniffing all the while. It did not take long. As they say, you can't miss it. On the city side of the riverside road was the shell of a bombed building that had been a cold-store. Mechanical shovels were digging into a mountain of rotting food and loading it onto trucks.
>
> Shortly after, on the river side, came Clarence Dock Power Station. Through the gate, past the Dockyard Police, and there she lay, my first ship and lifetime inspiration, HMS Bluebell.[3]

An odd name for a warship – one you might expect to see painted on the stern of a Thames Valley pleasure launch – but *Bluebell* was a Flower-class corvette. Nearly 300 of them were built during the war and they all had floral names, belying an enduring, hardy toughness that made them a mainstay of the Battle of the Atlantic. They were small, chunky and purposeful, a bare sixty-two metres long and displacing just over 900 tonnes, adapted from a civilian whaler design to be turned out cheaply and quickly in shipyards around Britain.

Only a year old when Shean joined her, *Bluebell* had already made her mark as one of the escorts for the legendary Convoy HX 112 from Halifax, Nova Scotia, across the North Atlantic to Liverpool, a bloody battle in March 1941 in which the honours were about even. The Germans sank six ships but the escorts destroyed U-boats commanded by two of the German Navy's top aces, *Kapitänleutnant* Otto Kretschmer's *U-99* and *Kapitänleutnant* Joachim Schepke's *U-100*. Kretschmer was captured and spent the rest of the war as a prisoner in Canada. Schepke, an ardent Nazi, died on his bridge when his boat was rammed and sunk by the destroyer HMS *Vanoc*. *Bluebell* rescued forty survivors from a sunken tanker.

Shean spent a week learning the ship before she sailed: the four-inch gun on the foredeck, two rails on her stern for dropping depth charges, quadruple pompom anti-aircraft guns port and starboard, a small bridge open to the elements, a single stumpy funnel, a best speed of around sixteen knots, a crew of some eighty men, almost all reservists. The captain was a former merchant officer, Lieutenant Commander Robert Sherwood of the Royal Naval Reserve.

They left Liverpool on 12 July, Shean racked by a bout of the seasickness that would plague his entire naval life.

> First afternoon at sea I studied my given action station back aft on the depth charges so that I would know it in the dark. We would be leaving the long twilight as we ran down our latitude towards Gibraltar. I prepared lists of depth charge settings for different submarine depths and fixed them adjacent to the rails and throwers. I was secretly disappointed to be stationed aft when I expected to be at the Asdic control position alongside the operator as we had trained to be at Rushcutter, but being green for lack of experience – besides seasickness – I accepted as the Captain's prerogative that this was where he wanted me.[4]

Bluebell was now part of the 37th Escort Group of two sloops and five or six corvettes running convoys to and from Gibraltar, at the mouth of the Mediterranean.

This first outing for Shean was the real thing on the playing field after all the training. There was so much to take in, from standing a watch on a dark night, to working with his depth charge crews, to the mundane business of keeping the ship's confidential books. There were thirty-three merchant ships in Convoy OG 68 – the O for Outward, G for Gibraltar – the biggest a 7200-tonne steamer of the Royal Mail Packet Line, the smallest an Irish freighter of not more than 900 tonnes with the Irish flag and 'EIRE' painted in big white letters on her hull. Arrayed in four stately columns, their smoke darkening the skies, the convoy sailed around the north of Ireland and then south down the twentieth meridian of west longitude, to send them out to sea as far as possible from enemy air bases in France before passing Spain and heading east to the Med, a distance of some 3800 kilometres. *Bluebell*, the junior ship – it depended on the rank and seniority of the captains – was invariably tail-end-Charlie, bringing up the rear, zigzagging to avoid submarines, chivvying the stragglers as the convoy crept along at perhaps eight knots.

Shean hated it at first. He was the only Australian on board and he was homesick, but the job had to be done. As he settled in conscientiously with the routine of the ship, as he became more at ease with the captain and his fellow officers, as he got to know the men on his depth charge team, *Bluebell* began to grow upon him. Lieutenant Commander Sherwood was a humane captain and a patient teacher, as Shean recorded:

> He would always come on to the bridge when I was on watch and make some remark to indicate that he was watching my progress. I was the first Australian he had sailed with, and our accents were quite different. One night, when I had been giving the quartermaster helm orders to follow a quick zig-zag pattern, the captain came onto the bridge and said 'Shean, I have been in the wheelhouse for the last hour and have not understood one word you have said. I don't know how the helmsman knows what to do.' I took note of this and tried to be more clear and deliberate . . .[5]

That first convoy arrived in Gibraltar without incident, a two-week voyage unmolested by the enemy. The Germans would not be so accommodating again. On the fourth night of the return journey to Liverpool, the U-boats attacked in the middle watch, about an hour after midnight, *U-372* firing a spread of four torpedoes from inside the convoy that sank two cargo steamers, *Belgravian* and *Swiftpool*.

The explosions woke Shean in his bunk and he was already pulling on his seaboots and his duffel jacket when the action station bells rang. *Bluebell* was ordered to pick up survivors in the inky dark:

We set about rigging the scrambling net over the starboard side as Bluebell, moving faster than usual, rolled her scuppers into the sea which gushed in and along the deck. The 'ding' of the engine room telegraph came clearly to our ears, and the vibration of shaft and propeller ceased. Looking ahead we could see a group of tiny red lights bobbing on the sea surface. A short run of the propeller astern and we were stopped close to the swimming seamen. Bob Sherwood could certainly handle his ship.

With heaving line and boathook we helped the ablest men close alongside and up into the net. Some voices called from the blackness. We could only call back, being forbidden to leave the ship. If their swimming mates could bring them close we could climb down the net and lift them aboard. Time was passing.

'How are you going, Shean?' asked the Captain down the voice-pipe. 'We can't remain stopped long or we will be the next target.'

'Aye aye sir. Give me a few minutes. Most of them are aboard.'

When all those within reach and the able swimmers were on deck I called the bridge.

'We have all we can save, sir. The other lights must be on dead men. They're all covered in oil.'

'Right, we must move.'

The telegraph rang and the steam engine turned the screw, faster as the swirl stretched out astern into the dark, towards a few points of red light. Those men nearly survived...[6]

Six ships were lost on that trip, five to U-boats, and one straggler bombed by one of the Luftwaffe's long-range Focke-Wulf Fw 200 Condor aircraft west of Ireland.

This would be the tenor of Shean's existence for the next year: long, sleepless hours of monotony and boredom crudely interrupted by the action stations alarm, by explosions and fire, by sinking ships and the cries of drowning men, by the pinging Asdic hunt for the enemy and the search for survivors, by the burnt and wounded laid out in the sailors' mess, coughing the poisonous oil fuel from their lungs, some of them to die and be buried at sea. This hideous drama played out with the unspoken subtext that the very next torpedo might be the one to pierce *Bluebell*'s thin hull plates and send her to the bottom.

After a while, Shean received his watchkeeping certificate, qualifying him to take charge of the ship, and he graduated to become an anti-submarine officer, supervising the Asdic operator ensconced in his tiny hut abaft the bridge. In November 1941, *Bluebell* was the first corvette to have radar installed, one of the early Type 271 sets, and Shean was put in charge of that too, on the vague idea that somebody had to do it and it might as well be him.

There were moments of respite. You could go swimming in Gibraltar or cross over into neutral Spain for a meal and a drink. With time off in Britain, Shean enjoyed long walks in the countryside and stayed with a welcoming family in a rural village in Sussex. On one long leave, he took a train to Scotland on a holiday arranged by the Australia House billeting service in London. At Aberfeldy, a picturesque little Highland market town on the River Tay, in Perthshire, he met a young woman, Mary Golding – 'a pretty girl with typical highland complexion'. When he returned to the ship they began to write to each other.

In all, Max Shean did twelve Gibraltar convoys. One of them was of such surpassing horror that it seared itself into the memory of all who were there. Convoy OG 71 sailed from Liverpool in the afternoon of 13 August 1941, collecting other ships from Milford Haven and the Clyde until there were twenty-three of them formed up in columns following the usual route north and west around Ireland's Bloody Foreland and then south. They carried coal, food and other supplies for the Mediterranean.

The commodore's ship was the small passenger steamer SS *Aguila*, popular in peacetime for its holiday cruises to Portugal and the Canary Islands, and now numbering among its passengers a detachment of 'Wrens': a nursing sister and twenty-one specially trained cypher personnel and telegraphists from the Women's Royal Naval Service. Most were in their twenties, and a few still teenagers, all of them excited to be posted to the British naval base at sunny Gibraltar. The escort was led by the sloop HMS *Leith*. There was an ancient destroyer, His Norwegian Majesty's Ship

Bath, an odd-looking four-funnelled vessel donated to Britain by the Americans under the Lend-Lease agreement and now crewed by men of the Royal Norwegian Navy. *Bluebell* was one of six corvettes, at her usual place in the rear as they ploughed along in calm seas beneath a blue summer sky.

The enemy found them two days later. One of the big, four-engine Focke-Wulf Condors appeared at midday on 17 August, when they were west of Ireland, circling well out of range of anti-aircraft fire from the escorts and shadowing them for a few hours, but then disappeared as suddenly as it had arrived. Not long after midnight, on the morning of 18 August, the first U-boat report arrived from the Admiralty: 'More than one U-boat may be shadowing convoy.' Intercepted wireless signals and sophisticated radio direction finding equipment enabled the Admiralty to plot the whereabouts of U-boats in the Atlantic with considerable accuracy and by midday they were reporting three or four boats.

That evening, two Junkers 88 bombers swooped down out of the setting sun, dropping eight bombs but scoring no hits before flying off in a blizzard of anti-aircraft fire. Shortly before 7 p.m. the Admiralty sent another of its ominous warnings to *Leith*: 'D/F [direction finding] bearings indicate four or five U-boats in the vicinity of OG71.'

The wolf pack was coming together.

Oberleutnant zur See Adalbert Schnee had left the French port of Brest on 14 August for his third patrol in command of *U-201*, a Type VII boat that was the mainstay of the German Navy's U-boat arm. Twenty-eight years old and a Nazi Party member, known to his admiring crew as *Der Schneemann* – 'the Snowman' – Schnee had learned his trade under Otto Kretschmer and was already an ace in the making, with six sunken ships and an Iron Cross to his credit.

U-boat headquarters in a chateau at Kerneval, on the French Atlantic coast – the *Befehlshaber der Unterseeboote*, or BdU – had received the sighting reports from the searching Condor and again from the Ju 88s, and had ordered Schnee to find OG 71.

On the night of 18 August he was following it astern on the surface with almost casual ease, sending back signals to the BdU, which despatched other boats to join him.

It was a sister boat which struck first. At 2 a.m. on the morning of 19 August, also shadowing astern on the surface, *Kapitänleutnant* Walter Kell in *U-204* saw the distinctive silhouette of the 'four piper' *Bath* zigzagging at twelve knots, well to the rear of the convoy. She was a sitting duck. He fired two torpedoes. One missed, but the other tore into the destroyer's engine room with a blinding flash and an explosion which broke her in half and sent her to the bottom in less than five minutes. Many of her survivors in the water were killed when her depth charges exploded as she went down. Fewer than fifty of her crew of 130 were saved by the corvette *Hydrangea*, which boldly went to their rescue.

But the night had just begun. Just five minutes later, *U-559* sank the collier *Alva* in yet another blinding explosion.[7] Miraculously, her crew of twenty-five took to a lifeboat and a couple of rafts and all were saved. As *Leith* and the corvettes began desperate but fruitless Asdic searches, the convoy commodore in *Aguila* ordered a change of course from due south to 162 degrees, in the hope of shaking off their pursuers. It did not work – quite the opposite.

Now it was the Snowman's turn. In *U-201*, Adalbert Schnee had overtaken the convoy on its port flank and the change of course actually put him in closer touch. At 4 a.m. he fired a spread of four torpedoes from his bow tubes at virtually point-blank range. The first slammed into the engine room of *Ciscar*, a 1800-tonne cargo steamer, and another struck her further aft in her No. 4 hold. She began to list to port and go down by the stern, and in less than a minute she had disappeared in a great, boiling bubble. Some of her crew were killed but fifteen men got away, including her master and the convoy vice-commodore, Captain Edward Hughes. Clinging grimly to a floating hatch cover, Hughes heard another two explosions in the distance.

Schnee's third and fourth torpedoes had also struck home – a perfect score.

There had been an impromptu concert that night in the saloon of *Aguila*. Spirits were high, enlivened by the presence of the twenty-two young Wrens in their white tropical uniforms, a welcome feminine leavening of this all-male war at sea. The commodore himself was there, a retired RN vice admiral named Peter Parker, together with the captain, Arthur Frith. A sailor banged away at the piano. The night ended with all the young women lined up to sing a sentimental favourite, 'The World Is Waiting for the Sunrise'.

Most people had gone to bed when *Bath* was hit. Captain Frith had his passengers woken as a precaution and the Wrens were gathered in the ship's library, next to the boat deck, fully dressed and with their lifejackets. After an hour or so they were allowed to return to their cabins but were told to stay clothed. Frith, too, returned to his cabin beneath the bridge.

Schnee's third torpedo of the night hit *Aguila* amidships on her port side, tearing into her stokehold and shaking her violently. The fourth, seconds later, struck in the engine room, cutting off all electrical power and plunging the ship into darkness. She slumped to port, sinking rapidly. Scrambling out of his stateroom, the captain almost stepped into the sea. *Aguila* was gone in less than two minutes. The corvette HMS *Wallflower* steamed to the rescue but found only sixteen survivors from her company of 161. Captain Frith was one but all twenty-two of the Wrens were gone.

All night and into the morning the escorts kept up an Asdic search but got not a contact. The U-boats had vanished as stealthily as they had come. As news of that devastating night reached the Commander-in-Chief Western Approaches back in Liverpool, he despatched two modern destroyers, HMS *Lance* and HMS *Gurkha*, already in the mid-Atlantic, to join the convoy. They arrived late that night. As the senior officer, *Ghurka*'s captain, Commander Charles Lentaigne, assumed command of the defence.

The next two days passed more or less quietly, the convoy unmolested and trudging along in its columns, *Gurkha* and *Lance* dashing about but finding nothing. A couple of Condors turned up to shadow them again from a distance, infuriatingly untouchable, a warning of more to come.

On the night of 21 August, *Bluebell* was ordered to set up a diversion in the hope of throwing the Germans off the scent and at 10 p.m. she left the convoy and steamed to the north-west at full speed. Max Shean was with his depth charge crew on the stern, bleary-eyed and weary like all of them. It seemed they had been at action stations since the dawn of time, sustained by the occasional cup of kye, the thick navy cocoa, and bully beef sandwiches sent up from the galley, snatching a little shut-eye when they could.

Promptly at midnight, when she was some sixty-five kilometres distant from the convoy, *Bluebell* launched into a mock battle, dropping depth charges, firing star shell and transmitting faked action reports by wireless. After half an hour or so she returned to her position on the starboard side of the convoy.

The ruse seemed to have worked. *Gurkha* had the latest radio direction-finding gear and she picked up signals which told Commander Lentaigne that the U-boats were heading in the direction of *Bluebell*'s fireworks. The night had been saved, but not for long. The next day, 22 August, the searching Focke-Wulfs were back again, and that afternoon two Ju 88s made another bombing run, although again without hitting anything. By now the convoy had come well south, to the west of Portugal, with another two days left before Gibraltar, and the wolfpack was regrouping. 'Reports of up to nine U-boats in your area,' said the Admiralty helpfully that afternoon.

The night brought more disaster, drowning and death. Another young U-boat ace, *Oberleutnant zur See* Reinhard Suhren, in *U-564*, fired his bow tube spread of four, first hitting the rescue tug *Empire Oak* and then one of the Irish ships in the convoy, *Clonlara*. Both went down quickly. *Empire Oak* had been carrying some survivors from *Aguila* and *Alva* and nine of them died, with fourteen of the tug's crew. *Clonlara* lost twenty of her thirty-three people.

The violence went on. Not long after midnight – now the morning of 23 August – Schnee in *U-201* returned to the slaughter, firing four and hitting first *Aldergrove*, a 1900-tonne freighter, which sank in six minutes with one man lost. Another of his torpedoes found the motor ship *Stork*, which, laden with jerrycans of aviation fuel, exploded in an appalling sheet of flame that lit up the convoy and the horizon in a hideous glare. Twenty-two men died; three survivors were picked up by the corvette HMS *Campion*. Another Norwegian freighter, *Spind*, was next. She had been trailing well behind the convoy when *U-552* missed her with two torpedoes but then surfaced and attacked her with the deck gun. Her crew of twenty-five took to the boats and lived.

Yet even this was not enough: there was a final act of this tragedy to come. A little after 5 a.m., the corvette *Zinnia* was zigzagging at her station on the starboard flank of the convoy, at fourteen knots. The order 'Port 10' had just been given and she was leaning into her next turn when a torpedo from Suhren's *U-564* struck her square on the port side, a little abaft the bridge. She broke in two around her funnel, hurling her captain, Lieutenant Commander Charles Cuthbertson, into the water and sucking him down as she went under. Lungs bursting, he struggled back to the surface and, half-blinded by fuel oil, saw the stern of his ship rear into the air and then slide out of sight. Some men in the water were killed by explosions – perhaps her depth charges going off, even though they had been set to safe. In a grim sunrise, seventeen of her sixty-five crew members, including the captain and his first lieutenant, were rescued by *Wallflower*, *Campion* and *Campanula*. Two of the seventeen later died of their wounds.

And that was it. Seven merchant ships and two escorts had been sunk. The U-boats had won. OG 71 simply could not endure another night of slaughter on that scale. Defeated, the Admiralty withdrew from the field, sending a signal that forenoon for the convoy to abandon Gibraltar and turn east towards neutral Portugal and into the River Tagus for the port of Lisbon. They made it there that night. The escorts, with their cargoes of wounded and dying survivors, limped on to Gibraltar and arrived on the afternoon of 24 August.

It was a bitter agony for the navy, a humiliation keenly felt. To have lost the merchant ships was one thing – only to be expected, no matter how hard you tried – but *Zinnia* had been one of their own, a 'chummy ship' in naval jargon, crewed by men just like themselves, many of them mates they'd made on a run ashore, all in the same uniform, doing the same jobs, sailors with families now to be plunged into grief at home. There but for the grace of God . . .

Another dimension of horror lay in the loss of the Wrens, which only gradually became known after the arrival at Gibraltar, and for which everyone felt some special responsibility. They had failed to keep them safe.

More bitter still was the gnawing recognition that they had not struck a blow in return. Not one punch. They had not even seen a U-boat, let alone pinned one down for an attack. In all the ships there was a sense of helpless shame at their impotence. Max Shean shared this feeling:

> We had lost seven ships and two of our escort, but not one U-boat sighting or Asdic contact had been made. What was wrong? It seemed we were ineffective, though nobody could tell what losses there would have been had we not been there. The lack of any opportunity to strike back was demoralising.[8]

The author Nicholas Monsarrat had been on that convoy, an RNVR lieutenant in *Campanula*. He drew a fictional account of OG 71 in *The Cruel Sea*, his epic novel of the Battle of the Atlantic; in his memoirs he would write that it had been his worst experience of the war, a nightmare.

Accorded an ecstatic welcome home to Brest, Adalbert Schnee had the coveted Knight's Cross pinned to his chest by the *Befehlshaber der Unterseeboote* himself, Karl Dönitz.[9]

From shaky beginnings, after a year Max Shean had come to love *Bluebell*, as sailors can do with a happy ship and a good captain. Yet he had become restless on the endless round of convoy after convoy, and in mid-1942, as he leafed through the Admiralty Fleet Orders that deluged a warship when it returned to port, one caught his eye. It called for 'volunteers for special and hazardous service, who are below age 24, unmarried, good swimmers and of strong and enduring physique'.[10]

Intrigued, he put his name down and in due course he was told to report to the Captain, 5th Submarine Flotilla at HMS

Dolphin – Fort Blockhouse at Portsmouth – where he was interviewed at length, given a physical examination, and then told that they would be in touch. 'All I can recall about the interview,' he later wrote, 'was being told that this "Special Service" was most terribly secret, so much so that I could not be told what manner of vessel we would serve in except that it was quite small and navigated with the use of a periscope.'[11]

He was accepted. On 14 September he stood forlornly on the wharf waving goodbye as *Bluebell* sailed to join the Russian convoy run to Murmansk, and then he took the train south. The next day Sub-Lieutenant Shean was at *Dolphin* again with eleven other volunteers to train as a submariner. A very special sort of submariner, as it would turn out.

The Italian Navy took a heavy hit when it was defeated by the Royal Navy's Mediterranean Fleet at the Battle of Cape Matapan in March 1941. It lost three cruisers and two destroyers, a battleship was damaged and 2300 men were killed, and it never ventured out in force again.

But the Italians did not give up. They had been working hard at underwater warfare with their human torpedo, the *Maiale*, and they scored a striking success with a raid on the Egyptian port of Alexandria, the British fleet headquarters. A few days before Christmas in 1941, in the dark of night on 19 December, a submarine launched three *Maiali*, led by their commander, *Tenente di Vascello* Luigi Durand de la Penne. They slipped into the harbour when the defence booms were opened to admit three British destroyers and headed for their targets, the battleships HMS *Queen Elizabeth* and *Valiant* and, they hoped, an aircraft carrier. De la Penne's pig broke down with engine trouble, his second crewman disappeared in the murk, leaving him alone. He had to physically push the thing towards *Valiant*, a long and arduous struggle.

> After about twenty more minutes, with increasingly longer periods of rest, for my strength was fast giving out, I hit the hull of the ship with my head. At last I had arrived! I was nearly exhausted.

> I checked my bearings, dragged the torpedo under the centre line of the ship, attached the warhead and set the fuses. I did not bother to set the clamps tight because by now I had no doubts as to our success. At the appointed time, everything would be blown up as planned – the ship, and the assault craft as well. Since its location on the bottom was so near the hull of the ship, the explosion would destroy both.
>
> I floated up to the surface and took off my respirator. As I was swimming away, someone on the battleship's deck almost above me saw me and ordered me to stop. I paid no attention and kept on swimming until a hail of machine gun bullets induced me to change my mind.[12]

De la Penne was hauled on board *Valiant*, together with his missing companion, who, slightly injured, was found clinging to the buoy on which the ship was moored. They were questioned but gave nothing away and were locked in a room below the waterline. The crew of the second pig attached their warhead to *Queen Elizabeth*'s keel exactly as planned and got away undetected, swimming ashore. The third pig could not find the aircraft carrier – in fact there wasn't one there – so the crew fixed their warhead to the bottom of a Norwegian tanker, *Sagona*, and also swam ashore. Tense and anxious, de la Penne was counting down the time:

> Day was breaking. This meant only ten minutes were left before the explosion. I asked to be taken to the ship's captain and warned him to give orders to abandon ship and save the personnel, for the ship would be blown up within a few minutes. He still tried to get me to talk, but receiving no reply, he had me sent back to the hold even as the loud speakers gave the orders which I had suggested. So it was that I was deep down in the hold when the explosion occurred. But destiny, or what you will, did not intend that I should die at that moment.
>
> The blast shook the vessel with extreme violence, the lights went off, and the hold was filled with smoke. But except for a pain in my knee, I was unhurt. The ship rapidly heeled over to port about five degrees and started to rest on the bottom. Groping my way up the ladder and through the open hatch to the upper bridge,

I went toward the stern where a number of officers were standing. They were watching the Queen Elizabeth, sister ship of the Valiant, which was anchored a hundred yards away from us. At that moment she, too, gave a terrific heave and blew up, belching scrap from her funnel and flooding the stern of the Valiant with gasoline.[13]

Eight sailors died in *Queen Elizabeth*, though none in *Valiant*, due to de la Penne's humane warning. Both battleships slumped in the water, settling on the harbour bottom. The tanker also sank and a destroyer secured alongside had her bow stoved in. It was shallow, the harbour floor only a couple of metres beneath the ships' keels when they were properly afloat, so to a casual observer they appeared to be only a little lower in the water.

To later Italian air reconnaissance, the ships looked unharmed from above, and the British said not a word publicly, although the news did leak out later. The crews of the second and third pigs were captured ashore a few days later and taken prisoner. All survived.

The raid had been a triumph of asymmetrical warfare, a David and Goliath encounter in which a small force, skilfully planned and led, had prevailed over a far larger and more powerful opponent. One daring thrust by a handful of submarine commandos had disabled the last two RN battleships in the Mediterranean, putting them out of action for months, a heavy blow causing a significant shift in the balance of naval power.[14]

The shock waves reached all the way back to London, then around the empire. Winston Churchill wrote to the Australian prime minister, John Curtin:

> I have already told you of the Barham being sunk. I must now inform you that the Queen Elizabeth and Valiant have both sustained underwater damage from a human torpedo, which put them out of action, one for three and the other for six months. As the enemy do not yet know about these three last-mentioned ships you will see that we have no need to enlighten them, and I must ask you to keep this deadly secret to yourself.[15]

A day later Churchill fired off a note to the Chiefs of Staff Committee:

Please report what is being done to emulate the exploits of the Italians in Alexandria Harbour and similar methods of this kind. At the beginning of the war Colonel Jefferis had a number of bright ideas on this subject, which received very little encouragement. Is there any reason why we should be incapable of the same kind of scientific, aggressive action that the Italians have shown? One would have thought we should have been in the lead.

Please explain the exact position.[16]

Colonel Rowland Jefferis was an army engineer, a confidant of Churchill and the officer in charge of a top-secret unit at the Ministry of Defence known only as MD1. Its business was to think up new and wonderful weapons of war. Unofficially it was known as 'Churchill's Toy Shop'; more orthodox – or less imaginative – officers who knew of its existence derided it as a haven for cranks and conjurors, which, to some extent, it was. But the prime minister's urging got things moving in the direction of Max Horton, who knew the man to do the job.

At the beginning of the war, William Richmond 'Tiny' Fell had been – in his own words – 'an elderly lieutenant commander, long since passed over for promotion'. Born a New Zealander, he had joined the Royal Navy during World War I, serving as a midshipman in the battleship *Warspite* at the great Battle of Jutland in 1916. He had done more than twenty years in RN submarines and commanded three of them, but in the first years of this war, in his early forties, he found himself captain of a former Belgian cross-channel ferry, HMS *Prince Charles*, requisitioned by the navy as a troop landing ship. It was hardly a plum job.

On leave for a week, by now a full commander, Fell dropped into Submarine Headquarters for a gossip with some old shipmates. He had served a few times with Horton in the old days. The admiral, hearing he was in the building, called him to his office, as Fell recounted:

He greeted me with 'Hello, Fell! What mischief have you been up to?' Then, scarcely waiting for my reply, said 'Would you like to come back to submarines?' I was struck dumb as this miraculous question penetrated, and he was already growing impatient by the time I could stammer out 'Yes, please sir.'

'Well,' said Max, 'go away and build me a human torpedo. I will see about your appointment and relief in Prince Charles.'

I stuttered out 'Human torpedo?' But he broke in, saying, 'I'm busy, but get on with the job right away and report as soon as you've got something. Good-bye and good luck.'[17]

In two days Fell had packed his bags and installed himself at HMS *Dolphin*. He had been given as much as anybody knew about the Italian raid on Alexandria and the *Maiali*, which was not a lot. Undaunted, he set to work with the engineer commander at *Dolphin* and together they began to sketch out what a human torpedo might look like and how it would work.

A third man turned up to pitch in, Commander Geoffrey Sladen, another submariner famed as a four-time England rugby cap, a feat which had won him the nickname 'Slasher'. He arrived with an invention of his own, a heavy twill and rubber diving suit with a helmet and an oxygen tank for breathing.

Fell and Sladen formed a unique double: Tiny easygoing and with affable Kiwi charm, Slasher a volatile, driving force. Against all the odds they revolutionised British underwater warfare. The decisions they made, the craft they created, the men they recruited and the wartime operations they planned and commanded would become the stuff of naval legend.

A surprising number of young Australians moved into their orbit and came under their spell, volunteers all. Some would burnish the legend themselves. Others would die in the attempt.

13
ATTACK THE *TIRPITZ*!

They threw you in at the deep end, literally. Sink or swim. On his first day at *Dolphin*, Max Shean and his fellow volunteers, wearing swim trunks, were introduced to the Davis Submarine Escape Apparatus, a rubber bag rather like a lung strapped to your chest, with a cylinder of oxygen below it, an air hose and mask, and a pair of goggles. Breathing with it on dry land was easy enough, even fun, but things quickly got serious.

With an instructor standing by, the dozen or so trainees were sent into a steel chamber at the base of a tall tank of water about three storeys high. As the door clanged shut behind them one man gave up then and there, screaming, 'Let me out, let me out!'

The chamber was filled with water and then you had to use the apparatus to breathe, very steadily, as you rose slowly to the surface. Max found it daunting at first but after a week of practice he felt he had it mastered. By then another three men had quit. Those still standing were given no idea of what they were to do with their newfound expertise until the instructor called them to a briefing. '[T]his was to be the shock of my life,' wrote Shean.

> The purpose of our recruitment was to take part in a most important, and therefore top secret mission. The vessel was a midget submarine designed to penetrate enemy harbour defences undetected. It had a 'wet and dry' compartment similar to the one which we had mastered (?) during the past week. This was to enable a diver, namely one of us, to get out while submerged in

an enemy harbour, to cut through anti-submarine nets, and to get back in again without upsetting the control of the submarine. The armament was a pair of explosive charges of two tons each, strapped to the sides of the boat, and the target was battleship Tirpitz.

Gasp![1]

Tirpitz! The very name had a sinister ring. *Tirpitz* was the ogre that haunted the nightmares of British naval war planners from the prime minister down. She was bigger, faster, stronger, more modern, more powerful than any single ship the RN could send against her, a colossus, a leviathan. Her mere being, even in harbour, was an existential menace. At sea, on the loose in the Atlantic, she could wreak untold havoc upon Britain's maritime lifeline.

The *führer* himself had attended her launching, at Wilhelmshaven in April 1939, strutting in the glow of a propaganda spectacle replete with all the Nazi trappings of uniforms, bands and bunting. A cheering, saluting crowd of thousands had been herded into orderly squares and given swastika flags to wave as the newsreel cameras rolled. The battleship had been named for *Großadmiral* Alfred von Tirpitz, the architect of the Kaiser's navy in World War I; his daughter, Frau Ilse von Hassell, was there to do the honours – reluctantly, for she was no Nazi. In fact, she despised Hitler – her husband, the diplomat Ulrich von Hassell, would be executed by the Gestapo for his part in the plot to overthrow Hitler in 1944 – but she had been ordered to attend. After an uncomfortable silence with him on the official platform, she mouthed the words: 'By order of the *führer* and Supreme Commander of the *Wehrmacht*, I christen you with the name *Tirpitz*.'

The great ship slid down the slipway to the roars of the masses and the thumping blare of *'Deutschland über Alles'*. Commissioned two years later, in February 1941, she was undeniably striking, her long, raked hull, single funnel and towering bridge structure exhibiting a *Bauhaus* elegance that British naval architects had never matched. At some 45,000 tonnes fully loaded, and heavily armoured, *Tirpitz* boasted eight fifteen-inch guns as her main armament and a bristling array of smaller-calibre weapons, including powerful anti-aircraft batteries. Driven by three steam turbines, she could turn on thirty knots, a full two knots better than the Royal Navy's newest battleships of the King George V class.

She was not worked up and ready for sea until the European autumn of 1941, but the potent threat she posed had already been demonstrated by her elder sister. When the battleship *Bismarck* had broken out into the Atlantic in May that year, she swiftly and shockingly sank the pride of the Royal Navy, the battlecruiser HMS *Hood*, and it had taken virtually the entire Home Fleet, straining every sinew, to hunt her down and destroy her. The Admiralty had no desire for a repeat performance.

Singularly, nor did the Germans. The loss of *Bismarck* had unnerved Hitler, who was not one-tenth the naval strategist he fancied himself to be, and he ordered that *Tirpitz* should be deployed only with the greatest caution, when the odds were overwhelmingly in her favour. In January 1942 she was moved to Fættenfjord, a long and narrow inlet near Trondheim, in occupied Norway, moored against a high cliff for added protection from the air, there to lie in wait for an opportunity to present itself.

Churchill urged his service chiefs to action:

> The presence of *Tirpitz* at Trondheim has now been known for three days. The destruction or even the crippling of this ship is the greatest event at sea at the present time. No other target is comparable to it. She cannot have ack-ack protection comparable to Brest or the German home ports. If she were even only crippled it would be difficult to take her back to Germany . . .
>
> The whole strategy of the war turns at this period on this ship, which is holding four times the number of British capital ships paralysed, to say nothing of the two new American battleships retained in the Atlantic. I regard the matter as of the highest urgency and importance. I shall mention it in Cabinet tomorrow and it must be considered in detail at the Defence Committee Tuesday night.[2]

The Royal Air Force had done its best to destroy *Tirpitz* in bombing raids over Wilhelmshaven, Kiel and Norway, to no result. Nothing. In ten raids from October 1940 to April 1942, they scored not a hit, not even a damaging near miss, but lost seventeen aircraft in the attempt.

Month after month, the great ship lay at anchor in Norway, her ship's company stale and bored. In March 1942, with three destroyers in company, she made a tentative sortie into the North Sea to seek out two British Arctic convoys, but failed to find them. On the way home she was discovered by the Home Fleet and unsuccessfully attacked by Albacore torpedo bombers from the carrier *Victorious*, with the loss of two aircraft. She returned safely to her Norwegian lair.

Then came a disaster which haunts the Royal Navy to this day, a cascade of errors and a litany of death brought on by the mere spectre of *Tirpitz*'s presence.

Convoy PQ 17, of thirty-five merchant ships laden with supplies for Soviet Russia, sailed from Iceland for the port of Archangel on 27 June, with a close escort of destroyers and corvettes and, in the background, a covering force centred upon the modern British battleship *Duke of York* and the American USS *Washington*. It was high summer, with barely an hour of night-time dark. The Germans found the convoy on 1 July and the sinkings began, by U-boats and Luftwaffe aircraft. On 4 July, the Admiralty had both aerial reconnaissance and decoded German signals indicating that *Tirpitz* was on the move with the heavy cruiser *Admiral Hipper*, and after a long and agonising strategy conference that night, the First Sea Lord, Admiral of the Fleet Sir Dudley Pound, took the momentous decision to cut and run. He ordered the naval escort to withdraw to the west at high speed and the convoy to scatter and proceed independently to Russian ports.

So the slaughter unfolded on the bleak North Sea, the U-boats and bombers swarming like sharks and scavenging sea birds for their prey. Twelve ships were sunk the very next day, and on it went. By the end, twenty-four of the thirty-five merchant ships of Convoy PQ 17 had been lost. *Tirpitz* did put briefly to sea but never reached the battlefield. After another fit of nerves, this time in Berlin, she was recalled, arriving back in Norway on 6 July. It was a resounding German victory and an Allied catastrophe – 'one of the most melancholy naval episodes in the whole of the war', wrote Churchill, with delicate understatement.[3]

The need to eradicate *Tirpitz* had become an overarching naval imperative, but clearly new methods were required.

The affable Commander Bill 'Tiny' Fell had carried out Max Horton's orders to create a human torpedo with alacrity. Experimenting at first with a log of wood in a test tank in Portsmouth, his collection of engineers produced what everyone came to call a 'chariot'.

Put together with riveted steel plates, not quite seven metres long and about a metre wide, battery-powered, it could travel underwater at a speed of 2.5 knots, at a maximum depth of twenty-seven metres, carrying a detachable warhead filled with 270 kilograms of the high explosive Torpex. Like the Italian *Maiali*, it had a crew of two riding astride, clad in Commander 'Slasher' Sladen's diving suits, one man to navigate and steer the beast and the other, seated behind him, to cut through protective anti-torpedo netting and plant the warhead.

In early 1942, Tiny popped over to the officer training school, HMS *King Alfred*, at Hove, near Brighton, and called for volunteers for a secret and hazardous mission. Ten men stepped forward. More came later, to undergo intensive instruction at Loch Cairnbawn, a distant and dismal inlet on Scotland's far north-west Atlantic coast a little south of the ominously named Cape Wrath. It was a gruelling regime. Encased in heavy twill and rubber diving suits with breathing apparatus strapped to their chests, for months these volunteers practised conning their cumbersome steeds, cutting nets and making realistic attacks on the battleship HMS *Howe*, sent to them for the exercise. Two men died on the training program in separate accidents.

By late 1942, Fell had his troops ready for Operation Title, a bold and ingenious attack on *Tirpitz*, which was then lying deep inside the Trondheim fjord. Two chariots and their crews, four men, would be carried there by a Norwegian fishing trawler manned by the Norwegian resistance. The chariots were secured beneath the hull of the trawler – named *Arthur* – by steel hawsers and ring bolts, and were, it was hoped, undetectable from the surface.

They sailed from Lunna Voe, in the Shetland Islands, on 26 October and, after bouts of seasickness, an engine breakdown and later a cursory German inspection, which detected neither the chariots nor their hidden crews, *Arthur* was poised in a secluded part of the fjord on 31 October. But in the night a storm blew up. The trawler was buffeted by wind and waves that grew steadily worse, and, with a dreadful grinding noise, the two chariots were torn from beneath the hull, vanishing to the bottom. All was lost. They had come within ten kilometres of *Tirpitz* only to fall at the final hurdle.

The Norwegians and the four charioteers made it ashore after scuttling *Arthur* and, with the help of the resistance, reached the border with neutral Sweden. There was a gunfight there with German border guards. Able Seaman Bob Evans was wounded and captured but the others made it across. Despite being in naval uniform and evidently not a spy, Evans, aged twenty, was tortured and shot by the Gestapo on the express order of *Generalfeldmarshal* Wilhelm Keitel, chief of the Armed Forces High Command.[4]

The stark reality was that, for all its meticulous planning and daring execution, yet another attack on *Tirpitz* had failed.

With his bags packed and having farewelled *Dolphin*, Sub-Lieutenant Shean was walking through the Portsmouth Dockyard to catch a train on his way to Scotland when HMS *Victory* caught his eye, her three great masts soaring above him. *Victory* had been Horatio Nelson's flagship at his three great battles – at the Nile, Copenhagen and Trafalgar – in a war against an earlier European tyrant. The 'Heart of Oak' was the eternal symbol of England's maritime greatness, her 'wooden walls'. A whim spurred him:

I walked over to her, for reassurance, perhaps. She was in her permanent dry dock. A bomb, not so long before, had hit the dockside and then the concrete plinth on which her keel rested. Climbing down under the ship's bottom I could see the splintered timber where the bomb had blown a hole through her planking. I took hold of a piece of oak which had projected from the keel and pulled. It came away in my hand so I slid it into the inside pocket of my uniform jacket.[5]

Shean kept this as a talisman through the war and for the rest of his life. He joined his fellow trainees at Euston Station and by train, ferry and truck they arrived at Port Bannatyne, on the island of Bute, in pre-war days a small and picturesque fishing village on the Firth of Clyde in Argyll, west of Glasgow.

There waiting for them was a sprawling and strikingly ugly Victorian Gothic pile of grey stone, all gables, turrets and a castellated tower, until only recently the 88-bedroom Kyles of Bute Hydropathic Hotel, where well-heeled guests had come to take the waters in elegant comfort. Now, requisitioned by the Admiralty, stripped of most of its luxury fittings and reborn as HMS *Varbel*, it was the top-secret headquarters of the 12th Submarine Flotilla. Sailors, officers and Wrens bustled about their business, an unceasing hum of activity.

All was to be revealed. At a lecture in the Grand Dining Room, their instructor suddenly stopped talking and pointed towards the wide window with its sweeping view of the bay.

'Look through the window now,' he said theatrically. 'You will see *X3* proceeding on the surface.'

The trainees crowded to the glass. There it was, a flattish, charcoal-grey shape like the back of a small, surfacing whale, cruising towards them low in the water with a slight froth of a wake. A midget submarine.

It was the first they had seen. Over the coming months, in long and arduous training, they would come to know all there was to know about these strange new craft: every nut and bolt, every pipe and tank and chamber and gauge and wheel and valve and lever, every one of their strengths and flaws, every one of their quirks and habits.

X3 was the first to take to the water, the prototype launched in March 1942.⁶ Eventually there would be twenty-five boats, modified and improved over the years, but remaining essentially the same. The hope was that they would undertake operations that were beyond the ability of the chariots.

The first operational boat would be *X5*, sixteen metres long, a tube of welded steel with a maximum diameter of 1.7 metres and a pointed bow, displacing thirty tonnes submerged. In the stern sat a 42-horsepower Gardner diesel engine, the same as those driving London's red buses, giving a maximum surface speed of around six knots. Two big Exide batteries of 112 cells did the job submerged at an economical two knots or a little more. At first there was a crew of three: the captain, the first lieutenant and a third man who was usually a senior stoker or an engine room artificer, a petty officer who would operate the machinery and sometimes act as a diver. A fourth specialist diver was added later.

The usable interior, where the crew lived and worked, was about half the length of a cricket pitch. In the bow was the bank of batteries with a bunk on top to crawl into, where you could sleep if you were prepared to wake up with a pounding headache from the hydrogen the batteries emitted. Clambering aft, squeezing through a bulkhead with a circular door about half a metre wide, you came to the 'Wet and Dry', or the W&D, a compartment which could be sealed and flooded to allow the diver to leave the boat through a hatch above his head, and which would then be pumped empty again after he returned. This space also contained the 'head' – the toilet – which flushed outboard but occasionally went nastily wrong, swooshing its filth around the interior.

Next was the control room amidships, with a chair for the man at the wheel; a main periscope and a smaller night periscope; a gyrocompass, the wheels, dials and controls; a device known as a Chernikeeff Log, which measured the distance run; and another narrow bunk. A small man could stand upright here, but only just, and most had to bend and crouch.

The engine room was aft, always reeking and thunderously noisy with a red-hot exhaust system when running on the surface. There was no place to wash or bathe, and no galley. Tinned food, such as it was, had to be heated in the control room with an electric pot and kettle. 'Pot mess', the crews called it. The air was recirculated, with the carbon dioxide exhaled by the men absorbed by a chemical of slaked lime called Protosorb, but after a while it became stale, fuggy and clammy. At best, in sheltered Scottish lochs, the X-craft was noisy, smelly, cramped and uncomfortable. In a big sea, surfaced or submerged, it was the belly of the beast.

There were only two weapons. Sometimes called side cargoes, they were charges fastened on either side of the hull, containing two tonnes of the explosive Amatol, released by turning a wheel in the control room. The diver would place them beneath the target and set a time fuse to allow the boat to escape.

Primitive as they appear today, the X-class midget submarine was then a miracle of technology and engineering, a weapon forged at impressive speed in the heat of war. It would prove its worth soon enough.

Max Shean was not the only Australian. There were four others at *Varbel*, impelled by the twin motives of patriotism and a desire for adventure.

Ken Hudspeth, twenty-four, was a trainee teacher at Southport, in southern Tasmania, when the war began. The Sea Scouts had given him his first taste of sailing as a boy, in dinghies and later in bigger yachts, and he was strong and healthy from his hobby of bushwalking. He was a natural fit for the RAN when he volunteered in 1940. He was given a quick commission as a sub-lieutenant in the RANVR, anti-submarine training at HMAS *Rushcutter*, then put on a ship to Britain in January 1941. The Royal Navy took him up and, like Shean, Hudspeth did his time on the North Atlantic convoys, gaining his watchkeeping certificate in the corvette HMS *Anemone* before applying for 'hazardous service'.

Unusually, Lieutenant Brian McFarlane was a regular officer of the RAN. Brought up near Mount Macedon, in Victoria, he came from a naval family. His father, John, had enlisted in the Royal Navy as a boy seaman in 1905, transferring to the RAN in 1912, and in World War I he was a warrant officer torpedo gunner in HMAS *Sydney* when she fought her historic battle with the German raider *Emden* in 1914. Remarkably, John McFarlane won a commission – not at all common in those days – and rose to become a commander and an aide-de-camp to the governor-general. Son Brian passed out of the Naval College in 1937 and was packed off to Britain for the customary finishing polish given to midshipmen, in no less than the battlecruiser *Hood*. Much of his time was spent in Britain. He had actually been on duty as officer of the day in HMS *Queen Elizabeth* during that Italian *Maiali* attack in Alexandria, which might just have aroused his interest in underwater warfare. He was shortish and invariably cheerful; everyone called him 'Digger'.

Jack Marsden shared a cabin with Max Shean. From the Adelaide suburb of Woodville, burly and exuberant – Shean called him a hard player – Marsden was probably too big for the confines of an X-craft, but there was not much to be done about that. Jack had come up the slow route, called up as an ordinary seaman in 1941, gaining his RANVR commission at HMS *King Alfred* in 1942.

And then there was Henty Henty-Creer, for whom the word 'flamboyant' seems an understatement. His father, Commander Reginald Creer, had been the commanding officer of the boys' training ship, HMAS *Tingira*, moored in Sydney Harbour, and the young Henty lived on board with his mother, Eulalie Henty, and two sisters until a spectacular divorce tore the family apart when the boy was eight.

Eulalie had caught her husband with a mistress and the newspapers gleefully trumpeted the lurid details from the Divorce Court: a private detective had burst through a window to catch Reg on the job and seized his trousers as evidence; the Commander claimed his wife was a drunk; she hit back that she and the three children had been forced to live in humiliating poverty in a tent at Collaroy Beach.

Eulalie got her divorce. A daughter of the pioneering Henty family from Victoria, she defiantly added her surname to her son's – thus Henty-Creer – and took the children globe-trotting, staying with relatives and friends in places as far-flung as Fiji, Malaya, Ceylon, Denmark and Switzerland. Eventually she installed the young Henty at an exclusive boys' school in London's Chelsea, where he befriended the son of the celebrity film director Alexander Korda. Eulalie's family money ran out during the Depression. Aged thirteen, Henty had to quit school; he asked Korda for a job and was given one. He began writing an autobiography:

> I was fascinated by this fantastic world of make believe – the mixture of art and artifice which is the essence of film-making. I saw commonplace faces given allure and beauty by the cameraman; I saw great actors and actresses moved by the director like puppets across the stage, 'cabined and confined' by the exacting tape measure; I saw great forests and palatial palaces grow overnight...[7]

By 1940, aged twenty-two, he had risen to become a cameraman on the film *49th Parallel*, a propaganda epic and box-office smash about the hunt for a U-boat off Canada, featuring the biggest stars of the day, Raymond Massey, Laurence Olivier and Leslie Howard. That piqued Henty-Creer's interest in submarines. He enlisted for the war as an ordinary seaman, was granted a commission as a sub-lieutenant in the RNVR, did the diving course at Blockhouse and duly ended up at HMS *Varbel*.

Tall, slender and boyishly handsome, with a shock of wavy copper hair, Henty Henty-Creer radiated worldly confidence and charm. Of the fifty energetic young officers – English, Scots, Irish, Australians, South Africans and Kiwi – all jostling to prove themselves at HMS *Varbel*, he was the shining star. The reserved and methodical Max Shean thought he was a show pony.

Their training went on winter and summer, in days of pale Scottish sunshine, in days when rain and cold mists shrouded the waters. All the operational submarines had arrived by the end of

Attack the *Tirpitz*!

January 1943, six of them, numbered from X5 to X10 and internally much improved on the prototypes. Now the job was to get to know them. Their target had not yet been officially revealed, although everyone reckoned it would be *Tirpitz*.

Early practice with the boats took place in Loch Striven, a narrow inlet of breathtaking beauty, its hills clad in golden gorse in early spring. Running north from HMS *Varbel* and Port Bannatyne for some thirteen kilometres, sparsely populated, it had been chosen as a fair approximation of a Norwegian fjord. A shooting lodge at the head of the loch, Ardtaraig House, cold and bleak, was requisitioned as another base for the crews and commissioned as HMS *Varbel II*.

First came work with the Sladen diving suits, the absurdly cumbersome garment they began to call 'Clammy Death'. Struggling into one was like trying to crawl into a car tyre. In the beginning you needed help to do it: feet and legs in first, then the upper part was pulled over your head; the Davis breathing apparatus was connected and the glass visor was screwed shut. With practice you could do it yourself, but it took time and invariably they leaked a little. You used them to leave the X-craft underwater, clambering into the W&D and sitting there on the toilet as the compartment was flooded. At his first try, Shean had to resist the urge to panic when the outer hatch refused to open:

> There I was, immersed in water in a dark steel chamber with a mere glimmer of light from the inspection window in the internal door, and the exit hatch was unyielding. Then I noted that I was still breathing, just a little faster. 'This won't do,' I told myself. 'Relax. Take your time. Everything will come right in the end.' I have always been unconvincing and would never have made a salesman. But in spite of all apprehensions and indications, the hatch did open as soon as water had flowed in through the widening gap at the seal to equalise the pressure difference which I was creating. Suddenly all was light. It was like Wagner's Sunrise that preceded Siegfried's Rhine Journey. I floated up, shut the hatch by the same, slow steady pressure, gave a thumbs up to the instructor through a small window and floated to the surface.[8]

Next came intensive training in driving the boats, taking turns either as the captain in the cramped control room or as the first lieutenant seated at the steering wheel and the main ballast vent and blow valves, or as the coxswain aft with the engine, electric motor and hydroplane controls. The principle was exactly the same as in a large submarine, but it took a delicate hand and a steady nerve to do it all in the right sequence and with the right orders: setting the hydroplanes to dive; achieving a bow-down angle; stopping the diesel and starting the electric motor and levelling at the required depth; pumping water in or out of the trim tanks to keep her where you wanted to be. One of the training officers got it wrong in the prototype *X3*, flooding her and sending her plunging to the bottom of the Loch, putting her out of action for months – an embarrassing and salutary lesson.

As first lieutenant, Henty-Creer made a mess of his debut too:

> For some ten minutes all went well at periscope depth – then all fogged up. Suddenly we hit a fresh water patch and she took a nose dive at a hell of a bow angle. With full rise on the after planes I tried to bring her up. Nothing happened and with the speed of an express train we headed for the bottom out of control – 30 – 50 – 60 – flashed by on the depth gauge.
>
> 'Blow ones!' I turned the high pressure air blow to my for'ard tank. 'Blow twos.' The bow slowly came up. The gyro repeat was spinning around out of control. Then we headed for the surface almost standing on our tail. It was so like coming out of a dive and going into a steep climb that all our new 'captain' had time to say was 'Hang on, here we go!'
>
> I heard afterwards that our return to the surface was spectacular in the extreme.[9]

Gradually it came together. Things that once had been dauntingly difficult became second nature, and after a hard day in the loch it was good to relax in the evenings around the wardroom fire at *Varbel II*, sipping gin or the flat Scottish beer. In the early days there had been an edgy stand-off, with some of the regular young RN officers looking down their noses at the upstart reservists who had come to join them, but these barriers gradually crumbled beneath the weight of their common purpose and a pride in doing it properly.

This disparate, thrown-together outfit was now dignified as the Royal Navy's 12th Submarine Flotilla, although it retained a Boys' Own, vaguely piratical air, grounded in the real though unspoken recognition that this was an elite body of men engaged on a unique enterprise. The submariner's much-loved, white woollen rollneck sweater and hefty sea boots became standard dress in the officers' mess, to the distress of one or two of the stuffier, shore-based RN officers.

Shean became close mates with Bill Whittam, an Englishman, a tall and athletic former commando and now sub-lieutenant, who had fallen head over heels in love with one of the Wrens, a cypher officer at *Varbel*. He and Bill enjoyed a regular early-morning run up into the lovely Scottish hills, relishing the quiet and calm, sometimes cutting wood to bring back for the fire. On Valentine's Day, 14 February 1943, Max was thrilled to get a card from Mary Golding, the Scots girl he had met in Aberfeldy. On leave, he made train trips to see her. That April, to his quiet satisfaction, he was promoted to lieutenant.

Winston Churchill and the Admiralty paused the Arctic convoys after the disaster of PQ 17, much to the displeasure of the truculent and demanding Soviet dictator, Josef Stalin. They were just too hazardous to sail in the long Arctic summer daylight. Yet *Tirpitz* and other heavy ships of the German surface fleet remained an ever-present danger, tying up the RN's Home Fleet when it could be put to better use protecting the Atlantic convoys. In early 1943 the pressure was on to send the midget submarines into action.

Max Horton had left Northways to become the new Commander-in-Chief, Western Approaches, running the Battle of the Atlantic from Liverpool. The new Flag Officer Submarines was the recently promoted Rear Admiral Claud Barry, who had been captain of *Queen Elizabeth* when the Italians attacked her in Alexandria. Barry, though, was a submariner through and through. As a lieutenant commander, he had brought one of the

J-class boats to Australia in the 1920s, where he married a young woman from Geelong. A very different character from the fearsome Horton, genial and portly, he nonetheless had the courage to resist the push from on high to move too soon.

Churchill had become obsessed with taking *Tirpitz* off the naval chessboard – he called the ship 'The Beast' – and, as was his wont, he pushed and nagged, firing off memo after memo to Pound, the First Sea Lord: 'I trust all concerned are alive to the importance of sinking this ship and that it is realised that reasonable losses must be risked in order to do so.'[10]

Barry held firm, knowing there was still work to be done. The X-craft crews needed to develop ways of cutting through the anti-torpedo nets of heavy steel cable suspended from floating buoys and surrounding *Tirpitz* underwater, and there was also the crucial question of how exactly the boats were to make the long haul from Scotland to the Norwegian coast. They could not do it under their own steam, let alone make it back home again.

Cutting the nets meant danger. One young diver, an RNVR sub-lieutenant named David Locke, had been killed on a practice attempt in May. It was thought he may have become disoriented and gone down too deep, then suffered an attack of oxygen toxicity. If you breathed pure oxygen under pressure at too great a depth, you could, without warning, have a quick and fatal seizure as your red blood cells and then your nervous system went haywire. The divers called it 'Oxygen Pete' and had a morbid ditty about it:

> Down at the depth of seventy feet
> Lives a guy by the name of 'Oxygen Pete' . . .

Thirty feet – about nine metres – was about as far as you should go. Despite a search, Locke's body was never found.

Max Shean was asked to work on the problem of the nets. These were woven in a diamond pattern, each diamond a little less than a metre wide. The X-craft had a wire-cutter stored in a compartment in the casing just for'ard of the W&D, a blade in a hook at the end of five metres of hydraulic hose, specially developed and classified top-secret. Shean, with his engineering mind, sketched out his ideas on a piece of paper with Henty-Creer around the fire in the wardroom, and the next day they took *X5* to a net set up in Loch Striven.

Keeping the craft at nine metres' depth, Henty-Creer nosed bow-on to the net and kept it there. Shean in his diving suit left the W&D and unleashed the cutter, hooking it over one of the net cables and squeezing the trigger. There was a hiss and the blade emerged to slice through the wire with a satisfying crunch. Four times more, and there was a hole large enough for *X5* to slip through, which she did. Max climbed back into the W&D. The whole thing had taken only twelve minutes.

There were several possibilities for getting the X-craft to Norway. The most obvious was to transport them on a mother ship, which could release them off the fjords, but that was quickly rejected: it would be almost inviting discovery by enemy air reconnaissance or some passing U-boat. The second idea, towing them behind fishing trawlers, was discarded for the same reason. Admiral Barry and his staff settled on submarines, the full-size version, which could tow submerged by day and surface by night to recharge their batteries and refresh their air supply.

That, too, was tested. Nothing was to be left to chance. The submarine HMS *Tuna* was despatched to Port Bannatyne for practice runs up the west coast of Scotland, and after some hair-raising trial and error, with the X-craft plunging and leaping like porpoises, it worked well enough, up to a maximum speed of ten knots.

The next issue to be settled was which cable to use for the tow. A steel hawser would be too heavy, dragging down the little X-craft by the bow. Nylon cables would be ideal, but these were only in the very early stages of development. Nylon was then a novel and expensive commodity, and the RAF had cornered the market in these cables for use in towing its gliders. Grudgingly, they offered up two of them to Admiral Barry, but that was it. The only other possibility was manila cable, heavier than nylon but lighter than steel. These were especially manufactured in a length of 200 metres, with a telephone line woven into them for communications between submarine and X-craft. It was not perfect, for manila towlines had been known to break under long and heavy strain, but it would have to do.

From the summer of 1943, things began to speed up. The attack was to be codenamed Operation Source. The men were officially told, to the surprise of no one, that the target would be *Tirpitz*, with secondary attacks on any other capital ships that might be with her. It would be a long, long journey to get there, more than a thousand sea miles. *Tirpitz* was known to be lying in Kåfjorden, a narrow branch of the much larger Altafjord, in far northern Norway, above the 70th parallel and therefore well inside the Arctic Circle. That put her out of reach of RAF bombers but within easy striking distance of the convoy routes to Russia.

The Admiralty left nothing to chance. A member of the Norwegian resistance, Torstein Raaby, was landed near Altafjord by submarine, equipped with maps, codebooks, a radio transmitter and a heavy wad of *krone*. Masquerading as a roadworker, he kept a close eye on *Tirpitz* and, at great risk, sent regular messages to London, including a map of the defences that surrounded her.

The season, the weather and even the phases of the moon would be critical. The planners determined that Operation Source would best be carried out in the third week of September, with the moon in its last quarter. Ideally, the X-craft would sail on 11 September for a passage of nine days. They would be unleashed from their towing submarines and sent in to Altafjord on 20 September, a Monday.

Then came the announcement they had all been awaiting: the final decision on captains and crews. In fact, there would be two crews for each craft. A passage crew of three men would be on board for the tedious but demanding tow from Scotland up the North Sea and then back home again. The operational crew, of four men, including a diver, would travel in the parent submarine to stay fresh and then transfer by dinghy to their X-craft for the attack itself.

Remarkably, of the six craft involved, three would be commanded by Australians. Henty-Creer was appointed to *X5*. Digger McFarlane, the regular RAN lieutenant, was given *X8*, and Ken Hudspeth, the Tasmanian schoolteacher, now also promoted to lieutenant RANVR, got *X10*. McFarlane was delighted to be assigned his friend Jack Marsden, the tall young man from Adelaide, as his first lieutenant.

The captain of *X6* would be Lieutenant Donald Cameron, a Scot from the Royal Naval Reserve, and one of the earliest of the submarine trainees. *X7* went to Lieutenant Godfrey Place, a regular RN officer. Slightly built, quirky and – to his friends – amiable but notoriously untidy, Place had done time in Mediterranean submarines, where he had already won the Distinguished Service Cross as third hand and then first lieutenant of HMS *Unbeaten*. He had been hired for X-craft during afternoon tea with an admiral at the Ritz Hotel in Piccadilly, who over scones and cucumber sandwiches had asked him if he would 'like a crack at *Tirpitz*'. Finally, *X9* went to Lieutenant Terry Martin, also RN.

Max Shean was devastated to be left out. He had done all and more that was asked of him, quietly and conscientiously, and to be passed over at this point was a cruel blow. Not even a first lieutenant. They told him he would be on standby, as a reserve in case anyone pulled out, but it was still a kick in the teeth. In particular, he was distressed that Henty-Creer had been preferred ahead of him, which he put down to his flair for showmanship and chatting up his elders and betters rather than any superior competence. Shean had done his time at sea in the Gibraltar convoys, while Henty-Creer had barely got his feet wet. There was a rowdy wardroom party that night to celebrate, the drinks flowing, but Max's heart was not in it.

The tempo quickened, inexorably. In summer the entire show migrated north to Loch Cairnbawn, codenamed Port HHZ. This would be the departure point. No leave was allowed.

There was now a mother ship for the X-craft, HMS *Bonaventure*, a requisitioned Clan Line freighter with large derricks, and a depot ship arrived for the six parent submarines, HMS *Titania*, commanded by Tiny Fell, the man who had developed the chariots. Then came the submarines themselves: HMS *Sceptre*, *Sea Nymph*, *Syrtis*, *Thrasher*, *Truculent* and *Stubborn*.

That added one more Australian to the cast: *Sceptre*'s commanding officer was none other than Ian McIntosh, now a lieutenant and wearing the cerise and white ribbon of the military MBE, awarded for his exploits in Lifeboat Seven, and the blue and white of the Distinguished Service Cross. His war had not lost its excitement, with service in two Mediterranean submarines attacking convoys, hunting U-boats, laying mines in enemy waters and running supplies to Malta. Perhaps its most interesting moment had come, though, when his second boat, *Thrasher*, was mistakenly but accurately depth-charged on the surface by a Fleet Air Arm Swordfish which had cocked up the recognition signals. That had been a near thing, *Thrasher* limping back to Port Said on her batteries alone. After that, McIntosh had done his Perisher, taken a turn driving a training boat and now commanded *Sceptre*, which he had commissioned on the Clyde, brand-new, still a few months short of his twenty-fourth birthday.

Towing and diving practice went on. The battleship *Malaya* put in an appearance, sent by the Admiralty to add realism to the exercise. At the last run of net-cutting trials, *X9*'s diver lost his nerve and pulled out, and Max Shean was named to replace him – a 'pierhead jump', as the navy calls it, joining a ship at the last minute before it sails. His relief was deep felt. He was wanted – he was in. He went to the intelligence briefings, where they were told how to evade capture and how to walk to Sweden if they had to, and were given survival kits and maps, as well as the names of Norwegian resistance agents, which they had to memorise.

Claud Barry had arranged with the RAF to station a pair of photo reconnaissance Spitfire aircraft in Russia to observe *Tirpitz* in her fjord, and there was an almighty panic after their first sortie on 7 September when they reported she was not there. Nor was her companion, the battlecruiser *Scharnhorst*. Only the heavy cruiser *Lutzow* was still in place. This was four days before Operation Source was due to begin from Port HHZ. The mystery was solved when, bizarrely, both ships, with an escort of no fewer than nine destroyers, turned up at the Norwegian island of Spitzbergen, on the edge of the Arctic Ocean, and bombarded Allied installations there, putting a battalion of troops ashore and setting fire to a coalmine. Sixteen Norwegians and one German were killed.

The Germans had grandly dubbed this Operation Zitronella, but it was an absurd pantomime, a sledgehammer sent to crack a nut; its main purpose seemed to be to demonstrate to an increasingly irritable Hitler that the German Navy's big ships were earning their keep. A sailor in one of the destroyers was discovered in hiding when the action started and was shot for cowardice on *Scharnhorst*'s quarterdeck. By 10 September both ships were back at anchor again, surrounded by their torpedo nets, and Iron Crosses were showered from on high in their hundreds.

In the last few days, the X-craft were hoisted one by one aboard *Bonaventure* to have their side cargoes – their explosives – fastened in place on each side of the hull. Admiral Barry arrived from London on 10 September to farewell the troops, and that night Tiny Fell threw a formal naval dinner for him and the X-craft officers on board *Tites*, as they called *Titania*. Not so the ERAs, the petty officers who tended the engines. They were given a barrel of beer in a cowshed on the shore.

Men on the eve of battle behave in different ways. Some withdraw into themselves, lost in thought. Some are sombre with anticipation, others affect a bold nonchalance, some are terrified but do their best to conceal it. Others are exuberant, exhilarated, as if this night might be their last and therefore not to be wasted. The ERA assigned to *X5*, Ralph Mortiboys, twenty-two years old, had a premonition that he would not return and declined the party in the cowshed, staying on board *Bonaventure* to write a farewell to his widowed mother.

By all accounts the officers' night was a rip-roaring success. Commander Fell, who dearly loved a social occasion, wrote that 'there was a tremendous dinner party in my cabin. A remarkable evening followed in the wardroom with nearly all hands in little more than bow ties and underpants, with morale sky high.'[11]

Max Shean joined in:

> After the dinner, some of the pent-up anxiety gave way to general revelry. A game started of collecting 'medal ribbons,' these being short pieces cut from braces which, in those days, were in general use to hold trousers up. Before long most of us had the shirts torn from our backs as well. I finished up in collar and cuffs.[12]

Admiral Barry, no stranger to a wardroom romp, kicked up his heels as well, later writing that:

> like boys on the last days of term, their spirits ran so high. This confidence was not in any way the outcome of youthful dare-devilry but was based on the firm conviction, formed during many months of arduous training, that their submarines were capable of doing all that their crews demanded of them, and the crews were quite capable of surmounting any difficulties or hazards which it was possible for human beings to conquer.
>
> It was in this spirit that they went out into the night in their tiny craft to face a thousand miles of rough seas before they reached their objective which itself, to their knowledge, was protected by every conceivable device which could ensure their destruction before they could complete the attacks.
>
> And the Tirpitz herself was tucked away close under the cliffs at the head of a narrow fjord 60 miles from the sea.[13]

They sailed the next afternoon.

14

MORE FRIGHTENED THAN I HAVE EVER BEEN . . .

The first to leave was *X6*, towed by *Truculent*, the sun beginning to set over the snow-dusted hills of the Loch as they passed into the North Minch, that turbulent strait in the Hebrides leading out to the North Sea. Admiral Barry was in a launch, waving as the 12th Submarine Flotilla put to sea. *Sceptre*, towing *X10*, was the last to depart.

The plan was to sail north-east on separate but parallel courses, submerged by day, on the surface at night when there was little risk of discovery. If all went well, this small armada would reach the arrival point off Soroy Island, on the Norwegian coast, in eight days, where the passage crews would leave by dinghy and the operational crews would take over. On 20 September, a Monday, the submarines would slip their charges and the X-craft would be on their own to enter the fjords. There was a known minefield off Soroy across the entrance to the main Altafjord, but the X-craft with their shallow draft should pass easily over it.

Inside Altafjord, they would first head south-east for about half the journey, some fifty kilometres, then turn south to slip into the small and narrow Kåfjorden, where *Tirpitz* lay moored and guarded by her torpedo nets. *Scharnhorst* and *Lutzow* should be there too. To give everyone time to get into position, to prevent things going off half-cocked, Barry had ordered that there should be no attack before 1 a.m. on Wednesday, 22 September. Among themselves, the X-craft captains agreed to lay their charges between 5 a.m. and

8 a.m., which should be timed to explode at 8.30 a.m. so as to give everyone a chance to get clear.

The first four days passed quietly enough, the passage crews toiling away at the exacting business of staying where they were supposed to be, constantly watching the depth gauges, the inclinometer bubble, nursing the electrical circuits and motors as they were towed along, taking turns to sleep. Every six hours or so, on a prearranged signal, they would surface to 'guff through' – to refresh the air in the boat – to run the diesels to charge the batteries, and to get rid of 'gash' (navy slang for garbage). In *Sceptre*, the two Australians, Ian McIntosh and Ken Hudspeth, were getting to know each other.

Trouble struck on the fourth day, Wednesday, 15 September. At four in the morning, *X8* suddenly nosedived, a sure sign that the towline to *Sea Nymph* had parted. Alarmed, the passage crew blew tanks and surfaced quickly and safely – but could see no sign of their parent vessel. Visibility was good but the sea was empty; *Sea Nymph* had inexplicably vanished. Mystified and perturbed, *X8*'s passage commanding officer decided that all he could do was maintain his course and press on.

Sea Nymph did not discover that she had lost her charge for another two hours. Her captain increased speed and turned back to retrace their steps on the surface, with extra lookouts on the bridge, in a sea that had begun to rise ominously. They searched all day and into the lowering night but found nothing, not a sign.

Next it was *X7*'s turn. At 3.30 that afternoon, her tow to *Stubborn* parted – those damn manila cables – and it took nearly an hour of fumbling and cursing to hook up an auxiliary line. But while that was happening, *X8* suddenly hove into view. The three boats set off again together, but during the night *X8* disappeared once more. *Stubborn* had ordered her to steer 046 degrees but she had misheard and headed away on 146 degrees. With a combination of good luck and good management, the still searching *Sea Nymph* found the wayward *X8* the next afternoon, 16 September, and took her in tow again. With her passage crew exhausted, Digger McFarlane agreed that his operational crew would take over.

Worse was to come. At 9 a.m. on 16 September, *Syrtis* surfaced and dropped three small grenades, or 'Suzies', as they were called – Signals-Underwater-Exploding – a message for *X9* to surface and recharge. Nothing happened. To their consternation, *X9* was no longer there. With *Syrtis* rising and falling in the swell, they hauled in the slack towline, only to have it snag on something beneath the stern. It was stuck.

The captain asked for *X9*'s diver to go down and take a look. That was Max Shean. But his diving suit was on the missing X-craft. He dressed in a pair of overalls, took one of the standard Davis escape sets and stumbled aft along the casing. It was madness, surely. They were on the edge of the Arctic Ocean in autumn, and the water temperature would be less than five degrees Celsius – near freezing.

'Be quick,' the captain said. 'If we're surprised by an enemy aircraft I'll have to dive.'

That was hardly encouraging, but there was nothing for it. With a lifeline attached and oxygen switched on, Shean jumped in.

> The water was absolutely clear. In the few moments that I could remain submerged I noted the shafts of sunlight descending into the depths. It made me feel giddy. I tried to see the propellers but, as Syrtis pitched in the heavy swell, the hydroplanes smacked the surface with an almighty splash, which forced me to the surface again. I was cold all over and more frightened than I have ever been . . . but there was no giving up . . .
>
> I swam along the surface to get clear of the hydroplanes and looked down. There were the infinite beams of light converging toward the great deep and there was the port propeller with the rope around it, not tight but in a big loop. That was fortunate so long as the propeller was not rotated. I looked up to the First Lieutenant on deck and removed my mouthpiece.
>
> 'Do not turn the port propeller. Let out some slack on the tow and carry it as far aft as you can.'
>
> This they did. I saw, to my enormous relief, that the bight of rope was now lying aft of the propeller.
>
> 'Right. Heave in now.'

The rope straightened above the propeller and slid across the top of the big shaft as the casing party heaved it aboard.[1]

Numb and shaking, blue with cold, Shean was still thawing out below when *Syrtis* swung around on a reciprocal course at speed to search for *X9*, butting into a rising swell. All that evening and night, extra lookouts on the bridge peered into the dark. Nothing.

The next day they came across a well-defined oil slick exactly where she should have been, but that was all. *X9* had gone to the bottom, carrying the three men of her passage crew to a terrifying death as she was crushed by the pressure and her plates caved in. It is likely that her end of the broken tow rope had weighed her down, sending her plummeting before they could blow tanks and bring her up. These were the first deaths of Operation Source.

Max Shean had lost a good friend, Paddy Kearon, a cheerful Irish sub-lieutenant who had been *X9*'s passage commanding officer. Only a few weeks before, Paddy had carried a letter to Mary Golding for him.

X8 caused more strife the next morning. Digger McFarlane and the first lieutenant, Jack Marsden, found her trim was all over the place and getting worse as she lurched and lunged beneath the surface, developing an ugly list to starboard. Nothing could keep her steady. They traced the problem to air escaping from the starboard-side cargo, the explosives capsule, and decided it would have to be jettisoned. They set the charge to safe but it blew up anyway, far enough astern to frighten the life out of them but doing no damage.

Hours later, a similar air leak developed in the port-side charge and, after setting the timer on that for a two-hour delay, they dumped it too. The timer failed and the charge exploded with phenomenal force, lifting *X8* like a windblown leaf and then slamming her down again. Her hatch burst open, the W&D was flooded, doors were distorted, pipes were fractured and they found she was taking on water and could no longer dive.

McFarlane talked it over with the captain of *Sea Nymph* and they agreed she could not keep going. That evening they scuttled her. That left only four of the six X-craft still in play, pressing on.

A little after midnight on the morning of 20 September, with *X7* in tow, *Stubborn* spotted a floating mine which had broken away from its mooring. From the bridge they watched in frozen horror as it bobbed astern and came gently to rest against the bow of the X-craft, its mooring rope hitched around the towline. It was an old-fashioned contact mine, a sphere with horns, but lethal nonetheless. If one of the horns were to strike a vessel's hull and break, a chemical reaction would detonate the explosive. Aroused from his supper, *X7*'s captain, Godfrey Place, crept out onto the casing and, hanging on for dear life, untangled the mooring wire and gingerly prodded the thing away with his foot. It passed astern.

That same morning at 3 a.m., *Syrtis*, on the surface, sighted a U-boat heading in towards the Norwegian coast. Everyone held their breath but the Germans did not see them, although they came within a range of 1400 metres, a sitting shot. But the towing submarines had strict orders not to attack anything less than a capital ship – a battleship or perhaps a heavy cruiser – and so *Syrtis* regretfully had to pass up a tempting opportunity.

By late Monday, 20 September, all the passage crews had finished their job and the operational crews were in place on board the small craft, the parent submarines withdrawing to wait for the return of their charges in assigned patrol areas at sea. If they returned. There were now two Australians left: Henty Henty-Creer in *X5* and Ken Hudspeth in *X10*. That night, under a breathtaking display of the Northern Lights, all four X-craft passed safely over the Soroy minefield and independently into Stjernsund, the broad waterway leading into Altafjord. Early on 21 September, they dived to a safe thirty metres or so, coming to periscope depth once in a while to check their positions. The day was beautiful, sunny and calm, the water a deep, glassy turquoise. This was Sami country, home to clans of fishermen and reindeer herders, with the occasional village dotting the steep green and brown banks of the fjord, patches of snow on the higher hills, and sometimes an unsuspecting trawler passing by.[2]

X5, *X6* and *X7* spent that night at a prearranged stop in the lee of an island, out of sight of each other but charging their batteries and making ready for the attack on the morrow. The last intelligence they had was that *Scharnhorst* and *Lutzow* were no longer in the fjords: they had apparently put to sea. *Tirpitz* would be their only target. *X5* and *X7* did catch a brief glimpse of each other, the two captains wishing each other 'good hunting'. Henty-Creer had been best man at Place's wedding back in April.

X6 was having problems with her periscope unaccountably fogging up and a slight list to starboard developing, but they thought it was manageable. Ken Hudspeth and *X10*, though, were in trouble. Her periscope hoist motor was playing up and she was struggling to keep her trim with her starboard side cargo flooding. Most worryingly, her gyrocompass failed. She paused for repairs in an isolated cove, Smalfjord, and then pressed on, but her troubles only mounted.

Early in the morning of 22 September, submerged but almost within sight of Kåfjorden, pretty well everything that could go wrong on *X10* did go wrong. The boat was leaking above the main electrical switchboard and, in a shower of sparks and a cloud of acrid smoke, all the fuses blew. Ken Hudspeth ordered periscope depth and the hoisting motor instantly burnt out, with more choking electrical fumes. And the magnetic compass had flooded. They were blind. Ken bottomed her at sixty metres before daylight set in and the crew began to make repairs.

So now there were three. Not long after midnight on 22 September, *X5*, *X6* and *X7* began their run towards the anti-submarine boom, which blocked the entrance to Kåfjorden, where the unsuspecting *Tirpitz* was skulking. The weather had taken their side, dawning to a grey, overcast day with a wind whipping up white horses helpful in concealing the wake left by a raised periscope. At about 4 a.m., *X7* had a stroke of luck. At periscope depth, Place saw a small German minesweeper coming out through a gap in the boom and, diving again to nine metres, he seized the opportunity to sneak through after her. There luck left him. He became stuck in torpedo nets which had protected the now-departed *Lutzow*, and it took a precious, anxious hour of bouncing and backing and filling to dislodge himself, all the while fearing the enemy must surely notice the bubbles of air venting from his main ballast tanks.

X6, an hour behind, slipped through the boom gap behind a small ferry, and she too dived as her captain, Donald Cameron, tried to fix the periscope, which had now clouded over. That done, he nudged forward again, only to have the thing go foggy once more and its motor burn out. It could now only be raised and lowered by hand. But he had passed through a gap in *Tirpitz*'s anti-torpedo net and was within striking distance.

Elegantly clad in neatly pressed jodhpurs and polished riding boots, *Vizeadmiral* Oscar Kummetz, commander of the *Kampfgruppe der Kriegsmarine*, the Navy Task Group, finished his breakfast, left his cabin in *Tirpitz* and went ashore to saddle his horse for his regular early-morning ride. The battleship's captain, *Kapitän zur See* Hans Meyer, also breakfasted in his cabin. *Tirpitz* went about her daily routine.

Shortly after 7 a.m., in the early light, a flak gunner on watch glimpsed a small, black, elongated shape in the water over near the shore. It looked like a submarine, he thought, and he reported it to his officer, who peered through his binoculars and saw nothing. If something had been there, it had disappeared. And anyway, how could a submarine be so close inshore? 'Probably a porpoise,' the officer said, laughing. Everyone relaxed.

It was in fact *X6*. Trying to close on *Tirpitz*, with her periscope all but useless, she had grounded inshore and lurched briefly to the surface. At the controls, her first lieutenant, Sub-Lieutenant John Lorimer, managed to bump and grind her free, but the shock of the grounding had disabled her gyrocompass and she was now blind. She surfaced again in a froth of bubbles, closer to *Tirpitz* now, and this time there was no mistake: she was seen for what she was. After a shocked pause, the battleship's alarms sounded and men began racing to their stations. *X6*'s luck had drained away. Down she went once more, and then up again for a third time, beneath *Tirpitz*'s port bow, to be met by rifle and machine-gun fire and hand grenades, some of the bullets rattling on her hull. Happily, *Tirpitz*'s bigger guns were unable to deflect to reach her.

Cameron now recognised that the game was up and he stood no chance of escape, but he would finish what he had come to do. At periscope depth, he ordered *X6* to go astern; scraping down the battleship's towering side, he released both charges abreast of Bruno turret.[3] Job done, he and his crew set about destroying their charts, smashing gauges and other secret gear, then they opened the Kingston valves as they surfaced for the last time. They left the hatch with their hands in the air. *Tirpitz* had a motor launch in the water and it took them off. The launch attempted to take *X6* in tow but she sank as they watched. Cameron and his three companions – Lorimer, diver Dick Kendall and ERA Eddie Goddard – were hustled up the battleship's accommodation ladder onto the quarter-deck, where they were surrounded by sailors with guns, their first sight of the enemy at close quarters. It was just after 7 a.m.

Kendall took in all he saw:

> Don walked over to me and said 'sorry about this.' The feeling was one of resigned expectation, what would happen when the cargoes blew. Would we be blown up too, after all we'd been through, would we be blown up by our own charges? This wasn't in the Manual at all. The over-riding sensation was one of relief that we'd done what we came to do.
>
> Don and John were moved away to be interrogated. Eddie and I were moved to a compartment on the port side, with a couple of guards.[4]

Free of *Lutzow*'s torpedo nets, Godfrey Place lined up *X7* for his attack on *Tirpitz* a few minutes after 7 a.m. He tried to squeeze beneath her anti-torpedo nets, first at twenty metres' depth and then again at twenty-seven metres, but got stuck each time. With more pushing and shoving he broke free, but his gyrocompass had also packed it in, spinning madly. To his astonishment, *X7* smacked straight into the battleship.

> We actually hit the target's side obliquely at 20 feet and slid underneath, swinging our fore-and-aft line to the line of her keel.

More Frightened Than I Have Ever Been... 263

The first charge was let go – as I estimated under the Tirpitz's bridge – and X7 was taken about 200 feet astern to drop the other charge under the after turrets. The time was 0720. It was just as we were letting go this second charge that we heard the first signs of enemy counter-attack – but, oddly enough, we were wrong in assuming they were meant for us.[5]

Now to escape. With the gyrocompass out of action, that meant groping in the dark to find a way back under the torpedo net, and for three-quarters of an hour or so they tried and failed, growing ever more concerned as the minutes ticked by that they might be blown up by their own charges. Finally they wormed over the top of the net – only to be spotted by the Germans, who opened up with machine guns. Place dived, becoming entangled in the net once more.

And then the charges went off, with a thunderous roar. They rocked X7 out of the net. Gauges and the trimming bubble were smashed and some leaks opened up. Crucially, her compass was still useless and she had very little compressed air left. If she were to dive again she might not be able to get back up. With a heavy heart, Place decided to surface for the last time. The Germans were still shooting.

As captain, Place felt he should go first into the gunfire. Opening the hatch, he gingerly extended an arm to wave a white submarine sweater in surrender. X7 had surfaced near a gunnery practice target, which she thumped into, and Place – still flapping the sweater – stepped onto it, unharmed by the bullets that were still flying. But the X-craft had been holed by the shooting in her starboard ballast tank, taking on a list, and her bows dipped on the impact with the target. Water surged through the hatch into the W&D, and Place watched in dismay as she went down for the last time, carrying the other three men with her.

He was taken to *Tirpitz*'s quarterdeck. In X7, lying on the bottom, the three planned their escape wearing the Davis breathing sets. Sub-Lieutenant Robert Aitken, twenty years old, was the diver, and later recalled:

> We all put one on and started to flood the boat. The hatch could not be opened until the boat was fully flooded to equalise the

pressure inside the boat with that outside. Unfortunately this took longer than we anticipated because some of the valves couldn't be fully opened. As the water crept up it reached the batteries which fused, giving off fumes, and we had to start breathing oxygen before the boat was fully flooded.

During that time there was nothing to do except wait. As soon as we went onto oxygen we could not talk to each other, the oxygen mouthpiece prevented that. There were no lights, we couldn't see each other and we were left with our own thoughts. I remember throughout that I was very confident I would escape. 'It couldn't happen to me, I was going to survive,' I thought.[6]

It took an age to get the water in, more than half an hour, which seemed like an eternity. It was ice cold, gripping them like a vice, and both the first lieutenant, Bill Whittam, and the ERA, Bill Whitley, eventually ran out of oxygen and drowned. On his own now and almost out of oxygen himself, Aitken clambered past their bodies and managed to force open the hatch at his third desperate attempt. Lungs near to bursting, he rose as quickly as he dared to the surface where, almost comatose, he was disappointed to see the target still afloat. The Germans picked him up in a boat and took him back to the ship.

There was pandemonium on *Tirpitz* when the charges went off. It was 8.12 a.m. Two great columns of water shot into the air, higher than her mast, and the ship heaved upwards like a bathtub toy, all 45,000 tonnes of her, and then slumped back again. *Tirpitz*'s log recorded: 'Two heavy consecutive detonations to port at 1/10 seconds interval. Ship vibrates strongly in vertical direction and sways slightly between the anchors.'[7] John Lorimer was in the captain's cabin being interrogated by Hans Meyer. Both men were thrown across the room. On deck, there was something close to panic as the Germans began firing at shadows in the water.

It is likely that the first charge exploding detonated all the others. The ship's hull was holed enough to flood part of the engine room with an estimated 450 tonnes of water and the pressure waves of the explosion ran through her innards, fracturing many of her engine mountings and throwing them out of alignment so that her propellers could not be turned. One of her rudders flooded through a stern gland. She was immobile. Electrical power was lost and all her lights went out, although that was quickly restored. More damaging, the four gun turrets of her main armament sprang from their roller bearings and were also rendered useless. Her aircraft catapult was wrecked. One man was killed and another thirty or forty were wounded to varying degrees.

The prisoners were lined up on the quarterdeck before a menacing squad of sailors with machine guns. In halting English, an officer demanded to know if there were more submarines out there. No one replied. They feared they were about to be shot. That pregnant moment was defused when Admiral Kummetz strode back on board, still in his riding jodhpurs, and spoke to the officer. The sailors lowered their guns.

This was not the last alarm. At 8.43 a.m. the Germans caught a brief glimpse of a midget submarine partly surfaced some 500 yards beyond the torpedo nets. Still on deck, John Lorimer saw it too and recognised a periscope. This could only be Henty Henty-Creer and *X5*. All hell broke loose: there was another fusillade from small and medium weapons and she disappeared very quickly. A launch from a destroyer was sent to the spot to drop depth charges. The German officer in charge of the launch, *Leutnant zur See* Eberhard Schmölder, recalled:

> I saw a third U-boat break the surface. I couldn't see in which direction it was heading or whether it was hit, as it was obscured by spray and the spouts of water thrown up by the shells. When it disappeared, firing ceased. I immediately made for the last place I had seen it. At 30-metre intervals I dropped five depth charges around the spot where it had disappeared. The last but one left on the surface an extra-strong eddy mixed with black bubbles of oil. Afterwards more oil rose to the surface and spread to form a large patch on the sea. The submarine had most certainly been badly damaged and put out of action.[8]

Lorimer, too, saw an underwater explosion and also an oil slick, and that was it.

It is impossible to piece together *X5*'s last hours. She may have penetrated the torpedo nets and placed her charges and was destroyed while escaping. Perhaps her gyrocompass also packed up and she was lost. Perhaps she did not make it through the nets at all. It remains a mystery. There have been searches on the floor of the fjord over the years but nothing conclusive was ever found. Henty-Creer and his crew – Sub-Lieutenant Tom Nelson, Midshipman Alistair Malcolm and ERA Ralph Mortiboys – all perished. Mortiboys' presentiment that he would not return had proved correct. The flamboyant Henty-Creer, always the life of the party, was no more.

After a while, an uneasy calm returned on board *Tirpitz*. To their credit, Admiral Kummetz and Captain Meyer ordered that the prisoners should be treated well. They were taken below, offered coffee and schnapps, and allowed to sleep. The next day they were sent south to prison camps in Germany, where they would spend the rest of the war.

Operation Source, though, was not over. By no means. *X10* spent the entire day of the attack sitting on the bottom as Ken Hudspeth and his crew worked methodically to fix the defects. Geoff Harding, *X10*'s diver, was just nineteen years old, an RNVR midshipman promoted early to acting temporary sub-lieutenant for this operation. He later recalled:

> Ken Hudspeth asked each of us whether we wanted to go in. Of course we all said yes but, after due consideration, Ken said it wasn't really practicable, which we already knew, and that if seen on the surface we might jeopardise the others' chances, and what fun it would be to lie on the bottom and listen for the bangs. If there weren't any, well, we'd think again and maybe 'have a bash' ourselves. At least if they did go off we were far away enough to remain undamaged. We continued to toil away at the long list of repairs.[9]

At 8.12 a.m. they did indeed hear the bangs, loud ones which were the side cargoes going off, followed at intervals by smaller explosions, probably depth charges. Geoff Harding again:

> I think we were all feeling a bit churned up inside. We were glad about the bangs but sorry they weren't ours. We were pleased that we didn't have to take the wreck of our boat into Kafjord but sad that we'd had such an appalling run of bad luck.
>
> By 1800, just twenty four hours after we had left Smalfjord in high spirits, we had been on the bottom for nearly sixteen hours. The air was becoming increasingly foul, making us disinclined to continue with the repairs, in fact we were just lying still and waiting for a good time to get away. It was not a happy party. We were desperately disappointed that, despite all our efforts, we had been unable to fulfill our task.
>
> Nobody said much, but I think each of us knew what the others were thinking. I looked at Ken and Bruce and Tilley, on different occasions, but conversation was obviously pointless.[10]

With the Norwegian night setting in, *X10* began to retrace her steps on the surface, heading towards the sea again to find her towing submarine, *Sceptre*. The cargoes were set to safe and released on the way. With the gyrocompass still out of action, Ken had to con the boat standing on deck in the icy cold and flurries of snow, hell-for-leather at her best speed of six knots, holding on for dear life, shouting helm orders down the hatch. Twice they saw patrol craft and dived to avoid them. Once when they surfaced again they found, to their dismay, that they had turned around 180 degrees and were doubling back. At 2.15 the next morning, 23 September, they reached Smalfjord again and found it deserted, as they had hoped. With the boat and the shore both covered in snow, they felt there was no risk of discovery and they spent the rest of the night on the surface, tethered to the bank with a grapnel, snatching what sleep they could.

After a makeshift breakfast they moved again at 11 a.m., and with the periscope lashed in the up position they dived to reach the southernmost edge of the minefield they would have to cross before reaching the open sea. That took most of the day. As the dark closed in at 6 p.m., *X10* surfaced and, with bated breath and fingers crossed, they passed over the minefield at full speed, reaching one of the designated recovery areas at around 11 p.m. There was nothing there, no submarine to be seen, the sea empty. Spirits sank, but all they could do was hang around waiting, taking turns to keep a lookout on the surface in the daylight hours. This they did for another thirty hours – an infinity, it seemed. Ken Hudspeth did his best to keep their hopes, if not high, then at least alive.

Time to try another option. Before dawn on 25 September, they abandoned that patrol area and set a course for another small inlet on Soroy Island, which they thought would be deserted, meaning they could get some rest before restarting the search. They reached that spot that afternoon and there they sat for another night and day, discussing what they might do if no submarine was found.

The alternatives were daunting. One thought was to put to sea again and try to make it around the top of Norway, through the notoriously turbulent seas off the North Cape, then south-east to the Russian port of Murmansk, where there was a British submarine base, a journey of some 800 kilometres. Another possibility was to abandon the boat and try to walk south to neutral Sweden, which was nearer. Although they'd been given maps and some instruction on how to do this, the reality would be a gruelling trek across a bleak, forbidding wilderness of bare tundra, glacial streams, snow-clad ranges and the occasional pine and birch forest.

Doubt gnawed at them, but not despair. Whatever his inner thoughts, Ken Hudspeth – twenty-five years old, the former Tasmanian schoolteacher – displayed a quiet calm and confidence, as a captain should. In the end they decided to stick it out and try another designated patrol area, and they moved to another nearby fjord.

Geoff Harding had the optimism of youth:

> A waterfall emptied into it on one side and we had great plans to swim ashore and get some fresh water. The sea was practically ice and it would have been a pretty chilly swim.

> As we were considering this we suddenly heard an aircraft. The last man had landed below and the plugs pulled out in about five seconds flat. Our periscope was still showing above the surface when we hit the bottom at nine feet. The chart had showed a lot of water there, too. It was a funny feeling doing a spectacular dive and landing on the bottom only nine feet lower down.[11]

Enemy or not, the aircraft did not molest them and after a decent interval they surfaced again. Cold though it was, they took the opportunity to strip off for a wash and then, refreshed, ate a hearty meal of tinned tomato soup and tinned chicken and vegetables, heated in the electric pot. Morale rose. Hudspeth decided to make one more attempt at contacting a waiting submarine, and on 27 September they motored on the surface to another defined area off Soroy, Oyfjord, which they reached that afternoon.

They kept a watch all night and for another day, and at five minutes before midnight on 28 September, salvation came to them, in a pinprick of red light dimly seen at first through snow and rain squalls. It was the infrared beam shone from a searching submarine, HMS *Stubborn*. They replied, and the two craft closed in a heavy swell, conditions so surging and lurching that it took almost an hour for the tow to be passed and made fast. They had to wait until daylight and an easing of the seas for *X10*'s exhausted but jubilant crew to transfer to the submarine, to be replaced by the passage crew from *X7*.

At 6 a.m. on 29 September, *Stubborn*, at a cautious four knots, set a course for the port of Lerwick, in the Shetland Islands, the agreed point of return. Still their troubles were not over. At midday on 3 October, in worsening weather, the tow parted again and *X10* broke adrift. *Stubborn*'s captain, Lieutenant Arthur Duff, asked Hudspeth and *X10*'s first lieutenant, Bruce Enzer, to go over in a dinghy to help the passage crew improvise a new tow with some of the submarine's spare periscope wires. A difficult and dangerous job, it took four and a half hours to do. Back again in *Stubborn* they set off, into the darkening night at three and a half knots. The official Admiralty report finishes the story:

About an hour later (1807) a signal was received in the Stubborn from the Rear Admiral Submarines, warning Lieutenant Duff that a gale was expected and directing him to embark the passage crew and to scuttle X10 at his discretion. The Stubborn was still some 400 miles from Lerwick; the chances of towing her there without a crew on board were slight and Lieutenant Duff decided to sink her. It was a hard decision to take after all they had been through together. By 2040 the three officers remaining in X10 were embarked, and five minutes later she sank in lat. 66°13'N, long. 4°02'E.[12]

So disappeared the last surviving craft of the 12th Submarine Flotilla. It was a crowded trip back. Digger McFarlane and the operational and passage crews of the scuttled *X8* were already on board. But the gale did not arrive and they reached Lerwick safely on 5 October. Never had a port looked more welcoming. After almost three weeks away, Ken Hudspeth had brought his men home. Operation Source had ended.

An RAF reconnaissance Spitfire flew over Altafjord the day after the attack, 23 September, but could observe only that *Tirpitz* was still afloat at her anchorage – depressing news when it reached the Admiralty and Claud Barry.

A day later, Berlin Radio, in a brief announcement, said that a British attack on *Tirpitz* by small submarines had taken place but failed. This was the first indication to the Admiralty that the raid had actually happened. But in the coming days the picture became clearer. After some bad weather lifted, another Spitfire flight on 28 September reported a large oil slick surrounding the battleship. On 30 September, still on her way home, *Stubborn* was able to radio Ken Hudspeth's account of hearing the detonations – more encouraging news. Far more satisfying, Enigma messages between *Tirpitz* and Berlin, decoded by the experts at Bletchley Park, the Government Code and Cypher School, began to reveal the scale of the damage done. The ship could not be moved, which ruled out a return to Germany for repairs, and it was thought she would be out of action until April 1944. Engineers and shipyard workers were despatched to Norway to work on her, and her crew would be sent home on leave in stages – another indication that she would not be putting to sea for some time.

So *Tirpitz* had not been sunk, as everyone had hoped, but Operation Source had achieved the next best result, removing her as a threat to the Arctic convoys. She was off the chessboard. *Scharnhorst*, her battlecruiser companion, which had been doing gunnery exercises at sea during the raid, returned to the fjords the next day, not moving again until 22 December, when she put to sea with escorting destroyers to fall upon a British convoy headed for Russia. With Enigma decrypts and superior radar, the British were able to follow her every move and she was destroyed and sunk by a force led by the battleship HMS *Duke of York* at the Battle of the North Cape four days later, on Boxing Day. Of her crew of 1968 men, only thirty-six survived. The cruiser *Lutzow*, with constant engine trouble, returned to Kiel.

By early November, Admiral Barry was able to compile a report to the Admiralty on Operation Source. Admirals have been known to gild the lily of their subordinates' exploits in the hope that the glow will reflect upwards, but in this case it was hardly necessary. Source had been carried out with skill and daring, in the best traditions of the RN. Nelson himself would have approved. The flaws were not of men but materiel, and there was probably a case for having the designer of the gyrocompasses taken out and shot, but Barry played it straight, beginning with the time-honoured salutation to his masters in Whitehall: 'Be pleased to lay before the Lords Commissioners of the Admiralty the following report . . .'

It was a long and detailed document, although still with significant gaps that would not be filled until much later. He hoped that the passage crew of the lost *X9* might somehow have made their way to the Norwegian coast. He approved the decision to scuttle the disabled *X8*. He also dealt with Ken Hudspeth and *X10*:

> The Commanding Officer expresses the highest opinion of all his crew throughout the whole time they were on board. They worked

long and arduously in the face of ever growing disappointment and at no time did their zeal or enthusiasm fail.

I consider that the Commanding Officer himself showed determination and high qualities of leadership in a gallant attempt to reach his objective. He was frustrated by defects for which he was in no way responsible and which he made every endeavour to overcome.

He showed good judgement in coming to his decision to abandon the attack, thereby enabling the craft to be recovered and bringing back valuable information.[13]

There was no news of what prisoners the Germans had taken, if any. The report ended with a flourish:

I cannot fully express my admiration for the three Commanding Officers, Lieutenants H. Henty-Creer RNVR, D. Cameron RNR and B.C.G. Place DSC RN, and the crews of X5, X6 and X7 who pressed home their attack and who failed to return.

In the full knowledge of the hazards they were to encounter, these gallant crews penetrated into a heavily defended fleet anchorage. There, with cool courage and determination and despite all the modern devices that ingenuity could devise for their detection and destruction, they pressed home their attack to the full and some must have penetrated to inside the anti-torpedo net defences surrounding the Tirpitz.

It is clear that courage and enterprise of the very highest order in the presence of the enemy were shown by these very gallant gentlemen, whose daring attack will go down to history as one of the most courageous acts of all time.[14]

The public first learned of Operation Source from an Admiralty communique of 11 October, which gave a factual account of the attack and named Henty-Creer, Cameron and Place, although with no word of their fate. It was front-page news, because it was a cheering victory at a dark hour of the war and also because this was the first indication that the Royal Navy actually possessed midget submarines. Australian newspapers picked up the local angle on Henty-Creer, his family and his movie career.

On 15 October, Barry wrote again to the Admiralty to urge the award of the Victoria Cross for the three commanders, lauding their 'cold, calculating and deliberate courage'. That recommendation made its laborious way through the usual bureaucratic channels. It was not until 6 January 1944 that the Admiral learned the names of the six men now prisoners of war in Germany at a camp named Marlag O, near Bremen. This information had been smuggled out in coded letters written home, along with more details of the attack. There was still no more information on Henty-Creer, but by now he and his crew were listed as missing, presumed dead.

At around that point Barry changed his advice. Cameron and Place should still get the VC but, as he put it, 'A recommendation with regard to Lieutenant Henty-Creer will be submitted at such time as a decision as to his ultimate fate is taken.'[15]

The two heard of their awards listening to a BBC Radio broadcast in Marlag O. Henty was awarded a Mention in Despatches, which, by a strange quirk of the rules, was the only other honour that could be given posthumously. At this distance it seems unjust, for the evidence suggests that Henty carried himself with the same courage and determination in the face of the enemy as did the other two. Certainly his distraught mother thought so. During and after the war, the formidable Eulalie Henty fired off letter after letter to the powers that be, demanding due recognition of her son, but to no avail.

In August 1944, Admiral Barry replied to her, sympathetically but directly:

> The facts of the case are these. There is positive evidence that Cameron and Place completed their attacks and caused all the damage. There is <u>no</u> evidence that Henty-Creer did, although we know he did all that he possibly could do. But it is <u>only</u> on positive deeds that it is possible to give the highest award and so I fear it is really impossible in your son's case.
>
> Had he been alive there is no doubt he would have had a higher award than a 'mention.' As you know, I could not possibly have more admiration for your son than I have and I would have given a

lot to see him given a higher decoration, but you will see from the frank description of the case I have given that there was no alternative. These are the facts of the case which will and must stand. You know how I feel for you in your great loss.[16]

Such are the fortunes of war. Eulalie never gave up. She fought for her boy for the rest of her days.

15

OPERATION POSTAGE ABLE

After the battle comes the anticlimax. When the nerves are taut and the adrenaline is running in the face of danger and possible death in action, you get on with the job, single-mindedly. There is neither time nor space for anything else, least of all introspection. When it's over and the adrenaline subsides, life returns to something like normal and the private thoughts crowd in: of moments won or lost, of what might have been, of friends who did not make it. For many, the aftermath of conflict brings on a tinge of melancholy and an urge to find refuge in peace and sanity away from the crudity of violence.

Max Shean sought his sanctuary at Aberfeldy 'in the depression period that follows all bouts of action', he wrote.[1] Mary Golding and her parents had invited him to stay at their small stone-walled cottage at 18 Kenmore Street. With a week's post-operational leave up his sleeve, he promptly accepted, and caught the train north from Glasgow, through Falkirk, Stirling, Perth and Dunkeld, into the heart of the highlands.

The Goldings welcomed him warmly. Mary's father, George, was a familiar local figure, the driver of the mail bus to nearby Glenlyon. He took Max for a drink to the local pub, the Black Watch Inn, a short walk down the street, and there the landlord conferred upon the visiting Australian the status of honorary local, which allowed him to buy nips of carefully rationed whisky. With its quiet paths through woods of birch and oak, with its gentle burns and meadows, with its homely, firelit cottages, Aberfeldy was balm to the soul. The Bard of Scotland, Robbie Burns, had set one of his poems there:

> Bonnie lassie, will ye go,
> Will ye go, will ye go;
> Bonnie lassie, will ye go
> To the Birks of Aberfeldy.
> A view along the ravine at the Birks of Aberfeldy.
> Now Simmer blinks on flowery braes,
> And o'er the crystal streamlets plays;
> Come let us spend the lightsome days
> In the Birks of Aberfeldy.[2]

News of the attack on *Tirpitz* came out in the papers and on BBC Radio while Max was there, and the good folk of Aberfeldy put two and two together to explain the presence of this young naval lieutenant in their midst, although, with polite Scottish discretion, nobody asked anything. He told only Mary that he had been part of it. Friends invited the two of them to dinner, as Shean related:

> Walking home in the twilight, we took a turn down the Kenmore Road, past the Twin Trees. It was said that if a lass could squeeze through the narrow space between the two trunks, she would marry. Mary stayed on the footpath, but I got to thinking that I was fond of her and could not imagine dropping her as a friend at any time. There seemed to be only one outcome.
>
> 'How would you like to come to Australia after the war? I know it is a big question for a girl to consider, so think it over in the next few weeks. There is no hurry.'
>
> 'Yes,' she said. 'I'll come.'
>
> That was the 14th of October 1943. We were officially engaged on the 18th, by which time I had bought a ring.[3]

Max had found his own 'bonnie lassie'. The next few days passed in a whirl of meetings with relatives, including a visit to the formidable Auntie Chris, a blacksmith's daughter and retired teacher who lived in the old smithy up the road in the village of Kinloch Rannoch. After a searching interrogation of the visitor from the other Perth a hemisphere away, she pronounced that he would 'do', and served tea and homemade shortbread on her best china. The wedding was set for the summer of 1944.

That done, Lieutenant Shean went back to war.

―

By now a steady stream of Australians – junior officers and men – was arriving in Britain to serve with the Royal Navy, more than 500 of them by 1944. They were impelled by a blend of duty: loyalty to King, empire and the distant islands they thought of as the Mother Country, overlaid by a youthful thirst for travel and adventure. Most had done their recruit training at *Cerberus* and then the *Rushcutter* anti-submarine course, with almost all the officers drawn in by the Yachties' scheme. Their welcome was generous, in the RN itself and with offers of hospitality in British homes from families keen to show their gratitude to kith and kin from the Dominions. Vera Lynn, the 'Forces Sweetheart', sang it in stirring strains:

> The Empire too
> We can depend on you
> Freedom remains
> These are the chains
> Nothing can break
> There'll always be an England . . .[4]

There were, though, isolated pockets of the old snobbery. In 1942, newly arrived to join the 10th Submarine Flotilla in Malta, Sub-Lieutenant Don Wilson, an RANVR officer, was taking in a morning view of the harbour from the flotilla headquarters in the old Lazaretto building when he ran into the second-in-command, a commander named Christopher Hutchinson.

'Good morning, sir,' said Wilson, saluting politely.

Hutchinson peered at him as if he had found a slug in his salad.

'Are you Wilson?' The accent was cut-glass. Hutchinson was the son of an Anglican canon.

'Yes, sir.'

'You're Australian?'

'Yes, sir.'

'I want you to know I don't like Australians. I hope you're not going to be as much of a bloody nuisance here as others have been.'

Hackles aroused, young Donald struck back, probably unwisely at a man three ranks above him. 'Sir, I'm very sorry to hear that but I can understand it, I suppose,' he said. 'I've met a couple of Englishmen that I wouldn't pull out of the drink if they were drowning.'

Hutchinson glared. 'Oh, it's going to be like that, is it?' he snapped. There the exchange ended, but forever after Don Wilson was marked down in the commander's books and singled out for niggling bullying.[5]

Fortunately, his captain in the submarine HMS *Untiring*, Lieutenant Robert 'Bobby' Boyd, was very different, an Ulsterman who had gone to sea in his youth as an ordinary merchant seaman and was now a reserve officer. The two got on famously, sharing some hair-raising exploits.

Born in 1917, Donald Rupert Wilson grew up at Chatswood, in suburban Sydney, enrolled at Shore, the Sydney Church of England Grammar School, where he did well academically and in rugby, rowing and cadets. His father, also Donald, had been an army lieutenant wounded at Gallipoli in 1915, suffering from what would now be recognised as post-traumatic stress disorder, and the Depression broke him, driving him to drink and frequent rage. The young man was forced to leave Shore in 1933 at the age of sixteen to take a job delivering gas bills to support the family; he completed his school Leaving Certificate at evening classes, and then worked for the British General Electric Company in Tasmania for two years. When his father died in 1939, Donald joined the army reserve, the Citizens' Military Forces, becoming a corporal in an artillery regiment.

Yet he had done a lot of sailing with a family friend, and when the call went out he was accepted as a Yachtie in May 1940. After the usual *Rushcutter* training and a short spell at sea off Sydney, Sub-Lieutenant Wilson sailed for Britain that November in the liner SS *Themistocles*. At the Quay to wave him farewell was Phyllis Westbrook, the woman he had married just five months earlier after a whirlwind courtship. They would not see each other again for five and a half years.

Landing at Liverpool in the depths of winter, he and a handful of other Australian officers were despatched to a base at Dunoon, on the Clyde in Scotland, where – inevitably – nobody had ever heard of them nor knew what to do with them. Off to London they went, where, after more hither and thither, Wilson was packed off to serve in armed trawlers based out of Harwich, on the English east coast. There he was shipwrecked and rescued, but he also gained his watchkeeping certificate, and in January 1942 he volunteered and was accepted for the submarine service.

It was the start of a wartime career of high adventure and achievement, bold and brave. Graduating second in his course, he chose the 10th Flotilla and was shipped out to Malta in a new submarine built for the Turkish Navy, *Murat Reis*, a passage much enlivened when the captain whimsically decided to test her safe depth and took her down to 150 metres, producing a volley of alarming creaks and groans and finally such a tremendous bang aft that they shot to the surface again at record speed. Sent further on to Alexandria, he hitched a ride in a Canadian Catalina aircraft, whose navigator got it all wrong and very nearly landed them at an airfield newly captured by the Germans and lined with Messer-schmitt fighters.

Don Wilson's first submarine was *P31*, later to be renamed HMS *Uproar*, which, by his own account, was not a happy ship. 'There were a lot of very disgruntled people in it. It's the only boat I've ever seen that had them,' he recalled.[6] He was in her for some six months. His next boat, *Untiring*, was chalk and cheese. After recovering from a bout of pneumonia, he joined her as first lieutenant in May 1943 while she was still building at the Vickers-Armstrong Shipyard, on the River Tyne at Newcastle. The U-class boats were modern but relatively small: fifty-eight metres long, 660 tonnes submerged, with a crew of thirty-nine. They had a diving depth of sixty metres, four 21-inch torpedo tubes for'ard and a three-inch deck gun. Capable of a little over eleven knots on the surface and ten submerged, they were not ocean boats but well suited for work in the Mediterranean.

After a couple of war patrols in the North Sea, *Untiring* reached Gibraltar that October. Wilson was by now an experienced submariner, twenty-six years old, sporting a handsome moustache and neatly pointed beard that lent him an almost Elizabethan air, the look of a seadog who might have walked a quarterdeck with Drake or Raleigh. Inevitably, the British called him 'Digger'.

Untiring's first crack at the enemy in the Med was with a German boat, *U-616*, which they met off the French port of Toulon early in the morning of 15 October 1942, when the Asdic operator reported 'hydrophone effect' – the sound of propellers.

> Bobby Boyd said 'Well, let's finish our breakfast and let's get up to periscope depth', which we did and we only waited 10 minutes I suppose before he sighted the boat, this submarine approaching. She was a lovely boat, a big lump of a boat and she was 5,000 yards away which was a bit far.
>
> We had it all our own way. We fired four torpedoes at him and he heard them coming and I was on the periscope at the time and I looked out and I saw him alter course 90 degrees till he was running absolutely straight away from us and he made smoke, he increased speed and we saw him go virtually into the blue. He dived and we sort of followed him but it was too late. He got away.[7]

There was no point in trying to chase and close. *U-616* was a Type VII boat, a full six knots faster on the surface. *Untiring* had better luck a few weeks later, on 15 December, after stalking a target for hours. Her log gives a straightforward account:

> 1215 hours – Sighted a ship off Monaco in position 43°41'N, 07°22'E. Range was 10,000 yards. Closed to investigate.
>
> 1420 hours – The target set course for Monaco harbour which she entered shortly afterwards. Untiring followed hoping to attack shipping in the harbour.
>
> 1556 hours – Fired one torpedo at the vessel sighted earlier from 550 yards. She was berthed so that she could be attacked from outside the harbour. A rumbling explosion was heard half a minute after firing and the bow of the target was seen to have disintegrated and she was settling by the bow. Untiring then retired from the area.[8]

The victim was a small German auxiliary vessel, *Netztender 44*, which had actually been loading mines. The explosion was volcanic, shattering almost every window along the Monaco waterfront and thereby providing *Untiring*'s crew with the cheerful boast that they were the submarine that broke the bank at Monte Carlo.

Experience taught them that the Mediterranean was a hard playing field for submarines. On sunlit days, summer and winter, the water could be so clear that a submerged boat was easily visible from the air, even a hundred feet down, a sitting duck for Axis bombers. Charts were not always reliable and sudden, bumping groundings were not uncommon, particularly along the African coasts. Many rivers emptied into the Med from its European shores, releasing layers of fresh and therefore less buoyant water, which could send a submarine into an abrupt, hair-raising plunge towards the bottom when you least expected it. There was little rest to be had in harbour, too, for Malta was ceaselessly pounded by the German and Italian air forces – the *Luftwaffe* and the *Regia Aeronautica* – often forcing the boats to spend the day submerged alongside the dock. When Italy surrendered in September 1943, the flotilla moved its headquarters to the tiny island of La Maddalena, off the coast of Sardinia.

The patrols were long and hard, sometimes lasting for up to three weeks, with the crews working watches of two hours on, four hours off. You never really got enough sleep. Much of the time it was monotony piled upon boredom, endless searching and waiting for a target to appear. *Untiring* had a good cook, though, the envy of the rest of the flotilla, and Don Wilson would occasionally bring out his wind-up HMV gramophone and a small collection of records for the crew to sing along. There was the rum ration, too, a tot for each member of the crew at 4 p.m., the start of the first dog watch.

On a clear summer night, surfaced in an easy sea, it was a pleasure to be on watch on the bridge with just a couple of lookouts for company, although the silvery wake in the moonlight could be a giveaway to enemy aircraft. Sometimes there were simple, unexpected delights, like schools of dolphins that would suddenly appear from nowhere, as Wilson noted:

> If you look up through the water you can see everything going on and to see the dolphins coming down ... they're a damn nuisance actually, you can't take your eyes off them but they'll give you away if anybody happens to be up on top looking at the dolphins. They will swim around you, around the conning tower and they nudge each other and push each other out and everything else and it's an absolute joy to watch. They stir the water up ...
>
> [T]hey're beautiful things and it was terrific but you couldn't do it for too long. You'd either take the boat down a bit deeper and leave them behind or they'd follow you for hours.[9]

Bobby Boyd knew his trade. In the two years Wilson was with him in *Untiring*, in fifteen war patrols, they hunted and sank a long list of German and Italian shipping: barges, freighters, storeships and submarine chasers, a minesweeper, sixteen vessels in all. At times they were also the hunted. On their seventh patrol, in January 1944, they were heavily depth-charged after an unsuccessful attempt on a convoy south of Saint-Tropez, perhaps the worst of many attacks they endured. These were the moments of real fear, of never knowing when the next clanging, echoing explosion might be the one close enough to tear open the hull and send you to the bottom. A couple of submarine chasers were after them, and for an hour they lay deep at seventy-five metres, beneath a layer of colder water which made it harder for the enemy to ping them, 'rigged for silent running', as it was called, waiting patiently as the explosions became less frequent and finally ceased. Don Wilson said:

> We had a bit of a conference and we said, 'Well, let's go up and have another look and see what we can find, if there's anything interesting going on.'
>
> We came up very slowly and we were up at over a hundred feet, 160 feet, I think we were, when Boyd said 'Somebody's pinging almost due astern of us and increasing in speed all the time' and he said 'Getting stronger and stronger.'
>
> We were coming up underneath a destroyer that we didn't know was there. It was only his good luck that he heard us coming and he increased speed and dropped a pattern right over us and it lifted the boat from 160 feet up to about 60 in less time than I'm

telling you this, just lifted it up bodily. All the lights went out, everything, and it was pretty unpleasant I can tell you . . .

We managed to avoid the four or five torpedo depth charges that they threw at us, that went all around us, and no one hit us exactly, thank God. I had to increase speed to get control of the boat to get down again, so I put all the planes to dive and I went ahead and I did a 90 degree turn to get out of the area.

Didn't matter, they knew we were there and they knew this kicked up a hell of a noise with the screws doing this, but I think they thought it was a final burst because we went straight back to being very silent and very slow, hardly any noise.[10]

It was enough. They got away. One of the signalmen had the job of tallying up all the depth charges exploding around them on all their patrols, but he gave up after 300. The next day they sank two German landing barges and were depth-charged once more in return, but they escaped again and a day later they were safely back at La Maddalena.

It was here that Wilson struck a spot of personal bother, in the words scrawled on his service record: 'Sentenced by disciplinary board, HMS Talbot, at La Maddalena on 28th February, 1944, to be severely reprimanded for drunkenness.'[11] There are no more details but it suggests a lively wardroom party after a return from a patrol, and perhaps a blow from his nemesis, the vindictive Commander Hutchinson. A black mark it was, but not black enough to prevent the award, a few months later, of the Distinguished Service Cross for 'outstanding courage and devotion to duty while on submarine patrols'.

Untiring left the Mediterranean in December 1944, returning to Rothesay, on the Isle of Bute, Scotland, not far from the midget submarine base at Port Bannatyne. And there Lieutenant Don Wilson made his farewells to the boat that had been his home for two years and began his Perisher, in January 1945. It was a singular honour, a vote of confidence, a rare and remarkable achievement for a young Australian Yachtie to be offered the chance, and he seized the opportunity with gusto. He passed with flying colours and in May 1945 he gained his first RN command, one of only three Australian RANVR officers to do so.[12] Best of all, it meant a return home. His submarine, HMS *Voracious*, was based at Sydney, and after those long years away he was reunited, at last, with his wife, Phyllis.

The Pacific War was almost over. *Voracious* spent the last few months of it on training exercises off Sydney without ever seeing the Japanese enemy, let alone firing a shot in anger. Don drove her until the end of October, and in March 1946 he left the navy and returned to civilian life to go farming.

But once a submariner, always a submariner. Years later, in the new century, *Untiring*'s encounter with *U-616* in 1942 would have a resounding coda. Don Wilson met the German captain, Siegfried Koitschka.

It was a long story. *U-616* had been forced to the surface by American destroyers off Algeria in 1944, where the crew surrendered and survived. *Kapitänleutnant* Koitschka – by then a recognised U-boat ace and a winner of the Knight's Cross – spent two years as a prisoner of war before returning home. In the 1970s, visiting the Royal Navy Submarine Museum at Portsmouth, he asked if anyone there might know who had attacked him back in 1942. Remarkably they did, and they put him in touch first with Bobby Boyd and then with Don Wilson. For years afterwards the two exchanged Christmas cards, and finally they met at Koitschka's home in Frankfurt in 2002. They were the same age, old warriors of eighty-five, and although Koitschka had not been well and it was a struggle for him, they embraced like brothers.

'I was not proud of everything in the war, but proud of the fact that I saved all my crew,' the German said. Warm and poignant, it was their only meeting. Koitschka died of a heart attack the very next day, the fifty-eighth anniversary of the loss of *U-616*.

Don Wilson died in 2009, aged ninety-two.

Back at work at *Varbel*, Port Bannatyne, in the winter of 1943, Max Shean found the 12th Flotilla regrouping after the *Tirpitz* attack. Six new and improved X-craft had been built at factories around Britain, numbered from X20 to X25, and there were new faces in training, too. To their delight, three of the Australians were given commands: Ken Hudspeth was appointed to *X20*, Max Shean to *X22* and, a little later, Brian McFarlane to *X24*. By January 1944 they were readying for the next operation.

Hudspeth, the cool and methodical Tasmanian, was assigned to Operation Postage Able, a risky run across the English Channel to the Normandy coast of occupied France to gather intelligence, to get the lie of the land for the Allied invasion planned for the coming summer. *X20* was shipped south by rail to Portsmouth. Hudspeth and his first lieutenant, Bruce Enzer, would carry three passengers, members of what was rather blandly known as a COPP, a Combined Operations Pilotage Party. They were, in fact, highly trained commandos, expert in the dark arts of infiltration and surveillance behind enemy lines and, if need be, in silently slitting enemy throats in the process. A naval officer, Lieutenant Commander Nigel Clogstoun-Willmott, was the team leader, with an army major from the Royal Engineers, Logan Scott-Bowden, and a Special Forces Commando, Sergeant Bruce Ogden Smith. In training exercises the soldiers found midget submarine life strange and oppressive at first, but after a quick course in steering and depth keeping they settled into it.

At 1 p.m. on Monday, 17 January, a small armed trawler towed *X20*, on the surface, around the great concrete lump of the Nab Tower in the channel beyond Spithead, outside Portsmouth, and headed south-east, towards a known German minefield off the French coast. Postage Able was underway. The objective would be the southern shore of the Baie de la Seine, an eight-kilometre stretch of long, low seafront eventually to be codenamed Omaha Beach and to become one of the landing places for the Americans on D-Day.

The Coppists, as they were called, had crammed an extraordinary amount of baggage into the little X-craft, including their heavy rubber swimming suits. The two soldiers, when they swam ashore, would each carry a torch, a trowel, wire-cutters, bags and tubes and an auger for collecting samples of beach sand and shingle. These samples would be used to assess if the ground was strong enough to support tank landings, a crucial question. They also had sounding gear and underwater writing tablets, a waterproof watch and compass; emergency rations; a Colt .45 pistol with two spare magazines and a slender, wicked-looking blade known as a Fairbairn-Sykes fighting knife. If all else failed, there was also a flask of brandy. Cylinders of air were welded to $X20$'s sides to give her more buoyancy with the extra bodies aboard and an echo sounder was squeezed in, along with a cumbersome car radio, an American Philco model, for Ken to receive prearranged coded weather forecasts broadcast by the BBC.

'Engine clutch out, tail clutch in, ready ahead, group down . . .' With Willmott navigating – he was an expert on the coast – they slipped the tow shortly before 10 p.m. and nosed south through the minefield on the surface, butting into a rough oncoming sea at about five knots. Hudspeth and Enzer took turns on deck, drenched to the bone. Willmott wryly wrote later in his report:

> It was found desirable for the officer on watch on the casing to be able to lift his head above water for breathing purposes.
>
> He is strapped to the induction pipe and has a bar to which he clings, with fervour, while floating on his front like a paper streamer on the bosom of the ocean, which has submerged the rest of the craft beneath him. Legs are liable to considerable injury.
>
> There is a vacancy in [the X-craft's] complement for an intelligent merman to fill this role.[13]

They dived in murky, overcast weather at 8 a.m. the next day, 18 January, heading towards the beach and bottoming at around 7.5 metres, where they ate and rested, the air growing ever heavier and more sour. Ken took them closer to the coast again in the midafternoon, creeping at periscope depth through a still sea to about 400 yards off the shoreline, opposite a village, Port-en-Bessin. They were now under the very noses of the enemy. Scott-Bowden, the engineer major, wrote:

> It was nearly high tide when we beached at periscope depth in about 7 or 8 foot of water on the left-hand sector of what was to be named 'Omaha' beach. Willmott took two bearings to fix our exact position and handed the periscope to me.

First I took a quick general view and was astonished to see hundreds of soldiers at work, and how hard they were working. We knew Field Marshal Rommel had recently taken command; he had certainly stirred things up.

From our low-level view and pointing slightly up due to the slope of the beach, it was often possible to see under the camouflage netting and so verify the types of gun emplacement being constructed.[14]

So far, so good. Then, just before 4 p.m., the sea was suddenly whipped up by a spray of bullets from the shore, not far from them. Had they been discovered? Had someone noticed the periscope? Ken hurriedly backed *X20* out into deeper water, relieved when the shooting stopped as suddenly as it had started. He noted in his report later:

> Explosions heard, splashes of projectiles observed inshore, and smoke from foreshore, continuing spasmodically for about five minutes. We were unable to establish that we were the target owing to the undesirability of further use of the periscope at that time, but the latter may have been sighted, though not necessarily identified.
>
> There is also the possibility of our presence having coincided with a routine firing as no shots appeared to fall very close.[15]

They could breathe again. After dark, they drew closer to the beach once more, surfacing shortly after 7 p.m., and the two swimmers, Scott-Bowden and Ogden Smith, slipped overboard and struck out for the shore. *X20* anchored some 500 metres out. At the water's edge, the two commandos set about their business, probing for what defences there might be, taking shingle samples from the beach. Then they froze, fearing they had been discovered. Scott-Bowden reported:

> Saw sentry with torch at back of beach about 200 yards away. Water was very smooth and surf negligible. Thought we might have been observed. Sentry continued to shine torch directly at us. We kept still. Other small lights were visible in the village.
>
> The sentry was joined by a second with torch. We 'edged' off silently and slowly backed into the water in a north-westerly

direction and came in again 350 yards to the west, approximately at our originally intended point of landing.[16]

But there was a sentry there too.

> [S]uddenly a powerful torch was beamed straight at us. We did not move, kept our faces down and took care to keep aligned with the beam as the gently rising tide could swing us broadside, showing our shapes.
>
> The sentry did not approach, but he kept his torch trained firmly on us. In time as the tide came in we eased gently back. He then swung his beam about and eventually switched it off. I have often wondered what he thought he had seen and whether he reported it?[17]

It was crucial that they not be discovered. Despatching the sentry would have been easy but would also have alerted the German command that something was up.

Their night's work done, the swimmers were back on board shortly before 10 p.m. and *X20* withdrew seawards, anchoring some two kilometres offshore to recharge batteries and get some fresh air into the boat. They repeated this routine for the next two days and nights, their submerged daylight hours passing in suffocating boredom. This was the dreary aspect of war, the tedium of waiting, waiting. With five souls on board, more than the midget submarine had ever been designed for, there was little room for movement. Even going to the head in the W&D compartment was an effort, the soldiers were afflicted by seasickness, and the stench of unwashed bodies grew ever stronger. Ken Hudspeth and Bruce Enzer took it more or less in their stride, as part of the job, but for the other three the strain began to show.

On the fourth day, 20 January, taking a quick look through the periscope, Hudspeth was startled to find they were in the middle of a French fishing fleet, about three dozen boats, some of them trawling with nets. One of the boats carried a German soldier on deck with a rifle slung over his shoulder, leaning back and smoking a pipe. They went deeper and circled around him.

That afternoon they again came under fire from the shore. Scott-Bowden held his breath, briefly fearing the worst:

> After raising the periscope briefly a few times, strange external rather unpleasant clanging noises started. Willmott soon saw small shells exploding close to the periscope.
>
> Had we been detected? We thought not. We were moving very slowly at about half a knot, with the small stick-like periscope exposed, at intervals, about a foot only. As it was not disturbing the water, perhaps it was thought to be a stray mine and was being used as a good aiming mark for target practice.
>
> The shooting had gone on intermittently for about 20 minutes without damaging the periscope. We would have been blinded if it had been hit.[18]

That afternoon, Willmott, the operation commander, decided they had done and seen enough. Time to go home. After sunset, Ken Hudspeth set a course nor'east to pass out through the German minefield and, that done, nor'west for the Isle of Wight and Portsmouth. At 6.30 p.m. the next day, 21 January, *X20*'s log laconically recorded: 'Secured alongside at Fort Blockhouse.'

Operation Postage Able had gone entirely to plan. It had been, in the words of the commander-in-chief at Portsmouth, 'a sustained and impudent reconnaissance under the very nose of the enemy'.[19] Scott-Bowden was hurried off to London, where he was interviewed at length by the American designated to command the invasion, General Omar Bradley. Willmott's report summed it up drily:

> All personnel remained reasonably fit during the operation. Benzedrine and hyoscine [a motion sickness pill] as prescribed, helped in some cases, although there were times when various members felt very bad. The effects, however, show themselves forcibly during the days after return to base.
>
> A fine spirit prevailed throughout amongst all hands, and in spite of the foul air, super-slum conditions and distasteful sewage system – a strain on the temper – no person was heard to pass strictures upon the habits or antecedents of any other. (At least in

that one's presence.) This I think reflects credit on the company, mixed as they were.

Lieutenant Hudspeth's grasp of submarine technicalities, coolness and dexterity in handling the craft submerged was of the highest order, and Sub-Lieutenant Enzer's skill and continual cheerful hard work must have been greatly responsible for the success of the expedition in that no major breakdowns and few minor ones occurred. The co-operativeness shown by these officers in circumstances which to them were unnatural, was unexceptionable.[20]

Ken Hudspeth was awarded a bar to his DSC.

In London, the Admiralty staff became concerned that the Germans might be planning their own midget submarine operations, possibly an attack on the battleships of the Home Fleet at Scapa Flow, their far-flung base in the Orkney Islands. They decided to test the defences there.

At *Varbel*, Brian 'Digger' McFarlane was ordered to head north with *X24* to do the job. He would be towed there by the submarine *Syrtis*. He made his plans, but *X24* was giving trouble, with one defect after another. It seemed she had been badly built. There were leaks here and there from glands and hull joints, with a new one springing up as soon as another had been fixed. The induction trunk for'ard of the periscope jammed, various valves got stuck, and one crucial hull joint was found to have been distorted and, scandalously, bodgied up with putty. She was simply not seaworthy. The flotilla made a swap. McFarlane would take *X22* for the job and *X24* would be given to Max Shean, with his engineering bent, to sort things out. McFarlane's first lieutenant would be another Australian, Jack Marsden, the burly young man from Adelaide who had shared a cabin with Shean when they were training. There were two more in the crew, both British, Engine Room Artificer Cyril Ludbrook and Able Seaman John Pretty.

They left Cairnbawn on a chilly winter's day in February, towed by *Syrtis*, the passage to take them north and east around mainland Scotland into the Pentland Firth and then up to Scapa. Sailors know the Firth to be one of the world's most treacherous stretches of water, linking the North Sea and the Atlantic, a bleak and miserable strait of tidal races, fast currents and whirlpools where wicked seas could be whipped up by sudden, gale-force winds.

On Monday, 7 February, *Syrtis* and *X22* were labouring on the surface through just that filthy weather somewhere north of John O'Groats, the big boat rolling and pitching and labouring, the little X-craft jerked and wrenched this way and that at the end of the tow. A big wave loomed over *Syrtis*'s stern, bigger than anything before. The officer of the watch, the first lieutenant, Charles Blythe, had time only to shout 'Hold on!' to the two lookouts on the bridge with him before the monster was upon them.

The submarine was pooped, pitching violently, her stern deep down, bow soaring into the air, then the bridge swallowed entirely under tons of icy water as the wave surged on. When she laboured to the surface again after what seemed an age, Blythe was gone.

Below, in the control room, alerted by the cries of 'Man overboard!' down the voice-pipe from above, the captain, Lieutenant Michael Jupp, acted instinctively. He ordered the boat into a hard turn to retrace her steps and asked for volunteers to go up to the bridge to look for his missing Number One.

In normal circumstances it was the logical thing to do, to head back on a reciprocal course to begin a search. But not in this case, with another vessel in tow, and Jupp should have realised it. *X22* would not, could not and did not follow in the same circle. She could only wallow to a halt, helpless in the peaks and troughs.

Syrtis's coxswain, Petty Officer Hugh Fowler, described it later: 'Answered call for volunteers up on the bridge. Saw the shape of a man, then realised it was the X-craft. Wave smashed her right under the bows of Syrtis, crunch, crunch, crunch. She is hit three times and the captain smells oil fuel as Syrtis rides on over X22.'[21]

With the tow parted, mortally holed, the little craft went straight to the bottom, carrying all four men with her. Brian McFarlane and Jack Marsden were thus the second and third Australians to be lost in midget submarines, after Henty Henty-Creer in Norway.

Digger had married a Frenchwoman, Jeanne Bestre, just five months before.

Lieutenant Blythe was not found either. Sailors can be superstitious, and in the flotilla *Syrtis* came to be seen as jinxed, an unlucky ship, everyone recalling that she had also lost *X9* on the *Tirpitz* operation. Her luck, such as it was, ran out the next month, March 1944, when she disappeared with all hands on a patrol somewhere off Norway, probably victim to a mine.

With *X24* back in working order – in all respects ready for sea – and Max Shean in command, she was sent up to Scapa Flow to do the test runs intended for *X22*. Taking no chances this time, *Bonaventure* hoisted her on board and carried her safely through Pentland Firth to the Orkneys, where she did her stuff without a hitch, slipping submerged through the defences with ease.

Back on the surface, passing the battleship HMS *Anson*, anchored in the Flow, Shean and his Number One, Sub-Lieutenant Joe Brooks, ventured to have a little fun with the frills of proper naval courtesy. They could see *Anson*'s crew peering curiously down at this strange little intruder with the White Ensign flying at the stern. Standing alert on the casing in full uniform with caps, the two of them came smartly to attention. Brooks piped 'the Still' on a bosun's call – a shrill, silver whistle used in naval ceremonies – and Shean crisply saluted *Anson*'s quarterdeck. The battleship, towering above them, could only reply in kind, all her officers on deck obliged to return the salute. Then, as prescribed, she piped: 'Carry on.' It was cheeky, a sardine making love to a whale, and the two enjoyed it hugely.

Emboldened by that success, and passing the flagship *Duke of York* the next day, Brooks flashed a lamp signal that read: 'What a big bastard.' The battleship replied only with a terse, one-letter acknowledgement. Shean had an attack of nerves, suddenly worried that the commander-in-chief, Admiral Sir Bruce Fraser, might assume the signal was for him. Fraser invited them to dinner the next evening, and it was a convivial affair, with no mention made. Much relief all round.

Fun over, it was back to work at Loch Cairnbawn, HHZ. The Admiralty planners had a new venture in mind, Operation Guidance, off to Norway again. This would be an attack on a large floating dock, known as the Laksevaag Dock, in the harbour at Bergen, on the Norwegian south-west coast. The Germans were using it for maintenance work, particularly for U-boats.

It would be a very different affair to the *Tirpitz* raid. The distance from the Orkneys across the North Sea to Bergen was much less than to Altafjord, a little over 480 kilometres, in every way an easier passage. Only one midget submarine would go, *X24*, under tow at first. On the minus side of the ledger there would need to be pinpoint navigation to get through two separate minefields, then into the long fjord leading to the dock and back out again. Bergen was a crowded harbour, alive with merchant shipping, fishing boats and local bits and pieces, and closely patrolled by the Germans in the fast coastal attack craft they called *Schnellboote* and the British knew as E-boats.

The risks were high but with careful planning they were manageable. Shean was delighted to learn that the towing submarine would be *Sceptre*, under the command of no less than Ian McIntosh: an all-Australian affair, the two happily told themselves. The engineering student from Perth and the career naval officer from Geelong Grammar had struck up a friendship and a good working rapport, trusting each other's competence, and they went to the task with the exuberance of youth. Max was now twenty-five, Ian still only twenty-four.

The planning was meticulous. Norwegian exiles in Britain familiar with Bergen and its approaches were invited to share their knowledge. They identified minefields, safe channels and lookout posts on the shore; one man who had worked for the dock company before the war told all he knew. Agents of the resistance in Norway reported what they could see and hear. RAF reconnaissance flights provided photographs and there were detailed discussions on how long *X24* should stay surfaced, how long submerged, how long at periscope depth and the like. Buoys and a net were set up in one of the more remote Scottish bays to simulate the dock location and layout, and *X24* spent days on end experimenting with getting in and out, this way and that. If all failed and they managed to make it to shore, there was a list of Norwegian agents who would help them, their names and addresses to be memorised.

There was one more detail, a curious piece of sailors' superstition described by Max Shean in his memoirs:

> My mother, in one of her letters, told me that her aged Uncle Charlie had died, that he had been a seaman in his youth in square riggers, and that among his belongings was a caul. This is a membrane which covers a baby's head at birth and [is] believed, by some, to be a lucky charm and a preservative against drowning. She enclosed it in the envelope.
>
> This was the first I had heard of such a thing, so I showed it to my crew, who immediately advised that it should be carried aboard X24. We already had Mickey Mouse, a Tiki donated by Bernie Tonks, Bonaventure's RDF officer from New Zealand, and a wishbone from some unfortunate chicken. With such an array of good luck, who needed skill?[22]

Their departure from HHZ was set for 9 a.m. on Sunday, 9 April.

16

'OKAY. WE'LL GO.'

This time no one was risking another disaster like the loss of *X9* or *X22*. On the first leg of the journey – to the lonely Burra Firth, at the northernmost tip of the Shetland Islands – *Sceptre* and *X24* were accompanied by the small submarine tender HMS *Alecto* and a Norwegian destroyer, *Narvik*. The seas stayed obediently calm.

At Burra the surface escort farewelled them, and Max Shean and the operational crew took over. Well before dawn on 12 April, they dived, still under tow and heading just a little south of east towards Bergen, at around eight knots. At twilight the next day, *Sceptre* at periscope depth spotted an outward-bound U-boat on the surface only 800 metres away, a point-blank target, but with gritted teeth Ian McIntosh had to let it go unmolested.

At 9 p.m. that night, Thursday, 13 April, it was time to part company. Shean and McIntosh spoke by telephone.

'I've brought you five miles closer to the land,' McIntosh said. 'This will give you a start. When you spot us tomorrow night, signal the letters "MAC" and I'll know who it is. Good luck. Slip now.'[1]

On *X24*'s casing, Shean went for'ard and released the tow rope, then ordered 'slow ahead'. The diesel rumbled into life and the black silhouette of *Sceptre* faded behind them into the night. Working up to full speed, *X24* headed closer to the Norwegian coast and turned south-east into Hjeltefjorden, a long and narrow stretch of water leading down towards Bergen. For all of them, it was their first venture into enemy territory. Occupied Norway lay all around. Shean noted an odd, tingling sensation in his legs, a ripple of excitement.

Yet it seemed almost too easy, no more challenging than one of their many practice runs in Scottish lochs. Sudden pockets of fresh water kept Joe Brooks working hard at depth-keeping, but there was no traffic at that time of night, the navigation lights on the channel were still lit red and green and it was just a matter of gliding down between them, past a known minefield, until Max decided to push his luck no more. They dived at 2.30 a.m., well before dawn on what was now Friday, 14 April, and forged onwards by dead reckoning at a depth of twelve metres.

Just before 6 a.m. they were ready for the next lap of the journey, a ninety-degree turn to port and a run down another stretch of water, Byfjorden, which would take them to the Laksevaag Dock. Their navigation had been spot on. The traffic was building now, the fjord getting busier, but they slipped through a second minefield easily enough with Shean at the periscope, Brooks at the controls, Engine Room Artificer Vernon 'Ginger' Coles at the steering position and the third hand, Sub-Lieutenant Frank Ogden, keeping the plot of their travels.

Now the going got tougher, more dangerous. A quick look through the periscope revealed a patrol boat of some sort, with the swastika flag and a sailor taking a leak over the stern, and another similar boat nearby, both uncomfortably close. They dropped down to seven metres again and then heard the ominous *ping, ping* of an Asdic pulse hitting their hull. Shean ordered a zigzag back and forth across the channel. It worked, for after about fifteen minutes the pings grew fainter and faded away. Presumably the German operator had written them off as a wayward school of fish or some such.

By 8 a.m., through the periscope again, Shean could see the dock itself about 800 metres away, flooded down and ready for a ship to enter. They crept forward, even as the traffic overhead grew busier still, daring to snatch only the briefest glimpses through the periscope. *X24* gently touched the bottom, as they had expected, and through the scuttle they could dimly detect what they took to be the dock's bottom above them, little more than a shadow.

To make sure, Shean backed out across the fjord, took a quick bearing, then went back in again.

> As before, X24 grounded, course was altered to port and at the same interval of time a shadow appeared. We carried on past it with the same result as before, with nothing else seen.
>
> 'That must be the dock,' I said. 'Port 30. Steady on the reciprocal course. We will attack.' I felt very dry in the mouth.
>
> As soon as the shadow reappeared we altered course to port and went astern, sat on the seabed, set four hours delay on the first (port) side cargo and released it. It peeled away without a hitch. Joe pumped her back to diving trim and we went ahead, dead slow, bringing up suddenly on a hard bottom . . .
>
> [W]e stopped the motor, sat on the bottom and released the starboard cargo with the same clock setting. It also peeled away correctly. I ordered slow astern with rudder hard a'port . . .[2]

Job done, it was time to go home. Ginger Coles suggested a celebratory tot of rum from a bottle that had found its way on board, but Shean said it could wait until they were clear. They headed back out the way they had come, submerged at around fifteen metres, the traffic still busy above them, working on dead reckoning. Shean decided they should work in two watches, to get some sleep.

> As daylight faded, the air was becoming heavy. We felt nausea and heads were beginning to ache (it was later found that the Protosorb air purifier was not functioning.) All would be better when on the surface, with the diesel running to change the air, but that was two hours away and we had to be alert on surfacing. This is the most risky time for a submarine that has been blind during the twilight. At the last daylight the waters were clear of vessels of any kind. We went deep and waited for darkness, still making economical speed for the open sea.[3]

An hour before midnight, Shean changed into a wet-weather suit and seaboots and switched the submarine lighting to red, which made it easier to see when you emerged from your cocoon into the night. 'Surface,' he directed. 'Blow main ballast.'

X24 rose as ordered, and as she broke the surface Shean stuck his head up through the W&D hatch for a look around. He saw the dark, unlit shape of some vessel dead ahead. 'Dive! Forty feet!' He pulled the hatch shut.

Down they went again, in a hurry, and as they levelled off they could hear the dreaded *ping, ping* on their hull. Max ordered a change of course, due west, to take them as close to the shore as possible in the hope that this might confuse the operator above. Evidently, it did, as the pings grew fainter and disappeared.

Back on course for the sea, but after leaving it another hour and a half to be sure, they went up to the surface again. There was no vessel in sight, but by now they were all feeling seriously sick from the foul air in the boat, from the lack of oxygen and carbon dioxide poisoning. The symptoms were plain: nausea, pounding headaches and stabbing stomach pains. Out on the casing Shean was violently sick, and so was Coles. The fresh air cleared them, and the diesel engine – also deprived of air – coughed and spluttered back into action again, its steady hum picking up reassuringly.

Despite his sickness, Frank Ogden had kept a meticulous track of their position and at 11 p.m. they found *Sceptre* exactly where she was supposed to be. They exchanged the prearranged MAC signal, and an hour after midnight *X24* was under tow with the passage crew on board. Max Shean and his men were relaxing at last in *Sceptre*'s wardroom.

There was an ecstatic welcome when they arrived back at HHZ early in the morning of 19 April, flags flying, sirens blasting. It was the first time an X-craft and crew had made it back from an operation – definitely something to celebrate. Captain Fell, as affable as ever, invited Shean and Brooks to his cabin for coffee and listened intently to their account of the trip, every detail. Then he gave them the bad news.

The Laksevaag Dock had not been destroyed. It was still floating in position, intact. RAF air reconnaissance photos showed that a ship berthed alongside the dock had been sunk instead. Intelligence had identified it as a German coal carrier, the 7200-tonne motor vessel *Barenfels*. There was no doubt about it.

It was a horrible kick in the guts. To have done everything by the book, to have carried out their job as asked, only to miss the target, was sickening, a cruel disappointment. Tiny Fell was generous, putting the best possible complexion on it, and later he threw a splendid dinner for them at *Varbel*, lauding their courage. A valuable German asset had been destroyed. It was important for the morale of the flotilla that this should be recognised. But it was not the dock, and everyone knew it.

Over the next few days, careful analysis discovered what had gone wrong. The maps Max Shean had been given were old and did not show the pier where *Barenfels* had been berthed, and the ship had not been photographed by the RAF in that position either. Nobody knew it was there. Coincidentally, the bottom of the dock and the bottom of *Barenfels* were about the same length, which added to the confusion. In sum, it was faulty intelligence, for which $X24$ and her crew could not be blamed. And nor were they blamed.

Shean offered to return immediately and finish the job, but was knocked back. For the rest of his life he lived with the haunting thought of what might have been. For the moment, he went on leave, gratefully accepting Joe Brooks's offer to stay with his family at Lowestoft, on the North Sea coast down in Suffolk, where they went sailing and celebrated Joe's twenty-first birthday. Then it was back to Aberfeldy and wedding plans, including the groom's job of trying to find a place for a honeymoon. This interlude was interrupted by an urgent phone call from *Bonaventure*, calling him back to work.

No explanation was given but when Shean arrived, highly curious, he was told that King George was paying a visit to Scapa Flow and had asked to see an X-craft and meet the crews. Off they all went, with the usual frenzy of painting and tidying and beautifying and rehearsing to make things ship shape for the royal gaze.

George VI duly appeared on a pleasant spring day in May. Uniformed as an Admiral of the Fleet, he knew what he was looking at, for he had been a midshipman in a gun turret of the battleship HMS *Collingwood* at the Battle of Jutland in 1916, the last British monarch to serve in action. He spent some minutes chatting with Shean, but declined an offer to be escorted below for a look inside. Probably for the best – the paint was still wet.

As the northern winter of 1944 became spring and then summer, the tide of war had turned against Germany: in the west and south it was flowing for the British and Americans and in the north and east for the Russians.

In late January, the Siege of Leningrad ended after nearly 900 days with the Germans in shattered retreat from the Soviet Red Army. In the air, the Allied bombing campaign by day and night was reducing German cities to smoking rubble. On land, the Allies were fighting their way north against fierce opposition in Italy. At sea, new technology, new weapons and many more warships were winning the battle against the U-boats in the Atlantic, with the United States and Royal Canadian navies hot on the hunt with the Royal Navy. Advanced radar was being installed in the escort corvettes and frigates, and the Leigh Light, a high-powered and dazzling long-range searchlight, was harrying U-boats on the surface at night. The arrival of the long-range Liberator bomber and light escort aircraft carriers closed what had been known as the mid-Atlantic gap, where the U-boats had once been beyond the reach of aerial reconnaissance; a new weapon known as the Hedgehog fired salvoes of mortar depth bombs ahead of an attacking destroyer, far more effective than the old way of rolling depth charges over the stern. Most of all, rapid decrypts of Enigma signals enabled Sir Max Horton and his Western Approaches staff in Liverpool to reroute convoys and send hunter-killer groups of frigates and destroyers to home in on gathering wolf packs. In the first three months of 1944, the German Navy lost sixty-one boats, an unsustainable rate of attrition that would grow worse as the year wore on.

At Norfolk House in London, a stately home of the Duke of Norfolk, planning for the greatest enterprise of all was underway. Operation Overlord, the long-awaited Allied invasion of Europe, was coming together under the leadership of the American General Dwight D. Eisenhower, designated the Supreme Allied Commander of the Allied Expeditionary Force.

'Ike', as he would famously be known, had graduated from the US military academy at West Point in 1915 but, to his chagrin, missed out on any combat role in World War I, never leaving the United States. At the beginning of 1941, the year America was bombed into World War II, he was a mere lieutenant colonel commanding an infantry battalion in faraway Washington State. Yet his superiors saw in him a talent – perhaps a genius – for staff work and military organisation, and by October that same year he was a brigadier general at the heart of power in Washington DC. With the staunch patronage of the US Army Chief of Staff, General George C. Marshall, Ike soared above his contemporaries. His successful command of Operation Torch, the Allied invasion of north-west Africa in November 1942, boosted his career again, and in February 1943 he was made a full four-star general.

The naval component – the task of carrying the armies across the English channel to France – was labelled Operation Neptune, and was put under the command of a British admiral, Sir Bertram Ramsay, who would have to find and deploy the ships and barges to do the job. Ramsay was undoubtedly the man for the task. He had commanded a destroyer in World War I and cruisers and the battleship *Royal Sovereign* in the post-war years, but, like Eisenhower, his great skill was as a staff officer, a planner.[4] As a vice-admiral, he had masterminded Operation Dynamo, the retreat from Dunkirk in 1940, gathering a fleet of ships big and small to bring more than 338,000 men back from France. He had led the naval element of Operation Torch and a year later he landed the British 8th Army in Sicily. Ramsay was sometimes described as 'difficult', for he did not suffer fools gladly, if at all, but unlike many of his generation he was capable of delegating responsibility, and he attracted intense loyalty from his staff.

The D-Day landings would be on an eighty-kilometre arc of the Normandy coast, on five beaches or sectors designated – from west to east – Utah, Omaha, Gold, Juno and Sword. The Americans would take Omaha and Utah; Sword and Gold would go to the British; the Canadians were assigned to Juno.

Around 132,000 men would storm ashore on the first day alone, an almost unimaginable number. Neptune, the sea operation, required 6483 vessels, from battleships to minesweepers, submarines and trawlers, including 4000 landing craft and some 200,000 men. In the air there would be waves of bombers and fighters, more than 12,000 aircraft, British, Canadian and American (and four heavy bomber squadrons of the RAAF).[5]

The coordination and the logistics were of eye-watering complexity for, in effect, everything would have to happen at once, like the opening bars of a symphony. The essential thing, the crucial thing, was to ensure that these thousands upon thousands of men and tanks and guns and supplies went ashore at exactly the chosen times and places. It would require pinpoint navigation. Much thought went into this and eventually someone at Norfolk House came up with the bright idea of sending midget submarines over first, to show the way. Ramsay agreed.

At the 12th Submarine Flotilla, two boats were given the job. *X23*, commanded by Lieutenant George Honour, an RNVR officer, would be the beacon off Sword for the British landings. Ken Hudspeth's *X20* was assigned to Juno for the Canadians. Navigating carefully into position, they would sit on the bottom just offshore until before dawn on D-Day, when they would surface and shine lights out to sea to guide the landing craft onwards. The Americans, perversely, had decided they had no need for midget submarines at Utah and Omaha beaches, which would prove a mistake.

This was christened Operation Gambit. Training began in April, with both boats sent from Portsmouth to the isolated Slapton Sands, in Devon, a stretch of coastline similar to Utah Beach and the stage for a dress rehearsal for Overlord, codenamed Operation Tiger. Some 30,000 American troops were to go ashore on the sands from landing craft, while ships offshore mounted a bombardment over their heads with live ammunition.

X20 almost came to grief on the way there, in misty weather, when her escorting trawler carelessly led her into the notorious Portland Race, a turbulent and dangerous stretch of water off the promontory of Portland Bill, in Dorset. Ken Hudspeth was on the casing, hanging on for dear life as *X20* was swamped and tossed on her side. Always the master of understatement, he wrote later:

'It was a highly exhilarating experience standing on the open deck with two feet of freeboard as she rolled nearly to her beam ends and those below were quite worried. It was the only moment of real danger I suffered in X-Craft.'[6]

Slapton Sands and Operation Tiger were a lethal shambles so disastrous that it shook even the usually imperturbable Eisenhower. On the first day, in a muddle over timings as they landed, some troops were killed by friendly fire from the bombarding ships at sea. The exact total was never released.

Worse was to come. Not long after midnight on the second day, a flotilla of nine German E-boats, detecting an unusual flurry of Allied radio transmissions, got among the landing craft like a pack of sharks and another 639 Americans were killed or drowned.

After a few hair-raising near misses from wayward surface vessels, the two X-craft escaped the carnage and legged it back home to prepare. There would be two Coppists travelling in each boat to help with the navigation and recognition signals, a crew of five in all, and they brought an extraordinary amount of gear that somehow had to be crammed into every nook and cranny. There were portable radar beacons, diving suits, flashing coloured lamps and their batteries, an assortment of pistols and Sten guns with ammunition, an eighteen-foot telescopic mast, and twelve Luftwaffe oxygen bottles – lighter and much better than the British version – to provide an extra day's air supply. To top it all off they squeezed in two RAF inflatable rubber dinghies. And even that was not all, for there were more bits and pieces tacked on outboard, including extra buoyancy chambers where the side charges would normally sit, two small CQR anchors (which looked rather like a plough and were good for mud and sand) stowed in the casing, an echo sounder, bollards fore and aft, and an upper-deck repeater for the gyrocompass. The regular crews felt like a travelling circus, missing only the elephants. They had also been given coded messages, to be broadcast by the BBC at night, which would let them know whether the landing was going ahead or postponed.

General Eisenhower had chosen Monday, 5 June for D-Day because there would be a full moon for visibility on the night crossing of the channel and for the Allied bombers, and a low but rising tide from dawn that would help the landing craft hit the beaches. The weather, though, would be critical, and as the day drew closer, the forecasters became more pessimistic. If things were too bad, a postponement for a day or two might be possible, but any longer delay was unthinkable. Eisenhower and his staff were preoccupied with the weather day by day, hour by hour as the forecasts changed.

The two X-craft crews had been told the date several weeks in advance, leaving Ken Hudspeth vaguely uncomfortable that he had been entrusted with so great a military secret. They slipped their moorings at Blockhouse on the evening of Friday, 2 June, out through the East Gate in the Portsmouth Boom, on the surface in an awkward, rising swell to find their escorting trawlers. Ken had with him his usual first lieutenant, Bruce Enzer, and his engine room artificer, Les Tilley, with two Coppists: Lieutenant Commander Paul Clark, a crack navigator, and his offsider, Sub-Lieutenant Robin Harbud. By the time they met the trawlers, the seas had turned difficult. *X20* was rising and falling beneath the stern of her escort, HMS *Darthema*, like a bucking horse, and time and again the trawler crew in a ship's boat could not get the towbar through its assigned hole in the submarine's bow. After half an hour of this, Hudspeth crawled forward on the casing in his underwear and, half-submerged like a drowning rat, shoved the thing into position.

They moved off, with *X20* having to stop after midnight to clear a bit of wire from a floating buoy that had fouled her propeller. Just before dawn, some ninety-five kilometres from the French coast, both X-craft slipped the tow. The trawlers disappeared and they were on their own, diving a little after 5 a.m. This was Saturday, 3 June, and they stayed submerged all that day as they ran on, raising the induction mast every five hours or so to 'guff through', or suck some fresh air into the boat. That night they surfaced in the dark to run the diesel to charge the batteries, and by dawn the next day, Sunday, 4 June, *X20* had reached her assigned position off Juno Beach without any further trouble, exactly as ordered. *X23* also reached hers.

They settled easily to the bottom about a mile offshore, taking it in turns for one man to stay awake as a watchkeeper while the others snatched some sleep. All day they spent there, whiling away the hours in boredom, occasionally rising to periscope depth for a sneaky look at what was happening on land. In $X20$, Paul Clark had positioned them midway between the white pillar of the Pointe de Ver lighthouse and the village and little port of Courseulles-sur-Mer, where they could glimpse the distant figures of locals going to church and German soldiers sunbathing on the beach. Their presence went unnoticed.

Things were not so sanguine 160 kilometres to the north, back in England. By this time Eisenhower's headquarters were at Southwick House, a white, porticoed Georgian mansion a little north of Portsmouth. Most commanders would have ensconced themselves in the grandest suite, but Ike had insisted on a spartan existence in a small tent and unheated trailer concealed beneath camouflage netting in a nearby wood, a camp codenamed Sharpener.

That Sunday the weather was dismal, the omens awful. Rain and wind whipped around the trailer. Storms drenched the armies encamped at ports all along the southern coast and waiting for the word to go. In the morning, a little before 4 a.m., Ike left Sharpener and was driven in his big Cadillac to the house.

His three commanders – land, air and sea – were waiting for him in the library. General Sir Bernard Montgomery, Air Marshal Sir Trafford Leigh-Mallory, Bertram Ramsay and their aides were seated in armchairs around a conference table, with a log fire burning in the grate. The meteorologists by now had almost the status of gurus and soothsayers, and their forecast was grim. The wind and waves, they said, would be too hazardous for the planned landing the next day, Monday, 5 June. They recommended a postponement for a day, when things might improve. Chain-smoking, Eisenhower asked around the room for opinions. Reluctantly, everyone agreed. D-Day would now have to be Tuesday, 6 June.

That Sunday night, both X-craft surfaced as ordered, the men grateful for the fresh air, and a little before 11 p.m. they fiddled with their radios to tune into the BBC, confident they would be told the invasion would begin at dawn the next day. It was a sour, puzzling disappointment when they heard one of the agreed phrases: *For Padfoot. Unwell in Scarborough.* It meant a postponement for twenty-four hours.

The men were incredulous, for the weather on the French coast had been good all that Sunday and it was inconceivable that it would suddenly turn foul by the next morning. There was nothing for it but the dreary prospect of whiling away another day stuck on the sandy bottom, hoping things might improve. After charging the batteries and refreshing the air in the boat they dived again before dawn, that Monday dragging on as if it would never end, the air growing more thickly unpleasant and tempers fraying. Hudspeth opened the Luftwaffe oxygen bottles one by one, which eased things a little. *X23*, off Sword Beach, endured the same long purgatory.

The decisive meeting at Southwick House took place at 4 a.m. on the Monday. The weather seemed no better, and Eisenhower was gloomy on the drive from Sharpener to meet the same cast of characters around the fire. The blackout curtains were closed, but they could hear the rain drumming on the French windows. Everyone dreaded another delay. If there was to be another postponement, the tides would not be favourable again for two weeks, an unthinkable time to keep armies, ships and aircraft straining at the leash, and even that would be without the full moon.

There was another consideration, too. Much time and creative effort had gone into leading the enemy to believe the invasion, when it came, would be further north, at the Pas de Calais, that point of France nearest to England across the Dover Strait. The signs were that this had worked, but further delay increased the chance of the Germans discovering the true picture.

As a steward passed around the tea and coffee, this time the senior meteorologist, RAF Group Captain James Stagg, described by Eisenhower as 'a dour but canny Scot',[7] was cautiously hopeful.

'Some good news, gentlemen,' he began. 'No substantial change has taken place since last time, but as I see it, the little that has changed is in the direction of optimism . . . the predicted good weather should last until tomorrow, with good visibility and winds not more than Force 4.' That meant a fresh breeze, with waves up to four feet high and whitecaps, but it was manageable.

After a brief, solemn discussion the commanders gave their assent, although Leigh-Mallory for the RAF was worried about too much cloud cover.

The final decision was Eisenhower's. Every eye was on him, the room silent save for a ticking clock on the mantelpiece. Ike was fifty-three years old, the third of seven sons of a rural worker from Abilene, Kansas. It is no exaggeration to say that the fate of the Western world now lay in his hands. He paused briefly in thought, then looked up and spoke words that would echo in history: 'Okay. We'll go.' The room erupted with applause and cheers.

The commanders then left but Eisenhower stayed on alone, contemplating what he had unleashed. He took up pen and paper and scrawled a note to himself, something he might say if the worst happened and Overlord turned into a catastrophe:

> Our landings in the Cherbourg-Havre area have failed to gain a satisfactory foothold and I have withdrawn the troops.
>
> My decision to attack at this time and place was based upon the best information available. The troops, the air and the navy did all that bravery and devotion to duty could do. If any blame or fault attaches to the attempt it is mine alone.[8]

That night, before bed, Admiral Ramsay wrote in his diary:

> Monday, June 5, 1944. Thus has been made the vital and crucial decision to stage the great enterprise which shall, I hope, be the immediate means of bringing about the downfall of Germany's fighting power & Nazi oppression & an early cessation of hostilities.
>
> I am not under delusions as to the risk involved in this most difficult of all operations ... Success will be in the balance. We must trust in our invisible assets to tip the balance in our favour.
>
> We shall require all the help that God can give us & and I cannot believe that this will not be forthcoming.[9]

Once again, *X20* and *X23* surfaced a little before midnight to tune into the BBC and this time they were not disappointed. Overlord was on. Their air refreshed, both boats dived again to make ready for the morning and at 4.45 a.m. they surfaced once more, in a rough and cross-grained sea.

Ken Hudspeth's first task was to erect the eighteen-foot telescopic mast that would carry their flashing light, a difficult balancing act as *X20* lurched and tugged this way and that at her anchor. But they got it going exactly as instructed: the light facing north and flashing the letter M for Mike – in Morse code, two dashes – every forty seconds, between bearings of 340 degrees and forty degrees. There was also a small electronic beacon transmitting the letter L, which could be detected by radar in the surface vessels. To top it off, they had a crude contraption officially called a rod sounder but usually known as a 'bong stick', a length of steel held underwater and banged by a hammer to be detected by Asdic.

As an added precaution, they had brought with them the biggest White Ensign they could lay their hands on, a flag grand enough to grace the mainmast of a battleship, and this they flew on the stern to make absolutely sure the oncoming swarm could see who they were. It would be a heavy irony indeed to be shot at or sunk by your own side. One plan was abandoned. The junior Coppist, Robin Harbud, was to have taken one of the RAF inflatable dinghies further along the beach to flash another guiding light, but they judged the sea to be too rough and the idea unworkable. *X23* came separately to the same conclusion at Sword, to the disappointment of both young officers, who had rather been looking forward to a starring role.

But they had a stunning view, front-row seats. Ken Hudspeth wrote: 'At last through the murk the first craft appeared and the lines of landing craft surging in the rising sea passed close on either side heading for the beaches, followed by seemingly endless streams of others, with the salvoes from the rocket ships pouring overhead.'[10]

Onward came the Canadians, their 3rd Infantry Division and the amphibious tanks of the 2nd Armoured Brigade, supported by the British No. 48 Royal Marine Commando, all forging towards Juno. Some soldiers waved as they passed *X20*. The rough seas had delayed them and they were behind schedule, but a little after 7.30 a.m. men of the Royal Winnipeg Rifles, the Canadian Scottish Regiment, the Canadian 1st Hussars and the Regina Rifle Regiment were beginning to land ashore, under heavy enemy fire.

Further offshore, warships of Ramsay's Force E, led by the cruiser *Belfast*, hurled a thunderous bombardment upon the German defences, the muzzle flashes of their guns stabbing through the murk. The whoosh and roar of the rockets overhead was new and startling, adding to the tumult. Plumes of smoke began rising ashore.

X20's crew watched, enthralled, acutely aware they were witness to a spectacle of power and violence on a scale unique in the history of warfare. Eventually it was time to go; their task was complete. Operation Gambit had worked, had shown the way. Ken Hudspeth, as matter-of-fact as ever, remembered:

> Our job was done and we had only to wait for an escort to our trawler waiting offshore, to shackle on the towline, quietly submerge and be comfortably towed through the swept channels to reach Dolphin in time for a bath and dinner. Something of an anticlimax, as the real war developed just across the water.[11]

One man's plans were badly upset. As the Allied armies streamed from their landing craft that morning, *Generalfeldmarschall* Erwin Rommel was away in Berlin. Assuming that the weather was too bad for an invasion, the commander of Germany's vaunted Atlantic Wall had left his headquarters in France on the Sunday to attend a birthday party for his wife and a meeting with Hitler. When the news reached him, he flew back to seize command.

The greystone Congregational church at Aberfeldy was packed to the gallery for the wedding. It was Wednesday, 14 June. Pretty well the whole village had turned out in Sunday best, mingling expectantly with the small sprinkling of naval officers, who cut a dash, to much local approval, in full uniform with medals and swords.

Max Shean almost didn't make it. With Overlord in full swing, travel in the British Isles had been sharply restricted, but at the last minute he and his best man, Joe Brooks, got permission to leave, and they arrived in Aberfeldy the day before. The timing was perfect. That very same day it was announced that Brooks had been awarded the Distinguished Service Cross and Shean the Distinguished Service Order for the Bergen operation.

None of the bridegroom's family was there, but his mother, Gladys, at home in Perth, had sent over a package of rich dried fruit and other hard-to-come-by Australian ingredients for the wedding cake, and a friend had magically found six bottles of Australian champagne. Mary Golding wore a floor-length white dress and a flowing veil. The Reverend Russell Lewis pronounced them man and wife, the register was duly signed and the wedding party was piped to the reception at the Weem Hotel, an old Georgian inn across the River Tay.

Shean was delighted that his boss from *Varbel*, Bill Fell, had made the trip to be there:

> I was both honoured and horrified to see Mary presented, by Captain Fell, with a framed photo of His Majesty and me standing on X24's casing. I had never said a word to any of Mary's folk about submarines! But it was an act of great kindness, especially as the picture was signed by many of my Bonaventure shipmates. The wedding breakfast was lovely, in spite of the severe rationing that had been in force for over four years. Having so many Navy there boosted me no end.
>
> Joe was to read the telegrams, to arrange all Navy messages of doubtful propriety last, not to be read. He arranged them in the desired order but forgot to stop, resulting in a climactic finish much appreciated, I might say, by most of the guests.[12]

The newlyweds took the night train to London, a thrill for Mary, who had never been there. Max had splashed out and booked two nights at the Royal Over-Seas League in St James's, the heart of London clubland, with leafy views over Green Park, and he had found seats for *The Quaker Girl*, a musical comedy at the Coliseum, near Covent Garden. But the war could never be far away. The sirens wailed as they left the theatre and searchlights began criss-crossing the sky. 'Probably a false alarm,' Max said reassuringly.

It was not. That very week, London was hit by the first of the V-1 flying bombs that Hitler called the *Vergeltungswaffe*, or 'Vengeance Weapon', and the British came to know as the buzz bomb or the doodlebug. They were, in effect, an early cruise missile, launched from scattered sites in coastal France. The V-1 engine had a low, ominous growl to it, which was fine so long as you could hear it above. The danger came when the noise suddenly stopped, which meant the engine had cut out and the thing was about to plunge to earth.

The Sheans heard that noise as they walked home through the blackout, and the explosions kept them nervously awake that first night. The next day they had a cheerful lunch with Ken Hudspeth and his future bride, Audrey Nicholson, an English girl, but it was something of a relief to get out of the capital and on to their next stop, The Compleat Angler, a warm, redbrick riverside hotel at Marlow, on the Thames in Buckinghamshire. For both of them it evoked happy memories of a favourite childhood book, Kenneth Grahame's *The Wind in the Willows*:

> The Compleat Angler was also the complete retreat, a lovely location on the river bank, no doubt with Moles, Water Rats and Toads thereabouts. The first night there were sirens again and more explosions, more distant this time . . .
>
> The weather was fine. We spent afternoons lying on the river bank, watching the RAF towing gliders packed with soldiers across to France. I felt uneasy that I should be enjoying peace while these men were flying into the thick of war. I hired a sailing dinghy from Henley and gave my reluctant bride her first taste of my favourite pastime. In the narrow river, with its busy traffic of tugs and barges, we were frequently sailing into the rushes and holding on until the wash subsided. There was a good fresh breeze and three times gear broke, causing moments of instability. I enjoyed it all and my bride put on a brave face out of duty, saving her comments till after the honeymoon.
>
> We trained back to Aberfeldy and I returned to Bute to resume international hostilities.[13]

Shean found that the pace at Kames Bay was quickening. Another attempt was to be made on the dock in Bergen, again with *X24*, but with a new crew and captain, Percy Westmacott, an RN lieutenant. Once again *Sceptre* and Ian McIntosh did the towing, leaving the Shetlands on 7 September in the jaws of a howling gale, which grew only uglier over the next few days.

Both boats submerged to thirty-six metres to escape the worst but, as ever, the weather held the upper hand. *X24* surfaced on 9 September to charge her batteries and guff through. Her diver, Sub-Lieutenant Derek Purdy, a newly joined Kiwi, was emptying gash from the hatch of the W&D when a big wave smashed them and sent the boat plunging down to six metres before they could regain control. When they surfaced again, Purdy was gone. *Sceptre* searched for him, with no luck. He was twenty years old.

They did the job, though. Westmacott had been thoroughly briefed by Shean and he followed the same route into the fjords, working from the same landmarks. They found the dock easily enough and placed the charges directly beneath it, north and south, then headed for the exits. *Sceptre* met them exactly as arranged and they were back home by 13 September. RAF reconnaissance showed the dock had indeed been sunk, along with a small merchant vessel of some sort. The crews bestowed a new honour on Ian McIntosh: he became known as 'Bring 'em Back Alive McIntosh'.

Shean spent the next few months helping to train new men joining the flotilla. Ken Hudspeth did too, but his time in submarines was coming to an end. Operation Gambit had been his last outing, winning him a second bar to his DSC for 'gallantry, skill, determination and undaunted devotion to duty'. In late September he left Bute and rejoined the surface fleet for the rather more sedate life of an anti-submarine officer in the destroyer HMS *Orwell*, where he eventually became her first lieutenant and saw out the war.

New and improved X-craft had been designed and were taking shape at several shipyards. That November, Shean was appointed Commanding Officer of J.3012, the construction number of a boat being built by Vickers at Barrow. The navy would call it *XE4*. The XE boats were a leap forward, in a good many ways. They were forty-five centimetres longer, to provide more storage space, and some aluminium was used on the casing to save weight. The bulk side charges were replaced by limpet mines, each carrying ninety kilograms of explosives, six of them attached to either side of the hull, and the diesel engine was better mounted, to run more quietly. The wheels that worked the main vent valves were replaced by levers, which were far quicker to operate. Best of all, as far as the crews were concerned, the XEs had air conditioning, which took away the stink of sweat and the humidity, making life submerged infinitely more bearable.

Max Shean stood by the build in Barrow and Mary joined him there for a week. They thought the boat should have a name as well as a number, and they settled on *Exciter*, which would not be officially recognised by the navy but would certainly do. One of the Vickers draftsmen designed an emblem, a seahorse with a trident prodding a whale. *XE4* was shipped by train to Bute, and on Monday, 4 December she was launched from a slipway across the bay from *Varbel*. Mary did the traditional honours, producing a bottle of Australian champagne saved from the wedding and smashing it across the bows.

Joe Brooks left the flotilla to rejoin the surface fleet, to Shean's disappointment, for he had lost a good mate and it would mean working up a new first lieutenant pretty much from scratch. As it turned out, Brooks's successor was a cheerful and capable Irishman, Sub-Lieutenant Ben Kelly, and he and Shean hit it off. The stalwart Ginger Coles stayed put.

So the training went on. Then, a few weeks before Christmas, the compact world of the 12th Submarine Flotilla was turned on its head. Tiny Fell called a meeting of his officers to give them the startling news that they would be joining the war against Japan in the Pacific. A new flotilla would be formed, the 14th. He would be its commanding officer. Six of the new XE boats would be hoisted and stowed on board the familiar old *Bonaventure* as the submarine parent ship, which would sail early in the new year, 1945, to carry them all across the Atlantic, through the Panama Canal and out into the Pacific to Australia.

As always with the navy, there was no time to lose. It was an organisational and logistics earthquake. *Bonaventure* had to be entirely self-sufficient in everything from fuel to machinery spare parts, weapons, medical supplies, food and drink for the ninety-two officers and 540 men who would make the journey. A big hangar was built on the after well deck, where four of the XEs would be housed to conceal them from inquisitive eyes. Two more would go in the for'ard hold. The days were crowded with gunnery and radar trials, steam trials, anti-mine trials, compass adjustments, all the rigmarole of readying a big ship for a long and far-flung deployment.

The amiable Captain Fell presided over all with his customary aplomb. 'The year 1944 ended in a whirl of parties, XE-craft launchings, trials, tribulations and gaieties,' he wrote.[14]

There would be more of the same in 1945.

17

OPERATION SABRE

Excited though he was to be going home to Australia after nearly four years away, Max Shean felt a pang at leaving Mary behind. They said their goodbyes on a bleak January day in Glasgow, he to join his ship, she to return to Aberfeldy, with no idea of how much longer the war would go on, nor when or where they might meet again.

Bonaventure sailed from the Clyde on 21 February with Tiny Fell in command, in a convoy which took them down to the Azores. From there they steamed on alone south-west across the Atlantic, zigzagging at a fast clip to avoid U-boats, pausing for a few days in the Gulf of Paria, to the west of Trinidad, to see how the XEs would perform in tropical waters. After that it was through the Panama Canal and up the American west coast to San Diego, then south-west again to Hawaii.

On the way, Shean heard that his first ship and his first love, the feisty little corvette *Bluebell*, had been sunk by a U-boat off the Kola Peninsula in the icy Barents Sea on 17 February. Later, he learned that she had exploded in a ball of flame and gone down in less than a minute, with only one man, a petty officer, surviving from her crew of ninety-one. It was a stab to the heart, for he had known most of them, including her captain, Lieutenant Geoffrey Walker, and the memory of her loss would stay with him always.[1] A good ship could do that to you.

The Americans welcomed them generously at Pearl Harbor on 7 April, where they marvelled at the food and drink and luxuries almost forgotten in wartime Britain. But there was bad news for Captain Fell. No one knew what to do with him and his midget submarines, nor if they should even go on to the war zone. Although *Bonaventure* was a British warship and therefore a part of the British Pacific Fleet, the Americans ran the war in this western hemisphere, under the hand of 'CincPac', the US Navy's Commander-in-Chief Pacific, Admiral Chester Nimitz, based in Hawaii, and so they had the final word.

Fell was shocked and appalled: 'We were not wanted by the Americans in the Pacific. They had no tasks for us and it appeared to the Admiral, who broke this news to me, that we might just as well go back to the UK, where the war was rapidly ending.'[2]

After a week of pleading, and volleys of signals back and forth, with Fell employing his considerable reserves of charm, the Americans shrugged their shoulders and waved *Bonaventure* on towards Australia. A rollicking ceremony at the crossing of the equator lifted spirits for a day – with Tiny himself resplendent as King Neptune – but the news got no better:

> During the voyage across the Pacific spirits fell steadily as doubts increased. Signals were intercepted which indicated that there was no employment for us and that the Americans did not want us in their war zone, which now lay between New Guinea and Japan. These signals leaked out and were soon around the X-craft crews; morale fell dangerously.[3]

The British Pacific Fleet of 1945 remains, to this day, the greatest collection of British and Commonwealth warships ever assembled. At its zenith it counted five battleships – *Howe, King George V, Duke of York, Anson* and *Nelson* – and some 200 hundred other vessels, including six fleet aircraft carriers and fifteen smaller escort carriers with more than 750 aircraft. There was a host of cruisers, destroyers, corvettes and submarines, the lot under their commander-in-chief, Admiral Sir Bruce Fraser, based in Sydney. Three Australian cruisers – *Australia, Shropshire* and *Hobart* – plus seven Australian destroyers and eighteen corvettes, were among the number, with Canadians and Kiwis too. Fraser had made his name as the man who had destroyed the German battleship *Scharnhorst* at the Battle of the North Cape in December 1943.

Yet not all was as it seemed. Behind the scenes, the fleet had a troubled birth in disputes about what it should actually do. Winston Churchill, ever the romantic imperialist, had a Kiplingesque vision of recapturing the colonies of Burma, Malaya, North Borneo and Hong Kong, proud ships sailing triumphantly into the old familiar ports, the White Ensign flying in a new golden dawn. His service chiefs – Navy, Army and RAF – dug in their heels and insisted that the fleet should join the Americans in the thrust north to Japan itself. The colonies could wait. Faced with their threats of resignation, Churchill backed away and surprised them by offering the fleet to President Roosevelt at the Allied summit meeting at Quebec in September 1944. It would be under overall American command, Churchill conceded, and Roosevelt accepted the offer.

That, though, aroused a thorny new problem. America's Chief of Naval Operations, Admiral Ernest King, famously foul-tempered and foul-mouthed, loathed the British in general and the Royal Navy in particular, and made no secret of it. It was said that he had been given a hard time as a junior officer on exchange visits with the Royal Navy during World War I and had neither forgotten nor forgiven. One of his own daughters reputedly said he was the most even-tempered man in the navy – always angry. He was also notorious for his seduction of junior officers' wives.

King had no choice but to accede to his president's acceptance of Churchill's offer, but he wanted no one to share in the glory of the defeat of Japan. He set about putting every obstacle in the way of the partnership actually working. He ordered that the British Pacific Fleet would get no logistical help from the US Navy – none at all. It would have to operate entirely on its own resources.

This was a heavy blow. In all its long existence, the RN had always fuelled and supplied its ships from well-established shore bases around the empire, from Scapa Flow and Portsmouth to Gibraltar, from Malta to Aden, from South Africa to Ceylon, from Singapore to Hong Kong. They were never far away. On the other hand, the Americans in the vast reaches of the Pacific ran a very different operation they called a fleet train, a huge and mobile armada of tankers and other supply and repair vessels, big and small, that could sustain the warships with everything from aircraft engines to ice cream, whether at sea or at island bases swiftly thrown together as they advanced. 'I don't know what logistics are,' King reputedly once said, 'but I want more of them.' And he got them, the burgeoning output of American industrial might.

Without their own bases, the British had no choice but to create a fleet train of their own, a formidable project, for their merchant navy had been decimated by the U-boat war and the remaining ships were labouring to carry essential supplies across the Atlantic. With a mighty effort, they scraped one together but in truth it was always the smaller, struggling cousin of the American superman.

There were other handicaps. The Americans insisted that the British adopt their signalling codes and procedures, which took a bit of mastering. The big new American Iowa-class battleships could turn on a spanking thirty-three knots, while British battleships could manage a top speed of twenty-eight knots at best. The US Navy had perfected the art of refuelling at sea, with ships steaming close together side by side, a far more efficient practice than the older RN method of hanging a hose over the stern of a tanker for a following ship to pick up. British ships used up to a third more fuel per sea mile than their American counterparts, and all of them – conversely – had around a third less refrigeration space for food, which meant more frequent replenishment. A final flaw was that Sydney, the only feasible home base for the British, simply did not have the skilled workforce or the repair and maintenance facilities to sustain such a complex fleet and, as the front line advanced, it was further and further from the action.

In practice, though, the partnership worked, because individual American commanders, including many senior admirals, had the common sense and decency to ignore Ernie King's order and helped out where they could, in matters big and small. The American commanding admiral at sea, the salty William 'Bull' Halsey, in his flagship, the USS *Missouri* – 'the Mighty Mo' – fostered a cordial friendship with his British opposite number, Vice Admiral Sir Bernard Rawlings.

'One of my most vivid war recollections is of a day when Bert's flagship, the battleship King George V, fuelled from the tanker Sabine at the same time as the Missouri,' Halsey wrote in his memoirs. 'I went across to "the Cagey Five," as we called her, on an aerial trolley, just to drink a toast.'[4]

No doubt it helped that – logistics problems or not – the always hospitable wardrooms of His Majesty's ships were well stocked with alcohol, while US Navy ships were dry.

It was plain, though, that the balance of sea power had shifted. Britannia no longer ruled the waves. American admirals generally had a flair for public relations, too, unlike their reserved British allies. Bull Halsey, who was usually photographed for the newspapers and newsreels in leather aviator jacket, with a khaki cap jammed at a jaunty angle on his nuggety head, glaring fiercely from his bridge at some far horizon, was a household name in both the United States and Australia, creating the distinct impression that he alone was in charge of beating the Japanese at sea.

Captain Fell and his six midget submarines would be but a small cog in this great American machine. They arrived in Brisbane on 27 April 1945.

Max Shean went ashore as soon as he could, found a public telephone and called his parents in Perth. His mother was surprised and delighted to hear that her son was home, even if he was on the other side of the continent.

Another Australian submariner, Sub-Lieutenant Ken Briggs, wangled two days' leave, just enough to get him home to see his parents at Glen Innes, in northern New South Wales, where he startled the life out of them by knocking on their bedroom door at half past one in the morning. He had been away for four years, leaving them as a boy of eighteen and returning as a man of twenty-two.

In his own words, Briggs had been 'a bit of a terror' at Glen Innes High School.[5] Looking for adventure, he headed for Sydney as soon as he could get away and at the age of seventeen forged his father's signature on the papers to sign up for the RAN. They called him up on his eighteenth birthday, 24 May 1941 – it was also Empire Day – and, after the usual few weeks of recruit and then anti-submarine training at *Rushcutter*, Ordinary Seaman Briggs shipped out for Britain on the liner *Aorangi*. His first taste of the war was serving on North Sea trawlers based out of Loch Fyne, near Glasgow in Scotland, a brief and uneventful interlude before he was posted south to Falmouth, in Cornwall, where he joined a flotilla of motor launches being sent to the Mediterranean in May 1942.

This was more like it. His new home, Motor Launch 469, was a Fairmile, one of a class of little ships newly designed and built by the British Fairmile company and turned out literally by the hundreds during the war.[6] Fast and highly manoeuvrable, they had a timber hull thirty-four metres long with a sharply raked bow, boasting two 650 bhp petrol engines that drove them along at a thrilling twenty knots. The armament varied over time, with a range of machine guns, and twelve depth charges on the stern for anti-submarine work. Briggs would be ML 469's Asdic operator, one of a crew of three officers and thirteen sailors.

With long-range fuel tanks mounted on deck, the trip south down the Bay of Biscay took them through a mountainous sea. Strong and fit, Briggs did not suffer the horrors of seasickness, but it was still a relief when the Atlantic rollers abated after a few days and they cruised unharmed into Gibraltar. There they began an ML's dogsbody life of running errands, once or twice dropping agents onto the coast of neutral Spain, searching for the occasional U-boat, and escorting Mediterranean convoys, which meant a lot of rescuing men from sunken ships, as Briggs later recalled:

> One I remember was one of the 'Strath' boats. They used to come from Australia, the 'Strath' Liners. It was in convoy and was torpedoed. By the time we looked around after the explosion, the vessel had gone. It obviously had blown up, but there were 40 Air Force people in the water who we picked up. Another convoy, one of the ships, an odd one, a cargo vessel, had ramps on the bows

which held a Hurricane fighter, and if they ran into a bomber raid, because there were no aircraft carriers and that with the convoy, they would launch the Hurricane and shoot him off.

But he had nowhere to land, so we'd get the job of picking the pilot up after he had parachuted out or his petrol ran out or what have you. They would have to just ditch the plane. We were only a few feet above the water. We could just grab them out of the water or hop in the water and help them up the side. We had scrambling nets which helped.

Anyone you could help you would help. If they were German air people you still had to help them.[7]

The Allies launched Operation Torch in November 1942, an American and British amphibious invasion of the French North African colonies of Morocco and Algeria. Ike Eisenhower was in command. More than 100,000 soldiers were to land ashore in a three-pronged attack: a Western Task Force at Casablanca, on the Atlantic coast, a Central Force at Oran and an eastern force at Algiers, both on the Mediterranean shore. The two navies, British and American, would deploy some 350 warships, great and small, and 500 transports and landing craft to make it happen.

The plan was to subdue or (if need be) crush the collaborationist Vichy French regime. That done, the invading troops would turn east to meet the *Panzerarmee Afrika*, the Germans and Italians under Erwin Rommel who were reeling from imminent defeat at El Alamein, in Egypt. Nobody knew if the French would resist. There were airy hopes that they would not fire on the Stars and Stripes, but at Oran, in particular, there were also bitter memories of the RN attacking and sinking French warships in the port to prevent them from passing into German hands after the fall of France in 1940.

ML 469 was assigned to the Central Force to take Oran. It began more or less to plan, shortly after midnight on 8 November, with the American 1st Infantry Division – 'The Big Red One' – and tanks of the 1st Armoured Division landing unopposed to the east and west of the Oran harbour. The French were taken by surprise. Then it all went wrong.

Just before 3 a.m., two former US Coastguard Cutters transferred to the RN and rebadged as HMS *Walney* and HMS *Hartland* dashed into the harbour itself, loaded with troops who were to seize the port facilities to prevent sabotage. The French, now aroused, fought back from both shore batteries and moored warships in a blaze of searchlights, shooting at virtually point-blank range. The little *Walney* was quickly reduced to a burning wreck and sunk, and shortly afterwards *Hartland* exploded and also went down, both with grievous loss of life. It had been a gallant folly. The battle was now on, and fiercely.

ML 469 spent that first morning in the harbour laying smoke-screens, and then came under fire the next day, twisting and turning as shells from a fort above the town landed around her, throwing up fountains of dirty brown water uncomfortably close, as Briggs recounted:

> Two shore batteries opened up on us. They were 9-inch guns mounted on the cliffs overlooking the harbour. I was on the wheel at that particular time and our senior lieutenant was directing. He and I cooperated. He was a New Zealander who was very kind to me. The two guns were synchronised. They couldn't both fire together which helped us.
>
> We would set on a course ... one gun would line you up and fire and we would alter course before the shell arrived and then get back on a course and the other one would do the same thing. So we were actually dodging the shells. By the time they left the guns and arrived at the ship we were 50 or 100 yards off.[8]

It was desperate stuff, but it worked long enough for ML 469's captain to call in support from the battleship *Rodney*, lying offshore. Her sixteen-inch guns pounded the fort to pieces.

In the end, Operation Torch was a victory despite some costly mistakes and bungles: landings at the wrong beach, paratroopers dropped in the wrong area, tanks and trucks unloaded in deep water, where they sank with their crews. In one absurd fiasco, fully laden soldiers could not be unloaded from a transport because the rungs on the rope ladders were spaced too far apart. But Allied might prevailed and the Vichy regime surrendered in confusion on 10 November – although, as Eisenhower recognised, the result might have been very different if the defenders had been seasoned German troops.

But with Torch done and dusted, with Rommel defeated at Alamein and with the Germans ensnared in the slaughterhouse of Stalingrad, on the eastern front, Churchill struck a note of optimism in a speech at the Mansion House in the City of London. 'This is not the end,' he said. 'It is not even the beginning to the end. But it is, perhaps, the end of the beginning.'[9]

Ken Briggs was one of very few Australians involved in Operation Torch. He found it exhilarating: the roar of carrier aircraft overhead, the thunder and shock of gunfire, the handful of French warships attempting to escape from the harbour either sunk or driven ashore.

Surviving unscathed, he spent another year in the Mediterranean in ML 469 until, in November 1943, out of the blue, he was offered a commission. The boy from Glen Innes would become an officer, to be trained at HMS *King Alfred*.

He almost didn't make it. On the way back to Britain, the convoy of landing craft he was travelling in was attacked by four Focke-Wulf Condor bombers in the Bay of Biscay:

> We had no guns so we couldn't fire back. They were pretty low. They attacked the first one on the right hand column. The two bombs hit and there was a cloud of smoke and it was gone. Then the second one, they did exactly the same to her. In that instance three of the sailors came out of the debris, the smoke, paddling what they call a Carley life raft. We picked them up. Then the next attack was on the vessel I was on, but instead of coming fore and aft they came across. They had us dead set in their sights.
>
> One of the bombs dropped on the port side and the other on the starboard side. Both exploded and kicked our vessel right up and completely clear of the water, but no damage done and no injuries. I would have been within 3 yards of where the bomb fell. I didn't even get concussed. I think we were lucky they landed in the water and it took all the blast . . .

He spent that Christmas at *King Alfred* and passed with flying colours to earn the single wavy gold stripe of a sub-lieutenant RANVR, but uncertain of what might come next. Somebody suggested he might be interested in becoming a clearance diver, cleaning up harbours of mines and unexploded bombs and shells and the like. Thinking there might be a demand for that sort of job after the war, he signed up and in quick time he found himself down at Fort Blockhouse:

> When I got to Portsmouth, again I went for an interview with a senior officer and we were sitting in his office a couple of floors up. He was asking me what I wanted to do and what have you and I went through the story.
>
> He said, 'You've volunteered and if you would like to look out that window, you'll see what you've just volunteered for.'
>
> Of course, I had a look out the window and I couldn't see it at first.
>
> He said, 'Have another look.'
>
> And there was a little midget submarine which was on the surface and he said, 'That's what you've just volunteered for. What do you think?'
>
> Anyway by this time I knew that midget submarines had carried out operations, so I said, 'Well, if other people can do it, I'm sure I can. Yes I'll be in it.'
>
> From then on the training started.[10]

They put him through the diving course day and night, working in the stiff and unyielding Siebe-Gorman diving suit on the bottom of Portsmouth Harbour, learning of the dangers of 'Oxygen Pete'. That done, it was up north to Scotland and the flotilla at *Varbel*, for yet more training in net-cutting and the arts and sciences of the midget submarine business. When the new *XE4* arrived, he joined her with Max Shean to become her diver, the two Australians together: Shean the painstaking perfectionist with his logical engineer's mind, Briggs fighting fit and game for anything. They made a good pair.

In Brisbane, Captain Fell set about finding something for his flotilla to do – some hostilities he could join. The war in Europe was in its last tumultuous days, the Red Army in the outer suburbs of Berlin. Hitler committed suicide in his bunker with his newly married mistress, Eva Braun, on 30 April. Japan, though, was fighting to the suicidal death at Okinawa, that small island some 650 kilometres south of the Japanese mainland, in a battle so protracted and bloody that they christened it '*kotetsu no hageshi kaze*' – the 'violent wind of steel'.

Nobody was at all interested in midget submarines. Fell flew to Sydney and obtained an audience with the British commander-in-chief, Sir Bruce Fraser, who heard him out politely but then told him he would have to deal with the Americans. Fell was downcast but did not give up, and in early May he began an extraordinary journey from Townsville, at times even begging a lift in whatever aircraft he could find that would deliver him to the US Navy base at Subic Bay, in the Philippines. Eventually he found himself comfortably seated on the verandah of Rear Admiral James Fife, the US Navy's Commander Submarines, South-west Pacific.

Fell began his pitch, exercising every ounce of persuasion he could muster to sell the virtues of midget submarines. Fife listened to him courteously for three hours, and the two hit it off well enough to enjoy a convivial dinner together that night, but the admiral regretted that he had nothing to offer. There were no worthwhile targets for midget submarines in his area. A disconsolate Fell left his new friend empty-handed:

> That first meeting with James Fife made a lasting impression on me. Not only was he full of tact and humour but his ability to grasp our problems and his genuine desire to help us towards a chance to show our teeth endeared him to me . . . I finally left him with the knowledge that he would do all in his power to help us, but that there was little hope that he or anyone else could promise us action . . .
>
> The sad journey back to Australia with practically no hope for our continued existence as a fighting unit was exhausting and acutely uncomfortable. We spent the night of the 24th in Peleliu,

the 25th in Manus and arrived in Townsville late on the 26th, having flown at 14,000 feet without oxygen or pressurization over the Owen Stanley Ranges.[11]

Bonaventure had moved to Cid Harbour, in the Whitsunday Islands off the Queensland coast south-east of Townsville, for the crews to train in warm, turquoise waters a world away from the cold grey lochs of Scotland. One of *XE4*'s two divers, Sub-Lieutenant Adam 'Jock' Bergius, a Scot himself, marvelled at his new environment:

> We found ourselves in a wonderland of colour and light: corals and fish and sea plants of every shape and colour and a world quite unknown, as any pre-war divers would have been in cumbersome suits with air pumped down to them from a boat on the surface. We could swim as free as fish and being on pure oxygen made no noisy bubbles to destroy the peace of the scene.[12]

Tiny Fell left them to it while he kept badgering anyone who might find him a path to get back into the war. He talked his way into staff meetings, and networked affably and energetically at dinners and parties. One meeting in Sydney gave him the depressing news that the XEs would be 'paid off' and *Bonaventure* converted into a mere supply ship for the Fleet Train, an ignominious fate.

As Fell left that discussion, all hope dashed, he was called into another office to meet a US Navy captain, Henri Claiborne, who was introduced as the American 7th Fleet's intelligence officer. Claiborne had one question: could XE-craft cut submarine telegraph cables? Fell had no idea whether they could or couldn't, but he cheerfully assured the American that this was no problem – where there was a will there was a way.

Claiborne explained his idea. The Allies – that is, the Americans and the Australians – had long ago cracked the Japanese naval and army codes and were able to read their radio messages as they were transmitted. But the Japanese also used underwater cables to communicate with their occupation forces in South-East Asia: one cable ran from Tokyo via Hong Kong to Saigon, in French Indochina, and another from Saigon to Singapore. These could not be listened to. But if they could somehow be severed, the Japanese would be forced to use radio for all their communications and the Allies could scoop up everything, an invaluable bonus.

Tiny Fell seized the idea like a drowning man grabs a lifebuoy. He and Claiborne refined their plans over the next few days, had them approved from on high, and then the captain flew back to Cid Harbour to brief his crews and get things moving.

The first task was to find the tools for the job: a way of locating cables on the sea floor then dragging them up out of mud or sand so that a diver could cut them. They settled on a device known as a 'flat fish grapnel', a steel hook arrangement that looked like the capital letter W, and had some made in *Bonaventure*'s workshop. You towed it along by a chain attached to the central peak of the W, while the prongs on either side dug into the seabed and, in theory, scooped up the cable you were looking for.

Improvising quickly, *Bonaventure*'s crew laid heavy steel hawsers on the bottom of the harbour. Max Shean set out in *XE4* with the chain and grapnel and – after a few days interrupted by a near cyclone – they began to get the hang of it, snaring the hawsers off the mud. As a reward, Max took his crew out to the deserted Haslewood Island, in the outer Whitsundays, for a few days, where they swam and lazed in the sun, foraged for oysters and caught lobsters to cook on an open fire, a calming interlude. Then Jock Bergius, unwary of the perils of life in tropical Australia, poked curiously at a stingray and was badly speared by its tail, which ended that idyll in a hurry.

Next, Fell took them all south down to Hervey Bay, on the Queensland coast south-east of Bundaberg, near a point named Mon Repos, where they knew there was a disused telegraph cable that would give them more practice. All the X-craft were unloaded from *Bonaventure* and they took turns searching and grappling, crisscrossing back and forth, with divers coming and going from the W&D compartments to practise cutting.

It went well at first – until it didn't. One of the divers from *XE3*, Lieutenant David Carey, left the craft and successfully cut the cable. Through the periscope his captain saw him surface and swim towards the submarine, where he stowed the grapnel and then entered the W&D. Suddenly and inexplicably, he jumped out of the hatch again and, as *XE3* surfaced, leaped over the side and vanished. They searched for him for hours but found no trace; his body was never recovered. Another young man gone at the age of twenty-two.

It happened again the next day, 22 June, this time with *XE2*. In his diving gear, Bruce Enzer followed the grapnel on the seabed, cut the cable and then returned, as planned, to the W&D. His captain had a vague hunch that something was wrong, though, so he surfaced near the small motorboat that accompanied them on these exercises. The boat pulled alongside and the coxswain asked Enzer, standing on the casing, if he was okay. Enzer punched the man on the jaw and then he, too, jumped into the sea, never to be seen again.

This was a hard blow, for Bruce Enzer had been a popular and experienced figure in the flotilla as first lieutenant for Ken Hudspeth on the *Tirpitz* attack back in 1943 and with him again for Operation Gambit, off the Normandy beaches, on D-Day. He had been one of the searchers looking for David Carey's body the day before.

The shock of these deaths was gut-wrenching, not least because they had happened far from any enemy, in warm and peaceful waters on what should have been a routine exercise. The gloom was palpable, hanging over *Bonaventure* like a stormcloud. Everyone had their guesses and their theories, but the only logical explanation seemed to be that both had spent too long too deep and suffered oxygen poisoning, the dreaded Oxygen Pete, which could cause a man to lose his reason.

Sick at heart, Tiny Fell came close to calling the whole operation off, but the crews persevered, successfully hooking the cable, and there were no more horrors. The job would go on. A week later, the captain flew north on another four-day epic of leapfrogging Pacific islands to present his plans to his friend Admiral Fife at Subic.

> In complete silence he read through the scheme my staff officer and I had compiled while I watched him and waited with my heart in my mouth. When he had finished he looked up over

his spectacles and said 'what about having a crack at the two 10,000 ton cruisers in Singapore while we are at the cables?'

The sheer delight at hearing these words was almost too much for me. I can only remember Jimmy Fife taking me off to the beautiful new mess that had just been completed and giving me an Old-Fashioned that nearly knocked my head off . . .[13]

The two cruisers were *Myoko* and *Takao*, both veterans of the war in the Pacific since its first days. To take them out, as well as the Saigon cables, would require a whole new set of operational plans, which Fell set to making.

He flew back to Australia to round up his troops and assign them their jobs. *XE1* and *XE3* were to go for the cruisers. *XE5* would cut the underwater cable at Hong Kong, and Max Shean's *XE4* would take on the Saigon cable. The whole show, three separate operations, would be launched from Labuan, a small island with a useful harbour off the northern coast of Borneo, and about equidistant across the South China Sea from Singapore and Saigon. Labuan had been liberated from Japanese occupation just weeks before in a textbook air and amphibious assault by two brigades of the Australian Army's 9th Division and the RAAF and RAN.

The first task was to go back to Subic Bay, to collect Admiral Fife and the RN submarines that would tow the XE-craft to their targets. *Bonaventure*, fully stored and loaded, the XEs on board, sailed from Brisbane on 8 July and reached Subic twelve days later, just in time to run into two unexpected and not entirely welcome events. The first was a sudden inspection visit by Jimmy Fife's boss, Vice Admiral Charles Lockwood, the US Navy's Commander Submarines Pacific, known officially by one of those much-loved American acronyms as COMSUBPAC and less formally to his sailors as Uncle Charlie. The second event was a fully fledged typhoon. To complicate matters, Uncle Charlie and the typhoon arrived together.

The admiral was a formidable figure. At the beginning of the war, the US Navy's submarine service had been in disarray, its boats outdated, unsuitable for long-range Pacific patrols and armed with torpedoes that regularly ran too deep or failed to explode.

Its tactics were outmoded and many of the submarine captains were cautious to the point of timidity. In 1943 Lockwood swept in like a tornado, winning a battle for better torpedoes over the opposition of desk-bound admirals in Washington, firing under-performing commanding officers, setting up new bases and inspiring new tactics. Tiny Fell was wary of Lockwood, because it was rumoured that he regarded midget submarines as nothing more than an interesting British toy.

The rain was sheeting down when Lockwood appeared at around noon, his barge curving alongside *Bonaventure*'s accommodation ladder through grey walls of water that grew denser as he was piped aboard, his khakis drenched. Tiny had assumed the visitor would be content with a meeting in his cabin and was surprised when the admiral insisted on going for a ride in an XE, typhoon or no typhoon.

Max Shean was summoned to do the honours. Lockwood scrambled nimbly on board *XE4* and disappeared down the hatch, Fell watching anxiously as the little craft faded into the murk and then dived. An hour passed and more, then more still, with heavier rain, the wind rising and the water in the bay steadily surging into whitecaps. The captain was beginning to contemplate the disturbing possibility that he had lost both a midget submarine and a senior Allied admiral when *XE4* appeared again, at last. Lockwood bounded back on board *Bonaventure*, enthusing that Shean had taken him for a couple of dummy attacks and how impressive they had been; he had been sceptical but was now a fan.

'The conversion of Admiral Lockwood from being an interested but definitely anti-X-craft man, to our most enthusiastic sponsor was indeed a triumph for Shean and the flotilla,' Fell wrote.[14] There would be plenty of opportunities to employ midget submarines as the war went on, they agreed, possibly well into 1946 if, as everyone feared, the Japanese fought a fanatical defence of their home islands against an Allied invasion.

By the time the admiral came to leave, the storm was upon them in full fury, the barometer dropping like a stone, the wind howling, the rain horizontal, the sea whipped to a rolling surf. Fell ran to the bridge and ordered 'slow ahead both engines', to take some of the strain off the two, bar-taut anchor cables holding the ship. The next few minutes were pure slapstick, never to be forgotten by those who saw it.

As Lockwood went down the ladder, a wave heaved his barge up beneath it, hoisting it several metres into the air with an awful splintering of timber. The admiral made a flying leap and landed on top of his coxswain in the boat, knocking him unconscious. As the barge slumped back into a trough, the coxswain prone on the deck boards, COMSUBPAC seized the helm himself, gunned the engine and, with a cheerful wave, ploughed off into the storm. Fife told Fell later that, on the way, Uncle Charlie had personally rescued four sailors he had found clinging to an upturned landing craft.

The tempest lasted another couple of hours, with some vessels big and small breaking away from their moorings and being carried towards hidden reefs, the bay in chaos. Most of the XEs were tethered to a boom outboard of *Bonaventure* and were more or less secure, but *XE6* had been swinging off a buoy, and Fell could only watch helplessly as she was dragged towards a line of breakers until, miraculously, the mooring line apparently snagged in some coral and held. By sunset the weather had subsided enough for the cleanup to begin.

Bonaventure sailed south-west for Labuan two days later, escorted by two destroyers and with Fife and his staff on board, providing the unusual spectacle of a British warship flying the blue and white, two-starred flag of a US Navy rear admiral. *XE5* was left behind in Subic Bay. She would go from there on her assignment to cut the Hong Kong cable. The rest reached Victoria Harbour in Labuan two days later, without incident, where they found their towing submarines *Spark*, *Stygian* and *Spearhead* ready and waiting for them.

The three assigned XEs were lowered into the water and prepared for their journeys. *XE4* was to travel around 1500 kilometres north-west, to the mouth of the Saigon River. Her mission would be known as Operation Sabre.

18

TO THE SAIGON RIVER

First off were *XE1* and *XE3*, heading south-west for Singapore on the somewhat pessimistically named Operation Struggle. Farewelled with a stirring speech by Jimmy Fife, they left the heat and humidity of Labuan in the midafternoon of 26 July, their passage crews on board, towed by *Spark* and *Stygian*, and accompanied for part of the trip by an American submarine rescue vessel, USS *Coucal*.

XE4 left just after breakfast the next day, with another florid farewell from the admiral, who clearly enjoyed these moments. 'You're the little guys with a lotta guts,' he told them. 'Good luck!'[1] Max Shean and his operational crew of four were on board the towing submarine *Spearhead* as they headed out on the surface for an hour in a calm sea, then dived. Lieutenant Willie Britnell and the three-man passage crew would handle the little craft for the next three days, a testing job requiring constant and tiring attention to keep the proper depth and trim at ten knots. The routine was to spend five hours submerged and then surface to guff up fresh air and top up the batteries. Operation Sabre was underway.

Max whiled away the time fixing the details of the job in his mind. The two cables lay at the mouth of the Saigon River, which empties into a wide bay bounded in the west by the delta of the Mekong River and in the east by a long peninsula called at the time by its French colonial name, Cap Saint-Jacques. (The next generation of Australians would know it as Vung Tau, a logistics base and rest and recreation centre during the Vietnam War.)

A tall, white lighthouse mounted on a hill on the tip of the peninsula would serve as a landmark.

The intelligence people back in Australia had produced an engineer from Cable & Wireless, the British company which ran most of the world's undersea communications cables, and he had been able to pinpoint on a chart exactly where *XE4* should search – to within fifty feet (fifteen metres), he claimed. The cables were running along what was virtually an underwater ridge known as the Formosa Bank, at a depth which varied from fifteen metres to thirty metres.

What the engineer could not tell them was the condition of the bottom. It might be sand, it might be rock. Almost certainly there would be silt from the river, with the cables buried beneath it, for they had been laid in 1871, he added helpfully. There would be only one way to find out.

The passage passed uneventfully in calm seas and without any sight of the little that was left of the Japanese enemy in these waters. An impressive sea snake was the only hostile creature they saw. On the fourth day, well before dawn, they surfaced for the changeover, the seas so calm that *XE4* was able to nudge astern of *Spearhead* and the crews simply stepped across. Max Shean noted that Willie Britnell and his men had left the craft in excellent condition.

On they went, briefly surfacing again at around sunset to look for the lighthouse, which was exactly where they expected to see it, about twenty-seven kilometres to the east-north-east. *Spearhead*'s navigation had been flawless. They surfaced once more, at nine o'clock that night, making for the lighthouse, but were disappointed to find it was not lit. The only other useful landmark was a range of mountains further inland – not exactly a reliable guide, but it would have to do.

The wind was rising now, setting up a short sea over the Formosa Bank, with water and spray sweeping over the casing. Coming up from below and just as he clambered out of the W&D hatch, a bigger than usual wave caught Shean by surprise and swept him overboard. Nobody noticed he had gone.

> XE4 was going slow ahead on engine and by the time I got my head above water I was back level with the rudder. I took several swift strokes and grabbed at the jumping wire which ran from the periscope guard to the rudder. At this speed of about two knots it was not difficult to pull myself hand over hand, forward along the wire and regain the casing, even with the binoculars hanging on their lanyard around my neck ... I had caught the wire after swimming the fastest few strokes of my life, so all was well.²

It could have been a disaster, a lonely, despairing death in an empty sea. If Max had not found the wire and grabbed it he would have been left floundering in *XE4*'s wake as she disappeared into the distance, the crew below entirely unaware. Eventually, when they noticed he was gone, they would have come back to search for him but there was no certainty they would have found him, alive or dead.

Very early the next morning, 31 July, they saw a couple of junks under sail, making to enter the river and heading straight for them. There was no telling what they were: innocent fishermen or some sort of Japanese patrol, but there was no point in taking chances so they dived again until 6 a.m. Then, back at periscope depth, it was down to work, streaming the grapnel at the end of its six metres of chain and nine metres of manila line.

First they would try for the Saigon–Singapore cable. Their initial run began at about 8 a.m., dead slow at less than two knots, Ben Kelly working constantly to keep the craft three metres from the bottom, Ginger Coles at the wheel. As far as they could tell, the grapnel was dragging over coarse sand on the Formosa Bank, but after about an hour of this it had caught nothing. Doubts began to creep in. They were exactly where the Cable & Wireless man had told them to be but were coming up empty-handed. They tried again, going back over their tracks, again with no luck, then once more for a third run. This time they were brought up short. The grapnel had snagged something.

Ken Briggs wriggled into his diving suit and went out through the W&D into water that was fifteen metres deep, which meant that he could stay there for fifteen minutes at most. When he came back within just five minutes to report that there was no sign of any cable, just a patch of hard clay, the disappointment was palpable. Perhaps they were on a fool's errand. Shean was feeling depressed but could not let it show, and after a short rest to gather his thoughts, he ordered the third run to continue.

Ten minutes later a sudden jerk brought them up short again. Max ordered full ahead, then full astern, but *XE4* would not budge. It must be the cable – it must be. Fingers crossed, Shean told Kelly to put her on the bottom and they settled there at thirteen metres. That was still a dangerous depth for a diver but manageable for a brief spell. Ken Briggs would be firmly attached to the cutter's hydraulic hose; if anything went wrong or he became overdue, they could surface and drag him up with them.

It was now just after midday. Ken dressed in his suit and went quickly into the W&D, closing the door behind him. Face mask on. Close off air. Switch on oxygen. Flood the compartment. Then open the outer hatch and into the sea. Get the cutter from its compartment on the casing. So far, it was well-practised routine, second nature.

The water at that depth was cold but not unbearable, and there was sunlight enough for reasonable visibility as he groped his way down along the grapnel rope towards the sea floor. And there it was. Hooked by the flukes of the grapnel, the cable lay partly covered by silt and mud and encrusted with weed and barnacles. Even so it was unmistakable. It had taken only minutes.

Briggs caught the cable in the jaws of the cutter and squeezed the trigger, releasing the blade to cut it once, then again. It worked perfectly, biting through cleanly and smoothly. The orders were clear: bring back a piece of cable to prove the job done. He severed a length of about sixty centimetres. In ten minutes he was home inside *XE4* again, excitedly displaying the trophy as he was helped out of his suit.

Now for the other cable, Saigon–Hong Kong. This time Jock Bergius would do the job.

Shean came to periscope depth to check his bearings and then dived down once more for the slow trawl with the grapnel. They jerked to a halt again at about half past one, the grapnel hooked and Bergius went out in his suit. This time the cutter did not work properly, failing to slice through the cable, so after a short struggle he returned to *XE4* to catch his breath and rest for half an hour. There was a second cutter, and when he took that out it worked perfectly, slicing off another length, which he had back on board within ten minutes.

The atmosphere in the boat by now was thick and foul, sour with the stench of sweat, but Shean brought them up to periscope depth and, elated, raised the induction mast to suck in fresh air to revive them all.

They had done it. Job completed, exactly as ordered. Shean rested them again on the seabed until it grew dark, then headed for the recovery rendezvous with *Spearhead*. That went like clockwork too. There was another possible leg to the operation – to sink any enemy shipping further up in the Saigon River – but *Spearhead*'s captain said aerial reconnaissance had found there were no worthwhile targets. So they headed for the barn, as Jimmy Fife would surely have said. *XE4* arrived back in the harbour at Labuan a little after sunset on 3 August, to a rousing reception.

Further to the south, *XE1* and *XE3*, on Operation Struggle, left their towing submarines an hour before midnight on 30 July, in sight of the Horsburgh Lighthouse at the very tip of the Malayan peninsula, and headed for Singapore. Their targets, the cruisers *Myoko* and *Takao*, were moored to the north of the island opposite the naval dockyard, in the Johore Strait separating Singapore from Malaya. That would mean some careful pilotage in narrow and congested waters, anticlockwise around Singapore from the east, negotiating a submarine boom and with every chance of enemy patrol craft making life difficult as well. Intelligence reports had confirmed that neither cruiser had moved for quite some time, but each was heavily armed with eight-inch guns and bristling with anti-aircraft weapons, all likely to be in working order and enough to cause trouble when the Allies went to retake Singapore.

XE3 cruised into the strait on the surface at night at a little over four knots, her captain, Lieutenant Ian Fraser, keeping a lookout on the casing. They hurriedly altered course to dodge a fishing boat which loomed out of the dark but apparently did not see them, and a little later they dived and sat on the bottom to avoid a big tanker and a small escort vessel. That gave them a problem, because the heavy bump when they came to rest on the seabed disabled the log that recorded their speed and distance travelled, meaning they would have to rely on guesswork and dead reckoning. Fraser, though, was a well-regarded skipper and a practised navigator. At just five feet four inches (162 centimetres) in his socks, he was perhaps the only man in the entire flotilla who could stand fully upright in an XE.

At 10 a.m. on the morning of 31 July, on schedule, *XE3* slipped at a depth of three metres through the submarine boom, a ramshackle affair with a gate that appeared to be left permanently open. There were surprisingly few ships or boats around but the water was an oily calm that left a telltale wake from the periscope, forcing Fraser to snatch only brief, infrequent glimpses. A couple of hours later, the unmistakable shape of *Takao* came into view, stark in that singular dark grey in which the Japanese painted their warships, moored right on the Malay shore.

XE3 lined up for her run in. Fraser took another quick look through the periscope and was stunned to find himself staring at a boat packed with Japanese sailors, perhaps twelve metres away, so close he could see their lips move as they talked. Surely one of them must see the submarine. 'Flood Q! Down periscope! Thirty feet!' he ordered.

XE3 lunged for the bottom, scraping forward across what sounded from the inside like small rocks or gravel until, with a crunch loud enough to wake the dead, she thumped into the side of the cruiser with the depth gauge showing just thirteen feet (four metres). Fraser decided to make another approach, so he backed off and began a new run from a different angle. This time he had better luck and managed to slip into a deeper pocket directly beneath *Takao*'s keel, although there was now only a little over a foot of water between the casing and the cruiser's heavily barnacled bottom.

XE3's diver, Leading Seaman James Joseph 'Mick' Magennis, a wiry Ulsterman from Belfast, entered the W&D and made to clamber out the hatch, only to find that they were so close under the cruiser that it would not fully open. Through the little night periscope, Fraser watched him writhing and squirming until he finally squeezed through and took six limpet mines from the starboard cargo container.

At this depth there would be no problems with the dreaded Oxygen Pete, but nothing ever went perfectly: the struggle out of the hatch had done something to Magennis's breathing apparatus, leaving a small but distinct trail of bubbles rising to the surface, a dead giveaway if anyone happened to glance over the side of the cruiser and see them.

The limpet mines had magnets for attaching them to the hull of the cruiser – in theory, it was a simple matter of pressing them on. But when Magennis tried to do this he found that the ship's bottom was so encrusted with weed and barnacles that the mines would not grip. Doggedly, laboriously, he used his diver's knife to scrape and hack away at the hull to clear six patches – three at the bow, three at the stern – where the mines could stick, and then set their timers. This exhausting ordeal took him half an hour but it seemed like a lifetime to the crew waiting for him to return.

Eventually he made it back, squeezing into the W&D again and closing the hatch, his hands badly lacerated by the barnacles, his body limp from fatigue. It had been a noble effort. Fraser ordered the release of the port-side cargo with its two tonnes of high explosive, which dropped away as normal, and then began to extract *XE3* from beneath her target, calling for half speed ahead, course 200.

She refused to budge. He tried full ahead but still there was no movement. He tried full astern but that was no good either, because at that point *Takao*'s keel was actually lower than *XE3*'s periscope standard, leaving nowhere to go. Another attempt at full ahead did not work either, the little craft straining and quivering but remaining fixed to the spot. There was no telling what she was stuck to, no knowing why she would not move, but it was beginning to look as if they might be trapped there, and the falling tide would bring the cruiser harder down on top of them, pinning them to the bottom. They could be caught with no way out, waiting there to be blown to pieces by their own charges.

A chill of fear began to rise, silently but inexorably. Perhaps they should abandon ship? Even that might be difficult, for the space for opening the W&D hatch was shrinking by the minute and it would be hard, if not impossible, for the bigger men to squeeze through. For those who might make it out, there was the certainty of capture by the enemy, and nobody had any illusions as to how that would end.

Ian Fraser kept his cool, as a captain must. There were still a few tricks to try. He pumped water from one ballast tank to another, fore and aft and then back again, and then several times more, the engine still running. He partially blew the No. 2 main ballast tank in the hope that this might dislodge them. This backing and filling took nearly half an hour, with the black blur of *Takao*'s keel still ominously, threateningly above them. One more try. And at long last something worked. Suddenly, inexplicably, they were free. *XE3* gave a lurch and a groan, and they could feel her beginning to shift beneath their feet as her propeller dug in. There was no explanation, but nobody needed one. They were moving.

With First Lieutenant Bill 'Kiwi' Smith, a sub-lieutenant from New Zealand, at the controls, *XE3* shot like a cork out of a bottle, so forcefully that before he could hold her she broke surface nearly fifty metres from the cruiser. Again nobody saw her. They went back down, only to find a new problem upon them.

They could not jettison the outboard container, which had held the limpet mines. It remained firmly stuck to their starboard side and, worse, it had flooded, the weight of the water leaving them dangerously lopsided. The emergency release gear did not work either. The only possible way to fix it would be for a man to go out into the water to remove the retaining bolts. Mick Magennis was still recovering from his wrestle with the limpet mines, so Fraser decided that he would do it himself. But the Irishman insisted that he was the boat's diver and it was his job. Armed with a spanner, it took him some ten minutes, another wait of what seemed like eternity until he appeared once more at the W&D hatch with a thumbs-up signal. The container slipped away.

From that moment, their luck got better. They were red-eyed and wrung out from lack of sleep and foul air, existing on Benzedrine to keep them going, but they were alive and free. Once or twice there was an alarm on the way out, an occasional ship which caused them to dive a few times, but they met *Stygian*, their towing submarine, as planned.

During her wait, *Stygian* had seen the distant flash of a tremendous detonation from the direction of the strait, which she took to be a cruiser blowing up. Her captain signalled *Bonaventure* and Tiny Fell back at Victoria Harbour in Labuan:

> Following from FRASER: 'My cruiser went upwards. What a bonfire. E.T.A. Victoria Noon 4th. Comment from our waiting position off Horsburgh Light: 'Spectacle great. Consider cruiser was well distributed over countryside . . .'[3]

They made it back to Labuan on 4 August as predicted, a day after *XE4*'s return, to yet another rousing reception.

XE1 did not fare so well. Misfortune dogged her all the way. It was the luck of the draw, but she encountered a lot of traffic on the way in, far more than *XE3* had met, forcing her captain, Lieutenant John Smart, to lie low for hours on end. His target, *Myoko*, was berthed further into the strait, some three kilometres beyond *Takao*, but darkness fell before he could reach her. Making the best of a bad job, he dropped his explosive side cargo alongside *Takao* and withdrew, also returning safely to Labuan.

The rejoicing soured and died a day later. Aerial reconnaissance flights over Singapore and the Johore Strait found the two cruisers still very evidently in one piece. A close inspection of the photographs showed *Takao* surrounded by a great pool of oil and very likely low in the water, but she had not been 'distributed over the countryside', as that optimistic signal had suggested. Ian Fraser and his crew were beyond disconsolate, and they badgered Captain Fell for permission to return immediately for a second strike, which he refused.

Further north, *XE5*'s attempt on the Hong Kong cable went badly. The tow broke on the way there, which delayed them by twenty-four hours, and when they finally arrived on the spot they found the water so muddy that the divers could barely see a metre in front of them. They searched back and forth for three days, found nothing, then gave it up as a bad job and returned under tow to Subic.

Behind a wall of silence and secrecy, the Americans conducted their first atom bomb test in the New Mexico desert at dawn on 16 July. It exploded successfully, with the energy of twenty-five kilotons of TNT.

The very next day, the leaders of the United States, Britain and the Soviet Union met at a former imperial palace at Potsdam, on the lakes south-west of Berlin, to plan the governance of occupied Germany and the shape of the post-war world. One result of this summit was an ultimatum to Japan demanding unconditional surrender. Known as the Potsdam Declaration, it was issued on 26 July by the new US president, Harry Truman, by Prime Minister Winston Churchill and by the Chinese president, Chiang Kai-shek. Its final clause carried a veiled hint of Armageddon: 'We call upon the government of Japan to proclaim now the unconditional surrender of all Japanese armed forces, and to provide proper and adequate assurances of their good faith in such action. The alternative for Japan is prompt and utter destruction.'[4]

In Tokyo, the Japanese government was racked by conflict and indecision, from the Emperor down. The militarists of the armed forces demanded that the war go on, to defend the sacred homeland no matter the cost in lives and treasure. The realists recognised that the game was up. Unable to agree, they played for time. The next day, the prime minister, Admiral Kantaro Suzuki, told journalists asking about the declaration that his government 'does not attach any important value to it at all. The only thing to do is just kill it with silence. We will do nothing but press on to the bitter end to bring about a successful completion of the war.'[5]

President Truman had before him the US War Department's latest estimate of the bloody cost of an invasion of Japan and perhaps another year of a fight to the death. It predicted as many as four million American casualties, including between 400,000 and 800,000 dead Americans, and between five and ten million dead Japanese.[6] He opted for the bomb instead.

On the morning of 6 August, a Boeing B-29 Superfortress named *Enola Gay* dropped an atomic bomb on the city of Hiroshima, in the south-west of the island of Honshu. Code-named 'Little Boy', and identical to one tested in New Mexico, it instantly killed tens of thousands of people and reduced the city to radioactive rubble. Tens of thousands more would die in the months that followed, perhaps as many as 140,000 people, with another 300,000 men, women and children known to the Japanese as *hibakusha*, or 'explosion-affected people'.

Later that day, the White House issued a press statement which said, in part:

> It is an atomic bomb. It is a harnessing of the basic power of the universe. The force from which the sun draws its power has been loosed against those who brought war to the Far East . . .
>
> We are now prepared to obliterate more rapidly and completely every productive enterprise the Japanese have above ground in any city. We shall destroy their docks, their factories, and their communications. Let there be no mistake; we shall completely destroy Japan's power to make war.
>
> It was to spare the Japanese people from utter destruction that the ultimatum of July 26 was issued at Potsdam. Their leaders promptly rejected that ultimatum. If they do not now accept our terms they may expect a rain of ruin from the air, the like of which has never been seen on this earth.[7]

This news, when it reached faraway Labuan, was a little garbled and not very revealing. The news sheet which appeared each morning on *Bonaventure*'s noticeboard called it an 'Atomatic Bomb', and very few people had any idea what that meant. The enormity of the destruction of Hiroshima became a little clearer over the next few days, and there was optimism in the wardroom that this must surely bring on a Japanese surrender. But in the meantime the war went on, and Tiny Fell decided there should be another operation to finish off those two Japanese cruisers at Singapore. *XE3* and Ian Fraser would be sent back in again, accompanied by *XE4* and Max Shean.

They were making their preparations when a second and bigger bomb was dropped on the city of Nagasaki, in Japan's south, on 9 August. Surely that must mean the end. There were wild celebrations on ships in the harbour that night, with star shells and flares shooting into the sky and fire hoses spouting floodlit fountains of water, until an angry order from the senior commander ashore called a halt.

It was not until noon on 14 August that Hirohito, the godly descendant of the Sun of Heaven, made his decision. To howls of dismay and shouts of *banzai*, he told his final Imperial Conference that he would accept the Allied demand for unconditional surrender. At noon the next day, he announced that surrender in a radio speech that contained one of the great self-serving understatements of all history:

> The war situation has developed not necessarily to Japan's advantage, while the general trends of the world have all turned against her interest...
>
> Moreover, the enemy has begun to employ a new and most cruel bomb, the power of which to do damage is, indeed, incalculable, taking the toll of many innocent lives. Should we continue to fight, not only would it result in an ultimate collapse and obliteration of the Japanese nation, but also it would lead to the total extinction of human civilization.[8]

XE3 and *XE4* were already at sea. They had left Labuan again for Singapore early that same morning. Not quite an hour into the trip, their two towing submarines received a signal calling the whole thing off. Return to base. Max Shean recorded the moment:

> 'This,' I thought, 'is our reprieve.' I lost no time in informing my crews. I had mixed feelings, of anticlimax due to the challenging operation for which we were prepared, now being unlikely to proceed, and intense relief in the knowledge that my crew and I would be spared the risk of extinction. We were saved by the bombs. Nobody expressed outrage that this was an unfair way to treat such an enemy.[9]

That same morning, the Australian prime minister, Ben Chifley, broadcast to the nation from an ABC studio in Canberra:

> The Japanese Government has accepted the terms of surrender imposed by the Allied Nations and hostilities will now cease. The reply by the Japanese Government to the Note sent by Britain, the United States, the USSR and China, has been received and accepted by the Allied Nations. At this moment let us offer thanks to God . . .
>
> And now our men and women will come home; our fighting men with battle honours thick upon them from every theatre of war. Australians stopped the Japanese in their drive south, just as they helped start the first march towards ultimate victory in North Africa. Australians fought in the battles of the air everywhere and Australian seamen covered every ocean. They are coming home to a peace, which has to be won . . .[10]

And so it was over. The signal had gone out from the Admiralty in London: 'Cease hostilities against Japan.' In *Bonaventure*, Captain Fell, Commanding Officer of the 14th Submarine Flotilla, recorded his reaction:

> The finality of those four words left me gasping. I felt utterly empty, deflated, without coherent thought. Late that night, while sirens screamed, rockets and tracer flamed and the roar of voices from the Army wafted out to us, I lay on my bunk looking back over the war years and thought how lucky I had been.[11]

For most of those who had faced the enemy, the immediate emotion was relief, a pervasive sense of deliverance from injury or death, the exhilaration of survival. But there was exhaustion, too, an overwhelming weariness that brain and body had unconsciously supressed in the daily business of simply staying alive, but which now descended like a dark cloud.

Darker still was the memory of those who hadn't made it, men who had been friends, shipmates, colleagues, comrades. Some had been like brothers, others perhaps just a face in the mess come and gone and now difficult to put a name to. All had shared the dangers. Twenty-three men lost their lives in X-craft of the 12th and 14th flotillas, either by enemy action or wretched accident. Three were Australians far from home: the flamboyant Henty Henty-Creer lay at the bottom of Altafjord, while the happy-go-lucky Brian 'Digger' McFarlane and that burly man of the world Jack Marsden from South Australia shared a sailor's grave in *X22* somewhere beneath the turbulent waters of the Pentland Firth.

In quick time, though, as the hope and dream of peace became reality, all else was eclipsed by a deep longing to return to home and family, to take off the uniform and to resume the civilian life that had been wrenched away what seemed like an age ago.

Always the meticulous planner, in the months before war's end Max Shean had explored the possibility of returning to the University of Western Australia to pick up the strands of the engineering degree he had begun in 1937 at the age of nineteen. He was now twenty-seven. Would they have him back? On spec, he wrote to ask one of his old professors if they would admit him and received an encouraging reply. The question was: how to get home and get a discharge from the navy? How could he get demobilised, or 'demobbed', as they called it?

His luck was in. *Bonaventure* was ordered first to Subic Bay, to collect *XE5* after her Hong Kong venture and then to proceed to Sydney. Shean and Ken Briggs could hardly believe their good fortune. They sailed from Labuan on 20 August, farewelled in the grand manner by their staunch friend and ally Admiral Fife, who issued the following signal:

> Upon release of the 14th Flotilla from my command I again wish to express appreciation for your co-operation and the fine spirit of willingness in accomplishing assigned tasks. I have the greatest admiration for the forthright sheer guts of you and your personnel. May Divine Providence continue to guide you and be with your future activities.[12]

It was strange, after so long, to hear no more the pipe of 'Darken ship' at dusk, to be sailing at night with all the lights on. It was almost a holiday cruise. They paused on the way to rescue the crew of an American army freighter which had run aground on the southern edge of the Great Barrier Reef. A few days out of Sydney, some bright spark on the flotilla staff asked Shean to lead a mock attack on the harbour as a publicity gimmick to show what midget submarines could do, but he refused, unwilling to perform like some circus act. The war was over, and there was always the risk of a collision in a crowded port. The idea was quietly dropped. By 5 September, *Bonaventure* was snugly and placidly anchored with the Sydney Harbour Bridge looming behind her.

To everyone's surprise, newspaper reporters were invited on board. The flotilla and its operations had been shrouded in secrecy for so long, and so successfully, that it was oddly uncomfortable to be thrust into the spotlight. Shean was persuaded to take *XE4* for a run out on the harbour for the photographers, and the resulting pictures appeared around the country. A reporter from the *Sydney Morning Herald* was allowed to crawl inside one of the midgets. 'A Grim Life,' said the headline.[13]

Captain Fell did the right thing. He sent Ken Briggs off on extended leave home to Glen Innes, and he took Max Shean with him on a flight to Melbourne to arrange his discharge at the Navy Office. It went like clockwork, the paperwork handled smoothly, as Shean recounted:

> So it was a quick farewell to Tiny Fell and we parted in Melbourne without more ado. My rehabilitation had begun. The RAAF would fly me home the next day. I boarded the Dakota at Essendon Airport and sat among a full complement of servicemen and women. There were two long seats, each occupying the full length of the cabin, against the sides. At Cook, the crew brought an urn of coffee for us passengers, a very kind action ...
>
> My family and friends were at the airport of course, sister Yvonne in her WRANS uniform. My mother had spent hour upon hour gazing, in solitude I believe, out to sea during the last five years, and now it was alright; her family was together again. Many a mother was still searching.[14]

Someone alerted the newspapers that the local hero was home, and on 16 September the *Sunday Times* in Perth ran a feature with the headline 'W.A. Submarine Ace Is Back to Civil Life Tomorrow':

Perth-born midget sub. Commander Lieut. Max H. Shean, RANVR D.S.O., whose pint-sized Exciter cut the Saigon-Japan Saigon-Singapore cables last July, and who nosed his way into Bergen to plant destruction under the keel of a 7500-ton ship, spends his last day in the Service in Perth today.

Son of well-known Crown Law official Harry Shean, Lieut. Shean will return to civil life tomorrow after a series of amazing adventures in one of the most hazardous branches of any war outfit.[15]

It would be Shean's first day back at his engineering studies, just another undergraduate in civilian clothing, although a little uneasily set apart from the others by his age:

> Monday morning I went to University and called on Professor Blakey, Dean of the Faculty. He welcomed me with more compliments than I deserved and advised where I would slot back into the somewhat altered course. I attended lectures the same morning, wondering whether the early wartime predictions of 'never settling down' would become an insuperable obstacle. I admit that I did feel out of place among this class of youth, five years younger than I. This was felt by them as well and took a matter of days to dispel.[16]

There was one more important matter to set right. Mary Shean farewelled the little greystone family cottage in Aberfeldy that Scottish autumn, took a train to Liverpool and on 5 October sailed for Australia on a passenger liner, SS *Umtali*. The young woman who had never been further than London, and then only once, was now voyaging to the other side of the world, to a strange country where she knew not a soul beyond the young husband she had only infrequently seen.

In truth, she was lucky to have found a berth. The passenger shipping fleet was strained to the utmost and there were literally hundreds of British war brides anxious to join their husbands in Australia, with their passages paid for by the Australian government. There were fifty-nine war brides on *Umtali* alone, some with children. Shean family relatives met Mary in Sydney, welcomed her warmly and put her on a train for the west, which must have given her pause for thought. As they rattled across the Nullarbor – such a stark contrast to the cool, heathered hills of Scotland – the temperature reached 104 degrees on the old scale (forty degrees Celsius). The Perth newspapers noted her arrival:

> Only child of one of the founders of the Aberfeldy (Scotland) scheme for the entertainment of Dominion servicemen reached Perth today – as the wife of a W.A. serviceman who had been one of the scheme's guests.
>
> She is attractive, brown-haired 23-year-old Mrs Mary D. Shean, wife of Mr Maxwell Shean DSO, former Naval Lieutenant and commander of a midget submarine, now of 178 Suburban Road, South Perth.
>
> Mrs Shean with 11 other servicemen's brides arrived by train from the Eastern States . . .[17]

The war had one last hurrah for Max Shean in 1945. On his farewell tour of Australia, Admiral Sir Bruce Fraser turned up in the west a few weeks before Christmas and asked to see the local boy. *The Daily News* produced an agreeable account under the headline 'Admiral Sends for Sub Hero':

> While at a civic reception in Fremantle yesterday Commander-in-Chief of the British Pacific Fleet Sir Bruce Fraser expressed a desire to meet Lieutenant M.H. Shean, D.S.O R.A.N.V.R, of Suburban Road, South Perth.
>
> R.A.N. officers interpreted the request as a command, and immediately took steps to find Lieutenant Shean. It was known that he had resumed his engineering course at the University of W.A., but he was not at the University or at home yesterday.
>
> Inquiries established that he was holidaying at Safety Bay so a naval car was sent there for him. When Sir Bruce Fraser reached the Naval Staff Office, Fremantle, at 5 p.m., Lieutenant Shean and his wife, who recently arrived from Perth (Scotland) were presented to him.
>
> The Admiral knew Lieutenant Shean well in Scapa Flow when the latter was operating in midget submarines in the North Sea, and again met him in the Pacific.

He was familiar with the operation which won Lieutenant Shean the DSO, when, in a small, specially constructed submarine, he cut a Japanese underwater cable near Saigon.

Sir Bruce chatted with Lieutenant Shean and his wife for nearly half an hour. He said to Lieutenant Shean: 'I suppose you are continuing your interest in submarines, but, of course, will want command of one of the bigger ones.'

Lieutenant Shean replied: 'If there is another war, and I sincerely hope there won't be, I will be ready, sir.'[18]

Ken Briggs's mother, Ethel, took the train to Sydney to meet her son. She had not seen him for four years. The country boy who had left in 1941 as the lowest of the low, an ordinary seaman, had returned home a young man of the world at twenty-two and, moreover, a naval officer. Another son, Ken's older brother Ross, was still away, a flight lieutenant with the RAAF in New Guinea.

Briggs made his farewells on board *Bonaventure* – she was to become a humble transport ship in the Pacific – and they returned to Glen Innes for a quiet homecoming, for his exploits had not yet become news. The navy put him on the books of HMAS *Penguin*, a shore base on the bushy slopes of Mosman, above Balmoral Beach in Sydney's Middle Harbour, where demobilisation was being managed, and he was told to take indefinite leave. Just report in occasionally to let us know where you are, they said.

Briggs took it easy, genuinely glad to be back in his boyhood surroundings, away from the war and the sea. Every couple of weeks he telephoned *Penguin* to report in until, on the third call, he got a sharp surprise. Where was he? They'd been looking for him. Get here immediately. He headed back as fast as he could, to meet with another shock when he arrived: he had been absent without leave, they said, and they were preparing a court martial for him. That would take a couple of days. In the meantime, he should wait on the quarterdeck, which, at *Penguin*, was a patch of lawn outside the main administration building.

Bewildered, Briggs did as he was ordered:

There's me, a brash youngster who reckoned he'd done as much as anybody in the world. So this was a bit frightening. And I had two days of that, reporting in each morning. And then at four o'clock in the afternoon I could go home, ready to report the next morning on the quarter deck ... no sign of a cup of tea or a sandwich or anything at all. You were there. 'You were a bad boy. Go there.'

The third day I thought, 'Oh no. They've got nothing on me and I don't think they're going to have anything on me. I might as well have something to do.' So I said, 'Well come on Kenny, you can go home now.' And that was in the middle of the afternoon. So I walked off the quarter deck, hopped on a tram that was taking me around to where I was boarding with an auntie of mine at Greenwich at the time.[19]

The tram took him along the harbour foreshores for a stretch. As it rattled past the zoo, Briggs saw the old *Bonaventure* herself, moored in the harbour. On an impulse he hopped off, somehow found a boat that would take him out to her and climbed on board, where he was met by none other than Tiny Fell.

Briggs explained his predicament. Fell was both amused and perplexed but, as ever, he had the solution at his fingertips. 'I'm having dinner with the commander of Balmoral tonight,' he said. 'I'll see what I can do.'

The captain was as good as his word. There had been an unfortunate mix-up, a misunderstanding, it turned out. Next morning at *Penguin*, the commander handed Sub-Lieutenant Briggs his demobilisation papers and on 17 December he was officially discharged from the navy.

There were still some loose ends to be tied up. On 13 November, Buckingham Palace announced the award of the Victoria Cross to Ian Fraser and Mick Magennis for their gallantry in *XE3* beneath *Takao*. Both men were still in Sydney with *Bonaventure*. After an audience with Sir Bruce Fraser, they were photographed for a newspaper publicity stunt with 'two blonde Miss Australia entrants, Miss Pat Craig and Miss Dawne Beresford'. Sydney's *Catholic*

Weekly proudly proclaimed that Leading Seaman Magennis was an old boy of De La Salle College, Belfast. He evaded the publicity by going to stay with a couple of elderly Ulsterwomen at Gosford, on the coast north of Sydney, for three days.

Magennis went missing the day before he was due to fly out to London, and both the naval police and newspaper reporters began a hunt for him. Quite by chance, a journalist from the *Daily Telegraph* found him at 7 p.m. that evening seated alone in a café with a hamburger and a cup of tea. He had been wandering the Sydney Domain for most of the day with just a shilling in his pocket, he told the reporter, who turned out to be another Belfast boy. The pubs had closed, as they did then, at six o'clock. The *Telegraph* noted:

> He had one bitter criticism – the near impossibility of getting a drink in Sydney. About girls, he said, he hadn't worried – he was too busy worrying about how to get a drink.
>
> That's why he thought lyrically of leave in Belfast – and Guinness' stout, McCaffrey's ale, and 10 o'clock closing.[20]

There were last curtain calls for the XE-craft, too. *Bonaventure* carried them to Melbourne and Hobart to show them off to the public that November, and *XE3* was taken by low loader to be the star of the show at a Pacific Victory Exhibition in Sydney's Lower Town Hall. The crowds flocked to see her.

And that was that. Their Lordships in London decided that *Bonaventure*'s flock was of no use in a post-war Royal Navy, and that there was no point transporting them back to Britain. In 1946, one by one, the midget submarines of the 14th Flotilla were unceremoniously and unsentimentally stripped and broken up for scrap in the dockyard at Sydney's Cockatoo Island. *Bonaventure* herself stayed with the navy for another couple of years, plodding back and forth on humdrum tasks, just another face in the crowd. She was sold to Britain's Clan Line in 1948 and renamed *Clan Davidson*, carrying passengers and the company's cadet officers to and from South Africa until she was scrapped in 1961.

Sic transit gloria.

19
ENTER THE OBERONS

World War II ended with Australia the proud owner of the world's fourth-largest navy, a fleet of 337 ships, big and small, manned by 39,650 officers and sailors.[1] It had been a remarkable achievement for a nation of a little over seven million people, at high cost. There were 1783 men killed in action and another 444 who died from other causes.[2]

The job at sea did not stop with the peace. There was a lot of cleaning up to do, from the disposal of Allied and enemy mines in waters up north to the despatch of ships to join the Commonwealth naval forces occupying Japan. Thousands of men, though, returned to their civilian lives and hundreds of ships were paid off; some were put into a mothballed reserve but most were sold for scrap. By 1947 there were just twenty-seven ships in commission and by 1949 the navy was down to just 10,188 personnel.

With the peace established, the 1950s and early 1960s saw a steady stream of war movies in the cinemas. The public wanted to celebrate the Allied victory and the studios churned out films to meet the demand, many with a naval theme. *The Cruel Sea* (1953), *The Battle of the River Plate* (1956), *Run Silent, Run Deep* (1958), *Sink the Bismarck!* (1960) and more were fusions of fact and fiction to varying degrees, all featuring popular actors adept at the jutting jaw, the stiff upper lip, the crisp word of command, the officer-like manner. They were big box office.

There were books, too, a flood of memoirs and first-hand accounts, generally in a cheap paperback format that sold like hotcakes. The end to secrecy brought the midget submarines into the limelight in words and pictures. The first book to hit the shelves was *Above Us the Waves* (1953), by C.E.T. Warren and James Benson, a factual account of both the chariots and the X-craft from go to whoa. Charles Warren had been a sub-lieutenant in the 12th Flotilla until he was badly injured when he lost control of a chariot in 1944. There was a pleasing David and Goliath element to the story, enhanced when someone did the sums and declared that HMS *Bonaventure* was the Royal Navy's most decorated ship, with four Victoria Crosses, eleven DSOs, seventeen DSCs, a host of lesser gongs and more than 100 Mentions in Despatches bestowed upon her people. That book was the platform for a film of the same name, released in 1955, a highly fictional account of a raid on *Tirpitz* that bore little resemblance to what actually happened on Operation Source but still captured big audiences.

The real-life actors had their exits and their entrances, and it seems appropriate to follow some in these pages.

One of *XE4*'s two divers, **Sub-Lieutenant Adam Bergius** was awarded the DSC for his cable-cutting exploits at Saigon. After the war he entered the family business, the distillers who make Teacher's whisky, and rose to become the company chairman. A keen sailor and farmer, he died at his home on Kintyre in 2011.

Another Scot, **Commander Donald Cameron**, commanding officer of *X6*, was awarded the Victoria Cross for his attack on *Tirpitz*. He saw out the war as a prisoner of war in Germany and returned to the Royal Navy in 1945. In 1951, with the rank of commander, he ran the submarine base at Portsmouth, HMS *Dolphin*, until ill health forced his retirement. He died in 1961.

After the war, **Chief Engine Room Artificer Vernon 'Ginger' Coles DSM** would maintain that Max Shean was the only captain he would sail with. The two remained close for the rest of their lives, writing regularly and visiting each other when they could. From 1945, Coles served in conventional submarines but left the navy in 1951 to work as a civilian engineer. He died at the age of ninety-four in 2014.

Captain William 'Tiny' Fell, the jovial father of the midget submarine, was awarded the DSC and made a Companion of the

Order of St Michael and St George and an Officer of the U.S. Legion of Merit. He retired from the Royal Navy in 1947 but continued to work for the Admiralty as a salvage expert. He retired to his New Zealand homeland in 1960 but kept in close touch with his flock. He died in 1981.

The amiable **Admiral James Fife Jr** stayed with the US Navy's submarine service after the war, commanding the Submarine Force, Atlantic Fleet from 1947 to 1950. He was later US Naval Commander-in-Chief, Mediterranean, until 1955. In retirement he served as the director of the Mystic Seaport museum in Connecticut, overseeing a big expansion program there. He died in 1975 and was buried at the Arlington National Cemetery in Virginia. A Spruance-class destroyer was named in his honour in 1980, the USS *Fife*.

The citation for **Lieutenant Commander Ian Fraser**'s Victoria Cross read that 'his courage and determination' in the attack on *Takao* was 'beyond all praise'. He left the navy in 1947 and set up a successful commercial diving firm, Universal Divers. He died in 2008.

Distraught at the loss of her son, **Lieutenant Henty Henty-Creer**, Eulalie Henty became fixed on the idea that he was still alive with a loss of memory and living with indigenous people in Norway. In 1950 she and her daughter Deirdre drove their small Hillman Minx car through the Arctic north to search for him, at times camping out in the freezing open. They found no trace. Eulalie also kept up a campaign for Henty to be awarded the Victoria Cross, to no avail. There were several attempts to find his remains or some sign of his submarine, X_5, on the bottom of Altafjord, but they too drew a blank.

Admiral Sir Max Horton, blunt and vigorous, was perhaps the foremost pioneer of British and therefore Australian submarine warfare. In November 1942 he was appointed the Royal Navy's Commander-in-Chief, Western Approaches Command, based in Liverpool, where he directed and won the Battle of the Atlantic against the U-boats. He died in 1951.

Lieutenant Commander Ken Hudspeth became the first Australian naval officer to win the DSC three times. He returned to Australia in December 1945 but was not demobbed until

February 1946, and he remained in the RAN reserve until 1965. In civilian life he returned to teaching in Tasmania, becoming principal of the state's Teachers Training College and serving a term as president of the Teachers' Federation of Australia. In 1959 he married Audrey Nicholson, the Englishwoman he had met during the war, and they had three sons. He died in 2000.

After the destruction of *Tirpitz*, **Generaladmiral Oskar Kummetz** finished the war as commander of the German Navy's Baltic Sea Command. The British held him as a prisoner of war from July 1945 until November 1946. As a civilian he made a living growing vegetables and later as a receptionist at a casino. He died in 1980.

Leading Seaman James 'Mick' Magennis was the only man from Northern Ireland to be awarded the Victoria Cross in World War II. The people of Belfast contributed to a fund for him, which raised the impressive sum of £3000, but the city council denied him the honour of the freedom of the city, most likely because he was a Catholic, and working class at that. When the money ran out he sold his VC to makes ends meet. He later made a living as an electrician, and died in 1986.

Vice Admiral Sir Ian McIntosh, the hero of Lifeboat Number Seven, captained conventional submarines with considerable success until the end of the war, sinking more than 15,000 tonnes of enemy shipping. In 1943 he married Elizabeth Rasmussen, the woman he had held in his thoughts during that lifeboat voyage. They had three sons and one daughter. He had hoped to return home to Australia to join the peacetime RAN, but when it did not acquire submarines he remained in the Royal Navy. There he built a soaring career, rising to become deputy chief of the British Defence Staff. His proudest moment, he said, came when, as captain of the aircraft carrier HMS *Victorious*, he brought her into Sydney in 1966, with his mother waiting on the dock at Garden Island. He died in 2003.

Konteradmiral Hans Karl Meyer, the captain of *Tirpitz*, survived the war and was held a prisoner by the British until January 1946. He was one of just six *Kriegsmarine* admirals who transferred to the newly formed West German Navy, the *Bundesmarine*.

He finished his career as commander of the naval academy and died in 1989.

Rear Admiral Godfrey Place – 'Freddy' to his friends – was perhaps the most celebrated of the midget submariners. Released from the German PoW camp *Marlag und Milag Nord* in 1945, he remained with the Royal Navy after the war. No longer interested in submarines, he qualified as a Fleet Air Arm pilot and flew Sea Fury fighters from the carrier HMS *Glory* during the Korean War. His aircraft was hit once in the port wing but he landed safely. He later commanded a destroyer, a frigate and the commando carrier HMS *Albion*, finishing his naval career in 1970 as the Director General of Naval Recruiting. He died in 1994.

With his engineering degree under his belt, **Lieutenant Commander Max Shean** worked for the City of Perth Electricity and Gas Department and the WA State Electricity Commission until his retirement in 1978. He and Mary had two daughters. He had a lifelong love of sailing and the sea and in 1979 celebrated the 150th anniversary of the settlement of Western Australia by sailing to Plymouth, England, in his yacht *Bluebell*, named for the corvette that was his first wartime ship. The return leg was the Parmelia Yacht Race from Plymouth to Fremantle, via Cape Town, which he won. Shean keep in regular touch with his midget submarine shipmates, most particularly Ginger Coles and Tiny Fell. A welcome guest at naval dinners and veterans' commemorations, he was admired and respected by later generations of Australian submariners. He died in 2009.

Lieutenant Lionel 'Bill' Whittam was Max Shean's onetime close friend and roommate, lost in *X7* during the *Tirpitz* raid. The Germans recovered his body from Altafjord and buried him with full naval honours. He lies now in the Commonwealth section of the Tromsø Military Cemetery, on the Norwegian north coast: it is the only known grave of a midget submariner who died on active service.

Lieutenant Commander Donald Wilson relinquished command of HMS *Voracious* at war's end and was demobbed in March 1946. He led a colourful life, farming in the New South Wales Southern Highlands and then outside Canberra, and later as a plantation owner in Papua New Guinea. He travelled widely, often for reunions with former shipmates. In Tibet he befriended the Dalai Lama.

Long and earnest were the debates about the future shape of the RAN: what it should actually do, and with what ships. Submarines barely got a mention. War at sea had been transformed by the soaring rise of air power, and the focus was for aircraft carriers to project that power. In 1947 the Labor federal government bought two light fleet carriers already being built in Britain, 20,000-tonne ships to be renamed HMAS *Sydney* and HMAS *Melbourne*, and the navy turned its hand to the ambitious project of creating a Fleet Air Arm from scratch.

With hindsight, this was not a bad call. *Sydney* and her embarked squadrons of Sea Fury and Firefly aircraft fought long and well in the Korean War, famously with snow heaped on the flight deck during the bitter northern winter of 1951.

There was at least a nod in the direction of submarine warfare – or, more accurately, anti-submarine warfare. From 1949, the British kept their 4th Submarine Squadron of three boats based at *Penguin* to provide training for Australian and New Zealand surface warships. Britain's staged withdrawal from 'east of Suez' changed the balance and the RN gave notice that its squadron would finish up Down Under in 1969. With the Cold War between the superpowers and their allies a grim reality, with a resurgent communist China, with the erratic Sukarno dictatorship ruling Indonesia, and with the Vietnam War escalating by the month, the horizon to the north of Australia was dark and uncertain.

The Australian government and the RAN drew a deep breath and bit the bullet. Once again there would be an Australian submarine squadron, the first since the dismal fiasco of the J-class boats in the 1920s. The early plan was for eight boats, but that was cut back to six when the money for two of them was diverted to buy Skyhawk jet fighters for the Fleet Air Arm.

In January 1963 the Menzies government placed its first order: four submarines of the new British Oberon class, to be built in the yard of the Scotts Shipbuilding and Engineering Company at Greenock on the Clyde. They would cost around £5 million each and the first keel was laid down in the summer of 1964.[3] It was a leap forward, a big one. There had been early thoughts of buying American nuclear boats but that was rejected as too costly and too high-tech. The Oberons were diesel-electric-powered, but the British had learned a lot from their own experience in World War II, both from the U-boats they had captured and from the leading German submarine designer, Hellmuth Walter, who worked for them after the war.

Displacing around 2400 tonnes submerged, not quite ninety metres long, capable of around twelve knots on the surface and up to nineteen knots at a stretch underwater, with a diving depth of 120 metres and boasting six forward torpedo tubes, the Oberons were a modern and potent weapon.[4] They had a 'snort' system, a development of the *schnorchel* used by the later U-boats: a long induction mast. In effect, this was a tube which could be raised above the surface to suck in air to recharge the batteries while the submarine itself remained concealed beneath the waves. Perhaps their most significant characteristic was their quiet. Specifically engineered for silent running, they proved very difficult to detect. There was one singular feature in the Australian boats: at the insistence of the RAN, they were fitted with showers for bathing. With the British scorning such effete luxury, RN boats were not.

The first to arrive in Australia was HMAS *Oxley*, the second of that name in the navy. After a truly sublime voyage – almost a holiday cruise via Bermuda, Jamaica, the Panama Canal and Hawaii – she slipped into Sydney Harbour on the surface on a sunny winter Friday, 18 August 1967, to a rousing welcome from the VIPs lined up with the band playing on the dock at HMAS *Platypus* in Neutral Bay, the RAN's purpose-built submarine base commissioned that same day. Her captain was an Englishman, Lieutenant Commander David Lorrimer, who had transferred from the RN to the RAN.[5] No Australian yet had the experience to do the Perisher.

Of more note to history, perhaps, was *Oxley*'s executive officer, 29-year-old Lieutenant Ian MacDougall, who would command submarines himself and rise to become a vice admiral and a much-respected Chief of the Naval Staff in 1991, the first submariner to reach the top job. The navy public relations people had inserted two journalists on board *Oxley* for the three-day trip from Brisbane to Sydney, a trick that paid off, with the reporter from the *Canberra Times* writing glowingly:

> It is obvious that in Oxley and her sister-boats Australia has acquired a deterrent punch which would require a potential enemy to deploy tremendous forces when intending to make a surface attack.
>
> At about $9.2 million a boat it is clear that we have acquired a bargain. Three earlier attempts to establish an RAN sub marine service have failed.
>
> In Oxley and her sisters there is a confident guarantee of success.[6]

There would be five sisters, six boats in all: first *Oxley*, then *Otway*, *Ovens*, *Onslow*, *Orion* and *Otama*, the last named for an Indigenous word from North Queensland meaning 'dolphin' and delivered in 1978. And the man from the *Canberra Times* had got it right: the O-boats, as they came to be called, would indeed prove a success.

Acquiring the submarines was the easy part, though, not unlike buying a car. You inspect the models available, choose what you want, pay your money and get one. Far harder was the job of creating the costly and complex infrastructure to support them. It would need to be a great enterprise built in Australia from the ground up: a squadron base with its maintenance, supply and repair facilities; a Submarine Warfare Systems Centre, with its simulators for teaching the dark arts and keeping pace with the constantly evolving science and technology of war below the surface; and a school for rookie crews, with a submarine escape training tank built at HMAS *Stirling*, at Garden Island, south of Fremantle in Western Australia. From a slow beginning, some things happened quickly; others ground along year after year in a swamp of bureaucracy or a shortage of funds.

Each crew would comprise seven officers and some sixty sailors. As ever with the navy, time was of the essence. From the day the purchase was announced, the rush was on to find bodies for the job, with volunteers called for and parties of officers and sailors packed off to Portsmouth for submarine training at Blockhouse, the now legendary HMS *Dolphin*, and then for experience in RN boats. In many cases, their families went with them. Young officers, at the beginning of their careers, were attracted to the submarine service by the novelty, by the aura of glamour and by the alluring prospect of responsibility and command at an early age, a leap up the ladder they might not expect in the surface fleet. In the early years, the commanding officers were all British. So, too, were many of the senior sailors. It wasn't until 1969 that an Australian-born officer gained a command, when Lieutenant Commander Ian Roberts took *Oxley* to sea from Sydney for the first time.

Finding and keeping crews was an endless struggle. Valuable senior men – highly and expensively trained petty officers and warrant officers with technical expertise – were all too frequently lured from the navy by the much better pay and easier family life on offer in Western Australia's booming mining industry. Funding was sometimes scarce but somehow it all happened because it had to. Steadily, surely, the 1st Australian Submarine Squadron came together, to be more than the sum of its parts, its motto 'Silent Service'. Sydneysiders became accustomed to the sight of the boats, with their bulbous black dome on the bow concealing the attack sonar and their tall, streamlined fin containing the conning tower, berthed in Neutral Bay like so many tethered porpoises or gliding silently out to sea with that unique submarine aura of purposeful menace. They were sleek and handsome with their slender masts raised high: the two periscopes, the snort, the radio and radar masts, the electronic warfare mast.

So they set to the job. In three decades, all six O-boats and their crews would give sterling service, from the northern Pacific to South-East Asian waters or deep into the Southern Ocean towards the Antarctic. There were war games with the Americans off the Australian coast or perhaps Hawaii, where, not a few times and to much joy, they silently penetrated the escort screen of destroyers to 'sink' one of the giant US Navy aircraft carriers. There were exercises with the army's SAS regiment, to practise landing commandos on some hostile shore, and more fun and games with the navy's own clearance divers. Often it was the humdrum job of acting as quarry for the surface fleet or the RAAF to give them practice at submarine hunting in waters closer to home, playing 'the clockwork mouse', as it was called. Sometimes it was just showing the flag to the taxpayers in ports around the country.

Any glamour was more imagined than real. There were moments of high elation, when a crew pulled off some intricate evolution or scored a big win in an exercise, but the plain fact was that life in an O-boat was, at best, uncomfortable: physically and mentally demanding. At worst, it could be squalid and dangerous. Sometimes the heaviest burden was simply the loneliness, the inner longing for home and family for days and weeks on end.

We can picture a typical long-distance patrol.

—

'Harbour stations!'

On a warm summer morning, under the watchful eye of the executive officer, a small handful of sailors makes ready to unleash HMAS *Oxley* from the bonds securing her to the continent of Australia, the submarine throbbing gently beneath their boots. As is the custom, the captain is the last to come on board, farewelled on the wharf by his boss, the submarine squadron commander, piped onto the casing by the piercing shrill of a bosun's call. It is the XO's job to present the captain with a submarine that is a going concern. They meet on the bridge atop the fin.

'All hands on board, all stores on board, ready for sea, sir.'

The orders for departure come in the familiar litany.

'Obey telegraphs!'

The response from the motor room is passed back up to the bridge by the coxswain on the helm in the control room below: 'Obey telegraphs. Both main motors ready. Group up!'

Time to go, to cast off the lines.

'Let go aft, let go the after spring . . . Group down . . . Port thirty, half astern port, slow ahead starboard . . . Stop starboard, let go for'ard, let go the for'ard spring . . . Midships . . . Half astern starboard . . .'

The manoeuvre is finely judged. A useful sou'west breeze helps bring *Oxley*'s bow around to the north and she eases away from the wharf, down Cockburn Sound, below Fremantle, and out to the Indian Ocean, beginning a journey that will take her away for forty-two days, six whole weeks. The parting is hardest for the family men perhaps, from the captain on down, for these are the days before email and they will have no communication with home for all that time. Wives will be left to cope alone with the domestic dramas: a sick child, a teenage rebellion, a flood in the bathroom, an unexpected bill, a tractor accident on the farm. Even in some grave crisis – a family death, say – the submariner will not hear of it until it is too late to do anything. The boat might be able to go into a friendly port – perhaps Singapore or Manila – to put him ashore so he can fly home, but there are no guarantees. Leaving is always a wrench, more for some than others, but it is part of the job. You signed up for it, you got on with it.

'Navigator, you have the submarine. Course 320 degrees.'

'I have the submarine, sir . . .'

Oxley heads north on the surface in transit to her operational area. The twin V16-cylinder Admiralty diesels drive her engines onwards, the bulbous sonar dome on her bow dips and rises again in a gentle sea, the officer of the watch and two lookouts high on the bridge constantly scan the world with binoculars. So far, so good.

They are alone on the ocean. The boat settles into her transit routine of three watches, each of four hours' duration. There are sixty-four men in her crew, seven officers and fifty-seven men, fully trained and qualified submariners and therefore entitled to wear the proud badge of two golden dolphins leaping towards each other beneath a red and gold royal crown, pinned on the left breast, a sure sign that you are superior to mere surface sailors, the 'skimmers', as they call them. Not everyone wins their dolphins; it is a tough test.

A lot of the crew have changed out of uniform and into what submariners call 'pirate rig', which is any old item of clothing that takes your fancy, quite likely a favourite T-shirt and a pair of football shorts. This is a submarine specialty, frowned on by the surface fleet, but it depends on the captain, really. Some happily condone pirate rig, others demand at least something that looks like an approved working uniform. The 'tiffies' – the engine room crew – are usually reckoned to be the most creative.

The rules are flexible, but only to a point. One captain famously entered the sonar room late one night to find the two operators stark naked.

'What the fuck do you think you're doing?' he barked.

'Nude watchkeeping, sir.'

'Fuck off and get dressed. You've got five minutes.'

Below, in the galley, just aft of the senior sailors' mess and for'ard of the control room, *Oxley*'s two cooks are already hard at work at their stove and pots and pans in a stainless-steel cubbyhole smaller than the bathroom of your average suburban two-bedroom flat. Conjuring small miracles, they will turn out four meals a day: breakfast, lunch and dinner, as well as 'midnighters' for men going on or coming off watch in the dark hours.

It is acknowledged by all and sundry, including the captain, that a leading cook and his offsider, an able seaman cook, are by far the most important people in the boat. Good cooks are a treasure beyond price; bad cooks can make a patrol a misery. The sailors queue to collect their meals, or 'scran', which they eat in their messes. The captain has a steward to serve him; he will breakfast alone with his thoughts in his cabin. There is an unspoken understanding that the steward will also look after the officers in their cramped wardroom, where, again by unspoken invitation, the captain will have his other meals.

Everyone has the same food. Tonight's menu has already been scrawled on the small noticeboard outside the galley:

Steak, mushroom sauce
Sausages
Chicken cordon blue
Garden salad
Potato wedges

In the coming weeks, the boat will take on the unique submarine odour of sweaty, unwashed bodies and dirty clothes, stale cooking smells and the sour cocktail of fumes from the engine room aft – an acrid stench to a newcomer, a fact of life for the old hands. *Oxley* and all the O-boats have air conditioning but it is never particularly effective; during ultra-quiet operations, it is turned off altogether.

There are three showers crammed into the port side with the toilets, or 'the traps', tiny alcoves where a man can barely stand, and you are lucky if you get a shower a week. More likely it will be a bowl of fresh water per day, first to clean your teeth and then to wash your undies, strictly in that order.

For sleeping, each man has a bunk, or 'rack', a narrow shelf half a metre wide and barely 1.8 metres long, with a thin mattress of sorts and a curtain you can close to shut out the crowded world around you. Rows of them are stacked in any space not filled with pipes, dials, gauges, screens, a forest of wheels and switches and levers, banks of electrical wiring. Only the captain has anything approaching privacy. His tiny cabin is next door to the control room, and contains his own rack, a small desk and foldaway washbasin, a compass, barometer, internal communications microphone and an all-important depth gauge. There is still not enough room to swing even a very small cat.

Off watch, you make your own entertainment. Some men read. You could catch a videotape movie on a boxy little screen or play cards, but that's about it. A few fitness enthusiasts might find space for push-ups and stretches on the deck of the torpedo compartment for'ard, a relatively open space in the boat, but many men return home from patrol with some extra flab and a distinctive pallor from the lack of sunlight. And the smell of diesel fuel, too. It gets into your skin and takes weeks to wash away.

Sometimes, just sometimes, there is blessed relief. During a surface passage, the happiest pipe in a submarine is 'Hands to bathe', which means fresh air, sunshine and a swim. If the weather is good and the seas are calm and there is time at hand, the XO might suggest it to the captain and, approved, the boat will glide to a stop. One or two sailors with rifles stand guard to watch for sharks while everybody else splashes exultantly in the blue, washing away the sweat and stink, hauling themselves back on board by means of ropes slung over the side. Afterwards, there might be a chance to throw out a fishing line, or perhaps a barbecue set up on the for'ard casing, the cooks turning on steaks and snags for a rare, glorious interlude before the routine begins again.

For now, *Oxley* ploughs on, with only the captain and the navigator aware of their destination, although everyone suspects it will be somewhere in the South China Sea. The days on transit pass by, watch on watch, in the humdrum of routine enlivened by the occasional drill to sharpen things up.

In the third week, a little after breakfast, the peace and quiet is shattered by the harsh honk of the klaxon. Two sharp blasts sound through the boat. A crash dive. The captain has decided to stir things along, to keep the crew on their toes.

'Officer of the watch, dive the submarine!'

'Dive the submarine, sir.'

A planned dive can be handled by the watch on duty, but a crash dive brings the captain automatically into control of the boat and the entire crew alert to their diving stations. The sleepers struggle from their racks. In the engine room, they crash-stop the diesels, the main motors now running silently on the batteries. If the diesels are not shut down on the instant, there would be a roaring gale as the superchargers suck the air out of the boat itself, creating an ear-popping vacuum.

In the control room, the coxswain takes the planes. 'Full dive on the planes, six down, ninety feet, then back to fifty-four!'

The main vents have been opened to flood the ballast tanks with sea water and the planes put hard to dive, to angle the submarine down, the engineer officer at ship control to keep the boat in trim.

On the second honk of the klaxon, the officer of the watch shuts the upper voice-pipe cock with a snap. The two lookouts with him leave the bridge first, scrambling down the ladder in the conning tower inside the fin, the second of them waiting at the bottom to report to the captain, a calm and deliberate figure.

'Officer of the watch in the tower, sir. The upper lid is shut. One clip . . . two clips . . . two pins!'

The submarine is now watertight. The lower hatch is then shut and also clipped. The needles on the two big black depth gauges begin to wind down clockwise – ten feet, twenty feet, thirty feet.

'Raise forward.'

The attack periscope glides upwards with a slight hum. Peering into it, the captain has one eye on the sonar dome on the bow, the other on a stopwatch. If your trim is perfect, it should take precisely one minute and five seconds for the dome to go underwater. Less than that means you are too heavy, and the officer of the watch will pump water from or between the tanks to achieve neutral buoyancy and horizontal balance. Longer and you are too light, requiring more water to be flooded in. It is a fine art that takes practice. *Oxley* is an efficient boat, well drilled. In less than two minutes she is underwater, invisible, only the swirl and wash of her exit to be seen, until that too disappears in the wide blue sea.

For the next three weeks, perhaps more, she will remain submerged, waiting, watching, listening. As her batteries are depleted, she will raise her snort, usually once every twenty-four hours under cover of darkness, sucking in air so she can run the diesels to recharge. This is a noisy business, increasing the risk of unwelcome attention, so the captain seeks the 'cover' on maritime traffic around and above her: fishing boats and tankers and container ships and cruise liners, all sorts of odds and sods, sometimes close, sometimes distant, sometimes the occasional warship, perhaps friendly, perhaps not, but all unknowing of the lurking presence below. *Oxley* leaves no trace of her existence. Her garbage, or 'gash', is compacted and ejected from the boat in a weighted bag that sinks to the sea floor. The main sewage tanks are blown, another noisy affair.

These can be the most testing days of a long-distance patrol, times that try the soul. Day and night cease to exist, the light of sun, moon or stars replaced by electric glare in the engine spaces or the dim glow of the gauges and screens and the red lighting in the control room. You know it is morning when breakfast appears but that's about it: scrambled eggs again, or just cereal, invariably known as 'soggies'. It is hot, too. In tropical waters the temperature of the hull rises, and with it the heat and humidity inside the boat itself, causing men to live in a perpetual sweat.

Boredom is an enemy, and the captain and his XO do their best to keep it at bay. There will be drills: simulated attacks or equipment failures, fire and flood exercises, anything to keep busy. Perhaps quiz nights and movies, or a slap-up Sunday lunch. An enterprising radio specialist with access to a typewriter might produce a ship's newspaper containing scurrilous articles about his shipmates. One creative captain was known to organise 'horse races' of sailors tied together with strips of cloth, galloping the length of the boat to cheers and hoots of laughter, and with a vigorous betting market on the results.

The key requirement is tolerance. That's sometimes a difficult thing for new men to learn, but you simply have to get along with the bloke next to you, no matter what his rank or what annoying habits or opinions or quirks of character he might exhibit. There is no alternative. This is as true for the captain as it is for the youngest sailor on board and submariners: they are a band of brothers, and pride themselves upon it. But more than that, binding them together as a crew is the overarching matter of trust. A careless mistake by any man can jeopardise the stealth and safety of the entire submarine and the lives of all who sail in her. You have to trust each other to get it right, to do the job properly.

From the early days of the squadron, the men who took the submarines to sea – officers and sailors – developed a unique ethos, a culture apart from the surface navy. They were special and they knew it, not in an overtly arrogant way, but the jobs they did and the lives they led were different. The golden dolphins were the external symbol of this but it ran deeper. Shared experience bound them together.

They were better paid, too. There was a submarine allowance on top of regular pay from the day you first qualified, and a seagoing allowance that included money for what the navy called 'hard lying', meaning a tough existence. Yet pay was always a vexed question, and every few years or so a squadron commander would find himself mounting a wage case to the powers-that-be with all the wile and vigour of a trade union boss. In the early 1970s, a delicious story did the rounds claiming that the Liberals' Malcolm Fraser, when he was defence minister, was bailed up and held captive in a boat's torpedo compartment until he agreed to a pay review. And there was a sense at times that submarine officers were on the outer with senior officers whose entire careers had been on the surface.

Especially in those early days, there was indeed a feeling in the rest of the fleet that submariners were eccentric, a bit of a circus act, all very well in their place and no doubt necessary, but not to be compared in substance with real sailors aboard carriers, destroyers and frigates, the 'Pusser' navy. Even today there is a hint of 'us and them'. The submariners held the skimmers in amused disdain and were not reluctant to show it. In an exercise in the narrow Capricorn Channel in the Coral Sea in 1980, *Onslow* adroitly evaded the frigate *Yarra* and two American destroyers to 'sink' the replenishment ships HMAS *Supply* and *Stalwart*, juicy targets. Afterwards, back in Cairns, *Onslow*'s captain, Kim Pitt, rubbed salt into the wounds by berthing alongside his victims, with their silhouettes painted in white on the Jolly Roger pirate flag flying from his communications mast.

Officers in the squadron felt, with some cause, that this rivalry hampered their promotion, which, for many years, seemed to stop at the rank of captain. It was not until 1986 that things improved. The Labor defence minister Kim Beazley set things to rights. Submarines particularly intrigued him. Handed a list of names to be promoted from captain to commodore, the genial but determined Beazley put his foot down.

'There'll not be one more commodore created until I see on my desk a recommendation for a submariner to that rank,' he said.[7]

The Chief of the Naval Staff, Vice Admiral Mike Hudson, backed down. Ian MacDougall, *Oxley*'s onetime XO and by now a captain and commanding officer of the squadron, was given the broad gold stripe on the way to flag rank. More would follow in time.

When trust was lost, when mistakes were made, when equipment failed or when the system itself broke down, bad things could happen. It might be a fire, a toxic gas leak, an engine stoppage or even – in one nightmare in 1988, still remembered with amused horror – the simple failure of a drain valve, which filled *Orion* with gash and sewage and a foul stench that took weeks to clear.

Sometimes it ended in tragedy. In 1981, nineteen-year-old Able Seaman Christopher Passlow died in *Onslow* during an exercise with a New Zealand frigate in the Tasman Sea when the diesel exhaust system was shut down while the starboard engine was still running. It was breakfast time. Choking black smoke and deadly carbon monoxide filled the boat within seconds, rendering most of the engine and control room people unconscious. Passlow was found slumped on the deck by the junior sailors' bathroom and could not be revived.

Onslow was only saved by the heroic efforts of her captain, Lieutenant Commander Jack Miers, an RN officer on exchange, who brought her to the surface with a handful of men fortunately unaffected by the gas. An enquiry decided that two tiffies had flicked the wrong switches, but some experienced submariners doubted it was human error and spoke of an oil leak in an engine supercharger. The RAN created the Christopher J. Passlow prize for the top trainee in the Stage III program each year, the final test at sea.

Worse was to come. In 1987, Able Seaman Hugh Markcrow and Seaman Damien Humphreys drowned when *Otama* dived with them still inside the fin. The boat was crowded with a bunch of trainees on board, eighty-four people in all, and the weather was filthy and getting worse when they left Sydney for Jervis Bay. The captain, Lieutenant Commander John Taubman, ordered the recovery of the towed array sonar, a long line of hydrophones trailed behind the boat, and Markcrow and Humphreys were sent up into the fin to secure it. Not long afterwards, Taubman dived *Otama* to escape the storm. Somebody should have told him that the two were in the fin but nobody did and nobody noticed. The men had no hope as the sea rushed in upon them.

It was another half an hour before their absence was reported. There was a long search, by sea and air, but their bodies were never recovered. A navy board of enquiry spread the blame thinly, including a finding that the two sailors themselves had failed to report to the petty officer of the watch before they went aloft, as they should have done. The squadron was shocked to the core and allegations of a whitewash persisted, with a sometimes acrimonious dispute between the senior officers involved; some claimed that Taubman appeared to be a protected species. Just the month before, going deep on exercises with a frigate, he had rammed *Otama* heavily into the sea floor.

These three were the only deaths in the thirty-three years of the O-boats' service. That there were no more speaks to the high competence and discipline of the men who took them to sea, for the risk was always with them. A relatively minor accident, mistake or breakdown in a surface vessel might be quickly and simply dealt with. It could easily become a disaster in a submarine. A surface vessel floats. A submarine is surrounded by water in three dimensions.

These things could happen in even the best-run boat. What counted was how you handled them. But then there were the good times, when all the training and discipline paid off in the satisfaction of a difficult and dangerous job well done.

As the 1960s became the 1970s, the Submarine Squadron grew in skill and potency, in men and machines. There was an ever-expanding body of sailors and officers who understood their boats and what they could do, and who were capable of teaching their successors. Green-as-grass Australian lieutenants and able seamen who had done their submarine training at *Dolphin* in Britain were rising through the ranks, officers to command their own boats, sailors to become petty officers and warrant officers, the backbone of the service.

But as the 1970s ticked over, the Oberons themselves were beginning to show their age. Not the hulls and engines, which were sound enough, but the sensors and weapons that were their reason for being. Much of the gear was little advanced beyond the technology of World War II, analogue stuff that looked ever creakier as the digital age began to dawn. The torpedoes, the British 21-inch Mark VIII, had been designed in 1925 and, although improved since then, were fast becoming obsolete. They were slow, at a maximum forty knots if you were lucky, and if you actually hoped to hit anything, they had to be fired from virtually point-blank range. If you were aiming to bag an aircraft carrier, say, you would first have to find your way inside the screening destroyers to get off your shots.

Once again, the government and the RAN had to make some hard decisions. Adding bits and pieces here and there would not do. There would need to be a full makeover for each boat, at a cost of untold hundreds of millions of dollars. It became known as the Submarine Weapons Update Program, with the inevitable navy acronym SWUP. Much scientific head-scratching went into deciding what was needed, what to acquire and where to acquire it from. The problem was aggravated by the fact that the Americans and British had turned their interest away from diesel submarines to go nuclear. The RAN would pretty much have to go it alone. Australian sailors, engineers and scientists would need to do the research and make the call. Methodically, the SWUP began to come together.

First cab off the rank was a digital Fire Control System, American-built but designed to Australian specifications, which could be operated by three men instead of seven on the old system. Then came new attack sonar and passive sonar, and a state-of-the-art gyrocompass that could perform all sorts of modern miracles of navigation. The sonar required an extensive remodelling of the Oberon's bow, with the lumpy old dome on the for'ard casing replaced by a more streamlined, teardrop model. The Mark VIII torpedoes gave way to the new American Mark 48, a vast improvement that carried its own sonar, an electronic box of tricks to seek and home in on its target at well over fifty knots. In theory, it could be fired from up to fifty kilometres away, although a captain would have to be either deeply timid or wildly optimistic to try that.

Released in a salvo, the Mark 48 was intended not to slam into a ship's hull in the old way but to run deeper and explode beneath the hull, to break a ship's back and sink it.

Later again, the Oberons got cruise missiles, grandly titled the UGM-84 Encapsulated Harpoon, to be fired from the bow torpedo tubes at other ships or submarines even beyond the horizon, skimming just a couple of metres above the waves at a speed of more than 850 kilometres per hour. This was a quantum leap into the missile age. The crews practised firing up to six missiles in quick succession from different points of the compass, setting them to converge on the one target, which would swamp the defences of the most capable anti-submarine vessel.

Oxley was the first to go under the SWUP surgeon's knife at the Cockatoo Island dockyard in Sydney, emerging from her refit in December 1979. She and her sisters became the most capable, most lethal diesel submarines in anyone's navy.

If the engines were the beating heart of the submarine, sonar was the eyes and ears. It had come a long way in the half-century since 1912, when an American device arrived on the scene, the Fessenden oscillator, splendidly named after its inventor. Magically, Mr Fessenden's contraption, huge and unwieldy, could transmit and receive sounds below the waves. Brought in shortly after the *Titanic* disaster, it was hoped it might be useful in detecting icebergs.

The British made leaps and bounds with Asdic during World War II, well ahead of the curve, and they shared the technology – for free – with the Americans from 1940. After the war the Americans forged ahead, refining and developing, and their name – SONAR – came into common use, an acronym for 'sound navigation and ranging'. Broadly, sonar comes in two sorts. Active sonar transmits a ping noise, which bounces back off an object in the water, but that ping can also be heard by other ships, including the enemy you are targeting. Passive sonar makes no noise but simply listens to what is going on around it – a far stealthier option, especially for submarines.

The jewel in the Oberons' crown was an Australian invention, developed in the 1980s, the Ping Intercept Passive Ranging System, which emerged from the acronym mill as PIPRS, pronounced 'Pippers'. This was a super sonar, created from scratch by two brilliant but unsung engineers at the laboratories of the Defence Science & Technology Organisation in Sydney, Tony Collins and Juoko Uusioja. Essentially, it intercepted the active sonar ping from somebody who was hunting you. The Oberons could therefore detect a searching enemy vessel well before they were discovered themselves – a priceless advantage.

There was nothing like PIPRS anywhere else in the submarine world; the US Navy were amazed when they learned about it. To the astonishment of the Americans and the British, the Australian Oberons could track twenty-four targets and attack two of them simultaneously, a revolutionary advance. Rather unsportingly, the Americans tried to lift the idea and reverse-engineer it for their own submarines, but for various technical reasons they could never quite get it to work.

Sonar operators – the men who did the listening and the searching – were the wizards and conjurors. They were intensely trained, in the early stages on land, listening endlessly to recordings of all sorts of ships and other underwater noises, learning to distinguish what was what. But it was experience at sea that truly counted as, over time, the best sonar men developed an almost uncanny sixth sense for what was happening around them far and near, friend or foe.

David Bryant was one of that special sonar breed. He grew up at Highett, south-east of Melbourne, the son of an electrical engineer and a teacher. As a youngster he read the works of that prodigious Australian writer J. E. Macdonnell, a former RAN sailor himself, whose book covers proclaimed, quite accurately, that he was 'Australia's leading novelist of the Navy'. With stirring titles like *Enemy in Sight* (1959), *Dive! Dive! Dive!* (1959), *Clear for Action* (1961) and *The Jaws of Hell* (1965), they fired the boy's imagination, awakening romantic dreams of life at sea. Dave also had some mates who had joined the navy and they looked good in their uniforms, he thought.

That did it. In 1965, at the age of seventeen, he left Highett High and signed up for what was then called an 'adult entry', three months' recruit training at *Cerberus* in Victoria, where they taught him port from starboard, how to march and salute, and the vital trick of folding those swaggering, bell-bottomed trousers into the correct number of creases. From there it was a spell at sea as an ordinary seaman in the carrier *Melbourne* and the destroyer *Vendetta*, then a course in sonar at HMAS *Watson*, the shore base on Sydney's South Head. It was in the Watson theatre that Bryant saw a navy recruiting film for submariners.

'There were these two guys with "HM Submarine" on their cap tallies standing in London and looking up at Big Ben,' Bryant recalls. 'And I thought I'd love to go and see Big Ben. And that was my motivation for joining submarines.'

He applied and was accepted. In the autumn of 1967, the navy sent him and two other young submariner hopefuls off to Britain in the liner *Fairstar*, in which they found themselves delightfully outnumbered by a shipload of Australian girls heading off to see Swinging London. Then it was to *Dolphin* for his submarine course, beginning with Part 1, the basics, where he found the Escape Tower 'pretty scary' at first. Then came Part 2, a sonar course, and finally Part 3, three months at sea as a trainee in HMS *Grampus*. This was the acid test. If you passed Part 3, you won your dolphins.

Grampus was at the time just ten years old, pretty much state of the art for the day, a diesel-electric boat at 2400 tonnes, one of eight of the Porpoise class originally intended as hunter/killer attack submarines. But they were found to be exceptionally quiet underwater, far quieter than anything in the other NATO navies, and very much better still than the comparable Russian Whiskey class. *Grampus* and her sisters were quickly switched to the role of intelligence gathering, of searching for and shadowing the Russians.

David Bryant's first patrol took him north towards the Arctic, through the Faroes Gap, north-west of the British Isles, that chokepoint the Russians had to use to leave the Norwegian Sea or the North Sea to head south into the open Atlantic. It was a hunting ground for both sides, a lonely place of hide-and-seek, and there began a steep learning curve for a nineteen-year-old able seaman from Australia encountering the rigours of life underwater.

'It was the cold war and everything was for real,' Bryant remembers. 'We were tracking the Russians and the Russians were tracking us. If you were on a patrol in Arctic waters it was very cold outside, and you had things called black heaters in the Brit boats. Inside, the temperature of the boat would be so hot that condensation would start to drip on you. As a trainee I was sleeping in the torpedo compartment. I had a bunk on top of a torpedo. You sleep in sleeping bags, and I used to pull a bit of plastic over the top so I didn't get wet. Otherwise I'd get soaked through with the condensation dripping on me. But I had to put up with drip drip drip, water dripping on the plastic keeping me awake. It wasn't much fun.'

Bryant was not the only novice on board *Grampus*: another three Australians, four Canadians and an Israeli were also learning the ropes. The captain, Lieutenant Commander Thompson, put them through the mill. On one foul winter's day in the Arctic Circle, the boat surfaced to recover a radio buoy she had been trailing. The winch had broken down and the buoy, floating astern on a mile and a half of heavy cable, had to be hauled in by sheer muscle, hand over hand.

Grampus pitched and wallowed in a heavy sea, waves breaking over, with an icy blizzard blowing and then some. Out on the narrow after casing with a small party of sailors, Dave Bryant found the sleet coming at him horizontally, lashing his face, stinging his eyes. The cold cut through his Arctic wet-weather clothing like razor blades. Struggling to keep their feet, slowly, ever so slowly, the men strained and heaved to drag in the cable with gloved hands. They did it in relays, spending only fifteen minutes out in the open before going below to the wardroom for a reviving tot of rum, then it was back up on deck again. It took three long, exhausting hours.

That was the thing about submarines. You never knew what you would be doing next. When the Arab–Israeli War broke out in June 1967 – the Six-Day War – *Grampus* spent a frantic seventy-two hours at Portsmouth loading for a full-scale, three-month war patrol: torpedoes, extra food, the lot. By the time they reached the Mediterranean it was all over, so they dawdled home on a leisurely cruise to Gibraltar, Oporto in Portugal and Lorient in France.

Another encounter with the French was not so happy. In January the next year, *Grampus* was snagged in the nets of a French trawler fishing illegally in British waters. The apoplectic fishing skipper radioed that he had been attacked and the French air force sent a plane that flew menacingly overhead with its bomb doors open. It took three hours to hack the boat free.

All the while, the young man was watching, listening and gathering experience, laying the foundations for a career. On watch, he would spend hours before the screens in the sonar room, headphones clamped to his ears, perfecting his trade. The recordings of underwater sounds they played you ashore were one thing. The reality at sea was more complex. Sound behaves very differently in water. It travels at a speed of around 1500 metres per second, about five times faster than in air, but that rate varies with the salinity and temperature of the ocean: faster in warm water, slower in cold. Far from being a silent domain, the oceans are often alive with noise.

'It's a bit like listening to an orchestra,' says Bryant. 'You can pick out the violins and the trumpets from everything else. You can distinguish what sort of ship it is from the number of blades on the shaft, the number of shafts it's got, whether it's a diesel or a turbine. You can pick up all these little nuances over time. You get better and better at it.

'Everything makes a noise. Rain makes a noise. Up north you hear ice which makes an incredible noise, crunching and groaning. A porpoise will come up and squeak in your hydrophones and just about knock your ears off. Fish are like birds. You have the dawn and evening chorus. When the dawn comes the fish wake up and start to eat, and they make an awful racket. When the sun goes down they do the same thing again. The biological noise, we call it.'

Bryant's time with the Royal Navy came to an end in 1968. He had enjoyed it, and learned a lot. They in turn had been hospitable, good shipmates, although there had been a certain unease when RN sailors realised that their Australian counterparts were far better paid. It was time to go. He was now a skilled sonar operator and ready for home. *Otway* was commissioned at Greenock in April that year, and he was in the crew that brought her out to Australia via the African west coast, for the Suez Canal was still closed after the war. They arrived in Sydney that October.

Dave Bryant spent twenty-three years in the RAN. He served in all six of the O-boats, a rare distinction, and finished his time in 1988 as a warrant officer.

'I loved it,' he enthuses. 'Absolutely loved it. It was the travel, going to different ports, it was the people, the mates that you made. It was just happy days, it was just so good. I liked the job. I was a very good sonar operator. I got a huge amount of job satisfaction.'

After the navy, submarines still held him in their grip. Out of uniform, he was headhunted for his experience by the Swedish Kockums company, which had the contract for the new Collins-class submarines for the RAN. He did fifteen years with them and another five years with the Australian Submarine Corporation, maintaining and servicing the Collins boats in Adelaide.

By any stretch it was a stellar career. Officers were all well and good, but skilled senior sailors like David Bryant were the backbone of the service and the navy. From all those years, over all those things seen and heard and done, there is a particular memory Bryant cherishes, as fresh in his mind as the time it happened many decades ago, a thing of wonder and beauty. It was when he was still a kid in *Grampus*, on watch at around 2 a.m., maintaining a lonely vigil in the high north latitudes.

'We were sitting there, nothing happening, at about 250 or 300 feet. And then I heard the whales,' he explains. 'They were calling each other from one side of the world to the other, across the Arctic Circle. It was amazing. You would hear the sound of the whale coming in and then it would pass over you . . . a bit like a racing car going past you. It was just extraordinary. And then you would hear it coming from the other direction. Everything else was deathly quiet, and this went on for about half an hour. It made the hairs stand up on the back of my neck.'

20

THE COLD WAR

The Oberons continued to play the clockwork mouse for anti-submarine exercises, a task everyone found tedious, not least because they thought the game was frequently rigged in favour of the hunting skimmer. There were many other tasks at sea they could perform with aplomb.

The ketch *One and All* had been a sturdy timber boat, built of Huon pine, when she took to the water back in 1878, not a yachtsman's pleasure craft but a bluff working vessel, twenty-five metres long, with two stumpy masts and a big hold to carry cargoes of salt. Nearly 100 years on, though, she was tired, in such bad shape that the Queensland Marine Board surveyors had refused to register her as a commercial fishing boat and warned that she was not fit for sea.

Undeterred, her owner, a film producer named Peter Dabbs, from Roseville in Sydney, had sailed her and a crew of six from Brisbane on a trip out to Middleton Reef, a low coral atoll in the Pacific near Lord Howe Island, some 600 kilometres from the Australian coast. On the way back, in rising seas, *One and All* struck a piece of flotsam, which sprang some hull planks. The only pump could not keep up with the inrushing sea and, after a struggle, Dabbs got off a mayday call, giving his position as about 90 miles nor'west of the reef. With his boat foundering beneath him, he sent a second message saying he was abandoning ship with his crew and taking to a life raft.

That was the last that was heard of them. It was the morning of Saturday, 2 October 1971. The RAAF began a search with relays of long-range maritime patrol Neptune aircraft from its base at Townsville.

A signal arrived in HMAS *Otway* early the next day, tagged IMMEDIATE and just in time for the morning ceremony of colours.

'Eight o'clock, sir!'

'Make it so!'

The submarine was to 'sail with all despatch' to join the search. A Sunday morning is not an ideal time for urgent action in even the best-run ship, and, compounding the problem, *Otway* was berthed in Brisbane for a flag-waving visit to celebrate Navy Week. Her ship's company was billeted in hotels ashore, including her captain, Lieutenant Commander Terry Roach. Summoned by the Officer of the Day, he hurried back by taxi. 'With all despatch' meant exactly what it said, and, reckoning there was no time to round up the rest of the crew, Roach decided to sail shorthanded with what he had, the outgoing watch and the incoming one, forty-five men instead of his full complement of sixty-eight, leaving even his XO behind.

The departure was tricky. The submarine was alongside at the RAN's local base, HMAS *Moreton*, at Bulimba on the Brisbane River, but it was facing upstream, away from the sea, and was hemmed in the navigable channel by large merchant ships in berths downstream. Making things even harder, there was a strong ebb tide. Normally, a tug would have been called to help out but there was no time for that either, and so, with finely judged helm and engine orders – 'Port thirty, half ahead starboard, full astern port' – Roach did a 180-degree turn and squeezed down the river with the ebb and out into Moreton Bay and beyond. By 9 a.m. he was well on his way.

A Queenslander, Terry Roach had entered the naval college at the age of thirteen with the intention of becoming a submariner, and he had served five years as a lieutenant in RN boats from the Arctic Circle to the eastern Mediterranean before doing his Perisher in 1970. *Otway* was his first command in what had been a colourful year. That April, below periscope depth off the American naval base at Subic Bay, in the Philippines, during a big international exercise, the boat had grounded on a large and unmarked

US Navy underwater rubbish dump, putting the sonar dome on the front of the keel out of action. When they opened it up back in dry dock in Sydney, they found it full of Dr Pepper cans and other barnacled American junk. In August, on an anti-submarine exercise off Jervis Bay, a practice torpedo dropped by a Wessex helicopter of the RAN's 816 Squadron went rogue and slammed into *Otway*'s fin, sticking there like a dart on a dartboard, to much hilarity. Accidents come in threes. A month later, again at Jervis Bay, a curious and possibly amorous whale nudged the attack periscope and bent it.

The sea was getting up as *Otway* headed south-east at her best twelve knots, helped along at first by the East Australian Current, which flows southwards off the coast. Terry Roach had no specific position to head to, just a general search area, with the hope that the RAAF might narrow that down. The crew would have to work watch on watch, filling in unfamiliar jobs where they could, hour upon hour, but it was at least on the surface, which simplified things. The coxswain, Chief Petty Officer John Curtain, and the chief tiffy, Ian Taber, found themselves doing the occasional periscope watch, and a stoker lent a hand in the galley to replace a cook who had been left ashore. They had no idea how many survivors there might be, or in what condition, but the captain laid his plans. His sailors rustled up spare clothing, made up bunks, planned meals and, as a rather macabre precaution, made space in the submarine's refrigerator to stow a corpse.

With the wind and seas still rising, *Otway* reached the search area that Wednesday with little or no hope of finding the proverbial needle in a haystack. It was a puzzling decision to send a submarine when a surface vessel, a frigate or a destroyer, would have been quicker to the scene and much better equipped for a rescue at sea. Evidently, there was not one available.

Locating the raft in those vast acres of ocean really depended on the RAAF. *Otway* had only two radio men instead of her usual four, and the radio supervisor, Brian Coultas, and his offsider, Leading Radio Operator Pollock, also took turns to work watches, long hours day and night, keeping in contact with the aircraft and the Sea Air Rescue Service headquarters back in Sydney.

For another two days nothing turned up and hopes faded. Then, on the Wednesday afternoon at three o'clock, an RAAF P-3 Orion spotted floating debris eighty kilometres to the north of the reef, and just in time. The search was due to be abandoned two hours later, at 5 p.m. The news media, now following the drama, had reported that the wife of one of the crew, a Mrs Anne Kenny of Brisbane, sent a telegram to the prime minister, Billy McMahon, appealing for the hunt to go on. 'For God's sake continue the search for seven Christian souls and for the sake of our five children,' she wrote.

The hunt went on for one more day, a last roll of the dice. Mrs Kenny's prayers were answered. Leaving the area and heading for home as darkness descended, the crew of one of the Neptunes spotted the distant glow of a red distress flare. Turning towards it and dropping down to ninety metres' altitude with searchlight blazing, they found a little orange rubber raft tossing in the peaks and troughs of a disturbed sea, and saw a figure waving from it.

Otway got the message. She was just 110 kilometres to the south, checking the debris found by the Orion. Terry Roach turned her around and headed for the position at best speed. As the Neptune left, an Orion arrived and dropped another raft, and flares to guide the submarine.

It was a pitch-black night. High on the bridge, the Officer of the Watch and four lookouts peered into the dark, whipped by a rising wind from the nor'east at forty knots and more, drenched by the spray from waves that were now around Sea State 5, classified as rough. Terry Roach stayed in the control room, seated at the search periscope. Radar was no help, because the raft was too small to be detected – and anyway, the waves were giving a jumbled sea return, confused images like confetti.

Guided by the intermittent, fitful light from the flares, they found their target at two o'clock on the Friday morning, almost to the minute. The survivors had scrambled into the larger RAAF raft. A cheer went through the submarine. The captain had laid his plans carefully, leaving nothing to chance, conscious that there were risks and hazards at every step. *Otway*'s deck guardrails had been put in place, unusual for a submarine at sea, and one of the sparkies, Peter Eastwood, had festooned them with a string of electric bulbs and hung another couple of floodlights from the fin.

With the submarine heaving and rolling beneath their boots, waves breaking over and wind lashing them, a handful of men on the casing struggled to secure the heavy wooden accommodation ladder in place. This would help the survivors climb over the bulbous ballast tanks to the upper deck, where they would be brought into the boat by the widest entrance available, the for'ard torpedo loading hatch, perhaps with a stretcher if necessary. A sentry was stationed there to slam the hatch shut if a wave looked like swamping it, which was very possible.

Slowly, carefully, Roach positioned *Otway* with the sea breaking on the starboard bow to provide a little lee as protection for the raft now wallowing on the port side. In an act of considerable courage, two men in wetsuits, the impressively bearded Lieutenant Rick Canham, the torpedo officer and leader of the boat's diving team, and his offsider, Able Seaman Bill 'Shorty' Needham, jumped into the sea to secure the raft and help the survivors onto the ladder. Warrant Officer Keith Hamilton recalled:

> Both casing and recovery parties wore life jackets, safety belts with a lanyard and safety hook to fix to the casing guard rails when needed. Two men were required to stand on the ballast tanks either side of the bottom of the boarding ladder to assist the survivors when leaving their life raft and found themselves up to their waists in sea water as it tried to snatch them away. A loud hailer provided communications. The weather, with wind and sea chop, was bad enough to test everyone's mettle.[1]

It took forty minutes for willing hands to haul all seven survivors on board: wet, hungry and exhausted but uninjured. They had a hot shower, were given clean clothing and then the light meal prepared in the galley. The flare the aircraft spotted had been their last.

Job done, *Otway* recovered the two rafts and set a course for Sydney, still on the surface, still watch on watch. It had been a flawless operation in which the failure of any of its moving parts – human or mechanical – could have wrecked the whole thing, with injury or worse. They arrived through the Heads on the Saturday afternoon, the seven survivors up on the fin, threading their way through the inevitable weekend hordes of sailboats, pleasure craft and ferries. TV news helicopters clattered overhead as they moved up the harbour and edged alongside at HMAS *Platypus*, to be met by no less than the fleet commander, Rear Admiral Bill Dovers.

There was a media scrum waiting there too. For *Otway*'s captain and crew, it was pleasingly novel. Unusually, the Silent Service had something to talk about.

'When we go to sea, we go to war.' It was a common saying in the squadron, not meant in a vainglorious way but as a statement of fact. Each time one of the boats headed out on patrol, it was indeed armed and ready for combat, and the ship's company knew it. To get this right required unremitting practice, from commanding officers to the most junior sailor, and although a lot could be simulated and learned ashore at *Watson* or *Platypus*, it was the real thing that counted most.

At around four o'clock of an October afternoon in 1976, in a sea like a mirror, *Otway* found exactly what she was looking for. Over the northern horizon came the 'Big E', the nuclear-powered aircraft carrier USS *Enterprise*.

To *Otway*'s new young captain, Lieutenant Commander Peter Briggs, she looked like 'a bloody big block of flats' and she was heading straight for him, steaming south into the wind to launch her aircraft. For a submariner, there could be no richer prize. *Enterprise* was the first nuclear-powered aircraft carrier, at a mighty 95,000 tonnes, powered by no fewer than eight reactors and at a length of 342 metres, to this day the longest warship ever built. With her big, square bridge island towering over her flight deck, she did indeed look like a block of flats, or perhaps as if a chunk of Manhattan had dislodged itself and floated down the East River out to sea.

Otway's job was to 'sink' her, then escape. This was Exercise Kangaroo II, seventeen days of a great and complex war game on and off the Queensland coast, involving some 30,000 men, forty ships and 250 aircraft from Australia, the US and New Zealand. *Otway* was a small but powerful cog in the machine.

Peter Briggs had a navy pedigree. On the mantelpiece in his boyhood home there was a framed photograph of his uncle, Ken Briggs, the man who had cut the underwater cable at Cap Saint-Jacques in 1945.

'I was a fifteen-year-old in rural Lismore, up on the New South Wales North Coast, and all my peers were aspiring to be bank tellers or school teachers, and I thought there's got to be something more to life than this,' Briggs recalls. 'Ken Briggs sat on the family mantelpiece in his sailor's rig all those years, so I applied for the naval college.'[2]

He graduated in 1964 and, after sea service in the destroyer *Vampire* and the carrier *Melbourne*, the navy sent him to Britain, first to HMS *Britannia*, the Royal Naval College at Dartmouth in England's west country, and then for warfare training. In 1966 he volunteered for submarine service with the RAN, not through any burning desire to become a submariner but because it meant he could stay longer in Britain, where he had fallen in love with a young Norwegian woman, Brit Petersen.

He finished the course at *Dolphin* by winning the Max Horton Prize as the top graduate, and in 1967, newly promoted to lieutenant, he was sent to one of the RN's early O-boats, HMS *Otter*. First they made him the torpedo officer – a sharp learning curve because Briggs knew nothing about torpedoes – and then he became *Otter*'s navigator, which brought him a shock of cold reality: his first grounding.

On a night training exercise to land some Royal Marines in Norway, submerged at 120 metres and unaware that a current was carrying him along, Briggs mistimed a turn and bounced off a sheer cliff on the side of the Hardanger fjord. *Otter*'s captain, thinking quickly, decided to report instead that they might have been hit by a practice torpedo during the exercise. In the dry dock back at the base at Faslane, on a quiet Saturday morning with no one around, they found an impressive lump of granite firmly lodged in a main ballast tank. The captain distributed bottles of Scotch to the dock manager and a few others, the hole was swiftly welded over and painted, and nothing more was said.

From that low point, Lieutenant Briggs's career began to climb. Back in Australia from 1968, he was navigator in *Ovens*, then sonar officer in *Oxley*. He passed the Perisher in 1975 and in December that year assumed command of *Otway*, her sixth captain. Now, off Lady Musgrave Island, on the southern tip of the Barrier Reef, all his training, and all his experience, would be put to the test.

He knew *Enterprise* was around somewhere because there were escorting destroyers fussing about here and there and 'dipping' helicopters clattering above, the big Sea Kings, which could lower their active sonar into the sea to search for him. The glassy calm was not helping. So he took himself off to gather his thoughts and gird his loins, as he describes:

> We got right behind the island in a bit of a radar shadow for patrolling aircraft or whatever. No one expects to find a submarine tucked up alongside an island. So we topped the battery right up during the day. Finished snorting at the end of the day and then basically at four knots, three or four hundred feet under the thermocline, we just stooged into the area. It took a while, more than twelve hours to get into the middle of it.[3]

The thermocline, the submariner's best friend, is where the warm and moving surface waters of the ocean meet the colder and calmer waters of the depths. That sudden, marked drop in temperature bends and deflects the soundwaves of a searching sonar, allowing a well-handled submarine below the thermocline to slip along undetected. So far, so good. But when *Otway* returned to periscope depth in the dark that night, she drew a blank – nothing. There were a few helicopters away in the distance but that was it. Briggs withdrew behind the island again, repeated the process and returned the next day. That was when he saw the block of flats in the crosshairs of his attack periscope.

The orders and responses came quickly, calmly:

'Close up the attack team ... Stand by Mark 48 attack. Two Mark 48, allocate five and six tubes ... Firing set up; bearing is that, the range is that ... put me ten port ... speed thirty knots ... Solution is set. Stand by check bearing and shoot ...'

It was perfection. Had this been the real thing, those two torpedoes would have left *Otway* at fifty knots and more, deep below the thermocline, their own sonar homing on the target, to explode directly beneath *Enterprise* and break her back. Bullseye. At best, she would have sunk; more likely she would have taken on a heavy list as the sea rushed in, slumped in the water, unable to fly her aircraft, and therefore to all intents and purposes out of action. The exercise umpire on board *Otway* scored it a direct hit – job done.

Next came the hard part, the escape, as Briggs recalls:

> We had to raise our radio mast, a bloody big telegraph pole, to report where we were and what we had shot at and the target's position course and speed, which we did. And that attracted attention. All hell descended on us, there were helicopters all over the place. We stooged off under the layer and headed south out of the area.[4]

It would be a long, slow, silent crawl. Every few hours or so, Briggs brought *Otway* back to periscope depth for a quick look around. He knew there would be aircraft hunting him, RAAF Orions and the fat-bellied American S-3 Vikings from the carrier. It was still mirror-calm. They did not find him, and he dived again and kept going, still heading south, hour upon hour, conscious that all the while his battery was running down.

After eight hours, it was flat. To snort would give his position away. All he could do was switch everything off and catch a 'stopped trim', as it was called. This meant keeping the boat at neutral buoyancy, suspended in the ocean, riding on the current. If she started to sink, she was heavy and so water would be pumped out of the trim tanks. If she rose towards the surface, she was too light and water would be flooded in. The air by now was growing foul and thick, with breathing an effort.

'We shut down everything we could, put everyone we didn't need to bed and started making oxygen by burning an oxygen candle and scrubbing the carbon dioxide,' Briggs explains.[5] The oxygen candle was a cylinder of chemicals – sodium chlorate and iron – which, set to burn at around 600 degrees, produced oxygen for the atmosphere inside the boat. The scrubber removed carbon dioxide gas by trapping it in soda lime. It was hardly ideal but it worked; you could at least breathe.

Otway drifted along on the southbound current at a couple of knots for still more hours until Briggs judged they were clean away and he could begin to snort again. Air returned to the boat, the diesels rumbled into action and life returned to something like normal. They set a course for Sydney.

It had been a textbook operation, one to be savoured and remembered. Peter Briggs rewarded his ship's company with a couple of stops for fishing on the way, a handy haul of fresh food for the galley.

Coastal waters, seas and oceans were principal theatres of the Cold War, above and below the surface. The navies of the Soviet Union and the Western bloc led by the United States circled each other like prize fighters in the ring, gloves raised, ready to strike.

The years after World War II saw the beginnings of a submarine arms race between the Russians and the Americans – and, to a lesser extent, the British – who strove to outdo one another in building bigger, better, faster and more lethally armed boats. Driven by the forceful and caustic Admiral Hyman Rickover, the son of Jewish immigrants from Russia and a man thought by some to be a genius, by others to be mad, the US Navy plunged headlong into the nuclear age.

Conventional diesel boats were abandoned. In the second half of the twentieth century, the US produced class after class of nuclear-powered submarine, some designed to attack enemy boats and surface vessels, others – the big Ohio class – to carry twenty Trident long-range ballistic missiles with nuclear warheads capable of striking targets in the Soviet Union from far at sea. The Russians did likewise, racing to keep up, culminating in the extraordinary Typhoon-class ballistic-missile boats, which, at an eye-watering

48,000 tonnes submerged, were the biggest submarines ever built, each a leviathan greater than the largest American aircraft carriers of World War II.

The stakes ratcheted higher when the Republican Ronald Reagan moved into the White House in January 1981. Determined to rise from the humiliation of the US defeat in Vietnam, and with the pugnacious British prime minister Margaret Thatcher at his shoulder, President Reagan abandoned the longstanding US policy of containment and détente, resolving instead to 'roll back' the Soviet empire by land and sea. The Soviet Union rose to the challenge.

The sea became a silent battleground. In a contest for supremacy, submarines met and shadowed and chased each other, chiefly (although not solely) in the North Atlantic, but also into the unlit black waters beneath the polar ice cap, submerged for weeks and months on end, their crews living on adrenaline, a knife-edge of stress. The Tom Clancy novel *The Hunt for Red October* (1984), which became a 1990 film, with its chilling confrontation between the Russians and Americans on the brink of a hot nuclear war, was fictional but grounded in a solid and uncomfortable foundation of fact.

The possibility of war was always on the horizon. The Cuban Missile Crisis of 1962 came within an ace of war when the captain of a Soviet submarine, *B-59*, very nearly fired a nuclear-tipped torpedo at American destroyers he believed were attacking him. Three officers had to sign off on the launch. The captain and the political officer signed but the third, the Executive Officer Vasily Arkhipov, refused.

In 1968, the brand-new British nuclear boat HMS *Warspite* got it badly wrong. Closely trailing a Soviet Echo II-class submarine, *Warspite*'s captain thought the Russian had done what the NATO navies called a 'Crazy Ivan', a sudden, sharp turn to shake off a pursuer. He went to follow. But there had been no turn. *Warspite*'s fin scraped along the Echo's bottom and was chewed by the blades of her two propellers, pushing her into a roll of a frightening sixty-eight degrees. When she came back again, she crunched into the Russian once more, forcing her into yet another roll. Both boats struggled to the surface, the Echo also damaged, *Warspite* leaping out of the water like a breaching whale. They parted company and *Warspite* limped back to Scotland at a little below periscope depth, listing heavily, her fin crumpled and leaking.

There were at least three collisions between American and Soviet submarines and probably more over the decades. The first came in 1974, when the USS *James Madison*, carrying sixteen Poseidon nuclear missiles, was struck by an unidentified Russian boat tailing her as she left the Scottish port of Holy Loch. The damage was relatively minor and both boats survived; the incident was covered up for forty-three years. In another clash – in 1992, near Kildin Island, a small Russian outcrop in the Barents Sea, off the port of Murmansk – the submarine *Kostroma* surfaced beneath the stern of the attack boat USS *Baton Rouge*, touching off a very public diplomatic storm and so damaging the American that she was eventually scrapped.

Less dramatically, a lot of effort went into the more passive business of intelligence gathering, with each side striving to assess the capabilities, the strengths and weaknesses, of their adversary's fleets and ships. Every class of ship has its unique acoustic signature: the noise of its engines and on-board machinery such as fuel pumps and air conditioning; the sound of cavitation, which is the generation of air bubbles caused by its turning propellers; the rush of displaced water as its hull moves through the sea. The earlier you can detect and recognise this individual signature in a prospective foe, the sooner you can prepare to deal with it, and the greater advantage you have. As the science evolved, it was possible to determine not merely the class of vessel but even individual ships by name.

So too with communications. It was useful to record and understand how your opponents talked to each other, what they said and how they said it. Photography of an enemy vessel, especially its hull underwater, could also tell you a lot. Submarines on intelligence patrols, armed with spyware of increasing sophistication, sought to gather all these things and more, to be analysed by experts ashore.

At which point enter the Australians. With the US Navy and the RN so heavily engaged in the Atlantic and the Northern

Hemisphere, it was suggested that the RAN might like to undertake 'ISR' operations – intelligence, surveillance and reconnaissance patrols – in the western Pacific. The O-boats, the British knew, were ideal for covert operations. Smaller and far quieter than nuclear submarines, they were especially suited for stealthy snooping in shallow coastal waters. The Americans agreed. So Australia was invited to join the Big League as a partner in a working alliance of the three navies. The RAN's submarine squadron acquired a new mission: intelligence. Not to put too fine a point on it, this meant spying, at the height of the Cold War.

The two newest submarines, *Orion* and *Otama*, were fitted with an array of the latest equipment for reconnaissance and surveillance, for gathering intelligence on the dangerous front lines. The nuts and bolts of this 'special fit' are secret even today, but there was seriously clever gadgetry for finding and listening to ships and recording the sounds they made, including their radio transmissions. Other gear could intercept missile telemetry. There were high-tech cameras for photographing and filming a target in close-up and with impressive clarity.

Only a select few people in the RAN and the defence scientific and intelligence communities were aware of what was happening, and they kept it to themselves, sworn to secrecy. There were no announcements, no discussions in federal cabinet and certainly no reports to parliament. There was not a hint in the media. The prime minister and the defence minister were aware, of course, but even then in no great detail. Much of what went on remains secret, for no Australian government of any political colour since has acknowledged what happened. The officers and sailors who took part were required to sign a binding commitment to silence, enforced by the federal *Crimes Act*, and to this day they will not talk about what they did. But enough has emerged over the years to reveal at least something of the nature of the complex and hazardous surveillance operations conducted by the Oberons against the Soviet and Chinese navies, and others, in dangerous waters.

The Australian people first heard of these in a detailed article in the *Australian Financial Review*, appropriately headlined 'The Mystery Boats', written in 2003 by the Melbourne journalist

Geoffrey Barker, a well-informed reporter with unmatched sources in the defence establishment. In 2013 he wrote another, for *The Australian*, labelled 'Cold War Exploits of Australia's Secret Submarines'. There have been more revelations in *Australian Submarines: A History*, an encyclopaedic two-volume work by the lawyer and former submariner Dr Michael White.[6]

What has become clear is that the Royal Australian Navy had been a serious player in the Cold War.

There was something of a test run in 1978, on *Orion*'s maiden voyage from Britain to Australia after her commissioning. It was essentially a Royal Navy operation, with *Orion*'s captain, Lieutenant Commander Rob Woolrych, given orders to keep his eyes open and see what he could see on the way out through the Mediterranean and into the Suez Canal. Woolrych was an experienced submarine commanding officer who had done the Perisher in 1972 and gone on to command *Otway* and then *Ovens*, but this intelligence-gathering role was new to most of his ship's company. Many Australians serving in British submarines, though, had been on RN intelligence patrols and knew how they worked. Woolrych's executive officer was Lieutenant Kim Pitt, who would become a quietly celebrated mystery boat commander himself.

Orion's motto was *Orbe circumcincto*, Latin for 'All around the world'. It seemed appropriate. She left the Portland Bill lighthouse behind on 13 March, punched her way on the surface through a ferocious gale in the Bay of Biscay, and then slipped past Gibraltar into the Med. Two Russian fishing boats took an unusually close interest in her off Malta. Towards the end of the month, she passed between the brand-new Soviet aircraft carrier *Kiev* and a cruiser of the Kara class, still on the surface.

She dived on 25 March, heading for North Africa and the coast of Libya, then ruled by the volatile, eccentric and staunchly anti-Western despot Colonel Muammar Gaddafi. For all his fiercely proclaimed Arab nationalism, Gaddafi was in fact a client of the Soviet Union, which, among other things, was training the Libyan air force. *Orion* remained off the coast for ten days, silently watching and listening, occasionally coming to periscope depth for what submariners habitually referred to as 'a quick look around', withdrawing out to sea at night to snort for battery charging and some fresh air. It was tedious, monotonous, relieved only by an Easter egg hunt: the captain's wife had bought them for the crew before they sailed. The details of what intelligence was scooped up remain secret.

Orion passed through the Suez Canal in late April, where, to their surprise, the canal pilot taking them through admitted that he was the commander of the Egyptian Navy's submarine squadron. Spying cuts both ways. There was some more listening done off the coast of Yemen, and then plain sailing down the Indian Ocean to arrive at HMAS *Stirling* in Western Australia on 23 June.

There had been some equipment failures. For a while a communications mast had to be held in place by a rope lashing, with a sailor standing by with an axe to cut it down if there was an emergency. A new one had to be flown out to meet the boat in Athens. The truly awful moment came in the Indian Ocean, when Woolrych decided on a whim to test one of his rear torpedo tubes and fired a 'water shot' – sea water expelled from the tube with no torpedo. The navigator rushed into the control room aghast. He had secretly stored a stash of expensive Greek brandy and ouzo there. When they opened the tube it was all gone, save for a few shards of glass.

The operation was judged a success. It had been a tentative step, but the RAN had arrived in the spying game. There would be many more intelligence patrols to come, growing in sophistication, daring and danger, authorised by the defence minister and under the direct command of the Chief of the Defence Force. In time, civilian intelligence officers – 'spooks' and linguists – would travel with *Orion* or *Otama*, stoically enduring the hardships of submarine life. The crews themselves would rarely, if ever, know where they were going, and sometimes the chart table would be screened by a black curtain. Secrecy was paramount.

Cam Ranh Bay lies on the south-east coast of Vietnam, some 300 kilometres north-east of what was once Saigon but is now

Ho Chi Minh City. It is a splendid deep-water harbour, a picturesque inlet off the South China Sea some thirty-two kilometres long and sixteen kilometres wide, providing a secure, year-round shelter from the typhoons that storm in from the Pacific Ocean.

Navies have long used it. The French as colonists and the Russians, too, when a squadron of the Tsar's Baltic fleet regrouped there in 1905 on its way around the world to a disastrous encounter with the Japanese at the Battle of Tsushima. The Vietnam War brought in the Americans, who, with their matchless energy, threw untold millions of dollars at rolling out a vast naval and air base with piers, ammunition dumps, warehouses and repair workshops, a fully functioning hospital, living quarters and messing facilities and the inevitable lavishly equipped Post Exchange, or PX, for several thousand men, plus a 3000-metre temporary runway for jet fighters completed from scratch in just fifty days. That done, they then built a permanent concrete runway of another 3000 metres.

They were there for less than ten years. Withdrawing from the war, the US abandoned Cam Ranh Bay in 1972 and turned it over to the South Vietnamese armed forces. That did not last long. In 1975, at war's end, the North Vietnamese Army captured the base virtually intact. With little use for it and with no navy or air force of its own to speak of, the communist government in Hanoi offered the bay to the Soviet Union, which happily signed a twenty-five-year lease and moved in to the excellent facilities so helpfully built by the Americans. By 1984, a top-secret assessment by the CIA reported:

> The Soviets have been increasing their air and naval presence and expanding facilities at Cam Ranh Bay, Vietnam, since 1979. In late 1983 they deployed naval Badger medium bombers, including strike models, to Cam Ranh; and they appear to be making preparations at the airfield to support long term deployment of Badgers. The number of Soviet naval ships routinely present at Cam Ranh port has increased steadily during the last few years.
>
> Soviet naval aircraft and ships operating from Cam Ranh Bay demonstrate visible Soviet support for the Vietnamese government and provide the Soviets with the capability to:

- Monitor and interfere with international shipping between the Indian and Pacific Oceans.
- Strike US air and naval bases in the Philippines.
- Threaten the southern coastal areas of China.
- Conduct surveillance of all of the South China Sea.[7]

The report went on to list Soviet ships that had used Cam Ranh, including cruisers, frigates, the new 40,000-ton aircraft carrier *Minsk*, and both conventional and nuclear submarines, some armed with cruise missiles. In short, the strategists at the CIA and the Pentagon saw a clear and mounting challenge to American hegemony in the Pacific, an incursion that had to be met and countered.

Surveillance of the port and its comings and goings was essential. Australian submarines, which could go in close where US Navy nuclear boats could not, would be very welcome. There was also the additional benefit of deniability: if something went awfully wrong and an Australian boat was apprehended or even attacked, provoking some international crisis, the Americans could throw up their hands in wide-eyed innocence and declare it was not their doing. The stage was set.

In October 1985, the heavy cruiser *Frunze* and two guided missile destroyers of the Soviet Navy were steaming in the tropical heat of the Indian Ocean a little above the equator, heading south-east towards the Malacca Strait, which separates the Malay Peninsula from the Indonesian island of Sumatra.

That course would take them down around Singapore and into the South China Sea. Following their progress by satellite, the Americans assumed they would call in at Cam Ranh and then perhaps continue on to the port of Vladivostok, in the Russian far east, to join the Soviet Pacific Fleet.

Commissioned only the year before and named for a hero of the Bolshevik Revolution, *Frunze* was on her first long deployment away from her home port at Kaliningrad, on the Baltic Sea. She had come the long way, south down the Atlantic and east around the Cape of Good Hope, calling at African ports to display the hammer and sickle flag. She and her slightly older sister *Kirov* were the pride of the Red Fleet, and with good reason, for they were elegant ships of awesome might and mass, unmatched by anything in the navies of the Western powers. Twin nuclear reactors drove them along, certainly to a speed of thirty knots and very probably a good bit more, but it was their sheer bulk that commanded respectful attention. At 28,000 tonnes fully loaded and a little over 250 metres long, *Frunze* was more than twice the size of the US Navy's guided missile cruisers, the 10,000-tonne Ticonderoga class.

And missiles she had aplenty. There were twenty silos clustered directly beneath her bridge at the beginning of an impressively long foredeck, which swept gracefully upwards to a flared bow. Western analysts assumed, correctly, that they contained the modern anti-ship cruise missile known to the Russians as *Granit* and to NATO by the appropriate codename *Shipwreck*, capable of delivering a nuclear warhead. She also carried surface-to-air missiles, anti-submarine rocket launchers, ten torpedo tubes and a range of conventional guns big and small. Not counting the world's aircraft carriers, *Frunze* was by far the greatest and potentially the most lethal surface warship afloat. So big, in fact, that the US Navy reclassified her as a battlecruiser, a term rarely heard since World War I. Yet so much about her remained unknown. The Pentagon was anxious to discover more. They asked the RAN if it could help.

By good luck, the frigate HMAS *Canberra* had been on an exercise in nearby waters and she was ordered to find *Frunze* and follow her. This she did. There was nothing secret about it, no cloak and dagger. For five days in the first week of November, the two steamed down the Malacca Strait together, sometimes *Canberra* trailing astern, sometimes out on the beam, literally within rifle shot, eyeball to eyeball, the frigate sending up her French-built Squirrel helicopter – nicknamed Cyril – to take photographs. The Russians took photographs as well. Long-range Orion P-3C surveillance aircraft from the RAAF base at Butterworth, in Malaysia, joined the party too.

And then the Australians departed as quickly as they had arrived, with an exchange of the elaborate farewell courtesies that were an incongruous ritual of the encounters of Cold War adversaries. Someone in *Canberra* had noted the date, 7 November, the day the Bolsheviks had stormed the Winter Palace at Saint Petersburg in 1917, the opening act in the Communist Revolution. A signal lamp flickered from *Canberra*'s bridge: 'Happy 68th anniversary. We leave you in peace.'

Frunze chattered back: 'Thank you very much for your co-operation. I wish you a pleasant voyage.'

The Soviet ships sailed on alone. Pleased with the achievement, the RAN cranked up the publicity machine, releasing a detailed account to the media. Unusually, the Fleet Commander, Rear Admiral Ian Knox, had been on board *Canberra* at the time, and the newspapers were given a photograph of him with the massive bulk of *Frunze* looming in the background. Defence Minister Beazley assured parliament that the RAN's 'surveillance of Soviet ships in the Pacific illustrated the sound working relationship between Australia and the United States'.[8]

There was more that was not revealed. *Orion*, with her high-tech surveillance gear, had been lying in wait off Cam Ranh Bay at the end of a long patrol, neatly positioned to intercept *Frunze* when she arrived. Kim Pitt, the executive officer on her commissioning voyage, was now her captain, a three-ringed commander.

It was 9 November, a Saturday. *Frunze* came up from the south, exactly as expected, and turned towards the bay at slow speed, perhaps five or six knots. Away in the distance, hovering at periscope depth, Pitt allowed himself a quick look around and then went deeper to creep towards the cruiser with infinite caution. The submarine was in the condition known as 'Ultra Quiet', with every possible mechanical or electrical sound silenced or muffled, but the risk was huge. One small error might bring on a collision or worse. It was a huge gamble.

Frunze, entering the harbour, was not using her sonar, was not expecting an intruder. On a Saturday and at the end of a long voyage, the Russians were relaxed, off their guard, intent on the business of finding their berth and looking forward to leave ashore.

Had they somehow discovered *Orion* lurking below, however, it was entirely conceivable they would assume they were being attacked – an act of war – and would hit back with everything they had. The Australian submarine and her crew might be captured, or even blown to bits. The diplomatic fallout would be immense, perhaps to the point of outright war. It did not bear thinking about.

Everything depended on the captain, who would have to bring extraordinary qualities to the task. In all his years of training as a junior officer and later doing his Perisher, Kim Pitt – like all his fellows – had been schooled to act with controlled aggression, to apply sudden, lethal force with stealth and skill. Now it was a very different game. Stealth was still required – more than ever, in fact – but aggression had no place in the equation. Just the opposite.

The wall of secrecy remains in place today. It has never been revealed what intelligence *Orion* obtained, nor how Pitt did it. But the drill, the manoeuvres, the evolutions for closing a target ship like this had been refined from lessons learned from years of ISR patrols and practised endlessly by every commanding officer.

The trick would be to place the submarine perhaps a kilometre astern of *Frunze* at periscope depth, for a quick look around to assess her course and speed, and then to dive deep and draw nearer, with the sonar operators calling the play: 'Green two getting louder . . . red three softer . . . right ahead . . .'

You could no doubt cut the air in the control room with a knife. The captain has in his head a three-dimensional picture of the two vessels, a mathematical juggling act: with breathtaking audacity, he is driving thousands of tonnes of submarine within metres of a vessel he can no longer see.

The coxswain nurses the helm with infinite delicacy, like a mother with a newborn baby, instantly responsive to orders. At a speed a knot or two more than the target, the submarine passes first down the starboard side, then the port, cameras photographing, sensors recording the acoustic signature. On a third pass the boat moves directly beneath the giant hull – just two metres below it – keeping pace, photographing her bottom: its shape, its sonar gear, its shafts and propellers, all grist to the intelligence analyst's mill. Done properly, the task takes around half an hour.

The job is completed. The big battlecruiser steams on into Cam Ranh Bay oblivious to the existence of the silent stalker below, which has probed and stolen her secrets. *Orion* heads for home, as quietly as she had come.

In his history, Michael White lists fifteen secret intelligence patrols by *Orion* and *Otama* between 1978 and 1992, but there may well have been more. Those who know will not say.[9] Geoffrey Barker's report for *The Australian* in 2013 suggests they ended after a near disaster, when *Orion* became entangled in the nets of a Chinese fishing fleet off Shanghai and only narrowly managed to free herself and escape.

Beyond that we know little more. The mystery remains.

21

IN MEMORIAM

One by one, the Oberons came to the end of their working lives. Over three decades, they had given sterling service, greater than their most ardent champions had expected, and they would live on in the affectionate memories of those who had taken them to sea. That was not always the case with submarines.

But by the last decade of the twentieth century, the art and science of undersea warfare had left the O-boats behind. In 1983 the Coalition government in Canberra invited seven European submarine builders to put forward their ideas for a replacement, to meet specific Australian requirements and to be built in Australia. There was fierce competition, a blizzard of allegations of skulduggery, incompetence and political meddling, and it wasn't until 1987 that federal cabinet approved the final design: the Swedish Kockums Type 471 submarine. There would be six boats, the Collins class, named for a hero of World War II, Vice Admiral Sir John Collins, the first Australian to become Chief of the Naval Staff. The contract was signed that June for $3.9 billion. The keel of the first boat, HMAS *Collins*, was laid down in South Australia in 1990 and she was formally commissioned in 1996, although a horror litany of design and technical problems meant she was not fully operational until 2000.

Oxley had been the first of the O-boats to arrive, and she was the first to depart, her Australian White Ensign hauled down for the final time at HMAS *Stirling* in February 1992 under the eye of the Chief of the Naval Staff, Vice Admiral Ian MacDougall, who had been her first executive officer. In twenty-five years she had travelled 403,056 nautical miles – almost 750,000 kilometres – in 54,910 hours underway.

MacDougall's career had flourished in parallel with the Oberons. He virtually grew up with them. He had joined the RAN as a fifteen-year-old cadet in 1954, and in the beginning he was a supply officer, but as a young lieutenant he switched to the seaman side of the trade and, with a bridge watchkeeping certificate under his belt, he moved to the submarine arm in 1963. By 1968 he was a lieutenant commander doing his Perisher in Britain, where his teacher was Commander John 'Sandy' Woodward, who would later gain fame leading the RN's taskforce in the 1982 Falklands War.

That done, MacDougall drove an RN O-boat, HMS *Otter*, and then, back home, HMAS *Onslow* from 1971. As a commander, he brought in the new Submarine Command Team Trainer at *Watson*, in Sydney. In 1985 he commanded the squadron at *Platypus* in Neutral Bay, going on to become the Fleet Commander as a rear admiral in 1989. In 1991 he would be the first submariner to surface at the top as Chief of the Naval Staff. That made him something of an iconic figure to the O-boat sailors – but from there opinions differed. Some thought MacDougall was a prickly bastard, exacting and difficult to work with. Others admired, liked and respected him, counting him as a lifelong friend. At his best he was a pragmatic reformer, running the RAN with a deft hand; to the dismay of some 'old salts', he was a firm advocate of women serving at sea. When he left the navy in 1994, he amazed almost everyone who knew him by becoming the first chief commissioner of the New South Wales Fire Brigades (which later became Fire and Rescue NSW), a job he held down for nine years and which won him the Australian Fire Service Medal. He died in 2020.

Otway was the next to leave, in 1994, with her casing and fin sold to the submarine museum in Holbrook, far from the sea in country New South Wales, where she sits today rather incongruously anchored in concrete and grass lawn. *Ovens* went the same year, to go on display on dry land at the WA Maritime Museum. *Onslow* is still afloat, a star attraction at the National Maritime

Museum at Sydney's Darling Harbour. *Orion*'s fin stands at the Naval Memorial Park in Rockingham, south of Perth.

Otama met a dismal end after she was decommissioned in December 2000 and bought for $50,000 by a tourist association at Hastings, in Westernport Bay south-east of Melbourne. She was to become a visitor attraction, but the money ran out and at one time she was put up for sale on eBay. Rumour had it that a criminal syndicate planned to buy her to run drugs. For twenty years she sat a few hundred metres offshore at Hastings, an ugly hulk rusting and rotting, until she was hauled away to be broken up in 2022.

A singular achievement of the Oberons and the men who took them to sea was their laying of the foundations for a permanent submarine service in the RAN. After them there was no going back. The Collins boats that replaced them undoubtedly had a difficult birth and they were initially much maligned, often for partisan political motives. They have never quite shaken off the 'Dud Subs' label slapped on them by an ill-informed media, but over the years they became one of the nation's most potent weapons, and they remain so at the time of writing. They have also served as mystery boats, a powerful intelligence asset.

Age is now catching up with them, too. The AUKUS agreement of 2021, in which the United States and the United Kingdom will assist the RAN to replace the Collins-class boats with nuclear submarines, is a logical, although undeniably controversial, evolution that will require a truly heroic commitment to pull off. Less understood is that AUKUS will also take Australia into the brave new worlds of artificial intelligence, cyberwarfare, autonomous warfare vehicles, and the eye-watering phenomenon of hypersonic missiles travelling at five times the speed of sound and more.

A pale September sun shone lightly on Saint Petersburg: on its grand palaces and museums, on the meandering Neva River, on the Admiralty building with its soaring spire, on the bronze equestrian statue of Peter the Great, the eighteenth-century tsar who had built this imperial capital on Russia's Baltic coast as his 'window on Europe'.

It was the northern autumn of 2018. At the Serafimovskoe Cemetery, a little outside the city, the beech trees were bare and despite the sunlight it was cold, minus five degrees Celsius. A small knot of figures, warmly clad against the chill, two of them elderly men carrying a wreath, approached a great block of black granite surmounted by a winged eagle and bearing, in gold letters, the word Курск.

Kursk. The name is burned into the Russian memory, much as 'Gallipoli' is hallowed by Australians. In the summer of 1943, the southern Soviet city of Kursk was the theatre of the greatest tank battle ever known, a blood-drenched Red Army victory over the German armed forces, in which hundreds of thousands of men were killed or wounded on both sides.

The respectful men at the memorial, though, were there to commemorate another tragedy of the name: the loss of the nuclear submarine *Kursk* and her crew of 118 men in the Barents Sea in 2000. That, too, hangs heavily on the Russian mind, not least for the official deceit and prolonged incompetence of the rescue attempt.

Kursk was a giant of what NATO labelled the Oscar II class, at 15,000 tonnes one of the largest cruise missile submarines ever built by any nation, and the pride of the Russian navy. Barely six years old, she was on a summer exercise with the Northern Fleet when leaking hydrogen peroxide fuel exploded inside a torpedo tube. That touched off another catastrophic explosion in several more tubes, and *Kursk* plunged to the seabed at a depth of 108 metres.

It took the navy sixteen hours to find her on the bottom and then, for four days, attempts to reach her with various rescue vehicles failed one after the other. Navy and government officials lied repeatedly to the media and the crew's relatives about the sinking, and refused help offered by the Americans, the British, the French and the Dutch. Public anger ran white hot when the waiting families, kept in the dark, saw TV news footage of the newly elected Russian president, Vladimir Putin, cheerfully sunning himself on holiday at a beach villa on the Black Sea. A Dutch salvage company that was finally allowed to reach the wreck found that twenty-three sailors had remained alive in a sealed compartment for at least six hours and perhaps several days.

One of the small party at Serafimovskoe that autumn morning in 2018 was Captain Igor Kurdin, a retired veteran of both the Soviet and then the Russian navies, and now commandant of the Saint Petersburg Submariners and Naval Veterans Club. The man standing with him was his guest, the former Australian warrant officer Dave Bryant, also retired and now the national secretary of the Submarines Association of Australia, a similar veterans group. Once, if their paths had crossed at sea, these two would have been Cold War antagonists, not out to kill each other but certainly keen to make life as difficult as possible. But that was then. This was now. Planning a holiday in Europe with his wife, Bryant had contacted the Saint Petersburg club to ask if he could meet them. The reply had been a prompt and welcoming invitation, which was gladly accepted.

The submariners of the world have a bond, a fellowship that transcends national frontiers, ideologies, even enmities. Ian MacDougall described it in a speech made not long after his retirement:

> Submarining has always been a lonely business. Perhaps because of that, we feel a strange kinship with the only other people who really understood what we were doing – other submariners, our allies but also our enemies. The admiration and sympathy allied submariners feel and felt for the German aces of the Second World War is completely incomprehensible to outsiders. The professional respect submariners feel for the Japanese midget submarines, which made their way in but not out of Sydney Harbour is not shared by the rest of the population. Those who served in British submarines during the cold war in the North Atlantic, patrolling the Faroes Gap and elsewhere, and doing what they could when they could, were the first to cry for the men of KURSK, men they would have used every professional skill they possessed to send to their watery graves only a couple of decades before, had the order come through.[1]

Pulling out all the stops, the Russians laid on a VIP program for the Australian. There was a visit to the Submarine Memorial Wall in beachside Sestroretsk, a tour of the Kronstadt navy base, with its great baroque wedding cake of the Saint Nicholas Naval

Cathedral; a splendid restaurant lunch and an inspection of the tsarist cruiser *Aurora*, which had famously fired the first shot of the Bolshevik Revolution of October 1917, and was now berthed in the Neva as a museum and flagship of the navy.

At the cemetery, Igor Kurdin and Dave Bryant paused in solemn silence, the slender Russian in a navy-blue pea coat over his old uniform, the grey-bearded Australian wearing a heavy windcheater with his submariner dolphins embroidered on the chest. The tombstones of lost submariners stood nearby. Kurdin had his own grim memories. One of his old boats, a Yankee-class ballistic-missile submarine, *K-219*, had been scuttled off Bermuda in 1986 after leaking fuel exploded in a missile silo, with four men dead, including a brave twenty-year-old sailor who had shut down both nuclear reactors but drowned in the act. Kurdin had written a book about it. In retirement, he acted as a mentor to veterans and bereaved submariner families.

The wreath was of soft blue and white flowers, the Russian naval colours, with a blue ribbon proclaiming in Russian that it was a tribute from the Submarines Association of Australia, and another ribbon with three simple words in English capitals: 'LEST WE FORGET.' The men laid it reverently on the cobbled base of the memorial and stepped back two paces. Dave Bryant recited 'The Naval Ode' combined with Laurence Binyon's 'For the Fallen', with its evocative fourth verse:

> They have no grave
> But the cruel sea.
> No flower lay at their heads,
> A rusting hulk is their tombstone.
> Afast on the ocean bed.

> They shall grow not old, as we that are left grow old;
> Age shall not weary them, nor the years condemn.
> At the going down of the sun and in the morning
> We will remember them.

> Lest we forget.

Captain Kurdin listened intently as an interpreter translated the lines. The Australian saw tears welling in his eyes.

Exactly at eight-thirty in the morning of 22 April 2015, a cool and cloudy Wednesday, the frigate *Anzac* sailed from the ferry wharf at Çanakkale, that small and ancient seaport on the Asian shore of Turkey, and out into the narrows of the Dardanelles Strait. On the bridge, the captain, Commander Belinda Wood, and her navigator were absorbed in the exacting pilotage that would take them north-east through the busy waterway and into the Sea of Marmara.

Gathered beneath an awning aft on the flight deck there were important people: no less than the Australian Chief of Navy, Vice Admiral Tim Barrett, and the Turkish Fleet Commander, Vice Admiral Veysel Kosele, with a group of other guests, Australian and Turkish, navy and civilian, including Terry Roach, the man who had done the *One and All* rescue in *Otway*, now retired as a commodore after forty-one years' service. In this Anzac centenary year, they were on their way to find an orange buoy floating on Marmara's waters, a buoy marking the resting place of Harry Stoker's submarine *AE2*.

It had been a long journey to get there, starting at a cocktail party in Istanbul in 1994, where the Australian ambassador to Turkey, David Evans, had begun chatting with a Turkish marine archaeologist, Selçuk Kolay, about *AE2*'s penetration of the Dardanelles. Kolay was the director of the Rahmi Koç Museum in Istanbul, a richly endowed gallery of land, sea and air transport artefacts, and his private passion was searching for historic wrecks scattered on the sea floor of Turkish waters. The talk with the ambassador piqued his interest, and he decided to look for the Australian boat.

Kolay spent months digging through Turkish, Australian, British and even German archives, only to find that none of them could agree where *AE2* had been scuttled and where she might be lying after nearly eighty years. Stoker had recorded the position as about seven kilometres north of Karaburun Point, on the southern shore, but Turkish estimates varied widely. Eventually, Kolay settled on an area of some thirty-five square kilometres, a large expanse of water to cover even with the sophisticated sidescan sonar and magnetic imaging he was using. Month after month, time and again, harried by bad weather and equipment failure, he drew a disappointing blank.

In 1996 he thought he had struck gold. He located a wreck of about the same shape and size as *AE2* at a depth of eighty-six metres. It turned out to be a small coastal steamer. Doggedly he pushed on, but it would be another two years before his persistence was rewarded. As the sun was setting on the evening of 11 June 1998, Kolay was about to finish for the day when the screen of the probing magnetometer discovered a large metallic body and exploded with light. The marine archaeologist felt in his bones that it could only be *AE2*.

A month later he and another two divers went down with a camera. He was right. She was lying upright at a depth of seventy-three metres, her lower hull lodged in mud as if she had sunk gracefully to the bottom. Heavy marine growth encrusted her – concretion, the experts call it – a hard, whitish carapace of calcium, shells and barnacles looking like coral to the untrained eye and dotted with feathery sea plants. She was draped here and there with old fishing nets that had snagged on her, but her stern was clearly visible, both propellers protruding. Best of all, her conning tower was instantly recognisable, guarded now by a large and aggressive conger eel, which had taken up residence there.

Next, to convince the Australians. That October, a diving team arrived from Australia to confirm Kolay's discovery and to report back to the federal government. Tim Smith, a maritime archaeologist with the NSW Heritage Office, waited on deck in the Rahmi Koç Museum's research and salvage vessel, *Saros*. He later reported what transpired:

> [T]he search team donned dive gear and entered the water over the wreck. Encumbered by up to 50 kilograms of mixed gas tanks and other equipment, the divers descended into the completely dark depths below. The only illumination was by torch light and

the demanding depth of 73 metres meant that only ten minutes could be spent on the bottom. The divers had a slow 80 minute ascent to the safety of the surface.

For those of us waiting on the research vessel, the scene when the divers broke surface was one of jubilation and emotion. Landing near the conning tower, the divers had been able to confirm that the wreck was indeed the Australian submarine. Even the conning tower hatch by which the crew made their escape was still ajar. Boat horns echoed around the Sea of Marmara as the team signalled the success of the moment. The mystery of the AE2 was finally solved.[2]

This was the beginning, though, not the end, for it posed as many questions as it answered. What, if anything, should be done with *AE2*? And who might do it?

In their retirement, as sailors will, the best of the Cold War Oberon men cherished their past: the boats they had served in, the things they had seen and done, the shipmates they had known. They nurtured these memories in two veterans' organisations, the Submarine Institute of Australia, and the Submarines Association of Australia – 'The first for thinking, the second for drinking,' as one member of both cheerfully explained.

Peter Briggs had left the navy as a rear admiral in 2001 after senior commands ashore. As president of the Submarine Institute from 2006 to 2009, he was ever conscious of those underwater warriors who had gone before, the pioneers of the RAN submarine service, and especially the gallant and ebullient Lieutenant Commander Harry Stoker.

He was not alone in this. A good many RAN people felt that Stoker and his ship's company had been allowed to fade into obscurity, their names forgotten, their deeds unsung. In the Australian story, Gallipoli was an affair of khaki and slouch hats, the legend of brave Anzac diggers confronting 'Johnny Turk' on beaches and ridges – all true enough, but incomplete. Few people had any idea that one of our submarines had been there in the Dardanelles, still less that it had played a pivotal role in the opening days of the campaign.

The navy's part needed to be told, and Briggs and Terry Roach fell to the task with enthusiasm. To do the planning, to cut red tape and raise funds, the Submarine Institute set up an AE2 Commemorative Foundation, approved by the Australian government and the RAN, but at arm's length. Project Silent Anzac was born.

It ran for years. The Turks were curious at first, and slightly suspicious. By the laws of war and the sea, they owned the wreck and everything in it, for Stoker had surrendered it to them and it lay in their waters. As they pointed out, it had been a victory for their ship, the *Sultanhisar*. What were the Australians up to? A conference of Turks and Australians at Ankara in 2008 began to bring things together. Some people wanted to raise *AE2* and place her on dry land as a memorial and a museum.

'Peter and I got involved because we thought it would be a tragedy if the Turks dragged the submarine out of the water and it broke on the way, and it would be demeaning if they put it on display and charged admission,' Roach says.[3]

When the cost of doing that was put at around $100 million and more, the idea was abandoned. She would be preserved in place. There was also the tricky question of her one unexploded torpedo and its obvious dangers. On the plus side, *AE2* was not a war grave. Nobody had died in her, meaning that there was no ethical concern about disturbing human remains.

The more Peter Briggs learned about Harry Stoker, the more he admired him, and with typical energy he mounted a campaign for a posthumous bravery award. The Admiralty had given four Victoria Crosses to RN submarine captains for daring deeds in the Dardanelles but there had been nothing for Stoker, who had shown the others the way. Briggs thought that unjust. If the British would do nothing, then perhaps the Australian government should. He compiled a closely argued case, pages of it, finishing with a flourish:

> Stoker's mission to penetrate the Dardanelles was no accident of history ... he actively sought out the opportunity and tackled it with unflinching courage, initiative and enthusiasm ...
>
> He successfully discharged and exceeded his challenging orders, achieving a major impact on the Ottoman defences, thereby

reducing Allied casualties, gaining a critical breathing space for the hard pressed Anzacs and making an inestimable contribution to the Anzac legend that was forged in the harsh crucible of Gallipoli. He led the way for a submarine campaign that was to deny the Ottoman forces free use of the Sea of Marmara for resupply, preventing them from achieving the preponderance needed to throw the Allies back into the sea, thereby preventing a debacle turning into a disaster.[4]

It was all true but it cut no ice. Best not to second-guess history, they said, not after such a long time, and that was that: regrettably, there could be no medal.

Gradually, Project Silent Anzac came together. The various Turkish authorities – and there were an awful lot of them – turned out to be friendly and 'open to persuasion', Roach found.[5] The plan was to have a full-scale, technically sophisticated exploration of *AE2* in 2014, in preparation for the Anzac centenary a year later. Ambassadors and ministers met, experts of all sorts were recruited. Ian Macleod, a corrosion scientist from Curtin University in Perth, Ken Greig, a former engineer officer in *Onslow* and *Ovens*, and Dr James Hunter, a marine archaeologist from the National Maritime Museum in Sydney, joined the team. There were endless meetings, conferences, workshops. At Corio Bay, near Geelong, they built a full-scale steel mock-up of the submarine's conning tower to work out how to insert a remote-controlled, roving underwater camera. There would also be a diving bell to take the divers down and a platform sunk as a base for them to work from.

For two weeks in June 2014, in mostly fair weather, operating from a Turkish support vessel, *Kapitani Derya-2*, divers and cameras slowly, methodically revealed the submarine's secrets. It was a triumph. Given the length of time she had been underwater, her hull was in remarkably good condition beneath the concretion and the sea plants. The experts thought it too dangerous for the divers to enter the boat, but the cameras revealed all. The interior was stunningly well preserved, the dials and gauges in the control room intact and their markings easily readable. Much of her original paint was still to be seen; the signalman's canvas sandshoes were discovered in the flag locker in the conning tower, with the remains of the flags themselves and *AE2*'s battle ensign. Harry Stoker's bedding was still there in his cabin, with a fluted lampshade above a port decanter on his desk.

They laid down what the scientists called a cathodic protection system, a string of big blocks of zinc that would attract the forces of corrosion away from the metal of *AE2*'s hull. Finally, a bright orange navigation buoy with a light was anchored above her to keep passing ships and fishing boats away.

And so it was that Commander Wood brought her ship there in the centennial year, on a glassy sea of steely blue-grey. With almost theatrical timing, the clouds drifted away to bathe *Anzac* in lambent sunshine as she glided to a stop, with a Turkish frigate watching on. The ceremony itself was polished perfection, the sort the navy does proudly and well: the White Ensign, a bark of orders, the stamp of gleaming boots; the sudden, always startling crack of a rifle salute. There was a solemn silence as the two admirals dropped a wreath of white and purple flowers into the water in memory of the four men who had died in the PoW camps, Petty Officer Stephen Gilbert, Able Seaman Albert Knaggs, Chief Stoker Charlie Varcoe and Stoker Michael Williams. Then the plangent bugle lament of 'The Last Post', the stirring arousal of 'Reveille'.

It was, thought Terry Roach, '[S]ome recognition of the dark blue threads in the khaki blanket that is the Australian Anzac legend. Lumps in throats and a tear in the eye of all Australians present.'[6]

The Silent Anzac lies there still.

With *AE2* done and dusted, Peter Briggs turned his hand to another project. The unexplained loss of *AE1* and the thirty-five souls of her ship's company who had vanished in the waters off New Guinea on 14 September 1914 had haunted the RAN for a century, and the descendants of the crew in Australia, Britain and New Zealand had no explanation for the death of their forebears, nor any place they could think of as a sea grave. Briggs set to solving the mystery.

People had looked before, many times. A naval officer with the Australian High Commission in Port Moresby, Commander John Foster, had searched on and off for years around the Duke of York group of islands, where *AE1* had last been seen by the destroyer *Parramatta* on her way back to Rabaul. In 1976 Foster persuaded the RAN to send the hydrographic survey ship HMAS *Flinders* to take a look with her sidescan sonar, but she found nothing. Fascinated, driven, he kept hunting, often at his own expense, searching archives and hiring divers in the hope that the submarine might have run aground on some uncharted rock or shallow coral reef. The celebrated French oceanographer Jacques Cousteau took a brief look as he was passing through the area in 1990, but also drew a blank.

Foster talked with islanders to probe their tribal memories, and on one expedition in 2003 he learned of a legend among the local Tolai people, who spoke of a 'devil fish' their forefathers had seen on the day of *AE1*'s disappearance, a discovery that spurred him on. The RAN made sporadic attempts as well. Another survey vessel, *Benalla*, and the minehunter *Yarra* were sent in 2007 but also came away empty-handed. John Foster died in 2010, mission incomplete.

With the *AE2* experience under his belt, Briggs hit the deck running. With one hand he did the spadework research, digging into the RAN records of a century ago, including the destroyer *Parramatta*'s last sighting of *AE1* in the midafternoon of that fatal September Monday, fossicking for some clue that might have been missed. The best guess still seemed to be a diving accident, although it was puzzling, with *AE1* due back in harbour by sunset, that her captain, Tom Besant, would have ordered a practice dive when the patrol was done and he was heading for home.

With his other hand Briggs began putting together a team to undertake a new search, which meant gathering the experts to run it and raising the money to pay for it. He set up another not-for-profit company, Find AE Ltd. Its first probe was an echo-sounder survey of the inshore reefs and waters of the Duke of York Islands in November 2015. That turned up nothing, which was disappointing, but at least it told them where the wreck was not. They would have to search in deeper waters.

Good fortune took a turn. John Mullen, a wealthy Sydney businessman and the chairman of Telstra, heard of the project. He had a passion for underwater exploration and maritime archaeology, which he pursued through his private Silentworld Foundation, hunting at first for colonial wrecks around Australia, and he was intrigued by the *AE1* operation. Mullen put up $500,000 of his own money and used his extensive contacts to find more sponsors. After some not-so-gentle arm twisting from Peter Briggs, the Department of Defence threw in another $500,000. A very big piece fell into place when Fugro, a Dutch-owned global geo-survey company, reported that it had a brand-new ship with the very latest technology operating in Papua New Guinean waters. Fugro was willing to make her available for a few weeks between jobs.

With her smart red hull, white upperworks and helicopter platform, MV *Fugro Equator* was perfect for the task. Her dynamic positioning system could hold her fixed to a spot above the ocean floor accurate to about ten metres, no matter what the state of the sea, winds or current. The jewel in her crown was a roving autonomous underwater vehicle, or AUV for short, a robot like a fat, orange-painted porpoise, battery-powered, equipped with echosounders and sonar capable of searching and mapping at depths of up to 3000 metres: so smart, so focused that it could spot a wine bottle lying on the bottom, they said. *Fugro Equator* sailed from Port Moresby on 14 December 2017, with Peter Briggs and his team on board, and in four days she was at the position where *AE1* was last seen, poised on the track the submarine should have taken back to Rabaul.

Time was money, and there was none to waste. The AUV went into the water at midnight on 18 December, creeping back and forth about thirty-five metres above the sea floor in parallel lines, like a tractor ploughing a field, scooping up data for twenty long hours until it was brought back on board again. A computer read the downloaded magic, projecting images on monitor screens in the ship's processing room for the analysts to assess.

At around 9.30 p.m. in the evening of 20 December, Briggs was in his cabin preparing for bed when he was summoned urgently to the room. The two analysts on duty were buzzing with excitement at a grainy, slender image on the screen. Briggs knew that they were looking at *AE1*. 'There it was, this great big lump of stuff on the bottom,' he recalls. 'It didn't look like a submarine; it looked like a pile of rocks. But it was 154 metres long, spot on the right length, and the height was sensible, too.'[7]

It was an electrifying moment. He and his team had been prepared to search for a week and more. Now there she was, discovered in the first few hours of the AUV search, an extraordinary stroke of informed guesswork met by good luck. But there was more to be done, more to ensure beyond any sliver of doubt that they had indeed found the holy grail. They sent down *Fugro Equator*'s drop camera, a large metal frame carrying high-powered LED lights and still and video cameras to film in colour, lowered from the ship by cable.

It took an agonisingly long time to descend through hazy green water, Briggs seated at a desk before the wall of screens in the processing room, the team behind him watching over his shoulder in tense silence. Nigel Erskine, Head of Research at the National Maritime Museum, was there and later described the experience:

> [T]he sudden appearance of a fish signals that we are getting close to the submarine.
>
> Moments later there are more fish and then, gradually, a recognisable shape of one of *AE1*'s hydroplanes comes into shot. It takes a moment to figure out which end of the submarine we are looking at before Peter Briggs begins to direct operations. In communication with the bridge, technicians in the processing room relay Peter's orders – 'Half a metre to starboard'; 'One metre forward'; 'Lower the camera half a metre' – and we gradually move along the submarine's hull, excited by the clarity of the pictures as more-recognisable features come into view. Up to this point the team had been unwilling to officially confirm the discovery, but any lingering doubts about the vessel's identity were now completely removed by the stunning pictures of the

submarine's fin, with the bridge helm and forward periscope clearly visible. After several hours the drop camera survey was finally completed and the room erupted in spontaneous applause.[8]

Briggs turned to the small knot of men watching on. 'There is no one around that looks like that,' he said. He was beaming with pleasure. 'We have found *AE1*.'

The search had been a triumph beyond their most optimistic hopes. They held a brief, solemn ceremony of remembrance on deck as the news flashed back to Australia, to the navy and the Defence Department, to the media and, above all, to the descendants of the lost men. Vera Ryan, from Sydney, the niece of Engine Room Artificer John 'Jack' Messenger, a 28-year-old from Ballarat, spoke for them all:

> He was never lost to the naval community. He was always, to them, waiting to be found. The submariners who followed, wearing his big boots, never gave up on him, and a dedicated, skilled team of people worked tirelessly to solve the mystery.
> And they found him.[9]

The discovery after 103 years made front pages around Australia, reported in detail under big headlines. Peter Briggs told *The Australian* that it had been:

> 'a very satisfying, sad feeling to discover the location of 35 English, Australian and one New Zealander who died doing their best for the country. It's a sombre moment, but also tinged with a warm glow of success . . .
> '[W]e've found the men of *AE1*, we've found the wreck, we've got some insight into its condition, and that opens the next chapter: learning exactly what happened to it. It will be quite a detective puzzle . . . what's happened will be an interesting challenge.'[10]

Viewing the camera images, Briggs and the other two submariners on *Fugro Equator*, Roger Turner (ex-RN) and Gus Mellon (a retired RAN engineer officer), had quickly noticed a critical fact. *AE1*'s hydroplanes, both fore and aft, were in the 'hard to rise' position. That meant, certainly, that she had dived and that Tom Besant had been trying to bring her back to the surface. For some reason, it had not worked. There could be no doubt about it: the submarine had kept going down, past her 'crush depth', where her hull could no longer withstand the pressure of water and she had imploded, the sea rushing in upon her.

But why had it happened? The question remained to be answered.

News of the *AE1*'s discovery quickly spread. The American billionaire and philanthropist Paul Allen, a co-founder of the Microsoft Corporation alongside the better-known Bill Gates, was an enthusiastic undersea archaeologist with his own survey ship, RV *Petrel*, and he offered it to the *AE1* team free of charge. This stroke of good luck was Peter Briggs's chance to get more answers, and he seized it with alacrity.

Petrel, splendidly equipped, had just come from discovering the wreck of the US aircraft carrier *Lexington*, sunk in the Battle of the Coral Sea in 1942 and found at a depth of 3000 metres some 800 kilometres east of the coast of Queensland. By April 2018 she was stationed above *AE1*, with Briggs and his small team on board. To deter possible scavengers, the wreck's exact location off the Duke of York Islands had been kept secret; it was reported only that she had been found at a depth of over 300 metres. She was a war grave, not to be disturbed or desecrated, although the Find *AE1* team was surprised and not a little annoyed to learn that Australian law only recognised and protected war graves on land, not at sea. (Disturbingly, that inconsistency has still not been fixed.)

Petrel's great asset for underwater exploration was the Triton 6000, a remotely operated vehicle, or ROV, a machine the size of a small truck armed with lights and cameras of all sorts and purposes and with a mechanical arm and claw, operated from a control room in the ship. Over two days, the ROV roamed above and alongside the submarine, pumping out exactly 8367 images and some twenty-five hours of full high-definition video.

Digital stills taken every five seconds by one of the cameras would eventually be mixed by the marine archaeologists at

Curtin University in Perth to compose a beautifully sculpted computer image of *AE1* at rest. The pictures were breathtaking, stunningly clear, showing her shattered, rusted hulk in shades of green and orange and ochre and encrusted with marine growth, anemones and feathery sea plants, the steel crushed in several places with jagged, gaping holes, through which eels and tropical fish in shades of fluorescent pink lazily came and went. There was no sign of human remains but soon enough some possible answers to the great questions began to emerge.

Firstly, why did she dive? Crucially, the images showed that the caps on her stern and bow torpedo tubes were open, suggesting that Tom Besant had taken her down to make ready for a torpedo attack. 'I think something frightened him,' Peter Briggs says. 'I think on the balance of probability he felt threatened by something and ordered a crash dive – "klaxon, klaxon and stand by bow and stern tube" . . . and down he went.'[11]

This was not mere guesswork but the considered judgement of an experienced submarine commanding officer who had weighed the evidence piece by piece. What might that threat have been? The German administration had a small vessel in the area, *Kolonial Gesellschaft*, a little, single-funnelled steamship that plodded from island to island on the Kaiser's business. The destroyer *Yarra* had glimpsed her the previous night, and it is plausible that *AE1* encountered her again on her way back to Rabaul – perhaps caught by surprise as she rounded a jungled point. It was known that *Kolonia*, as she was usually called, carried a Maxim one-pounder machine gun mounted on her foredeck – not by any means a heavy weapon but more than enough to punch holes in a submarine's pressure hull from close range. Without a deck gun of her own, *AE1*'s only defence would have been to dive and then attack with torpedoes.

Four days later, the cruiser *Encounter* found *Kolonia* aground on New Britain island, abandoned and with the gun missing, but shell cases were scattered about the mounting on her deck, suggesting the gun had been fired. Her crew and passengers, some of whom were German army reservists, eventually turned up in Rabaul and surrendered, but – incredibly – nobody thought to question them.

Why did the dive lead to disaster? Shockingly, the ROV revealed that the submarine's main ventilation valve had been left more than half-open. This was an inlet to admit fresh air into the submarine when surfaced, aft of the conning tower, about 150 centimetres wide, manually operated by turning a wheel: it should have been closed immediately the order to dive was given. Evidently, and tragically, it was not. The sea would have surged in unstoppably, flooding her stern section as she went under. As soon as he realised what was happening, Besant would have ordered an emergency return to the surface, but the submarine – growing heavier, losing buoyancy with every passing second – would have been sinking by the stern. And here another stab of ill fortune played its fatal part: only one of her two motors was working, so only one propeller shaft was turning. She had sailed from Rabaul that morning with her starboard main motor out of action, and the port motor alone did not have the power to take her back to the surface. Down, down she went.

Those last moments would have been terrifying. Men stationed aft must have struggled and quickly drowned in the rush of water from the open valve. In the control room, Besant would have been shouting orders for full power on the port motor, shouting orders to surface while the helmsman and the planesmen struggled at their controls and tonnes of sea water surged towards them. Electrical power would have been lost, stopping the motor and plunging the boat into darkness and beyond hope.

Death must have been instantaneous as *AE1* sank below her crush depth and the pressure hull imploded on the way down to eternity.

Danger stalks the submariner still.

In February 2003, off Western Australia, the Collins-class boat HMAS *Dechaineux* came within seconds of disaster and death when a simple sea water hose burst, flooding the lower motor room. She was on the limit when it happened, near her deep diving depth, with no margin for safety. (The exact figure is classified but it's below 180 metres.)

Dechaineux's captain, Commander Peter Scott, confronted exactly the same peril that had beaten Tom Besant in *AE1*. As he described it later in his memoirs:

> The emergency orders ring out and are immediately acknowledged by the operators. The panel watchkeeper cracks the valves to hear the rattle, blast and hiss of high-pressure air pushing into the ballast tanks. The Chief of the Boat lifts and artfully holds the nose of the submarine. The revolutions come on and we start to surge forward. They know the drill and are already onto it.
>
> In an instant, everything has changed. We have gone from knowing the state of our submarine in intimate detail to endless unknowns.
>
> Breathe.
>
> My heart is beating through my neck. I know – we all know – that if we go down in this depth of water we will be crushed by the pressure before we hit the bottom. Once the pressure hull splits the ocean's onslaught will be absolute in its violence. Though it be the world to us, the ocean would fill our submarine as effortlessly as it would fill my lungs, without a moment's hesitation or a skerrick of remorse. There is no coming back.
>
> Breathe.[12]

A lone sailor stationed in the cramped lower motor room, Able Seaman Geordie Bunting, was nearly drowned when the force of the torrent jammed him beneath the exit ladder. He was saved when two mates, Greg Sullivan and Michael Morris, risked their own lives to haul him upwards through a narrow hatch. Training and discipline held fast. Luck came good, as Scott described:

> After hanging in suspense for what seems an eternity, the descent below Deep Diving Depth is mercifully arrested. The depth gauge needle twitches . . . then twitches again . . . and we finally begin to rise, wrestling from the grip of the depths. Our steadily building speed, driven by the immense power of the propellor, brings life and lift to the hydroplanes. The emergency blow on the main ballast tanks begins to overcome the external pressure, disgorging 400 tonnes of sea water back out into the ocean.[13]

Dechaineux burst to the surface like a breaching whale, then slumped back into the Indian Ocean to limp back to HMAS *Stirling*. It had been a close-run thing, a hair's breadth between life and death. Another few seconds, another few tonnes of water, and she and her ship's company of fifty-five would have been lost like *AE1*.

Essentially, a submarine – any submarine – is an inert metal tube only brought to life by the men, and now men and women, who serve in it. At their best, they are a unique breed, as described eloquently and persuasively by Ian MacDougall:

> The world has never actually been able to make up its mind about what it thinks of submariners and so has chosen not to think about us much at all. It's just too difficult to decide whether we are a group of gallant warriors saving our countries or a shaggy bunch of overgrown adolescents in peculiar pullovers, prone to sinking anything that floats simply for our own amusement.
>
> They find the hard questions with which we deal too slippery to come to grips with – should we be picking up survivors, or machine-gunning them in the water? Should we operate like regular forces and give the enemy a fair chance at us or is it really necessary for stealth to be our shield? Are we too sneaky and devious to be tolerated in the Pantheon of Heroes or are we the bravest men they have ever known? Don't we, of all military forces, cost too much with our constant demand for better boats, better equipped, grubbing up money which could be so much more worthily spent on surface classes and preservation of the pink-nosed paper rat?
>
> We could have fixed all that of course – we could have explained loudly and often, in short sentences using simple words, why it is important that any island nation has a submarine force and just how submarines and submariners project that force. We could have detailed our operations and told our 'warries' out loud, sung our own praises and waved our own banners. We could have had our pictures in the paper and our heads on television, spilled our

secrets and pushed our own barrows. We could have lobbied and campaigned for medals and ribbons and cured the empty chest disease that afflicts so many here today. And the public would have listened and watched and loved us because this is a country so hungry for heroes that it applies the word to people who play sport for money.

Unique in this, as in so much else, we chose not to. We had other priorities. The efficient and effective performances of our duties. Support for our own and friendly forces. The gathering of useful intelligence. The preservation of the lives of our people. The protection of our country. We chose to keep secrets, not to tell them.

Sometimes this cost us dear. We kept secrets from those who love us, even the most trustworthy. We shut them out of the most demanding, dangerous, and gruelling aspects of our lives. We came home silent and shaky. We dreamt bad dreams and woke coughing our lungs up. We smelt bad most of the time. We pretended, with much less than complete success, to be normal. We asked them to share that pretence with us, and God love them, they did. And, the problems continue today – in our bodies, our minds and our way of relating to the world. It is a price we gladly paid and keep on paying. We are proud of what we did and of the men we did it with.[14]

Those men hold that pride close in their retirement. The men and women who sail our submarines today know the history of their calling and accept the risks they face. They follow in the wake of those who went before them with confidence and courage, proud wearers of their hard-won dolphins, modestly content that they do their duty.

I met a lot of them while writing this book. They are quality people, fine Australians. My admiration for them is unbounded.

ACKNOWLEDGEMENTS

Many people helped me to write this book, some of them old friends, others newly encountered. In every case their kindness and their interest were truly gratifying and they added immeasurably to the story.

The idea for *Dive!* came from the Chief of Navy, Vice Admiral Mark Hammond, when we met at a café overlooking the Fleet Base at Woolloomooloo early in 2023. A distinguished submariner himself, he encouraged me all the way and has done me the honour of writing the foreword.

Many other naval friends pitched in as they have done with earlier books, including the all-seeing, all-knowing Lieutenant Commander Desmond Woods; Commander Greg Swinden; Commodore Ivan Ingham; and Rear Admiral Lee Goddard. They were ever available for advice and suggestions. Vice Admiral Peter Jones, a fine historian and biographer himself, cheerfully answered my more obscure questions.

Retired RAN submariners are a close-knit fraternity and they offered unstinting comment and interest. I'm especially grateful to Commander David Nicholls, the Executive Director of the Submarine Institute of Australia. Commander Peter Horobin was a fountain of fact and information, often delightfully sardonic and amusing, taking no end of trouble to point me in the right direction. Commander Frank Owen, Commodore Peter Scott, Commodore Terry Roach and Rear Admiral Peter Briggs were invaluable sources for both the big picture and small but important detail. Many of them gave me hours of their time, in conversations and in writing. Warrant Officer David Bryant's memories and yarns were a delight. Best of all, each of these men trusted that I would strive to get the story right.

Though we have not met, I am also grateful to Dr Michael White – sailor, barrister and historian – whose two encyclopaedic volumes of *Australian Submarines: A History* were a priceless reference point. The works of the distinguished naval historians David Stevens and Tom Frame were as reliable as ever. At the British end, I thank Barrie Downer of the Barrow-in-Furness Submariners Association for information he provided.

The Royal Australian Navy Sea Power Centre in Canberra is a priceless national asset, a treasure trove of naval knowledge. My thanks to its Commanding Officer, Captain Alastair Cooper; the Head of Navy History & Heritage, Miesje de Vogel; and to Rob Garratt, Petar Djokovic and John Perryman.

Family of people mentioned in the story were a pleasure to talk to. I thank Dacre Stoker of South Carolina, USA, for permission to quote from the memoirs of his kinsman Commander Harry Stoker. Vera Ryan, a descendant of John Messenger of *AE2*, offered great help, as did Ruth Shean, the daughter of the matchless X-craft submariner Max Shean. The family of the late Vice Admiral Sir Ian McIntosh, including Alistair McArthur, kindly gave permission for me to quote extensively from his fascinating letter to his mother. Further afield, my thanks also to Tom Pringle, Roll Keeper of the Dull and Weem parish church in Scotland, for tracking the details of Max Shean's wartime marriage.

The Melbourne journalist Geoffrey Barker, who wrote with authority about defence matters and especially on Australian submarines in the Cold War, very generously offered me the benefits of his research, and chapters of an unpublished book. That was a lode of gold.

Jennifer Bucher and Janet Greenlee of Vulcan Inc. swiftly and kindly arranged for me to use the MV *Petrel* pictures of *AE1* on the sea floor. Associate Professor Andrew Woods, of the Centre for Marine Science and Technology at Curtin University in Western Australia, and Dr James Hunter, the Curator of Naval Heritage and Archaeology at the Australian National Maritime Museum in Sydney, steered me in that direction. They do sterling work.

Publisher Allen & Unwin gave permission to quote from *Beneath the Dardanelles* by the Turkish writers Vecihi and Hatice Basarin. Every effort has been made to track the owners of other copyright where necessary, but many are simply lost in the shadows of time. If any come forward, I will be happy to acknowledge them in future editions.

Once again, my warmest thanks to my friends at Penguin Random House. Alison Urquhart, the non-fiction publisher, and Catherine Hill, the managing editor, are the steadfast, loyal and inspiring book people that authors dream of encountering. Julian Welch did a marvellous edit on the manuscript, sprucing up my prose and saving me from a good few tricky errors of fact.

My elder son, James Carlton, a talented computer artist and games designer, did the beautiful line illustrations and maps for *Dive!*, as he has done for my earlier books of naval history. My other son, Lachlan, and my wife, Morag Ramsay, happily tolerated my long spells locked away in my study.

My gratitude goes to everyone mentioned here. Each, in their own way, has enriched the book. Any errors of fact or opinion are all mine.

BIBLIOGRAPHY

Books

Affleck, James (ed.). *Geelong Grammarians at World War Two*. Old Geelong Grammarians Inc., Melbourne, 2002.

Ambrose, Stephen E. *D-Day: June 6, 1944: The Climactic Battle of World War II*. Simon & Schuster, New York, 1995.

Basarin, Vecihi and Hatice. *Beneath the Dardanelles*. Allen & Unwin, Sydney, 2008.

Bastock, John. *Australia's Ships of War*. Angus & Robertson, Sydney, 1975.

Bean, C.E.W. *Official History of Australia in the War of 1914–1918 – Volume I – The Story of ANZAC*. Australian War Memorial, Canberra.

Beesly, Patrick. *Very Special Intelligence*. Hamish Hamilton, London, 1977.

Beevor, Antony. *The Second World War*. Weidenfeld & Nicolson, London, 2012.

Besant, Arthur Digby. *Besant Family Pedigree*. Besant & Co., London, 1930.

Billett, Janet Roberts. *The Yachties*. Australian Scholarly Publishing, Melbourne, 2023.

Bishop, Patrick. *Target Tirpitz*. Harper Press, London, 2012.

Braeuer, Luc. *U-Boat Ace Adalbert Schnee*. Schiffer Publishing, Pennsylvania USA, 2015.

Brenchley, Fred and Elizabeth. *Stoker's Submarine*. HarperCollins, Sydney, 2001.

Brodie, C.G. *Forlorn Hope 1915: The Submarine Passage of the Dardanelles*. Frederick Books, London, 1956.

Burnell, Frederick Spencer. *Australia versus Germany: The Story of the Taking of German New Guinea*. George Allen & Unwin Ltd, London, 1915.

Byrski, Liz. *Spectacular Australian Sea Rescues*. New Holland, Sydney, 1997.

Caddick-Adams, Peter. *Sand & Steel*. Penguin Random House, London, 2019.

Churchill, Winston S. *The Second World War. Vols I, II, III, IV, V, VI*. Houghton Mifflin, Boston, 1958. *The World Crisis, Volume I*. Thornton Butterworth, London, 1923.

Cunningham, Admiral of the Fleet Viscount Andrew. *A Sailor's Odyssey.* Hutchinson, London, 1951.
Dönitz, Großadmiral Karl. *Memoirs: Ten Years and Twenty Days.* Weidenfeld & Nicolson, London, 1959.
Edwards, Bernard. *The Cruel Sea Retold.* Pen & Sword, Barnsley, UK, 2009.
Eisenhower, Dwight. *Crusade in Europe.* New York, Doubleday, 1948.
Fell, Captain W. R. *The Sea Our Shield.* Cassell & Co., London, 1966.
Fisher, Admiral of the Fleet Lord. *Memories and Records.* George H. Doran, New York, 1920.
Frame, Tom. *No Pleasure Cruise.* Allen & Unwin, Sydney, 2004.
Frame, T. R. and Swinden G. J. *First In, Last Out.* Kangaroo Press, Sydney, 1990.
Fuhrer Conferences on Naval Affairs. Chatham Publishing, London, 2005.
Fyfe, Herbert C. *Submarine Warfare Past, Present and Future.* Grant Richards, London, 1902.
Gallagher, Thomas. *Against All Odds.* Pan Books, London, 1971.
Gilbert, Martin. *The Second World War.* Weidenfeld & Nicolson, London, 1989.
——*First World War*, Weidenfeld & Nicolson, London, 1994.
Gill, G. Hermon. *Australia in the War of 1939–1945. Royal Australian Navy 1939–1942*, and *Royal Australian Navy 1942–1945.* Australian War Memorial, Canberra.
Hall, Keith. *X3 to X54: The History of the British Midget Submarine.* History Press, London, 2023.
Halsey, Willliam F. & Bryan, J. *Admiral Halsey's Story.* McGraw-Hill Inc., New York & London, 1947.
Hamilton, General Sir Ian. *Gallipoli Diary.* George H. Doran, New York, 1920.
Hamilton-Kenny, Fred. 'Letter Diary, 29 August–19 October 1914'. State Library New South Wales, MLMSS 930/Item 1.
His Majesty's Submarines. HM Stationery Office, London, 1945.
Hough, Richard. *The Great War at Sea.* Oxford University Press, Oxford, 1983.
Hunting Tirpitz. Admiralty Records. University of Plymouth Press, Plymouth, 2012.
Jacobsen, Alf R. *X-Craft Versus Tirpitz.* Sutton Publishing UK, 2006.
James, Robert Rhodes. *Gallipoli.* Pimlico, London, 1999.
Jones, Peter. *Australia's Argonauts.* Barallier Books, Geelong, 2016.
Jose, A. W. *Official History of Australia in the War of 1914–18, vol. IX. The Royal Australian Navy.* Angus & Robertson, Sydney, 1938.
Kemp, Paul. *Underwater Warriors.* Brockhampton Press, UK, 1996.
Kennedy, Ludovic. *Menace: The Life and Death of the Tirpitz.* Sphere Books, London, 1981.
Kerr, Greg. *Lost Anzacs: The Story of Two Brothers.* Oxford University Press, Melbourne, 1997.
Kinder, Harry. Private diary.

King-Hall, Commander Stephen. *North Sea Diary 1914–1918*. Newnes, London, 1927.

Konstam, Angus. *Tirpitz in Norway*. Osprey Publishing, Oxford, 2019.

Lund, Paul and Ludlam, Harry. *Nightmare Convoy*. Foulsham & Co, London, 1987.

Mackay, Ruddock F. *Fisher of Kilverstone*. Clarendon Press, Oxford, 1973.

MacKenzie, S. S. *Official History of Australia in the War of 1914–18, vol. X. The Australians at Rabaul*. Angus & Robertson, Sydney, 1938.

MacKenzie, William. *The Secret History of SOE*. St Ermin's Press, UK, 2000.

Massie, Robert K. *Dreadnought: Britain, Germany and the Coming of the Great War*. Jonathan Cape, London, 1991.

——*Castles of Steel: Britain, Germany, and the Winning of the Great War at Sea*. Random House, New York, 2003.

McGuire, Frances. *The Royal Australian Navy*. Oxford University Press, Melbourne, 1948.

Mitchell, Pamela. *The Tip of the Spear*. Richard Netherwood, UK, 1993.

Monsarrat, Nicholas. *The Cruel Sea*. Cassell & Co., London, 1951.

——*Three Corvettes*. Cassell & Co., London, 1975.

——*Life Is a Four Letter Word, vols I and II*. Cassell & Co., London, 1970.

Moore, Robert. *A Time to Die*. Random House, London, 2002.

Morgenthau, Henry. *Ambassador Morgenthau's Story*. Doubleday, Page & Company, Garden City & New York, 1918.

Rohwer, J. and Hummelchen, G. *Chronology of the War At Sea 1939–1945*. Greenhill Books, London, 1992.

Seal, Graham and Blake, Lloyd. *Century of Silent Service*. Boolarong Press, Queensland, 2013.

Sebag-Montefiore, Hugh. *Dunkirk*. Viking, London, 2006.

Shean, Max. *Corvette and Submarine*. Privately published, Perth, 1992.

Smyth, Jennifer. *The Long Silence*. Privately published, Melbourne, 2007.

Sontag, Sherry and Drew, Christopher. *Blind Man's Bluff*. Hutchinson, London, 1988.

Spurling, Kathryn. *The Mystery of AE1*. Missing Pages Books, Canberra, 2014.

Stevens, David (ed). *The Royal Australian Navy in World War II*. Allen & Unwin, Sydney, 1996.

——*The Royal Australian Navy: A History*. Oxford University Press, Melbourne, 2001.

Still, John. *A Prisoner in Turkey*, The Bodley Head, London, 1920.

Stoker, Commander H. G. *Straws in the Wind*. Herbert Jenkins Ltd., London, 1925.

Suckling, Charlie. Private diary.

The Submarine Commander Pocket Manual 1939–1945. Casemate Publishers, Oxford, 2018.

Van Der Vat, Dan. *Stealth at Sea*. Weidenfeld & Nicolson, London, 1994.

Walker, Frank and Mellor, Pamela. *The Mystery of X5*. William Kimber, London, 1988.

Warren, C. E. T. and Benson, James. *Above Us the Waves.* George Harrap, London, 1953.
Watkins, Paul. *Midget Submarine Commander.* Pen & Sword, Barnsley UK, 2012.
West, Frank. *Lifeboat Number Seven.* William Kimber, London, 1960.
Wester-Wemyss, Admiral of the Fleet Lord Rosslyn. *The Navy in the Dardanelles Campaign.* Naval & Military Press, UK, 2010.
Wheat, John Harrison. Diary. NSW State Library. collection.sl.nsw.gov.au/record/9Bv70PO9.
White, Dr Michael. *Australian Submarines, a History, Vols I and II.* Australian Teachers of Media Inc., Melbourne, 2015.
Zetterling, Niklas and Tamelander, Michael. *Tirpitz.* Casemate Publishers, UK, 2009.

Reports, documents

'Main Report – Finding the Men of AE1 – 20 December 2017, Version 2', November 2018. Fugro Equator.
Mercan, Evren. 'The Impact of Allied Submarine Operations on Ottoman Decision-making during the Gallipoli Campaign'. *Journal for Maritime Research*, 2017.
'Operation Silent Anzac, Report to the Australian Government on the Assessment Phase, HMAS *AE2*, 2008'. *AE2* Commemorative Foundation.
'Project Silent Anzac, Report to the Australian & Turkish Governments', February 2015. *AE2* Commemorative Foundation.
'Research Vessel Petrel, Baseline Survey of HMAS *AE1*'. Australian National Maritime Museum, Sydney, 2018.

Websites

There is simply no space to list the dozens upon dozens of websites used in research for this book. But I have selected some of the more significant for further reading:

Australian National Library, Newspapers, trove.nla.gov.au/newspaper
Australian National Maritime Museum, sea.museum
Australian War Memorial, awm.gov.au
Drebbel's Submarine, sea.museum/2013/11/07/drebbles-submarine
HMAS *Onslow* Virtual Tour, sea.museum/2021/videos/360-degree-tour-of-onslow
Holbrook Submarine Museum, holbrooksubmarinemuseum.com.au/index.php/about-us/hsm
Imperial War Museum, London, iwm.org.uk
Military History, Department of Veterans' Affairs, anzacportal.dva.gov.au
National Archives of Australia, naa.gov.au
National Museum of the Royal Navy, nmrn.org.uk
RAN Sea Power Centre, navy.gov.au/spc-a

Royal Navy Submarines Association, rnsubs.co.uk
Submarine Institute of Australia, submarineinstitute.com
Submarines Association Australia, submarinesaustralia.com
US Navy History and Heritage Command, history.navy.mil
Wikipedia also provides a useful guide to almost every ship and many of the people, battles and incidents appearing here.

ENDNOTES

Chapter 1: Damned Un-English
1. The Hon. Robert Boyle, *New Experiments Physico-Mechanical: Touching the Spring of the Air and Their Effects*, Oxford, 1662, p. 188.
2. William Brenchley Rye, *England as Seen by Foreigners in the Days of Elizabeth & James the First*, John Russell Smith, London, 1865.
3. Gerrit Tierie, *Cornelis Drebbel (1572–1633)*, H.J. Paris, Amsterdam, 1932.
4. Louis Figuier, *Les merveilles de la science*, Furne Jouvet, Paris, 1867.
5. Herbert C. Fyfe, *Submarine Warfare Past, Present and Future*, Grant Richards, London, 1902, p. xiv.
6. The wreck of the *Hunley* was raised in 2000 and is on display at a museum in Charleston.
7. Fyfe, *Submarine Warfare Past, Present and Future*, p. 28.
8. Robert K. Massie, *Dreadnought: Britain, Germany and the Coming of the Great War*, Jonathan Cape, London, 1991, p. 452.
9. RN Subs, 'Story of the First Dive', n.d., rnsubs.co.uk/articles/service/first-dive.html.
10. H.G. Wells, *Anticipations of the Reaction of Mechanical and Scientific Progress Upon Human Life and Thought*, Chapman & Hall Ltd, London, 1902, chapter 6.
11. The journalists would heap praise upon Fisher in their reports. He, in turn, would write to the Admiralty modestly deploring this unexpected and embarrassing publicity.
12. Ruddock F. Mackay, *Fisher of Kilverstone*, Clarendon Press, Oxford, 1973, p. 297.
13. Winston Churchill, *Great Contemporaries*, Thornton Butterworth, London, 1937, p. 265.
14. Fisher agitated to make a swift, pre-emptive strike on the German fleet in harbour at Kiel on the Baltic. King Edward VII talked him out of it.
15. Admiral of the Fleet Lord Fisher, *Memories and Records*, George H. Doran, New York, 1920.

16 Fisher, *Memories and Records*.
17 Her rusting remains still sit in Half Moon Bay, east of Melbourne.
18 HMCS stood for 'Her Majesty's Colonial Ship'.
19 Lord Tweedmouth, quoted in G.L. McCandie, *The Genesis of the Royal Australian Navy*, Government Printer, Sydney, 1949, p. 183.
20 Creswell, Ibid, p. 206.
21 *The Age*, 12 December 1907.
22 Approximately $9 million in 2024.
23 *Evening News*, 16 December 1907.
24 *Lone Hand*, 1 August 1908.
25 A.W. Jose, *Official History of Australia in the War of 1914–18, Volume IX – The Royal Australian Navy, 1914–1918*, Australian War Memorial, Canberra, 1928, p. xxvii.
26 *The Argus*, 26 March 1909.
27 Quoted in David Stevens (ed.), *The Royal Australian Navy: A History*, Oxford University Press, Melbourne, 2001, p. 20.
28 McCandie, *The Genesis of the Royal Australian Navy*, p. 277.
29 McCandie, *The Genesis of the Royal Australian Navy*, p. 288.

Chapter 2: Straws in the Wind
1 Harry Kinder, Private diary.
2 *Hansard, House of Commons*, 11 June 1913.
3 The origins of the term 'the Andrew' are lost, but it may refer to one Andrew Miller, who ran a famously brutal press gang during the Napoleonic Wars.
4 Arthur Digby Besant, *Besant Family Pedigree*, Besant & Co., London 1930, p. 243.
5 Besant service record, UK National Archives, ADM 196/143/268.
6 Henry Stoker, *Straws in the Wind*, Herbert Jenkins, London, 1925, p. 65.
7 Stoker, *Straws in the Wind*, p. 7.
8 As a young man, he added the name Dacre to become Henry Hugh Gordon Dacre Stoker, in the hope of receiving a handsome inheritance from a rich uncle of that name. It didn't happen.
9 Stoker, *Straws in the Wind*, p. 16.
10 Stoker, *Straws in the Wind*, p. 17.
11 The gunroom was the midshipmen's quarters in a big ship.
12 Stoker, *Straws in the Wind*, p. 19.
13 Stoker, *Straws in the Wind*, p. 21.
14 Fisher had two great passions outside the navy: dancing and listening to Anglican sermons. He did both to excess.
15 Stoker, *Straws in the Wind*, p. 44.
16 Stoker service record, UK National Archives, ADM 196/143/268.
17 Stoker, *Straws in the Wind*, p. 48.
18 Kinder, Private diary.
19 National Archives of Australia MP472/1, 16/14/4771.

Chapter 3: Australia Welcomes Her Defenders

1. Thomas Besant, 'Submarines AE1 and AE2 – propellers – damage', NAA, MP472/1, 16/14/5983.
2. Kinder, Private diary, p. 14.
3. Besant, 'Submarines AE1 and AE2 – propellers – damage'.
4. Henry Stoker, 'HMA Submarines AE1 and AE2 – voyage to Australia [including log book]', NAA, MP472/1, 16/14/4771.
5. *Sunday Times*, 7 June 1914.
6. Stoker, *Straws in the Wind*, p. 50.
7. 'Three badges' were awarded for twelve years' good conduct.
8. Stoker, 'HMA Submarines AE1 and AE2 – voyage to Australia [including log book]'.
9. Stoker, *Straws in the Wind*, p. 51.
10. The young officer's name is lost to history. Presumably he had come from Yarmouth for the ride.
11. Stoker, *Straws in the Wind*.
12. *Sunday Times*, 7 June 1914.
13. Stoker, *Straws in the Wind*, p. 53.
14. Stoker, *Straws in the Wind*, p. 55.
15. *Sydney Morning Herald*, 6 May 1914.
16. *Sunday Times*, 7 June 1914.
17. *Northern Territory Times and Gazette*, 7 May 1914.
18. *Express & Telegraph*, Adelaide, 6 May 1914.
19. *Sunday Times*, 7 June 1914.
20. Stoker, *Straws in the Wind*, p. 55.
21. Kinder, Private diary, p. 15.
22. Besant, 'Submarines AE1 and AE2 – propellers – damage'.
23. *Evening Telegraph*, 23 May 1914.
24. *Sydney Morning Herald*, 25 May 1914.
25. *The Sun*, 25 May 1915.
26. Stoker, *Straws in the Wind*, p. 60.

Chapter 4: The Unthinkable

1. Franz Ferdinand was both.
2. *Sydney Morning Herald*, 1 July 1914.
3. Speech at the *Berliner Schloss*, 31 July 1914.
4. Winston S. Churchill, *The World Crisis*, Volume I, Thornton Butterworth, London, 1923.
5. *The Age*, 6 August 1914.
6. Stoker, *Straws in the Wind*, p. 61.
7. 'Table money' was an entertainment allowance. All up, equivalent to $360,000 in 2024.
8. Alec Doyle, 'Diary', AWM RR/85/073. Doyle would become the RAN's first engineer admiral.
9. Gerald Hill, 'Memoir', AWM IDRL/351.

10 S.S. MacKenzie, *Official History of Australia in the War of 1914–18*, vol. X. *The Australians at Rabaul*, Australian War Memorial, 10th edition, 1941.
11 Patey, 'Private papers', Australian War Memorial, AWM 2DRL/795.
12 NSW State Archives and Records, NRS 13660 [4-71511].
13 Fred Hamilton-Kenny, 'Letter Diary, 29 August–19 October 1914', p. 12, State Library New South Wales, MLMSS 930/Item 1.
14 MacKenzie, *The Australians at Rabaul*, p. 35.
15 MacKenzie, *The Australians at Rabaul*, p. 50.
16 *Sydney Morning Herald*, 6 October 1914.
17 Doyle, 'Diary'.
18 Gus Shea, 'Private papers', AWMPR 00895.
19 *Advertiser*, 10 November 1914.
20 Ambrose O'Hare, 'Diary', AWM, MLMSS 1840.
21 Frederick Spencer Burnell, *Australia versus Germany: The Story of the Taking of German New Guinea*, George Allen & Unwin Ltd, London, 1915, p. 131.
22 Burnell, *Australia versus Germany*, p. 132.
23 Burnell, *Australia versus Germany*, p. 136.
24 Hamilton-Kenny, 'Letter Diary, 29 August–19 October 1914', p. 21.
25 Hamilton-Kenny, 'Letter Diary, 29 August–19 October 1914', p. 18.
26 *Sydney Morning Herald*, 15 September 1914.
27 *Sydney Morning Herald*, 15 September 1914.
28 *Sydney Morning Herald*, 15 September 1914.
29 Kinder, Private diary, p. 18.

Chapter 5: Goodbye to *AE1*
1 Kinder, Private diary, p. 19.
2 John Harrison Wheat, 'Wheat war diaries and narratives, February 1914–ca. 1920', Item 01, p. 16, State Library New South Wales, 9Bv70PO9.
3 Stoker, *Straws in the Wind*, pp. 65–67.
4 Stoker, 'Loss of Submarine AE1. Submitting report from Lieut Stoker as to the reasons he assigns for above loss', NAA: MP472/1, 16/14/8314.
5 RAN Statement, 19 September 1914.
6 *Daily Telegraph*, 21 September 1914.
7 *Advertiser*, 21 September 1914.
8 *The Sun*, 20 September 1914.
9 Hamilton-Kenny, 'Letter Diary, 29 August–19 October 1914', p. 134.
10 Hamilton-Kenny, 'Letter Diary, 29 August–19 October 1914', p. 135.
11 Stoker, *Straws in the Wind*, p. 72.
12 MacKenzie, *The Australians at Rabaul*, p. 111.
13 Stoker, *Straws in the Wind*, p. 74.
14 Sir John Forrest, a former explorer, was the first premier of Western Australia, the first federal MP for Swan and a long-term federal cabinet minister.

15 William Morris 'Billy' Hughes was the seventh prime minister of Australia, serving from 1915 to 1923.
16 Stoker, *Straws in the Wind*, p. 77.
17 Henry Morgenthau, *Ambassador Morgenthau's Story*, Doubleday, Page & Company, Garden City & New York, 1918, p. 13.
18 'Treaty of Alliance Between Germany and Turkey 2 August, 1914', The Avalon Project, Yale Law School, avalon.law.yale.edu/20th_century/turkgerm.asp.
19 Morgenthau, *Ambassador Morgenthau's Story*, pp. 64–65.
20 Quoted in Martin Gilbert, *First World War*, Weidenfeld & Nicolson, London, 1994, p. 104.
21 Winston S. Churchill, 'Guns of August 1914–2014 – "The terrible 'ifs' accumulate": The Escape of the Goeben', *Finest Hour*, no. 163, 6 February 2015. (Reprinted from Winston Churchill, *The World Crisis 1911–1914*.)
22 Minute by Churchill, 30 October 1914, Public Records Office, Kew, UK, Admiralty 137/96.
23 Morgenthau, *Ambassador Morgenthau's Story*, p. 161.

Chapter 6: Generally Run Amuck
1 Quoted in Gilbert, *First World War*, p. 124.
2 Lord Hankey, *The Supreme Command, 1914–1918: Volume I*, Routledge, London, 1961, pp. 265–56.
3 Quoted in Ruddock F. Mackay, *Fisher of Kilverstone*, Clarendon Press, Oxford, 1973, p. 482.
4 Stoker, *Straws in the Wind*, p. 86.
5 Kinder, Private diary, p. 26.
6 Chris Buckey, Simon Harley & Tony Lovell, (editors-in-chief), 'Sackville Hamilton Carden', The Dreadnought Project, dreadnoughtproject.org/tfs/index.php/Sackville_Hamilton_Carden.
7 C.G. Brodie, *Forlorn Hope 1915: The Submarine Passage of the Dardanelles*, Frederick Books, London, 1956, p. 53.
8 Stoker, *Straws in the Wind*, p. 92.
9 Sir Ian Hamilton, *Gallipoli Diary*, George H. Doran, New York, 1920.
10 Hamilton, *Gallipoli Diary*.
11 Hamilton, *Gallipoli Diary*.
12 Hamilton, *Gallipoli Diary*.
13 Hamilton, *Gallipoli Diary*.
14 Quoted in Robert K. Massie, *Castles of Steel: Britain, Germany, and the Winning of the Great War at Sea*, Random House, New York, 2003, p. 462.
15 Massie, *Castles of Steel*.
16 Massie, *Castles of Steel*.
17 Paul McNeil, 'Submarine E15', 31 May 2015, timedetectives.blog/2015/05/31/submarine-e15.
18 Brodie, *Forlorn Hope 1915*, p. 13.

19	Stoker, *Straws in the Wind*, p. 101.
20	Wheat, 'Wheat war diaries and narratives, February 1914–ca. 1920', Item 01, p. 13.
21	Charles Suckling, Private papers, p. 12.
22	Stoker, *Straws in the Wind*, p. 102.
23	Kinder, Private diary, p. 26.
24	Kinder, Private diary, p. 27.
25	Stoker, *Straws in the Wind*, p. 105.
26	Stoker, *Straws in the Wind*, p. 106.

Chapter 7: Abandon Ship!

1	C.E.W. Bean, *Official History of Australia in the War of 1914–1918 – Volume I – The Story of ANZAC*, Ch XII, The Landing at Gaba Tepe.
2	Kinder, Private diary, p. 27.
3	Suckling, Private papers, p. 9.
4	Stoker, *Straws in the Wind*, p. 108.
5	1 point is 11.25 degrees of the compass.
6	Wheat, 'Wheat war diaries and narratives, February 1914–ca. 1920', Item 01, p. 15.
7	Kinder, Private diary, p. 30.
8	Stoker, *Straws in the Wind*, p. 118.
9	Wheat, 'Wheat war diaries and narratives, February 1914–ca. 1920', Item 01, p. 17.
10	An Australian soldier, quoted in Robert Rhodes James, *Gallipoli*, Pimlico, London, 1999, p. 115.
11	Hamilton, *Gallipoli Diary*.
12	Hamilton, *Gallipoli Diary*.
13	Hamilton, *Gallipoli Diary*, p. 129.
14	Royal Australian Navy, 'HMAS *AE2*', navy.gov.au/hmas-ae2.
15	Hamilton, *Gallipoli Diary*.
16	Stoker, *Straws in the Wind*, p. 122.
17	Kinder, Private diary, p. 34.
18	Vecihi Basarin and Hatice Basarin, *Beneath the Dardanelles: The Australian Submarine at Gallipoli*, Allen & Unwin, Sydney, 2008, p. 112.
19	Stoker, *Straws in the Wind*, p. 137.
20	Kinder, Private diary, p. 35.
21	Basarin and Basarin, *Beneath the Dardanelles*, p. 119.
22	Stoker, *Straws in the Wind*, p. 138.
23	Kinder, Private diary, p. 37.
24	Kinder, Private diary, p. 37.
25	Stoker, *Straws in the Wind*, p. 141.

Chapter 8: Arrival at Prisoner Avenue

1	Basarin and Basarin, *Beneath the Dardanelles*, p. 128.
2	Suckling, Private papers, p. 37.

3   Wheat, 'Wheat war diaries and narratives, February 1914–ca. 1920', Item 01, p. 24.
4   Suckling, Private papers, p. 23.
5   Suckling, Private papers, p. 24.
6   Kinder, Private diary, p. 52.
7   Senate, *Hansard*, 20 May 1915.
8   Senate, *Hansard*, 20 May 1915. Bridges had actually died two days earlier, on 18 May.
9   *Sydney Morning Herald*, 21 June 1915.
10 *Courier*, 22 September 1915.
11 Stoker, *Straws in the Wind*, p. 221.
12 Morgenthau, *Ambassador Morgenthau's Story*, p. 259.
13 Kinder, Private diary, p. 79.
14 Quoted in Greg Kerr, *Lost Anzacs: The Story of Two Brothers*, Oxford University Press, Melbourne, 1997, p. 159.
15 Herbert Brown, Private papers.
16 M. Williams to W. Hughes, National Archives, MP472/1.
17 John Still, *A Prisoner in Turkey*, The Bodley Head, London, 1920, p. 202.
18 Wheat, 'Wheat war diaries and narratives, February 1914–ca. 1920', Item 01, p. 54.
19 Archibald was the great-grandson of Admiral Thomas Cochrane, Earl of Dundonald, a storied hero of the Napoleonic Wars and the inspiration for the novelist Patrick O'Brien's character Jack Aubrey.
20 Stoker, *Straws in the Wind*, p. 269.
21 Stoker, *Straws in the Wind*, p. 273.
22 Stoker, *Straws in the Wind*, p. 286.
23 Wheat, 'Wheat war diaries and narratives, February 1914–ca. 1920', Item 01, p. 58.
24 Wheat, 'Wheat war diaries and narratives, February 1914–ca. 1920', Item 01, p. 74.
25 Wheat, 'Wheat war diaries and narratives, February 1914–ca. 1920', Item 01, p. 79.
26 Wheat, 'Wheat war diaries and narratives, February 1914–ca. 1920', Item 01, p. 89.

Chapter 9: Entrances and Exits
1   Craig Tibbitts, 'Casualties of War', *Wartime*, no. 85, 2019, awm.gov.au/wartime/article2.
2   *London Gazette*, 22 April 1919.
3   Stoker, *Straws in the Wind*, p. 304.
4   Stoker, *Straws in the Wind*, p. 314.
5   *Sydney Mail*, 6 May 1925.
6   *Western Mail*, 13 May 1926.
7   *The Sun*, 11 August 1935.
8   Stoker, Scrapbooks.

9   Quoted in Fred and Elizabeth Brenchley, *Stoker's Submarine*, HarperCollins, Sydney, 2001, p. 207.
10 Morgenthau, *Ambassador Morgenthau's Story*, p. 386.
11 Still, *A Prisoner in Turkey*, p. 145.
12 See collection.sl.nsw.gov.au/record/92eVVVNY.
13 Massie, *Castles of Steel*, p. 780.

Chapter 10: First to the Perisher
1   Quoted in Peter Jones, *Australia's Argonauts*, Echo Books, Geelong, 2016, p. 158.
2   *The Sun*, 15 July 1919.
3   *Herald*, 16 July 1919.
4   Quoted in Michael White, *Australian Submarines: A History*, Vol. I, Australian Teachers of Media Inc., Melbourne, 2015, p. 223.
5   *Naval Defence: Report of Admiral of the Fleet, Viscount Jellicoe of Scapa on Naval Mission to the Commonwealth of Australia, May–August 1919*, Melbourne, Government Printer, 1919, p. 222.
6   Peter Smith, 'Captain Frank Edmund Getting, RAN – 1899–1942', Naval Historical Society of Australia, navyhistory.au/captain-frank-edmund-getting-ran-1899-1942.
7   Approximately $66 million in 2024.
8   *The Sun*, 21 August 1942.
9   *Daily Telegraph*, 21 August 1942.

Chapter 11: Lifeboat Number Seven
1   House of Commons, *Hansard*, 26 September 1939.
2   Winston Churchill, *The Second World War, Volume 2: Their Finest Hour*, Cassell, London, chapter 2.
3   'McIntosh, Ian Stewart (Oral history)', Imperial War Museums, Cat. no. 11950, iwm.org.uk/collections/item/object/80011690.
4   A light vessel was in effect a lighthouse on a ship.
5   Whale Island, at Portsmouth, was the Royal Navy's gunnery school.
6   Ian McIntosh, Letter to his mother, quoted in James Affleck (ed.), *Geelong Grammarians at World War Two*, Old Geelong Grammarians Inc., Melbourne, 2002.
7   A counter stern: the upper deck is longer than the waterline, overhanging the water like a shelf.
8   'McIntosh, Ian Stewart (Oral history)', Imperial War Museums.
9   If there was a warship, it never appeared. *Thor* returned safely to Hamburg on 30 April, after 329 days at sea and having covered over 100,000 kilometres. On the way home, she destroyed three more merchant ships and forced the surrender of yet another British armed cruiser, HMS *Voltaire*. Kähler was awarded Nazi Germany's highest decoration, the Knight's Cross with Oak Leaves, and survived the war as a rear admiral.
10 Frank West, *Lifeboat Number Seven*, William Kimber, London, 1960, p. 17.

11 West, *Lifeboat Number Seven*, p. 32.
12 McIntosh, letter, p. 513.
13 McIntosh, letter, p. 513.
14 West, *Lifeboat Number Seven*, p. 53.
15 McIntosh, letter, p. 517.
16 West, *Lifeboat Number Seven*, p. 85.
17 Ian McIntosh, 'Lifeboat No. 7 – 23 Days at Sea', Naval Historical Review, September 2008, navyhistory.au/lifeboat-no-7-23-days-at-sea.
18 West, *Lifeboat Number Seven*, p. 105.
19 McIntosh, letter, p. 520.
20 West, *Lifeboat Number Seven*, p. 114.
21 McIntosh, 'Lifeboat No. 7 – 23 Days at Sea'.
22 McIntosh, 'Lifeboat No. 7 – 23 Days at Sea'.

Chapter 12: Special and Hazardous Service
1 'McIntosh, Ian Stewart (Oral history)', Imperial War Museums.
2 Max Shean, *Corvette and Submarine*, self-published, Perth, 1992, p. 6.
3 Shean, *Corvette and Submarine*, p. 21.
4 Shean, *Corvette and Submarine*, p. 27.
5 Shean, *Corvette and Submarine*, p. 36.
6 Shean, *Corvette and Submarine*, p. 38.
7 *U-559* would also sink the Australian sloop HMAS *Parramatta* in the Mediterranean in November 1941. In October 1942 she was captured disabled on the surface and her Enigma codebooks were seized by the RN.
8 Shean, *Corvette and Submarine*, p. 48.
9 Schnee survived the war. He later ran a sailing school on the island of Elba. Taking little trouble to hide his Nazi past, he was a longserving chairman of the *Verband Deutscher Ubootfahrer*, the Association of German U-boat crews.
10 Shean, *Corvette and Submarine*, p. 118.
11 Shean, *Corvette and Submarine*, p. 120.
12 Commander Luigi Durand de la Penne (as told to Captain Virgilio Spigai), 'The Italian Attack on the Alexandria Naval Base', *Proceedings*, vol. 82, no. 2, usni.org/magazines/proceedings/1956/february/italian-attack-alexandria-naval-base.
13 De la Penne, 'The Italian Attack on the Alexandria Naval Base'.
14 After the Italian armistice, de la Penne was released from a PoW camp to fight on the Allied side. In 1946 he was presented with the *Medaglia d'oro al Valor Militare*, the Gold Medal for Military Valour. Delightfully, it was pinned to his chest by the Royal Navy's Vice Admiral Sir Charles Morgan, who had been captain of *Valiant* when de la Penne attacked her.
15 Churchill to Curtin, 19 January 1942. HMS *Barham*, a battleship, was torpedoed and sunk by *U-331* in the Mediterranean on 25 November 1941 but the U-boat captain did not see the result of his work.

16   Winston Churchill, *The Second World War, Volume IV: The Hinge of Fate*, Houghton Mifflin, New York, 1950, Appendix C.
17   Captain W.R. Fell, *The Sea Our Shield*, Cassell, London, 1966, p. 11.

Chapter 13: Attack the *Tirpitz*!
1   Shean, *Corvette and Submarine*, p. 122.
2   Winston Churchill to Chiefs of Staff Committee, 25 January 1942.
3   Winston Churchill, *The Second World War, Volume IV: The Hinge of Fate*, Houghton Mifflin, New York, 1950.
4   One of the crimes for which Keitel, a Hitler sycophant, was hanged in 1946.
5   Shean, *Corvette and Submarine*, p. 122.
6   The names $X1$ and $X2$ had already been used for other vessels.
7   Frank Walker & Pamela Mellor, *The Mystery of X5: Lieutenant H. Henty-Creer's Attack on the Tirpitz*, William Kimber, London, 1988, p. 25.
8   Shean, *Corvette and Submarine*, p. 136.
9   Walker & Mellor, *The Mystery of X5*, p. 141.
10   Churchill to Pound, 5 May 1943.
11   Fell, *The Sea Our Shield*, p. 180.
12   Shean, *Corvette and Submarine*, p. 169.
13   His Majesty's Submarines. HMSO, 1945.

Chapter 14: More Frightened Than I Have Ever Been . . .
1   Shean, *Corvette and Submarine*, p. 174.
2   The Sami people, indigenous to northern Norway and Sweden, were once known as Lapps, living in Lapland. The term is no longer used.
3   The British gave their gun turrets an initial: A and B turrets for'ard, X and Y aft. The Germans used names: Anton, Bruno, Caesar, Dora.
4   Pamela Mitchell, *The Tip of the Spear*, Richard Netherwood, UK, 1993, p. 99.
5   Quoted in Fell, *The Sea Our Shield*, p. 193.
6   'X-craft and Operation Source', WW2 People's War, BBC, 7 November 2004, bbc.co.uk/history/ww2peopleswar/stories/77/a3237077.shtml.
7   *Tirpitz* log, 22 September 1943, *The London Gazette*, 10 February 1948.
8   Quoted in Alf R. Jacobsen, *X-Craft Versus Tirpitz: The Mystery of the Missing X5*, R. Sutton Publishing, Gloucestershire, 2006.
9   Mitchell, *The Tip of the Spear*, p. 92.
10   Mitchell, *The Tip of the Spear*, p. 92.
11   Mitchell, *The Tip of the Spear*, p. 94.
12   Admiralty account, 1944, HMSO.
13   Barry to Admiralty, 8 November 1943.
14   Barry to Admiralty, 8 November 1943.
15   Barry to Naval Secretary to First Lord, 2 February 1944.
16   Barry to Eulalie Creer, private correspondence, quoted in Walker & Mellor, *The Mystery of X5*.

Chapter 15: Operation Postage Able

1. Shean, *Corvette and Submarine*, p. 178.
2. Robbie Burns, 'The Birks of Aberfeldy', 1787. 'Birks' is the Scots word for birch trees.
3. Shean, *Corvette and Submarine*, p. 179. The Twin Trees, ancient oaks, are still there.
4. Ross Parker and Hughie Charles, 'There'll Always Be an England', 1939.
5. Interview with Donald Wilson, 12 May 2003, Australians at War Film Archive, australiansatwarfilmarchive.unsw.edu.au/archive/121-donald-wilson.
6. Interview with Donald Wilson, 12 May 2003.
7. Interview with Donald Wilson, 12 May 2003.
8. 'HMS *Untiring* (p. 59)', uboat.net/allies/warships/ship/3564.html ADM 199/1818.
9. Interview with Donald Wilson, 12 May 2003.
10. Interview with Donald Wilson, 12 May 2003.
11. recordsearch.naa.gov.au/ Donald Rupert Wilson.
12. The other two were Lieutenant Commanders Geoffrey Gellie and William Littlejohn, both from Melbourne.
13. Quoted in Rob Crane, 'January 1944', *COPP Survey*, coppsurvey.uk/january-1944.
14. Quoted in Rob Crane, 'January 1944'.
15. Quoted in Rob Crane, 'January 1944'.
16. Quoted in Rob Crane, 'January 1944'.
17. Quoted in Rob Crane, 'January 1944'.
18. Quoted in Rob Crane, 'January 1944'.
19. Quoted in Paul Kemp, *Underwater Warriors*, Brockhampton Press, UK, 1996, p. 169.
20. Quoted in Kemp, *Underwater Warriors*.
21. Mitchell, *The Tip of the Spear*, p. 120.
22. Shean, *Corvette and Submarine*, p. 205.

Chapter 16: 'Okay. We'll Go.'

1. Shean, *Corvette and Submarine*, p. 209.
2. Shean, *Corvette and Submarine*, p. 213.
3. Shean, *Corvette and Submarine*, p. 214.
4. In 1919, Ramsay, then a commander, had been an aide to Admiral of the Fleet Lord Jellicoe on his fact-finding inspection of Australia's naval defences.
5. Squadrons 460, 463, 466 and 467.
6. Ken Hudspeth, 'X-Craft: X20 in the English Channel', *Naval Historical Review*, September 1994, navyhistory.au/x-craft-x20-in-the-english-channel.
7. Dwight Eisenhower, *Crusade in Europe*, New York, Doubleday, 1948, p. 249.

8 Quoted in Peter Caddick-Adams, *Sand and Steel: A New History of D-Day*, Penguin, London, 2019, p. 350. An aide found the note months later and kept it for posterity.
9 Quoted in Stephen E. Ambrose, *D-Day: June 6, 1944: The Climactic Battle of World War II*, Simon & Schuster, New York, 1995.
10 Hudspeth, 'X-Craft: X20 in the English Channel'.
11 Hudspeth, 'X-Craft: X20 in the English Channel'.
12 Shean, *Corvette and Submarine*, p. 225.
13 Shean, *Corvette and Submarine*, p. 226.
14 Fell, *The Sea Our Shield*, p. 209.

Chapter 17: Operation Sabre
1 One of the dead was an Australian, Lieutenant William Twiss RANVR, of South Australia.
2 Fell, *The Sea Our Shield*, p. 213.
3 Fell, *The Sea Our Shield*, p. 214.
4 William F. Halsey III & J Bryan, *Admiral Halsey's Story*, McGraw-Hill Inc., New York & London, 1947, p. 262.
5 Interview with Ken Briggs, 3 October 2003, Australians at War Film Archive, australiansatwarfilmarchive.unsw.edu.au/archive/1019.
6 Thirty-five of them were built in Australia for the RAN.
7 Interview with Ken Briggs, 3 October 2003.
8 Interview with Ken Briggs, 3 October 2003.
9 Winston Churchill, Mansion House speech, 10 November 1942.
10 Interview with Ken Briggs, 3 October 2003.
11 Fell, *The Sea Our Shield*, p. 218.
12 Quoted in Keith Hall, *X3 to X54: The History of the British Midget Submarine*, The History Press, London, 2023.
13 Fell, *The Sea Our Shield*, p. 224.
14 Fell, *The Sea Our Shield*, p. 228.

Chapter 18: To the Saigon River
1 C.E.T. Warren & James Benson, *Above Us the Waves*, George Harrap, London, 1953, p. 220.
2 Shean, *Corvette and Submarine*, p. 242.
3 Quoted in Mitchell, *The Tip of the Spear*, p. 190.
4 'Potsdam Declaration', *Atomic Archive*, atomicarchive.com/resources/documents/hiroshima-nagasaki/potsdam.html.
5 Quoted in Richard B. Frank, *Downfall: The End of the Imperial Japanese Empire*, Penguin, New York, 1999, p. 235.
6 Samuel J. Cox, 'H-057-1: Operations Downfall and Ketsugo – November 1945', Naval History and Heritage Command, January 2021, history.navy.mil/about-us/leadership/director/directors-corner/h-grams/h-gram-057/h-057-1.html.
7 'Announcing the Bombing of Hiroshima', *American Experience*, PBS, pbs.org/wgbh/americanexperience/features/truman-hiroshima.

8 Hirohito broadcast speech, 15 August 1945.
9 Shean, *Corvette and Submarine*, p. 252.
10 'Chifley Victory Speech', Anzac Portal, Department of Veterans' Affairs, anzacportal.dva.gov.au/resources/chifley-victory-speech.
11 Fell, *The Sea Our Shield*, p. 246.
12 *Signals*, 19 August 1945.
13 *Sydney Morning Herald*, 7 September 1945.
14 Shean, *Corvette and Submarine*, p. 254.
15 *Sunday Times*, 16 September 1945.
16 Shean, *Corvette and Submarine*, p. 254.
17 *Daily News*, 29 November 1945.
18 *Daily News*, 8 December 1945.
19 Interview with Ken Briggs by Rob Willis and Olya Willis, 20 June 2009, Oral History and Folklore Collections, National Library of Australia.
20 *Daily Telegraph*, 25 November 1945.

Chapter 19: Enter the Oberons
1 The order was US Navy, UK Royal Navy, Royal Canadian Navy, then the RAN, which included 2617 women in the WRANs.
2 David Stevens, *The Royal Australian Navy: A History*, Oxford University Press, Melbourne, 2001, p. 151.
3 In today's dollars, approx $171.2 million.
4 For various technical reasons the two rear tubes were eventually sealed and not used.
5 Lorrimer had been a sub-lieutenant in the sloop HMS *Amethyst*, trapped by the Chinese communists for three months in 1949 in what became known as the Yangtse Incident.
6 Frank Cranston, *Canberra Times*, 24 August 1967.
7 Conversation with the author, 22 October 2023.

Chapter 20: The Cold War
1 *The Centenary of Australian Submarines*, Submarine Institute of Australia, 2014.
2 Conversation with the author, October 2023.
3 Conversation with the author, October 2023.
4 Conversation with the author, October 2023.
5 Conversation with the author, October 2023.
6 White, *Australian Submarines*.
7 Directorate of Intelligence, 'The Soviet Air and Naval Presence at Cam Ranh Bay, Vietnam: An Intelligence Assessment', CIA, June 1984, cia.gov/readingroom/document/cia-rdp91t01115r000100190003-2.
8 *Canberra Times*, 15 November 1985.
9 White, *Australian Submarines*.

Chapter 21: In Memoriam

1. Ian MacDougall, Speech at the National Patron of the Submarines Association Australia, at the Holbrook submarine memorial, 9 June 2001.
2. Tim Smith, 'Report on the Inspection of *AE2*', NSW Heritage Office, 1998.
3. Conversation with the author, 3 December 2023.
4. Peter Briggs, Submission to the Defence Honours Tribunal, 2011.
5. Briggs, Submission to the Defence Honours Tribunal.
6. Email to the author, 4 December 2023.
7. Conversation with the author, 21 November 2023.
8. Nigel Erskine, 'Finding AE1', *Signals*, no. 122, March 2018, sea.museum/2018/03/21/finding-ae1.
9. Submarine Institute of Australia, *Finding the Men of AE1*, 11 June 2020, youtube.com/watch?v=Mv5z2ZoJRdM.
10. *The Australian*, 21 December 2017.
11. Conversation with the author, October 2023.
12. Commodore Peter Scott, *Running Deep: An Australian Submarine Life*, Fremantle Press, Fremantle, 2023, p. 182.
13. Scott, *Running Deep*, p. 183.
14. MacDougall, Speech at the National Patron of the Submarines Association Australia, at the Holbrook submarine memorial, 9 June 2001.

INDEX

Note: in the text, ship and base names are in italics. In the index, ship names only are in italics.

A-class submarines 9, 190
  A1 9
  A5 9
  A8 9
  A9 9
  A10 29
Abbott, Chief Petty Officer Harry 'Scratcher' 41
Abdül Hamid 4
Aberfeldy 275–6, 299, 309–10, 311, 315, 347
Aboukir, HMS 91
Above Us the Waves (1953) 353
acoustic signature 389
Adamant, HMS 37, 113
Admiral Hipper 237
AE1, HMAS 20, 24–5, 33, 65, 83
  finding the wreck 410–15
  first crew 24–32
  German New Guinea 66–7, 77–8
  journey to Australia 36, 38–9, 40–58
  loss of 79–86, 183, 415–17
AE2, HMAS 20, 24, 33–6, 65, 83, 90, 91, 183, 405–10
  AIF personnel, escorting 93
  Dardanelles campaign x, xxi, 102–8, 112–20, 122–8, 130, 131–9
  diagram xvii
  finding the wreck 405–10
  first crew 26, 30, 31, 41
  German New Guinea 66–7, 77–8
  journey to Australia 37–9, 40–58
  media reports on loss of 144–5
  POWs, crew as 140–60

Project Silent Anzac 408–10
propeller, problems with 44–5, 48, 55, 57, 87
Suva 87–8
Afion Kara Hissar 142, 148, 149, 151–2, 159, 160
AG Vulcan 179
AG Weser 179
Agamemnon, HMS 110
Agincourt, HMS 95
Aguila, SS 222, 224, 225, 226
Aitken, Sub-Lieutenant Robert 263–4
Ajax 188
Albion, HMS 104
Aldergrove 226
Alecto, HMS 295
Alexandria 160, 196, 198, 279
  Italian Naval strike on 229–32, 233, 243, 247
Allen, Paul 415
Allied Expeditionary Force 300–2
Altafjord 250, 255, 259, 293, 345, 356
Alva 224, 226
Anemone, HMS 242
Anson, HMS 292, 316
anti-submarine training 182–3, 217–18, 277
Antrim, HMS 182
Anzac 405, 410
Aorangi, SS 68, 320
Arab-Israeli War 375
Ari Burnu 121
Ark Royal, HMS 134
Arkhipov, Executive Officer Vasily 388

Armenian genocide 142, 149–50, 173
Arnauld de la Perière, Lothar von 175
Arnold-Forster, Lieutenant Forster Delafield 6–7
Arthur 239
Asdic 182–3, 190, 218, 221–2, 224, 225, 280, 296, 308, 372
Asquith, Henry 101, 102, 171
Athena, SS
Atlantic, Battle of the 183, 197, 218, 228, 247
atom bomb 341–3
AUKUS agreement (2021) 401
Aurora 404
Australia, HMAS 19, 23
  WWI service 62, 64–5, 68, 80, 87, 90, 193
  WWII service 316
Australian Imperial Force (AIF) 79
Australian maritime strategy x–xi, 13–20
Australian Naval and Military Expeditionary Force (ANAMEF) 66, 73
Australian Submarine Corporation 377

B-class submarines 9
  B2 9
  B6 114
  B8 29
  B11 98–9, 114, 162
Bacon, Captain Reginald 9
Baie de la Seine 285
Baker, Alberta 84
Baker, Cyril 84
Barenfels 298–9
Barker, Geoffrey 391, 398
Barrett, Vice Admiral Tim 405
Barrow 30–1
Barry, Rear Admiral Claud 247–8, 249, 253–4
  Operation Source 252, 253, 255, 270–3
Barton, Edmund 13
Batavia 48, 190
Bath 222–3, 224, 225
Baton Rouge, USS 389
The Battle of the River Plate (1956) 352
battlecruisers 10, 11, 18–19, 97, 236, 395
  Dardanelles campaign 97, 104, 110
  German Navy 252, 271
  HMAS *Australia see Australia*, HMS
  Royal Navy 97, 104, 110, 236, 243
battleships 5, 10–11, 17–18, 32, 56, 101
  Battle of the Atlantic 175, 235–8
  Dardanelles campaign 97, 104, 106, 110, 11, 114
  German Navy 235–6, 261–2, 270, 317

'Great White Fleet' 16
King George V class 236
post-WWI treaty conditions 178, 180
Royal Navy 229–31, 237, 271, 292, 316, 318–19
Turkish, seizure of 94, 96
US Navy 236, 237, 318
Beatty, Admiral Sir David 188
Beazley, Kim 368, 396
Beck, Wally 208–9
Belemedik 150–1, 155, 158
Belfast 309
Belgravian 220
Bellinger, Eva 173
Benalla 411
Benson, James 353
Beresford, Dawne 350
Bergen 293, 295, 310, 311, 347
Bergius, Sub-Lieutenant Adam 'Jock' 326, 327, 335–6, 353
Bermuda 214, 358
Berrima, HMAS 66–8, 71, 73, 93, 102
Besant, Annie 25
Besant, Edgar 25–6, 84
Besant, Lieutenant Commander Thomas 25–7, 32, 36, 45, 65, 75, 82, 83,
  AE1, journey to Australia 41, 42, 52–3, 57
  German New Guinea 67, 77–8
  loss of *AE1* 80–2, 84, 411, 414, 416, 417, 418
Besant, Sir Walter 25
Bestre, Jeanne 292
Binyon, Laurence 404
  'For the Fallen' 404
Birdwood, Lieutenant General William 129–30
Bismarck 236
Black Sea 94, 96
Blanche Bay 62, 68, 74, 77
Bletchley Park 270
Bligh, Lieutenant William 195
Bluebell, HMS 218–23, 226, 228–9, 315
  Convoy OG 71 222–3, 226
Blythe, Lieutenant Charles 291–2
Board of Invention and Research 182
Bolsheviks 161, 171
Bonaparte, Napoleon 2
Bonaventure, HMS 251, 253, 292, 299, 313, 345–6, 353
  Pacific War 315–16, 326–31, 340, 342, 344
  post-war service 349–51
Bond, Lieutenant Tom 73

boredom 46–7
Bounty, HMS 195
Bouvet 104, 110, 111
Bowen, Lieutenant Rowland 70, 71
Boyd, Lieutenant Robert 'Bobby' 278, 280, 282, 284
Boyle, Lieutenant Commander Edward 113, 133, 162
  J-class submarines 183–5
Boyle, Robert 182
Bradley, General Omar 289
Brandt, Captain Frank 38, 45, 89
Braun, Eva 325
Bray, Jack 24–5
Bray, Petty Officer Cecil 124, 168, 169, 191
Breslau 96
Bridges, Major General William 129, 145
Briggs, Ethel 349
Briggs, Flight Lieutenant Ross 349
Briggs, Lieutenant Commander Peter 383–7
  AE1, finding 410–16
  AE2, finding 407–8
Briggs, Sub-Lieutenant Ken 319–24, 334–5, 345–6, 384
  return home 349–50
Brisbane, HMAS 169
Britain
  post-WWI armament 181–3
  Royal Navy *see* Royal Navy
Britannia, SS 26, 27, 83
  Lifeboat Number Seven 201–14
  sinking of 198–201
British Mediterranean Fleet 103
British Pacific Fleet 316–18
Britnell, Lieutenant Willie 332, 333
Brock, Sir Osmond de Beauvoir 191
Brodie, Lieutenant Commander Charles 106, 107, 113–14, 129–30
Brodie, Lieutenant Commander Theodore 113–14, 124
Brooks, Sub-Lieutenant Joe 292, 296, 297, 299, 309–10, 313
Broomhead, Harry 42
Brown, Stoker Petty Officer Herbert 150, 169
Bryant, David 373–7, 403–5
bulkheads 12, 33
Buller, Midshipman Reg 71
Bunting, Able Seaman Geordie 418
Burnell, Fred 73
Bushnell, David 2
buzz bombs (doodlebugs) 310–11

C-class submarines 9, 15, 16, 19
  C11 9
  C12 26
  C14 9
  C30 26
Cam Ranh Bay 392–4, 396
Cameron, Lieutenant Donald 251, 272, 353
  Operation Source 251, 261–2
Campanula, HMS 227
Campion, HMS 227
Canberra, HMAS 193–4, 395–6
Canham, Lieutenant Rick 382
Canopus, HMS 89, 104
Cantlie, Commander Colin 189
Cap Saint-Jacques (Vung Tau) 332
Cape Helles 97, 120
Cape Matapan, Battle of 229
Carden, Vice Admiral Sackville 105, 106
Carey, Lieutenant David 327–8
Cary, Lieutenant John Pitt 102, 138, 153, 169–70
Cerberus 13
Cerberus (base) 277, 374
Challenger, HMS 22
Chanak (Çanakkale) 123, 125, 405
chariots 238–9, 251, 353
Charlemagne 104, 111
Chauvel, General Henry 160
Chelmer 107
Chiang Kai-shek 341
Chifley, Ben 344
Churcher, Lionel 131
Churchill, Winston 24, 56, 60, 109, 170, 172, 197, 231–2, 323
  Battle of the Atlantic 197, 236, 238
  'Churchill's Toy Shop' 232
  colonial imperialism 317
  Dardanelles campaign 100–2, 104, 106, 112, 113, 171
  Potsdam Declaration 341
  Special Services 232, 247–8
  WWI 91, 95, 97
Cid Harbour 326, 327
Ciscar 224
Claiborne, Captain Henri 326–7
Clan Davidson 351
Clark, Lieutenant Commander Paul 304–5
Clemenceau, Georges 177
clinometer xiv
Clogstoun-Willmott, Lieutenant Commander Nigel 285–6, 289–90
Clonlara 226
Cochrane, Lieutenant Commander Archibald 153, 154, 155

Cockatoo Island 57
Cold War 357, 375, 387–92
  arms race 387–8
  'ISR' operations 390–2, 396–8
Coles, ERA Vernon 'Ginger' 296, 297, 298, 313, 334, 353, 356
Collie, Captain Alexander 200
Collingwood, HMS 299
Collins, Tony 373
Collins-class submarines 377, 399, 401, 417
  Collins, HMAS 399
  Dechaineux, HMAS 417–19
Collins, Vice Admiral Sir John 399
collisions
  Cold War 388–9
  early submarine 9
Combined Operations Pilotage Party (COPP) 285
Commonwealth Naval Force 13, 14, 18–19, 22
conning tower 6, 12, 34
convoys (WWII) 252
  37th Escort Group 219
  Convoy HX 112 218–19
  Convoy OG 68 219–20
  Convoy OG 71 222–8
  Convoy PQ 17 237, 247
Cook, Joseph 60
Coptic 218
Coral Sea 62, 415
Cornwallis, HMS 104, 105
Coultas, Brian 380
Courtney, Stoker John 72
Cousteau, Jacques 411
Cradock, Rear Admiral Sir Christopher 'Kit' 89
Craig, Pat 350
'Crazy Ivan' 388
Creer, Commander Reginald 243
Cressy, HMS 91
Creswell, Captain Randolph 170
Creswell, Lieutenant Colin 170
Creswell, Lieutenant Edmund 170
Creswell, Rear Admiral Sir William Rooke 14–16, 19, 170
  loss of *AE1* 84
crew 32–3, 299, 367–8, 403, 419–20
  clothing 21
  early volunteers 21–39
  long-distance patrol 361–7
  Oberon-class 359–60
  'pirate rig' 362–3
  prisoners of war 140–60, 262, 264–5, 272, 353, 356, 410
  wages 367–8

The Cruel Sea (1953) 352
cruise missiles 372, 395
  Granit 395
  Shipwreck 395
Cuban Missile Crisis 388
Cullen, Ruby 171
Cullen, Stoker Jim 158, 159, 171
Cunningham, Ernest Semple 'Dick' 164
Cunningham, Jean 164
Curtain, Chief Petty Officer John 380
Curtin, John 231
Cuthbertson, Lieutenant Commander Charles 227
Cyclops, HMS 192

D-class submarines 9–10, 22
  D2 22–3
D-Day landings 285–6, 301–9
Dabbs, Peter 378
Damascus 159, 160
Dardanelles 96, 97, 98, 116, 405
  AE2 attack (1915) x, xxi
  British assault on 105–6, 109–19
  plan to take 100–2
Darthema, HMS 304
Darwin 50–4
Davis Submarine Escape Apparatus 234, 245, 257, 263
de la Penne, *Tenente di Vascello* Luigi Durand 229–31
de Robeck, John 106, 109, 111, 112, 114–15, 118, 129
Deakin, Alfred 'Affable Alfie' 13–19
Dechaineux, HMAS 417–19
Denison, Sir Hugh 191
Diesel, Rudolf 12
Djemal Pasha 94, 160
dog watches 32
Dolci, Monsignor Angelo 148
Dolphin, HMS (Blockhouse) 22, 23, 191, 198, 228–9, 233, 234, 239, 244, 289, 304, 309, 324, 353, 360, 374
dolphins
  golden 362, 367, 374
  watching 281–2
Dominion Yachtsmen Scheme 217, 277
Dönitz, *Großadmiral* Karl 179–80, 197, 228
Doyle, Lieutenant Alec 63, 71
Dreadnought battleship 10
Drebbel, Cornelis ix, 1–2
Dresden, SMS 89, 91
Duff, Lieutenant Arthur 269–70
Duke of York, HMS 237, 271, 292, 316
Dunkirk, retreat from 216, 301

Index

E-boats (*Schnellboote*) 293, 303
E-class submarines 12–13, 19, 112, 183–4
   E1 12
   E4 23
   E5 23–4, 37
   E7 151, 153
   E9 83
   E11 112, 162
   E14 112–13, 131, 133, 162, 183
   E15 112–14, 115, 124, 143–4, 153
   E47 170
Eagle, HMS 2
Eastwood, Peter 382
Echo II-class submarine 388–9
Eclipse, HMS 38, 41, 42, 44–6, 89
Edward VII, King 11
Eisenhower, General Dwight D.
   'Ike' 300–1, 303–7
   Operation Overlord 303–7
   Operation Torch 321, 323
El Alamein 321, 323
Electric Boat Company 4–6
Elwell, Lieutenant Commander
   Charles 71–2, 76
Emden, SMS 61, 64, 79–80
   destruction of 90–1, 243
Empire Oak 226
Encounter, HMAS 68, 76, 79, 87, 416
Enigma 270, 271, 300
Enola Gay 342
Enterprise, USS 383, 385–6
Enver Pasha 94, 96, 142, 148, 160, 171
Enzer, Lieutenant Bruce 269, 328
   Operation Overlord 304
   Operation Postage Able 285, 288, 290
Erebus, HMS 196
Erin, HMS 95
Erskine, Nigel 413
Evans, Able Seaman Bob 239
Evans, David 405
Exercise Kangaroo II 384–7

Fairstar 374
Falconer, Bill 'Sparks' 102, 128, 130, 171
Falkland Islands, Battle of (1914) 91
Far Eastern Imperial Fleet 186
Fearless, HMS 163
Fell, Commander William Richmond
   'Tiny' 232–3, 310, 346, 350, 353–4, 356
   human torpedo, development of 238–9
   Operation Guidance 298–9
   Operation Source 251, 253
   Pacific War 313–16, 319, 325–31, 340, 342, 344

Ferdinand, Archduke Franz 58, 59
Fessenden oscillator 372
Fife, Rear Admiral James 325–32, 336, 345, 354
Fife, USS 354
Finlayson, Lieutenant Commander
   John 68–9
Fire Control System 371
Fisher, Admiral Sir John Arbuthnot
   (Jacky) 8–11, 18, 28, 91, 97, 171
   Board of Invention and Research 182
   Dardanelles campaign 101–2, 105
Fisher, Andrew 16, 92
Fitzgerald, Lieutenant Geoffrey 144, 146–8
Fleet Air Arm 357
Flinders, HMAS 411
Focke-Wulf Condor aircraft 221, 223, 225, 226, 323
Formidable, HMS 100
Formosa Bank 333–4
Forrest, Sir John 92
Foster, Commander John 411
Fowler, Petty Officer Hugh 291
Francis, Colonel H.V. 52
Fraser, Admiral Sir Bruce 292, 316–17, 325, 348–51, 354
Fraser, Lieutenant Ian 336–40, 342, 350
Fraser, Malcolm 368
Frew, Dr Robert 154–5
Frith, Captain Arthur 225
Frunze 394–7
Fugro Equator, MV 412–14
Fulton, Robert 2–3

Gaba Tepe 120, 121, 128, 130
Gaddafi, Colonel Muammar 391
Gallipoli x, 97, 128–31, 149
   casualties 149
   landings 119, 120–1, 128–9
Garden Island 55, 56
Gaulois 104, 110, 111
Gelebek 158
George V, King 18, 62, 170
George VI, King 299
German New Guinea 17, 62, 66
   German defence of 70–3
   map (1914) xx
   surrender 86
Germaniawerft 179
Germany 300
   arms race 10–11, 17–18
   East Asia Squadron 61–5, 88–9, 91
   Imperial Navy (*Kaiserlichemarine*) 178

Germany *continued*
  Navy Task Group (*Kampfgruppe der Kriegsmarine*) 261
  post-war disarmament 177–80
  Realm Navy (*Reichsmarine*) 178
  Turks, alliance with 94–6
  War Navy (*Kriegsmarine*) 179
  World War I, start of 59–60
Getting, Captain Frank 184, 187–90, 193–4
  Oxley, HMAS 190–2
Getting, George 188
Getting, Hazel 194
Getting, Paul 187
Gibraltar 14, 29, 30, 39, 42, 192, 219–22, 226–8, 279, 317, 320, 376, 391
Gilbert, Petty Officer Stephen 151, 410
Glasgow, HMS 89
Glorious, HMS 188
Glossop, Captain John 49–50, 52, 54, 90
Gneisenau, SMS 61, 89, 90
Goddard, ERA Eddie 262
Godley, Major General Alexander 129, 130
Goebbels, Joseph 197
Goeben 96, 97, 101
Gold Beach (D-Day) 301
Golding, George 275
Golding, Mary *see* Shean, Mary
Goltz, Colmar Freiherr von der 95
Good Hope, HMS 89
Grace, Dr W.G. 191
Grace, Rear Admiral Henry 191
Grampus, HMS 374–7
Grampus-class submarines 216
Grantala, HMAS 68
Greig, Ken 409
Grubb, Sir Howard 9
Guépratte, Admiral Émile 111
Guild, James 84
Guild, Stoker William 84a
Gurkha, HMS 225–6
gyrocompass 10, 38, 42, 124
  modern updates 371
  torpedo shots, lining up 189
  X-class submarines 260, 261, 262, 266, 267, 271

H-class submarines
  H29 189
Haber, Dr Eduard 68, 76, 86
Hacikiri 155
Haggard, H. Rider 32
Haggard, Lieutenant Commander Geoffrey 32, 40–1, 88, 123, 138–9, 171–2
  POW 152, 153

Halsey, Admiral William 'Bill' 318–19
Hamilton, General Sir Ian 108–9, 111, 119, 129–31, 133, 149, 172
Hamilton, Warrant Officer Keith 382
Hammond, Vice Admiral Mark xii
Hampshire, HMS 173
Hankey, Colonel Maurice 101
Harbud, Sub-Lieutenant Robin 304, 308
Harcourt, Lewis 63
Harding, Geoff 266–9
Harman, Sub-Lieutenant Ken 208–9
Hartland, HMS 322
Hassell, Ilse von 235
Hassell, Ulrich von 235
hazards 9–10, 23–4
Hedgehog 300
Hela, SMS 83
Heligoland 83
Henderson, Sir Reginald 18
Henty, Deirdre 354
Henty, Eulalie 243–4, 273–4, 354
Henty-Creer, Lieutenant Henty 243–4, 260, 272–4, 291, 345, 354
  Operation Source 250, 251, 265–6
  Special Services training 246, 248–9
Herbert, Lieutenant Douglass 32
Herbertshöhe 68–9, 76–7, 86
Heritage, Major Frank 74
Hilfskreuzer IV 199
Hill, Lieutenant Gerald 63
Hirohito, Emperor 343
Hiroshima 342
Hitler, Adolf 172, 179, 196–7, 235–6, 253, 309, 310, 325
Hobart, HMAS 316
Hochseeflotte 11
Hodge, Petty Officer Harry 44
Hogue, HMS 91
Holbrook, Lieutenant Norman 98, 162
Holland, John Philip 4–5
  Holland VI 4–5
Holland, USS 5
Holland I, HMS 6–7
Holmes, Colonel William 66, 68, 70, 74, 80, 86
Honour, Lieutenant George 302
Hood, HMS 236, 243
Horton, Vice Admiral Max 83, 215–16, 232–3, 238, 247–8, 300, 354
Houdini, Harry 30–1
Housatonic, USS 4
Howard, Leslie 244
Howe, HMS 238, 316
Hudson, Vice Admiral Mike 368

Hudspeth, Lieutenant Ken 242, 285, 311, 312, 354–5
  Operation Gambit 304, 306, 308–9, 312, 328
  Operation Postage Able 285–90
  Operation Source 250, 256, 259–60, 266–70, 271, 328
  Operation Tiger 302–3
Hughes, Billy 151, 177, 381
Hughes, Captain Edward 224
human torpedo 181
  British 233
  Il Maiale, 'The Pig' 181, 229–31, 233, 238, 243
Humphreys, Seaman Damien 369–70
Hunley, Horace Lawson 3–4
  H.L. Hunley 3–4
Hunstone, Marie 174
Hunter, Dr James 409
Hutchinson, Commander Christopher 277–8, 283
Hydrangea 224
hydroplanes xiv, 34, 36, 46, 117, 414

Implacable, HMS 28
Indefatigable, HMS 97
Indomitable, HMS 97
Inflexible, HMS 104, 110, 163
Irresistible, HMS 104, 110–11
Italy
  Decima Flottiglia Motoscafi Armati Siluranti (Decima MAS) 181
  human torpedo *see* human torpedo
  Regia Aeronautica 281
  Regia Marina 180–1
  Second London Naval Treaty 180

J-class submarines 183–5, 187, 190, 248, 357
  J2 184
  J3 183
  J5 184
  J7 187
James Madison, USS 389
Japan 313, 325
  atom bomb 341–2
  Circle Three shipbuilding program 180
  Darwin, bombing of 173
  Imperial Japanese Navy 180
  occupation of 352
  post-WWI navy 178
  Second London Naval Treaty 180
  surrender 344
  threat to Australia 186
Jarman, Able Seaman Jack 25

Jed, HMS 128
Jefferis, Colonel Rowland 232
Jellicoe, Admiral Sir John 101, 105, 186–7
Johore Strait 336, 340
Jolly Roger pirate flag 83–4, 215, 368
Junkers 88 bombers 223, 226
Juno Beach (D-Day) 301, 302, 304, 308
Jupiter, HMS 28
Jupp, Lieutenant Michael 291
Jutland, Battle of 232, 299

K-class submarines 162–5
  K3 163
  K4 163
  K6 163
  K9 162, 165
  K13 162, 163
  K14 163
  K17 163, 164
  K22 163, 164
Kabakaul 68, 70
Kåfjorden 250, 255, 260
Kähler, *Kapitän zur See* Otto 199–201
Kapitani Derya-2 409
Kearon, Sub-Lieutenant Paddy 258
Keitel, *Generalfeldmarshal* Wilhelm 239
Kell, *Kapitänleutnant* Walter 224
Kelly, Sub-Lieutenant Ben 313, 334, 335
Kendall, Dick 262
Kenny, Anne 381
Kenny, Surgeon Fred 67, 74–5, 78
  AE1, loss of 80–1
  Suva 87–8
Kephez Point 98, 113, 117
Kerneval U-boat HQ 223
Kerr, Corporal George 150
Keyes, Commodore Roger 38, 105, 106, 111, 113, 114, 118–19, 129–31, 139, 172
Kiev 391
Kinder, George 21
Kinder, Henry James Elly (Harry) 21–4, 172
  AE2 33–6, 42, 54, 55, 78
  Dardanelles campaign 104, 115, 117, 122, 126–7, 132, 136
  loss of *AE1* 81
  POW 143–4, 149–50
King, Admiral Ernest 317–18
King Alfred, HMS 238, 243, 323–4
King George V, HMS 316
Kirov 395
Kitchener, Field Marshal Lord Horatio Herbert 100, 106, 108–9, 111, 170, 173
Knaggs, Able Seaman Albert 151, 410

Knox, Rear Admiral Ian 396
Kockums Type 471 submarine 399
Koitschka, *Kapitänleutnant* Siegfried 284
Kolay, Selçuk 405–6
Kolonial Gesellschaft 416
Korda, Alexander 244
Korean War 357
Kosele, Vice Admiral Veysel 405
Kostroma 389
Kretschmer, *Kapitänleutnant* Otto 219, 223
Kum Kale 97, 120
Kummetz, *Generaladmiral* Oscar 261, 264, 355
Kurdin, Captain Igor 403–5
Kursk 402–5
Kut-al-Amara 149, 157

La Maddalena 281, 283
Labuan 329, 331, 336, 340, 342, 343, 345
Laksevaag Dock 293, 296–8, 312
Lance, HMS 225
Larkins, Sub-Lieutenant Frank 184
Leacock, Olive 29, 161
League of Nations 177
Lee, Sergeant Ezra 2
Leigh Light 300
Leigh-Mallory, Air Marshal Sir Trafford 305, 307
Leipzig, SMS 61, 89
Leith, HMS 222, 223, 224
Lemnos 104
Lemp, *Oberleutnant* Fritz-Julius 196–7
Leningrad, Siege of 300
Lentaigne, Commander Charles 225–6
Lewis, Reverend Russell 310
Lexington 415
Liberator bombers 300
Loch Cairnbawn 251, 293
Locke, Sub-Lieutenant David 248
Lockwood, Vice Admiral Charles 'Uncle Charlie' 329–31
Lombok Strait 48
long-distance patrol 361–7
Lord Nelson, HMS 110
Lorimer, Sub-Lieutenant John 261, 262, 264–6
Lorrimer, Lieutenant Commander David 358
Ludbrook, ERA Cyril 290
Luftwaffe 221, 237, 281
Lusitania, RMS 197
Lutzow 252, 255, 260, 262, 271
Lynn, Vera 277
Lyons, Lieutenant Frank 202–7, 211–13

MacDougall, Vice Admiral Ian 358–9, 368, 399–400, 403, 419–20
Mack, Frank 59
Mackintosh, Able Seaman Patrick 193
Macklin, Chief ERA Herbert 151
Macleod, Ian 409
McFarlane, John 243
McFarlane, Lieutenant Brian 'Digger' 243, 285, 291–2, 345
  Home Fleet defences, testing 290–2
  Operation Source 250, 256, 258, 270
McIntosh, Vice Admiral Ian 195–216, 311–12, 355
  Lifeboat Number Seven 201–14, 252
  Operation Guidance 293, 295
  Operation Source 251–2, 256
  SS *Britannia* 198–201
McKenna, Sir Reginald 16
McKinnel, Norman 165
McVicar, Bill 202–7, 209, 212, 214
Magennis, Leading Seaman James Joseph 'Mick' 337–8, 339, 350–1, 355
Majestic, HMS 104, 114
Malaya 252
Malcolm, Midshipman Alistair 266
Maloney, Beatrice 84
Maloney, Petty Officer John 84
Malta 43
Marconi wireless transmitters 9, 38, 102, 128
Markcrow, Able Seaman Hugh 369–70
Marrack, Commander Hugh 191–2
Marsden, Lieutenant Jack 243, 250, 258, 290–1, 345
Marshall, General George C. 301
Marshall Islands 63, 64–5
Marsland, Ellie 84
Marsland, John 43, 47, 51–2, 53, 84
Marsland, Nellie 43
Martin, Lieutenant Terry 251
Maslum Bey 151–2, 173
Massey, Raymond 244
May, Alfred 113
May Island 162–3, 183
Mediterranean Ocean 281
Mehmed V, Sultan 94, 97
Mekong River 332
Melbourne, HMAS 19, 357, 374, 384
Mellon, Gus 414
Merlin, HMS 170
Mersin 155, 156
Messenger, Elizabeth 84
Messenger, ERA John 'Jack' 84, 414
Messerschmitt fighters 279

Index

Mesudiye 98
Meyer, *Konteradmiral* Hans 261, 264, 266, 355–6
mice, use of 9, 10
Middleton Reef 378
Midilli 96
Miers, Lieutenant Commander Jack 369
Millen, Edward 19
Minsk 394
Missouri, USS 318
Moffat, Iris 72
Moffat, Signalman Robert 72
Monmouth, HMS 89
Monsarrat, Nicholas 228
  The Cruel Sea 228
Montcalm 87
Montgomery, General Sir Bernard 305
Moore, Annie 84
Moore, Colonel Henry 84
Moore, Lieutenant Charles 32, 40
  loss of *AE1* 81, 84
Moreton, HMAS 379
Morgenthau, Henry 94, 95, 112, 147–8, 173
Morris, Michael 418
Mortiboys, ERA Ralph 253, 266
Motor Launch (ML) 469 320–3
Mudros 104, 105, 106, 112, 114–15
Mullen, John 412
Müller, Captain Karl von 90
Munro-Ferguson, Sir Ronald 89–90
Murat Reis 279
Musashi 180
Myoko 329, 336, 340

Nagara Point 125
Nagasaki 343
Nairn, Alec 192
Narvik 295
Nasmith, Captain Martin 112–13, 162
  'Is-Was' 188
Nauru 17, 63, 64
Nautilus 2
'The Naval Ode' 404
Naval Scare (1909) 17
Nazis, rise of 179
Needham, Able Seaman Bill 'Shorty' 382
Nelson, Admiral Horatio 41, 239, 271
Nelson, HMS 316
Nelson, Sub-Lieutenant Tom 266
Neptune aircraft 379, 381
Netztender 44 281
New Britain (*Neupommern*) 62, 69
New Guinea 63
Nichols, Alice 146

Nichols, Petty Officer Alex 146, 155–8, 168, 173
Nicholson, Audrey 311, 355
Nordenfelt, Thorsten 4
North Cape, Battle of the 271, 317
North Solomon Islands 18
nuclear power 371, 387–8, 395, 401
Nürnberg, SMS 61, 89
NV *Ingenieurskantoor voor Scheepsbouw* (IvS) 179

O-class submarines (Oberon) 357–72, 378, 399–401
  diagram xix
  'ISR' operations 390–2
  long-distance patrol 361–7
Oberon, HMS 192
Onslow, HMAS 359, 368, 369, 400
Orion, HMAS 359, 369, 390–2, 396–8, 401
Otama, HMAS 359, 369–70, 390, 398, 401
Otter, HMS 384, 400
Otway, HMAS 190–3, 358–9, 377, 379–87, 391, 400–1, 405
Ovens, HMAS 359, 385, 391, 400
Oxley, HMAS 190–3
Oxley, HMAS (second boat) 358–68, 372, 385, 399–400
  search and rescue 378–83
ocean currents xiv–xv
Ocean, HMS 104, 111
Odessa 96
Ogden, Sub-Lieutenant Frank 296, 298
Ogden Smith, Sergeant Bruce 285, 287
O'Hare, Private Ambrose 73
Ohio class submarines 387
Okinawa 325
Olivier, Laurence 166, 244
Omaha Beach (D-Day) 285–6, 301, 302
One and All 378, 405
Operation Dynamo 301
Operation Gambit 302–9, 312, 328
Operation Guidance 293–9
Operation Neptune 301–2
Operation Overlord 300–2
Operation Postage Able 285–90
Operation Sabre 331, 332–6
Operation Source 250–72, 328, 353
  casualties 258, 264, 266
  map xxiii
  prisoners of war 262, 264–5, 272
Operation Struggle 332, 336–41
Operation Tiger 302

Operation Title 238–9
Operation Torch 301, 321–3
Operation Zitronella 252–3
Oran 321–2
Orwell, HMS 312
Oscar II class 402
Osprey, HMS 182
Ostend 172
Otranto, HMS 89
Ottoman Turks 59, 93, 159–60, 161
Overseas Patrol Submarines 190
Oxley, John 190
oxygen toxicity (Oxygen Pete) 248, 324, 328, 338

P-3 Orion aircraft 381, 395
P31 279
Panama Canal 90, 218, 313, 315, 358
Parker, Vice Admiral Peter 225
Parramatta, HMAS 19, 25, 55, 62, 68, 77, 79, 87, 90, 411
Passlow, Able Seaman Christopher 369
Paterson, Lieutenant Halliday 32
Patey, Vice Admiral Sir George 57, 62, 87, 89–90
   AE1, search for 79–80
   East Asia Squadron, searching for 62–4, 88
   German New Guinea 67–9, 73–8
Pearce, George 84, 92–3, 144–5
Pearl Harbor 315
Penguin, HMAS 349–50
   4th Submarine Squadron 357
periscope 9, 12, 34
Perisher 187–9, 191, 252, 283, 358, 379, 391, 397, 400
Petersen, Brit 384
Petrel, RV 415
Philip, Hoffman 148
Philippines 325
Phillip, Captain Arthur 41
Pidcock, Dorothie 167
Ping Intercept Passive Ranging System (PIPRS) 373
Pitt, Captain Kim 368, 391, 396–7
Pitt the Younger, William 3
Place, Rear Admiral Godfrey 251, 260, 272, 356
   Operation Source 251, 259, 260, 262–3
Platypus, HMAS 184, 185, 190
Platypus, HMAS 358, 383, 400
Plongeur 3
Pockley, Captain Brian 71
Pollock, Leading Radio Operator 380

Porpoise, HMS 216
Porpoise-class submarines 374
Port Bannatyne 240, 245, 249, 283, 284
Port HHZ 251, 252, 293–4, 298
Port Said 103, 252
Poseidon nuclear missiles 389
Potsdam Declaration 341
Pound, Sir Dudley 237, 248
Pretty, Able Seaman John 290
Price, Lieutenant Edward 153, 154, 155
Prince Charles, HMS 232
Prince George, HMS 104
Princip, Gavrilo 58, 59
prisoners of war 140–60
   death of 149, 150–1, 155, 410
   escape attempts 152–9
   Operation Source 262, 264–5, 272, 353, 356
   Red Cross parcels 146, 152
   treatment of 141, 143–4, 147, 149, 152
Project Silent Anzac 408–10
Protector, HMAS 67
Protector, HMCS 14
Purdie, David 202–6
Purdy, Sub-Lieutenant Derek 312
Putin, Vladimir 402

Queen Elizabeth, HMS 101, 104, 109–10, 113, 118
   human torpedo assault on 229–31, 243, 247

Raaby, Torstein 250
Rabaul 411, 416
   World War I 62–3, 66–74, 79–80, 87
radar 300
   Type 271 222
Ramsay, Sir Bertram 301, 302, 305, 307, 309
Rasmussen, Elizabeth 214, 216, 355
Rawlings, Vice Admiral Sir Bernard 319
Reagan, Ronald 388
Reardon, Able Seaman John 84
Reardon, Catherine 84
reconnaissance and surveillance
   Cold War 390–2, 396–8
   Operation Gambit 304, 306, 308–9, 312, 328
Renown, HMS 8
Reşadiye 94
Rickover, Admiral Hyman 387
Riza, Captain Ali 134–5, 137, 140
Roach, Lieutenant Commander Terry 379–82, 405, 408–10

Index

Roberts, Lieutenant Commander Ian 360
Rodney 322
Rommel, *Generalfeldmarschall* Erwin 309, 321, 323
Roosevelt, Franklin D. 317
Roosevelt, Theodore 16
Royal Arthur, HMS 165
Royal Australian Naval College 19
Royal Australian Navy (RAN) 19, 183–4, 352
  Admiralty control, under 63–4
  1st Australian Submarine Squadron 360, 370
  first submarines commissioned 38–9
  'ISR' operations 390–2
  post-WWI 186–7
  post-WWII 357
  Volunteer Reserve 217
  war games 360, 383–7
Royal Navy 16, 19, 27–8, 175–6
  Australians serving with 277–8
  Cape Coronel, defeat at 88–90
  Eastern Mediterranean Squadron 103
  first submarines 5–7, 8–11
  first WWI submarine success 83–4
  14th Submarine Flotilla 313, 344, 345
  Fourth Cruiser Squadron 89
  Home Fleet 101, 236, 237, 247, 290
  Mediterranean Fleet 43
  Periscope School, 'Perisher' 187–9, 191, 252, 283, 358, 379, 391, 397, 400
  shore bases around the empire 317–18
  12th Submarine Flotilla 247, 270, 284–5, 302, 313, 345
  US Navy, relationship with 317–19
Royal Sovereign, HMS 301
rules-based order xi
Run Silent, Run Deep (1958) 352
Russia 94 *see also* Soviet Union
  Kursk, loss of 402–5
  WWI 59–60, 83, 161
Ryan, Vera 414
Ryrie, Major General Sir Granville 191

saddle tanks 33
Sagona 230
Saigon River 332
Samson, Private Harold 158
Saros 406
Savo Island, Battle of 193–4
Scapa Flow 173, 290–2, 299, 317, 348
Scarlett, Hugh 65
Scarlett, Lieutenant Leopold 65, 75, 78
  loss of *AE1* 80–1, 84

Sceptre, HMS, 311–12
  Operation Guidance 293, 295, 298
  Operation Source 251, 252, 255–6, 267
Scharnhorst, SMS 61, 89, 90, 252, 253, 255, 260, 271, 317
Schepke, *Kapitänleutnant* Joachim 219
Schmölder, *Leutnant zur See* Eberhard 266
Schnee, *Oberleutnant zur See* Adalbert 223–4, 225, 226–7, 228
Schnorchel xiii
Scott, Commander Peter 418
Scott-Bowden, Major Logan 285–7, 289
Scullin, James 193
Sea Air Rescue Service 380
Sea of Marmara 94, 101, 105, 106, 109, 113, 116, 131–9, 405, 409
Sea Nymph, HMS 251, 256, 258
search and rescue 378–83
Sebastopol 96
Second London Naval Treaty 180
Seddülbahir 97
Shaw, Lieutenant Norman 189–91
Shean, Gladys 309, 346
Shean, Harry 347
Shean, Lieutenant Max 216–22, 243, 244, 253, 275–7, 290, 294, 312, 353
  Convoy OG 71 222–3, 226, 228
  discharge 345–7
  Home Fleet defences, testing 292
  marriage 309–11
  Operation Guidance 295–9
  Operation Sabre 331, 332–6
  Operation Source 252, 257–8
  Pacific War 319, 329, 330–6, 342–3
  post-WWII 347–9, 356
  Special Services training 228–9, 234, 239–40, 242, 245, 247–9, 251, 284–5
  XE boats 312–14, 324, 327, 329, 330–6, 342
Shean, Mary (nee Golding) 222, 247, 258, 275–7
  marriage 309–11, 313, 315, 347–8, 356
Shean, Yvonne 346
Sherwood, Lieutenant Commander Robert 219, 220, 221
Showers, Sub-Lieutenant Harry 164, 183
Shropshire, HMAS 316
Siebe-Gorman diving suit 324
silent running 282, 358
  'Ultra Quiet' 396
Simpsonhafen 62–3, 69, 77, 80, 90
Singapore 47–8, 54, 186, 190, 317, 329, 342–3
  Operation Struggle 332, 336–41

Sladen, Commander Geoffrey 'Slasher' 233, 238
  diving suits 233, 238, 245
Slapton Sands 302–3
Smalfjord 260, 267
Smart, Lieutenant John 340
Smith, Lieutenant Bill 'Kiwi' 339
snorting xiii, 358, 385, 386
Solomon Islands 18, 62, 193
Somerville, Commander Fred 113
sonar 371, 372–3, 376
  active 372
  Asdic *see* Asdic
  operators 373
  passive 372
  PIPRS 373
Sopwith Schneider floatplane 134
Soroy Island 255, 259, 268–9
Souchon, *Konteradmiral* Wilhelm 96–7
Soviet Union 179 *see also* Russia
  Cold War conflict 387–91
  Vietnam, in 393–4
  WWII 237, 300, 341
Spark 331, 332
Spearhead 331, 332, 333
Spee, *Vizeadmiral* Maximilian von 61–2, 64–5, 79, 87
  Cape Coronel, victory at 88–90
  death 91
Spind 227
Spitfire reconnaissance aircraft 252, 270
Stagg, Group Captain James 306
Stalin, Josef 247
Stalwart, HMAS 368
Still, Lieutenant John 152
Stirling, HMAS 359, 392, 419
Stoker, Bram 27
Stoker, Hope 29
Stoker, Iris 29
Stoker, Joan 29
Stoker, Lieutenant Commander Henry x, 26, 27–32, 37, 39, 65, 78, 91–2, 161–2, 168–9, 405, 407–9
  acting career 165–7
  AE1, loss of 80, 82
  AE2, journey to Australia 41–50, 52–3, 57
  Dardanelles campaign 102–7, 112–20, 122–8, 130, 131–9, 162, 407–9
  death 169
  Distinguished Service Order 162, 166
  K-class submarines 162, 164–5
  memoir, publication of 166
  Pearce, meeting with 92–3
  POW 140–8, 152–5, 161

  retirement 167–8
  Suva 87–8
  Sydney, on 57
  World War I, start of 61
  World War II service 167
Stoker, Olive 29, 161
stokers 22
Stork 226–7
Street, Able Seaman Harold 72
Stubborn, HMS 251, 256, 259, 269–70
Stygian 331, 332, 340
Subic Bay 325, 328, 329, 331, 341, 345, 379
Submarine Attack Teacher 189
Submarine Institute of Australia 407–8
Submarine Warfare Systems Centre 359
Submarine Weapons Update Program (SWUP) 371–2
submarines ix, xiii, 56–7, 419–20
  commander training 187–90
  crew *see* crew
  diving xiv, 36, 365–6
  invention of 1–8
  life aboard 361–7
  post-war numbers 178
  sources of power xiii, 12
  surfacing xv, 33, 36
Suckling, Margaret 174
Suckling, Stoker Charlie 115–16, 122, 141–3, 174
Suez Canal 44, 94, 102, 190, 391–2
Suffren 97, 104, 111
Suhren, *Oberleutnant zur See* Reinhard 226
Sullivan, Able Seaman Timothy 72
Sullivan, Greg 418
Sultan Osman 95
Sultanhisar 134–5, 137, 140–1, 408
Supply, HMAS 368
Sussex, HMS 196
Suzuki, Admiral Kantaro 341
Swiftpool 220
Swiftsure, HMS 104
Sword Beach (D-Day) 301, 302, 306, 308
Sydney, HMAS 19, 62, 80, 243, 357
  AE1 and *AE2*, escorting 47–51
  Emden, destruction of 90, 243
  German New Guinea 68, 87
Syme, David 172
Syme, Marjorie 172
Syrtis, HMS 251, 257–8, 259, 290–2

Taber, Ian 380
Takao 329, 336–40, 350, 354
Talaat Pasha 94, 160
Tannenberg, Battle of 83

Index 455

Taubman, Lieutenant Commander John 369–70
telegraph cables, cutting 326–9, 340–1, 347
  Operation Sabre 332–6
Tenedos (Bozcaada) 103–4, 109, 110–11, 115, 118
Terror, HMS 165
Tesei, Teseo 181
Thatcher, Margaret 388
Themistocles, SS 278
thermocline 385–6
Thor 199–201
Thrasher, HMS 251, 252
Thursby, Rear Admiral Cecil 129–30
Ticonderoga class cruisers 395
Tilley, ERA Les 304
Tingira, HMS 243
Tirpitz 235–9, 245, 247–8, 270–1, 355
  attack on xxii, 250–70, 276, 285, 293, 328, 353
Tirpitz, *Großadmiral* Alfred von 11, 235
  risk theory 11
Titania, HMS 251, 253
Tonks, Bernie 294
torpedo tubes 12, 33, 35
torpedoes
  American Mark 48 371–2
  British 21-inch Mark VIII 371
Torres Strait 54
Toschi, Elios 181
Treaty of Versailles 178, 179
Trident long-range ballistic missiles 387
Triton 6000 415
Triumph, HMS 104, 114
Trondheim 236, 239
Truculent, HMS 251, 255
Truman, Harry 341
Tuchman, Barbara 173
Tuna, HMS 249
Turkish Forces 279
  WWI, entry into 93–8
Turner, Roger 414
Turtle 2
Typhoon-class ballistic-missile boats 387–8

U-boats xiii, 11, 172, 174–5, 178–80, 252, 259, 293, 300, 358
  Battle of the Atlantic 197, 218–19
  Befehlshaber der Unterseeboote (BdU) 223–4
  convoys, attacking 218–21, 224–8, 237–8
  Type VII 179–80, 223–4, 280
  U-9 91

U-24 100
U-30 196–7
U-68 179
U-99 219
U-100 219
U-201 223–4, 226–7
U-204 224
U-320 197
U-372 220
U-552 227
U-559 224
U-564 226, 226
U-616 280, 284
  wolf-packs 179, 223, 226–8, 300
ultrasonic sound 182–3
Umtali, SS 347
Unbeaten, HMS 251
Untiring, HMS 278–84
Upolu, HMAS 67, 78, 87
Uproar, HMS 279
US Navy 16–17, 317
  fleet train 318
  Royal Navy, relationship with 317–19
  USSR, conflict with 387–8
  war games 360, 383–7
Utah Beach (D-Day) 301, 302
Uusioja, Juoko 373

V-1 flying bombs 310–11
Valiant, assault on 229–31
Vampire 384
Vanoc, HMS 219
Varbel, HMS 240, 242, 244–5, 247, 284, 299, 313, 324
Varbel II, HMS 245, 246
Varcoe, Chief Stoker Charlie 150, 410
Vaughan, Chief Petty Officer Charlie 24, 37, 134
Vendetta 374
Vengeance, HMS 104
Vérité 97
Verne, Jules 3
Verner, Commander Rudolf 110
Vernon, HMS 188
Vichy French 321–2
Vickers 5, 12, 20, 30, 45, 57, 94, 192, 312
Vickers-Armstrong 279
Victorious, HMS 237, 355
Victory, HMS 21, 41, 239–40
Vietnam War 357, 388, 393
Vindictive, HMS 196
von Sanders, *Generalleutnant* Otto Liman 94, 134–5, 141
Voracious, HMS 284, 356

Walker, Lieutenant Geoffrey 315
Wallflower, HMS 225, 227
Walney, HMS 322
Walsh, Commander John 194
Walter, Hellmuth 358
Wangenheim, Baron Hans von 94
war books 352–3
war brides 347–8
war movies 352
Warrego, HMAS 19, 62, 68, 79, 87, 90
Warren, C.E.T. 353
Warren, Lieutenant Bill 77–8
Warspite, HMS 232, 388–9
Washington, George 2
Washington Naval Conference (1922) 179
Washington, USS 237
Weddigen, *Kapitänleutnant* Otto 91
Wells, H.G. 7–8
West, Frank 202–3, 205–9, 211–12
Westbrook, Phyllis 278, 284
Westmacott, Lieutenant Percy 311–12
whales 377
Wheat, John 81, 115, 125, 127, 168, 174
  POW 143, 152, 155–60
White Australia policy 186
White, Dr Michael 391, 398
Whitehead, Robert 4
Whitley, ERA Bill 264
Whittam, Lieutenant Lionel 'Bill' 247, 264, 356
Wilhelm II, Kaiser 11, 59–60, 94, 100
Williams, Able Seaman Billy 71, 75–6
Williams, Margaret 151
Williams, Stoker Michael 'Bill' 151, 410
Wilson, Donald (father) 278
Wilson, Lieutenant Commander Don 'Digger' 277–84, 356–7
Wilson, Rear Admiral Arthur 6, 84
Wilson, Woodrow 173, 177
  '14 Points' 177
Women's Royal Naval Service (Wrens) 222, 225, 228
Wood, Albert 182
Wood, Commander Belinda 405, 410
Woolrych, Lieutenant Commander Rob 391, 392

World War I 100
  British submarine success 83–4, 98–9
  casualties 161
  media coverage 83
  post-war disarmament 177–80
  start of 59–61
World War II 196, 300, 343–4, 352

X-class submarines 241–2, 248, 284–5, 312
  books about 353
  diagram xviii
  training 245–7
  transportation of 248, 249, 251–3, 255–61, 290–2, 293, 295, 304, 311–12
X_3 240, 241, 246
X_5 240, 249, 250, 253, 354
X_6 251, 255, 259–62, 272
X_7 251, 256, 259–60, 262–3, 269, 272, 356
X_8 250, 256, 258, 270, 271
X_9 251, 252, 257–8, 271, 292, 295
X_{10} xxii, 250, 259–60, 266–70, 271
X_{20} 285–90, 302–8
X_{22} 285, 290–2, 295, 345
X_{23} 302–8
X_{24} 285, 290, 292, 293–9, 311–12
XE-class submarines 312–14
  post-war 351
  transportation of 331, 332–3
XE_1 329, 332, 336, 340
XE_2 328
XE_3 327–8, 329, 332, 336–40, 342–3, 350, 351
XE_4 (*Exciter*) 312–13, 324, 326, 327, 329–36, 340, 342–3, 346
XE_5 329, 331, 340–1, 345
XE_6 331

Yalta 96
Yamato 180
Yarmouth, HMS 46, 47
Yarra, HMAS 19, 62, 68, 78, 79, 416
Yavuz Sultan Selim 96
Yozgad 155

Zeebrugge 172
Zeir Bey 152
Zinnia 227